LEVINAS AND BUBER

LEVINAS & BUBER

Dialogue & Difference

Edited by
Peter Atterton,
Matthew Calarco &
Maurice Friedman

Duquesne University Press
Pittsburgh, Pennsylvania

Library of Congress Cataloging in Publication Data

Lévinas and Buber : dialogue and difference / edited by Peter Atterton,
Matthew Calarco, and Maurice Friedman.
    p. cm.
Includes bibliographical references (p.) and index.
    ISBN 0–8207–0349–4 (cloth) — ISBN 0–8207–0351–6 (pbk.)
    1. Lévinas, Emmanuel. 2. Buber, Martin, 1878–1965. I. Atterton,
Peter, 1961– . II. Calarco, Matthew, 1972– . III. Friedman, Maurice S.

B2430.L484L465   2004
181'.06—dc22   2003023594

CONTENTS

III. Religion

IV. Heidegger, Humanism, and the Other Animal

ACKNOWLEDGMENTS

We thank the copyright holders for granting permission to reproduce the following material in this book:

Martin Buber, "Autobiographical Fragment no. 17," in *The Philosophy of Martin Buber*, Paul Arthur Schilpp and Maurice Friedman, eds. (La Salle, Ill.: Open Court, 1967), 31–3. Copyright 1967 by Open Court.

Emmanuel Levinas, "Interview with François Poirié," in François Poirié, *Emmanuel Levinas: Qui êtes-vous?* (Lyon: La Manufacture, 1987), 123–24. Copyright 1987 by La Manufacture.

Stephan Strasser, "Buber und Levinas: Philosophische Besinnung auf einen Gegensatz," *Revue Internationale de Philosophie* 32 (1978): 512–25. Copyright 1978 by Revue Internationale de Philosophie.

Robert Bernasconi, "'Failure of Communication' as a Surplus: Dialogue and Lack of Dialogue between Buber and Levinas," in Robert Bernasconi and David Wood, eds., *The Provocation of Levinas: Rethinking the Other* (London: Routledge, 1988), 100–35. Copyright 1988 by Routledge.

Neve Gordon, "Ethics as Reciprocity: An Analysis of Levinas's Reading of Buber," *International Studies in Philosophy* 31 (1999): 75–93. Copyright 1999 by Binghamton University Press.

Maurice Friedman, "Martin Buber and Emmanuel Levinas: An Ethical Query," *Philosophy Today* 45 (2001): 3–11. Copyright by Duquesne University Press.

Andrew Kelley, "Reciprocity and the Height of God: A Defense of Buber against Levinas," *Sophia* 34 (1995): 65–73. Copyright 1995 by Andrew Kelley.

Andrew Tallon, "Intentionality, Intersubjectivity, and the Between: Buber and Levinas on Affectivity and the Dialogical Principle," *Thought* 53 (1978): 292–309. Copyright 1978 by Fordham University Press.

A   Michael Theunissen. *Der Andere*. Berlin: Walter de Gruyter, 1977.

AQE   Emmanuel Levinas. *Autrement qu'être ou au-delà de l'essence*. The Hague: Martinus Nijhoff, 1974.

APB   Emmanuel Levinas. "A propos de Buber: quelques notes." In *Qu'est-ce que l'homme? Philosophie/psychanalyse: Hommage à Alphonse de Waelhens (1911–1981)*. Bruxelles: Facultés universitaires Saint-Louis, 1982, 127–33.

BH   Martin Buber. *A Believing Humanism: My Testament, 1902–1965*. Trans. Maurice Friedman. New York: Simon and Schuster, 1967.

BMM   Martin Buber. *Between Man and Man*. Trans. Ronald Gregor Smith. London and New York: Routledge, 2002.

BMP   Emmanuel Levinas. "Martin Buber, Gabriel Marcel and Philosophy." Trans. Esther Kameron. In *Martin Buber. A Centenary Volume*. Eds. Haim Gordon and Jochanan Bloch. New York: Ktav Publishing House for the Faculty of Humanities and Social Sciences, Ben-Gurion University of the Negev, 1984, 305–21.

BP   Emmanuel Levinas. "Martin Buber, Gabriel Marcel et la Philosophie." *Revue Internationale de Philosophie* 32 (1978): 492–511.

BV   Emmanuel Levinas. *Beyond the Verse: Talmudic Readings and Lectures*. Trans. Gary D. Mole. London: Athlone, 1994.

CPP   Emmanuel Levinas. *Collected Philosophical Papers*. Trans. Alphonso Lingis. Duquesne University Press, 1998.

DEE   Emmanuel Levinas. *De l'existence à l'existant*. Paris: Vrin, 1947.

DF   Emmanuel Levinas. *Difficult Freedom*. Trans. Seàn Hand. Baltimore: Johns Hopkins University Press, 1990.

DL   Martin Buber. *Dialogisches Leben*. Zurich: Gregor Muller, 1947.

DP   Martin Buber. *Das dialogische Prinzip*. Heidelberg: Lambert Schneider, 1984.

DVI   Emmanuel Levinas. *De Dieu qui vient à l'idée*. Paris: Vrin, 1982.

ED   Jacques Derrida. *L'écriture et la différence*. Paris: Seuil, 1967.

EDE   Emmanuel Levinas. *En découvrant l'existence avec Husserl et Heidegger*. Paris: Vrin, 1974.

EE   Emmanuel Levinas. *Existence and Existents*. Trans. Alphonso Lingis. The Hague: Martinus Nijhoff, 1978.

EG   Martin Buber. *Eclipse of God*. Trans. Maurice Friedman et al. Atlantic Highlands, N.J.: Humanities Press, 1988.

GAA   Zachary Braiterman. *(God) After Auschwitz*. Princeton: Princeton University Press, 1998.

GE   Martin Buber. *Good and Evil: Two Interpretations.* New York: Scribner's, 1986.

HMM   Martin Buber. *Hasidism and Modern Man.* Trans. Maurice Friedman. New Jersey: Humanities, 1988.

IR   Jill Robbins, ed. *Is It Righteous to Be? Interviews with Emmanuel Levinas.* Stanford, Stanford University Press, 2001.

IT   Martin Buber. *I and Thou.* Trans. Walter Kaufmann. New York: Scribner's, 1970.

ITN   Emmanuel Levinas. *In the Time of Nations.* Trans. Michael B. Smith. Bloomington: Indiana University Press, 1994.

IW   Martin Buber. *Israel and The World: Essays in a Time of Crisis.* New York: Schocken Books, 1948.

KM   Martin Buber. *The Knowledge of Man: A Philosophy of the Interhuman.* Trans. Maurice Friedman and Ronald Gregor Smith. New York: Prometheus Books, 1998.

LC   David Hartman. *A Living Covenant: The Innovative Spirit in Traditional Judaism.* London: Macmillan, 1985.

LR   Emmanuel Levinas. *The Levinas Reader.* Ed. Seàn Hand. Oxford: Blackwell, 1989.

MB   Paul A. Schilpp and Maurice S. Friedman, eds. *Martin Buber. Philosophen des 20. Jarhunderts.* Stuttgart: Kohlhammer, 1963.

NP   Emmanuel Levinas. *Noms propres.* Montpellier: Fata Morgana, 1976.

NTR   Emmanuel Levinas. *Nine Talmudic Readings.* Trans. Annette Aronowicz. Bloomington: Indiana University Press, 1994.

O   Michael Theunissen. *The Other.* Trans. Christopher Macann. Cambridge, Mass: MIT Press, 1984.

OB   Emmanuel Levinas. *Otherwise Than Being or Beyond Essence.* Trans. Alphonso Lingis. Duquesne University Press, 1998.

OGM   Emmanuel Levinas. *Of God Who Comes to Mind.* Trans. Bettina Bergo. Stanford: Stanford University Press, 1998.

OJ   Martin Buber. *On Judaism.* New York: Schocken Books, 1967.

OS   Emmanuel Levinas. *Outside the Subject.* Trans. Michael Smith. Stanford: Stanford University Press, 1993.

OT   Emmanuel Levinas. "On the Trail of the Other." Trans. Daniel J. Hoy. *Philosophy Today* 10 (1966): 34–46.

PF   Martin Buber. *The Prophetic Faith.* New York: Harper and Row, 1949.

PI   Martin Buber. *Philosophical Interrogations.* Eds. Sydney Rome and Beatrice Rome. New York: Holt, Rinehart & Winston, 1964.

PM   Emmanuel Levinas. "The Paradox of Morality: An Interview with Emmanuel Levinas." Trans. Andrew Benjamin and Tamra Wright.

	In *The Provocation of Levinas: Rethinking the Other.* Eds. Robert Bernasconi and David Wood. London: Routledge, 1988.
PMB	Paul A. Schilpp and Maurice S. Friedman, eds. *The Philosophy of Martin Buber.* La Salle, Ill.: Open Court, 1967.
PN	Emmanuel Levinas. *Proper Names.* Trans. Michael B. Smith (Stanford: Stanford University Press, 1996.
TA	Emmanuel Levinas. *Le temps et l'autre.* Montpellier: Fata Morgana, 1979.
TAT	Steven Kepnes. *The Text as Thou: Martin Buber's Dialogical Hermeneutics and Narrative Theology.* Bloomington: Indiana University Press, 1992.
TeI	Emmanuel Levinas. *Totalité et infini: Essai sur l'exteriorité.* The Hague: Martinus Nijhoff, 1961.
TI	Emmanuel Levinas. *Totality and Infinity.* Trans. Alphonso Lingis (Pittsburgh: Duquesne University Press, 1969).
TO	Emmanuel Levinas. *Time and the Other.* Trans. Richard Cohen. Pittsburgh: Duquesne University Press, 1987.
US	Emmanuel Levinas. "Useless Suffering." Trans. Richard Cohen. In *The Provocation of Levinas: Rethinking the Other*, Eds. Robert Bernasconi and David Wood. London: Routledge, 1988.
W	Martin Buber. *Werke. Erster Band. Schriften zur Philosophie.* Munchen: Lambert Schneider, 1962.
WD	Jacques Derrida. *Writing and Difference.* Trans Alan Bass. London: Routledge & Kegan Paul, 1978.
WM	Martin Buber. *The Way of Man: According to the Teachings of Hasidism.* New Jersey: Citadel Press, 1966.
WMB	Martin Buber. *The Writing of Martin Buber.* Ed. Will Herberg. New York: Meridian Books, 1974.

Peter Atterton, Matthew Calarco & Maurice Friedman

Dorthin
führt uns der Blick,
mit dieser
Hälfte
haben wir Umgang.
There
our looking leads us,
with this
half
we keep up relations.

— Paul Celan

Martin Buber (1878–1965) and Emmanuel Levinas (1906–1995) knew each other as associates and friends. Indeed, Buber instructed Maurice Friedman, one of the editors of this volume, to include contributions by Levinas to both *The Philosophy of Martin Buber* volume of *The Library of Living Philosophers* and the Martin Buber section that heads up *Philosophical Interrogations*. Buber devoted a page to Levinas in the "Replies to My Critics" section of *The Philosophy of Martin Buber*, and there is a six-page exchange between Levinas and Buber in *Philosophical Interrogations*. Levinas attended the Centenary Conference on Buber's thought at the Ben Gurion University of the Negev in Beer-Sheva, Israel, in 1978, and gave a paper that was subsequently published in the volume that grew out of that conference. Levinas devoted several studies to Buber to which the latter responded on more than one occasion.

But although the dialogue between Buber and Levinas was certainly instructive at times — and showed the esteem in which Levinas held Buber, in particular — it just as often exhibited a lack of dialogue and a failure to communicate. The present volume is intended to resume the dialogue between the two philosophers. The objective is not to assimilate their respective views to each other, but to point out their differences — differences that both Levinas and Buber agreed were required for genuine dialogue to begin. Hence our title for this volume: *Levinas and Buber: Dialogue and Difference.*

BUBER'S PHILOSOPHY OF DIALOGUE AND ITS INFLUENCE ON LEVINAS

The fundamental fact of human existence, according to Martin Buber's philosophical anthropology, is that of person to person. In Buber's classic presentation of his philosophy of dialogue, *I and Thou*, he is concerned with the difference between mere existence and authentic existence, between being human at all and being more fully human, between partial and fuller relationships with others. Emmanuel Levinas's phenomenological approach begins with the experience of the face (*le visage*) of the other, with whom I relate face-to-face. The main dynamic behind this relation is ethics. I recognize the otherness of the other by not competing with him or her but by responding to him or her in a relation of discourse.

When two persons "meet" each other, according to Buber, there is an essential remainder common to each of them that reaches out beyond the special sphere of each. That remainder is the basic interhuman reality, the "sphere of the between" (*BMM*, 203f.). The participation of both partners is indispensable to this sphere. The unfolding of this sphere is the "dialogical." The meaning of this dialogue is found in neither one nor the other of the partners, nor in both taken together, but in their encounter. *The psychological, that which happens within the souls of each, is only the secret accompaniment to the dialogue. It influences the dialogue but does not define it.*

In a dialogic relation, the "barriers" of individual being are breached and "the other becomes present not merely in the imagination or feeling but in the depths of one's substance, so that one experiences the mystery of the other being in the mystery of one's own" (*BMM*, 170). The I-Thou relationship is direct, mutual, present and open; I-Thou is a dialogue in which the other is accepted in his or her unique otherness and not reduced to a content of my experience. We may move in the direction of greater wholeness through greater awareness and fuller response in each new situation. "The inmost growth of the self does not take place, as people like to suppose today," writes Buber, "through our relationship to ourselves, but through being made present by the other and knowing that we are made present by him." (KM, 71)

Being made present as a person is the heart of what Buber calls confirmation. The confirmation of the other must include an actual experiencing of the other side of the relationship so that one can imagine quite concretely what another is feeling, thinking and knowing. This "inclusion" does not abolish the basic distance between oneself and the other. It is rather a bold swinging over into the life of the person one confronts, through which alone I can make her present in her wholeness, unity and uniqueness.

This experiencing of the other side is essential to the distinction that Buber makes between "dialogue," in which I open myself to the otherness of the person I meet, and "monologue," in which, even when I converse with her at length, I allow her to exist only as a content of my experience. I can only become truly aware of another as I perceive her in her wholeness as a person, and that means to perceive that dynamic center that stamps on all her utterances, actions and attitudes the tangible sign of uniqueness. As long as the other is for me the detached object of my contemplation or observation, she will not yield her wholeness and its center to me, and I shall not be aware of her as a *person*, only as an *individual*. Only when I risk and reveal myself as she risks and reveals herself will I grasp her uniqueness and she mine.[1]

The essential problematic of the sphere of the between, writes Buber, is the duality of being and seeming. The being person looks at the other as one to whom she gives herself. She is not uninfluenced by the desire to make herself understood, but she has no thought for the conception of herself that she might awaken in the other person. The seeming person, in contrast, is primarily concerned with what the other person thinks of her. The origin of the tendency toward seeming is found in the human need for confirmation. It is no easy thing to be confirmed by the other in our being; therefore, we seek to get confirmed through what we appear to be. To give in to this tendency is our real cowardice, to withstand it is our real courage (*KM*, 68). Whatever the word "truth" may mean in other spheres, in the interhuman realm it means that we impart ourselves to the other as what we are. This is not a question of saying to the other everything that occurs to us, but of allowing the person with whom we communicate to partake of our being. The self as such is not ultimately essential, but the meaning of human existence again and again fulfills itself as self — through dialogue. The essential element of genuine dialogue is "seeing the other" or "experiencing the other side."

In the spokenness of speech, the between becomes real in the relationship of two or more persons. When the word really becomes speech, when it is actually spoken, it is spoken in the context of relationship, of the meeting with what is other than us. It takes its very meaning from the fact that it is said by one person and heard by another. The hearer adds a different dimension and relationship to the word that is spoken, even as he or she stands on a different ground from the speaker. One must keep in mind, therefore, the genuinely two-sided and dialogical character of the word as the embodiment of the between when it is spoken. The mystery of word and answer that moves *between* human beings is not one of union, harmony, or even complementarity, but of tension. Two persons never mean the same thing by the words that they use, and no answer is ever fully satisfactory. At each point of the dialogue, understanding and misunderstanding are interwoven. From this tension of understanding and misunderstanding comes the interplay of openness and closedness and of expression and reserve that mark every genuine dialogue between person and person. Thus the mere fact of the difference between persons already implies a basic dramatic situation as an inherent component of human existence as such, something that drama only reproduces in clearer and heightened form (see *KM*, chapter 5). It is this recognition of *difference* that explains the polarity, the vis-à-vis *and* the tragic conflict that may arise because "each is as he is."

"Dialogue between individuals is merely a sketch," says Buber in his essay, "Dialogue." Only dialogue between real persons is dialogue in the full sense of the term. But one does not become a real person by turning away from others and focusing on one's own individuation, with the hope of later turning more effectively to others: "By what could a man from being an individual so really become a person," writes Buber in this same essay, "as by the strict and sweet experience of dialogue which teaches him the boundless contents of the boundary?" (*BMM*, 21). The way to dialogue is dialogue itself, that incessant dance of distancing and relating that makes up our human life together. Our going inward to solitude and our going out to meet others from that solitude is "the systole and diastole" of the soul.

Responsibility means to respond, and this is the basis of ethics as Buber sees it. I cannot respond until I am in the situation, until I am face to face with you. Although genuine response is response of the whole person, we ought not think of the question of how to be a whole person but only of how, in any given situation, to respond more wholly rather than less so. In every situation we are asked to respond in a unique way. Therefore, our wholeness in that situation is unique, too. This integration through responding entails making a genuine decision. Decision here is not a conscious matter but the movement of the whole person. Genuine guilt, by the same token, arises because we have failed to respond or have responded with less wholeness and awareness than we might have. The corollary of dialogue, confirmation, inclusion and the interhuman is what Buber calls *existential guilt*. In contrast to inner or neurotic guilt, existential guilt is an event of the "between" that can be healed only through illuminating the guilt, persevering in that illumination, and repairing the injured order of existence through an active devotion to it. Guilt does not reside in the person, says Buber. Rather, one stands, in the most realistic sense, in the guilt that envelops one. Similarly, the repression of guilt and the neuroses that result from this repression are not merely psychological phenomena, but real events between persons (see *KM*, chapter 6).

Buber's I-Thou relationship has obvious parallels to Levinas's face-to-face, in which I recognize the otherness of the other not by competing with him but by responding in a relation of *discourse*. Both Buber and Levinas place the relationship with otherness — or the readiness for such an encounter — at the beginning of experience. Both consider the encounter as oriented toward the other prior to theoretical understanding and knowledge. And finally, both posit the relation with the Thou as in some sense incorporating or deriving from the relation with the absolutely Other called God.

Nonetheless, and despite Levinas's many writings on Buber, it is not easy to determine how much Buber influenced Levinas's thinking. Why not? The question is a difficult one not only because the notion of "influence" in philosophy is itself problematic, but also because Levinas was reading the dialogical philosophies of Franz Rosenzweig and Gabriel Marcel at the same time as he was reading Buber.

Levinas seems to have preferred Buber's rendering of the I-Thou relation to that of Marcel. However, Levinas does not present a consistent reading of Buber. In his postwar writings up to and including *Totality and Infinity*, it seemed that Levinas was primarily concerned with distinguishing his own ethical philosophy from Buber's. Despite the centrality of the category of relation in Buber's writings, Levinas suspected that Buber's thought was unable to account for the radical "separation" between the I and the other. In a series of lectures presented in 1946/7 at the College Philosophique, published under the title *Time and the Other*, Levinas explicitly opposed his own use of the phrase "I-Thou" (*moi-toi*) to "Buber's sense, where reciprocity remains the tie between two separated freedoms, and the ineluctable character of isolated subjectivity is underestimated" (*TO*, 93–94). This was not Levinas's only criticism of Buber during this phase of his thinking, but it remained the key one.

Levinas would add to the criticism in *Totality and Infinity*, where the "I-Thou" is charged with being self-sufficient and forgetful of the universe (*TI*, 213). Buber is not mentioned here by name, but earlier in the book Levinas had written, "the I-Thou in which Buber sees the category of the interhuman relationship is the relation not with the interlocutor but with feminine alterity" (*TI*, 106). It seems fairly clear that Levinas at this time associates Buber's I-Thou with love, which, as a relationship with the feminine in the intimacy of the home, excludes the third party. To be sure, it is not easy to reconcile this reading of Buber with Levinas's remark later in *Totality and Infinity*: "Love does not simply lead . . . toward the Thou. It is bent in another direction than that wherein one encounters the Thou" (*TI*, 106). Whatever we are to make of the discrepancy, it is clear that Levinas was prepared to use Buber both as a useful resource when seeking to avoid the neutral discourse of ontology, and as a foil for his own views when it was necessary to distinguish his own thinking from Buber's.

This is the case in Levinas's first essay devoted entirely to Buber entitled "Martin Buber and the Theory of Knowledge" (1958). Assimilating Buber's philosophy to "an entire movement of contemporary thought" (*PN*, 19), Levinas praised "Buber's fundamental contribution to the theory of knowledge" and attributed "great spiritual importance" (*PN*, 23) to the gesture of attaching primacy to the I-Thou relation over the I-It. He went on, however, to pose several "objections" to Buber, the chief of which was again directed at the "reciprocity of the *I-Thou* relation" (*PN*, 32). According to Levinas, by making the relationship a reciprocal one, Buber failed to bring out the essentially nonformal *ethical* character of the "meeting." This led Levinas to present Buber's I-Thou as a relation of "totally spiritual friendship." "We may ask ourselves whether clothing the naked and feeding the hungry are not the true and concrete access to the otherness of the other person — more authentic than the ether of friendship" (*PN*, 33). Buber, however, always rejected the label of spiritualism, claiming that to give the relation a character in advance would be an illegitimate delimitation of its content, which can only be revealed to the parties who stand within it and bring one another to their respective Thou.

Another conclusion that we draw from Levinas's works up to and including *Totality and Infinity* is that Buber is a thinker who, although concerned with ethics, is unable to go beyond the philosophical tradition that has always subordinated ethics to ontology. Inasmuch as Buber suggests that one can come to *know* the independent other and explicitly enter into *community* with her or him in the I-Thou relation, Buber comes dangerously close to reenclosing the other within the confines of knowledge and comprehension — for Levinas, an ontological gesture par excellence.

However, by 1978, the year in which Levinas published "Martin Buber, Gabriel Marcel and Philosophy," Levinas's reading of Buber appears to have undergone a significant transformation. Levinas's earlier worries about formalism, reciprocity and spiritualism in the I-Thou relation are set aside, and in their place we find Levinas praising Buber's notion of dialogue as containing a trace of original responsibility and ethical saying.

In many ways, the changes in Levinas's reading of Buber reflect the changes Levinas's own thinking underwent between *Totality and Infinity* and *Otherwise Than Being*, prompted in some measure by Derrida's reading of Levinas in his 1964 essay "Violence and Metaphysics." Now, rather than presenting Buber as a philosopher of consciousness, Levinas views him primarily as a philosopher of coexistence and sociality who challenges the philosophical tradition's epistemological or ontological bent. At the same time, Levinas does not attempt to establish a *homoiosis* between his thought and Buber's: "Here we are certainly taking a few steps to one side of Buber — not to 'understand him better than he understood himself,' but to rejoin him and to recognize him as a pioneer" (*BMP*, 316).

CONTINENTAL PHILOSOPHY AND LEVINAS'S PHENOMENOLOGICAL APPROACH

Levinas's last commentary on Buber sums up well Buber's place in and influence on Continental philosophy as well as his influence on Levinas himself:

> That valuation of the dia-logical relation and its phenomenological irreducibility, its fitness to constitute a meaningful order that is autonomous and as legitimate as the traditional and privileged *subject-object* correlation in the operation of knowledge — that will remain the

unforgettable contribution of Martin Buber's philosophical labors. . . . Nothing could limit the homage due him. Any reflection on the alterity of the other in his or her irreducibility to the objectivity of objects and the beings of beings must recognize the new perspective Buber opened — and find encouragement in it (*OS*, 41).

For the professional philosopher and the intellectual historian it may be helpful to say here a word about Buber's relationship to Kant. Buber took over from Kant the concept that the sense world is only the world of appearance, the real world being for Kant, but not for Buber, a *Ding an sich* that we can never know. Buber went beyond Kant in insisting that it is precisely through the sense world — our fellow human beings, animals, the rest of nature, even art — that we meet the eternal Thou and that we do so through genuine I-Thou relationships. Whereas Kant relied on reason, Buber relied on experience and religious intuition.[2] For this reason too Buber was open to the influence of post-Kantian thinkers, such as J. G. Hamann, Søren Kierkegardand Wilhelm Dilthey,[3] who insisted on a spiritual transcendence with which we can be in relationship, that there was a hidden power, spiritual in character, that manifests itself in human life.

Expanding on Levinas's commentary, we could describe Buber's place in and influence on Continental philosophy in two ways. Buber is, first of all, the foremost of the dialogical existentialists, or existentialists of dialogue, a group which includes other philosophers such as Gabriel Marcel, Karl Jaspers, Albert Camus, and even Franz Kafka.[4] Secondly, he stands at the head of the stream of philosophers of dialogue, stretching from Hermann Levin-Goldschmidt to Hans Georg Gadamer, Jürgen Habermas, and Levinas himself, whether they acknowledge Buber's influence or not. However, Martin Buber did not construct a systematic philosophy, much less a phenomenology, and though it would be possible to present Buber's thought as a coherent and unified philosophy, academic philosophers will probably always prefer Emmanuel Levinas with his phenomenology and rigor. Although Buber's work has for many decades been more widely read and discussed both within and outside philosophy, Levinas's thought is very much in the ascendancy, especially in Continental circles.

Known primarily by French philosophers as a Husserl and Heidegger scholar throughout the 1940s and 50s, Levinas came to be regarded as an important philosopher in his own right soon after the publication in 1961 of his first master work, *Totality and Infinity*. Although many of the central themes presented in that book had appeared in earlier books and articles, it was not until they were presented in *Totality and Infinity* as part of a systematic phenomenology of ethical life that readers began to realize just how innovative and fecund Levinas's thinking was. Derrida's 1964 essay "Violence and Metaphysics" helped to demonstrate the philosophical rigor of Levinas's work and its complex relations to the phenomenologies of Hegel, Husserl and Heidegger, while simultaneously sealing Levinas's reputation as a thinker of equal rank to these highly regarded German philosophers. Soon thereafter other major Continental theorists, including Jean-François Lyotard and Luce Irigaray, published essays on Levinas's thought, acknowledging their debt to his work and extending it into new areas of discussion. This trend has continued over the past several decades with a host of other notable Continental theorists — including Paul Ricoeur, Maurice Blanchot, Enrique Dussel and Zygmunt Bauman — all paying homage to Levinas's work. There are also indications that Levinas is starting to make the crossover into Anglo-American philosophy, as evidenced by the inclusion of an essay by Hilary Putnam in the recently published *Cambridge Companion to Levinas* (2002) and several publications on Levinas by Edith Wyschogrod, who was the first person in America to emphasize Levinas's philosophical significance.

Much of Levinas's thinking goes beyond what traditionally goes by the name of philosophy. Traditional philosophy claims to give us knowledge of the nature of reality, and thus of the ultimate grounds of everything that exists. As such it has been "ontology," an account of the nature of *Being in general*. Insofar as philosophy is concerned with Being in general, the relation with particular beings is subordinated to an *impersonal* rational structure. This rule of sameness and identity characteristic of philosophy leads to the suppression and domination of individuals.

Ontology as first philosophy is a philosophy of power. It issues in the State and in the non-violence of the totality, without securing itself against the violence from which this non-violence lives, and which appears in the tyranny of the State. Universality appears as impersonal; and this is another inhumanity. (*TI*, 46)

Levinas's critique of the totality is not an existentialist revolt against the system à la Kierkegaard, a revolt waged in the name of authenticity or personal salvation. "It is not I who resists the system," according to Levinas, "it is the other" (*TI*, 40). The other here means *the other person* (*autrui*). The other is not merely other *than* me, which would be to define him or her in terms of me, and thus make alterity merely relative. The other is *absolutely* other in the sense that his or her identity is *ab-solved* or separated from mine. The other remains radically exterior, outside of all philosophical intelligibility and concepts. Levinas is uncompromising on this point. The other is radically incomprehensible, unknowable and nonthematizable. *He or she cannot be comprehended as such.*

The phenomenology to which Levinas turns to validate his philosophical conclusions begins with the experience of the face (*le visage*) of the other. The main dynamic behind the face-to-face relation is ethics. The other and I do not relate to each other as two hostile forces involved in a Hegelian struggle for recognition, but in a relation of *discourse*. This should not be confused with the mundane traffic of information from one being to the next. Behind what is actually "said" (*le dit*), according to Levinas, there is "the saying" (*le dire*) of what is said. This saying is straightaway ethical inasmuch as it first comes to me from the other and consists in the biblical command: "You shall not commit murder."

The prohibition against violence, however, does not exhaust the meaning of ethics and the face. When facing the other there is a constraint to *give*, not just fine words and praises, not just hymns and encomiums, but with full hands. "No human or interhuman relationship can be enacted outside of economy; no face can be approached with empty hands and closed home" (*TI*, 172). The other is essentially proletarian, destitute. He or she is "the widow, the orphan and the stranger" spoken of in the Book of Jeremiah (Jer 22:3). It is precisely as destitute that the other manages to contest all possession. Faced with the neediness of the other, I never knew I had so much, I never knew I was so rich. I am not rich because I have a surplus beyond what I need. I am rich because the other always has less than he or she needs. The face is the face of deprivation and need. In *Totality and Infinity*, Levinas writes:

> This gaze that supplicates and demands, that can supplicate only because it demands, deprived of everything because entitled to everything, and which one recognizes in giving . . . this gaze is precisely the epiphany of the face as a face. The nakedness of the face is its destituteness. To recognize the Other is to recognize a hunger. To recognize the other is to give. But it is to give to the master, to the lord, to him whom one approaches in a dimension of height. (*TI*, 75)

"Height" is the most elementary fact of morality according to Levinas. The other dominates me from a position of height. We, I and the other, are not equals. The relationship between us is fundamentally nonreciprocal or asymmetrical in the sense that what I have the right to demand of the other is incomparable with what the other has the right to demand of me. This recognition of the rights of the other over my own is what Levinas terms goodness. "Goodness consists in taking up a position such that the other counts more than myself" (*TI*, 247).

Levinas's thinking is thus an attempt to rethink the meaning of ethics after the failure of ethics, when the heavens are vacant and reason alone is unable to provide a good enough reason to be good. But it does not strive on that account to be anything other than reason. Although Levinas seeks to go beyond the philosophical tradition, he does not attempt to go beyond philosophy *as such*. He indeed insists that his thinking "means to be philosophy" (*OB*, 155). It thus aspires to a neutral and objective language — the language of Greece — even if the meaning that inspires it is closely connected with the spiritual vocation of the particular cultural experience called Judaism.

The reader of Kant or Mill — and perhaps Buber — will doubtless reject Levinas's seemingly implausible claim that ethics is not reciprocal. For if ethics is not reciprocal, then it is not universal, and thus is nothing I can prescribe to the other.

Another claim that is likely to puzzle philosophers trained in the Western philosophical tradition is Levinas's insistence on the other rather than reason and autonomy as the only possible source of morality. In Levinas's theory, freedom is not held to be morally justified in itself but requires justification from the other. Left to its own devices — or vices — freedom shows itself to be arbitrary and violent. Face-to-face with the other, I am not an innocent spontaneity, but murderer, someone whose natural instinct is to be indifferent to the other. The other calls into question "the naive right of my powers, my glorious spontaneity as a living being" (*TI*, 84) through what is ordinarily called conscience.

Again this does not presuppose any freedom on my part. "Freedom is at the same time discovered in the consciousness of shame and concealed in the shame itself. Shame does not have the structure of consciousness and clarity" (*TI*, 84). Levinas attempts to show how the other is capable of justifying the exercise of freedom, not in the sense of a theoretical demonstration or proof of freedom (which Kant showed is impossible), but rather in the sense of making it just: "To justify freedom is not to prove it, but to render it just" (*TI*, 83).

There is a twofold sense in which it can be said that ethics is prior to freedom. First of all, I do not choose to relate to the other ethically, a choice that would have to precede the encounter with the other, and thus would be an expression of my arbitrary spontaneity and ipso facto unjustified. Second, I find myself always already bound to the other — ligated — in a relationship of obligation preceding the will and consciousness. Levinas calls this preconscious bond "metaphysical Desire." Desire is thus to be distinguished from need, which can in principle be satisfied, e.g., the need for food, the fine car, the loyal friend. Desire is essentially dissatisfied, perpetually hungry. Or rather, as Levinas likes to say, in remembrance of Shakespeare (e.g., *Anthony and Cleopatra* 2.3), it is satisfied only when it is unsatisfied, nourished as it were by its own hunger (*TI*, 34).

The satisfaction of need, however, has an important role to play in ethics. In Levinas's ethics, we find none of the idealized asceticism of the type Nietzsche denounced in the third part of *On the Genealogy of Morals*. Levinas insists that one must first enjoy what one gives before one can make of it a gift to the other. Hence responsibility is described in poetical fashion as "the tearing away of the mouthful of bread from the mouth that tastes it in full enjoyment. . . . It is a gift, not of the heart, but of the bread from one's mouth, of one's mouthful of bread" (*OB*, 74).

It is this "one-for-the-other" of responsibility that ultimately defines the self according to Levinas. I am me in the sole measure that I am responsible, a noninterchangeable I. The other is my charge and mine alone. Only I can answer before and for the other, which amounts to a privilege and an election with regard to responsibilities I do not choose and from which no one can release me. The self is thus characterized by Levinas as a "hostage," someone who is put in the place of another, carrying his or her woes, ready to substitute itself for the other.

Accordingly, the self is a *subjectum* (*sub-jacere*, to throw, place, or set under) in the sense that it is subjected or subordinated to the responsibility that ultimately serves defines it. The relation with the other is the sole *principium individuationis.* The self is a subject, then, not in any traditional Cartesian or humanist sense. Self-presence, the presence of self to self in the interiority of consciousness (the *cogito*), which Descartes took to be the first certainty, is secondary to the relation with other. Responsibility is literally *an-archic*, without any principle or origin in consciousness or thought. It is not as if I provide myself with some principle or rule for acting ethically. I do not weigh up what I have actually done and try to make amends. Responsibility is more immediate than that insofar as I feel myself obligated by the other prior to the onset of reflection. The other commands me before my really hearing it, a command that is not understood, not thematized as such. It is similar to the case where someone is commanding one to listen, as though the imperative "Listen!" preceded — or indeed followed — itself.

This strange, illogical notion of a "command before understanding," where the other is capable of obligating prior to consciousness and deliberation, is what Levinas in *Otherwise Than Being* calls the "trace" (a term most commonly associated with Derrida, but which

Derrida, in *Of Grammatology* explicitly attributes to Levinas).[5] The language of the face is the trace of "a past that has never been present," that is, a past that has never been present to consciousness in the form of memory. I have always already been responsible for the other without knowing it. Here, again, there is no choice. "To leave men without food," says Levinas, quoting a talmudic source, "is a fault that no circumstance attenuates; the distinction between the voluntary and the involuntary does not apply here" (*TI*, 201).

BUBER, LEVINAS AND JUDAISM

While Buber influenced many religious thinkers and theologians, he was not himself a theologian, if by theologian one means someone who accepts certain dogmatic principles on faith. Buber was too bound to experience to ever be that. In this he differs from the great Jewish religious philosopher Abraham Joshua Heschel, even though he was Heschel's friend and had a profound influence on him. In Hasidism, the communal Jewish mysticism of eastern Europe during the eighteenth and nineteenth centuries, the holiest teaching is rejected if it is found in someone only as a content of that person's thinking. This must not be understood as a contrast between feeling and thought. It is not the dominance of any one faculty but the unity of all faculties within the personality that constitutes the wholeness of the person, and it is this that Buber calls "spirit." "Spirit is . . . the totality which comprises and integrates all man's capacities, powers, qualities and urges" (*IW*, 175). But human wholeness does not exist apart from real relationship to other beings. In *I and Thou* Buber defines spirit in its human manifestation as "a response of man to his *Thou*" (*IT*, 39).

Like Buber, Levinas repudiates theology, and for similar reasons. He insists that ethics, which he sometimes calls "metaphysics," is not a theology — not even a negative one — and even resorts to the term "atheism" to stress the fact that it is not even based on traditional theism. "The atheism of the metaphysician means, positively, our relation with the Metaphysical is an ethical behavior and not theology, not a thematization, be it a knowledge by analogy, of the attributes of

God. God rises to his supreme and ultimate presence as correlative to the justice rendered unto men" (*TI*, 78). Few claims in Levinas's philosophy come across more forcefully than the claim that there can be no relationship with God separated from the relationship between persons. For Levinas, the interhuman is the only manner in which the Eternal Thou "comes to mind" or *presences* — a claim Buber would be inclined to grant were it not for the fact he also thought it was possible to have an I-Thou relation with the rest of nature, which Levinas for the most part strenuously denied. (See Peter Atterton's essay in this volume.)

Nonetheless, both Buber and Levinas were deeply rooted in Judaism. Whereas Buber emphasized the biblical covenant, the prophets, and the teachings and tales of the Hasidim, Levinas emphasized the Talmud, and the Hebrew Bible read through the lens of the Talmud. Buber would go on to translate the Hebrew Bible into German (with Franz Rosenzweig). Levinas, on the other hand, would produce a number of talmudic commentaries based on the Haggadah, having been trained quite late (in the 1950s) in the Midrash by "*le maître prestigieux*," the enigmatic M. Chouchani (who was also the teacher of Elie Wiesel). Levinas was, in addition, an unyielding opponent of myth and mysticism, preferring study over zeal and emotion, which were important to Buber's understanding of Judaism.

It has become almost fashionable to describe Levinas as a Jewish philosopher. However, the term is one that Levinas himself treated as suspect, implying as it does something less than pure philosophical rigor. When asked in an interview whether the term "Jewish philosopher" had any meaning for him, he said, "To be considered a Jewish thinker is not in itself something that shocks me. I am Jewish and certainly have readings, contacts and traditions which are specifically Jewish and which I do not deny. But I protest against the formula when by it one understands something that dares to establish between concepts relations which are based uniquely in religious traditions and texts, without bothering to pass through the philosophical critique" (*IR*, 61). Levinas went on explain that there are two ways of reading a biblical verse. The first way is uncritical, and consists in appealing to the tradition "without distrusting and without even taking account of the presuppositions of that tradition" (*IR*, 61). The second is critical, and consists in translating what is said there into a philosophical thinking that has independent warrant. "The verse must be phenomenologically justified" (*IR*, 62).

This is not to say that one would search in vain for references to the Bible or the Talmud in Levinas's work. They are legion. Plentiful too are borrowings from contemporary Jewish sources, such as Rosenzweig's *Star of Redemption*, said in *Totality and Infinity* to be too often present to be mentioned (*TI*, 28), and Buber's *I and Thou*, which is commended in the same work for its "essential contribution to contemporary thought" (*TI*, 68). Clearly Levinas is more than happy to draw on Jewish sources for purposes of attestation, though he claims to find independent validation for what is attested there outside religion. "I illustrate with verse, yes, but I do not prove by verse" (*IR*, 62).

"God," says Buber in his classic work *I and Thou*, "is the Being that is directly, most nearly, and lastingly, over against us, that may properly only be addressed and not expressed" (*IT*, 80 f.). God is the "absolute Person" who is met whenever we meet our fellow human beings or the world as "Thou." God is the "eternal Thou" who cannot become an "It." The true God can never be an object of our thought, not even the "Absolute" object from which all others derive. We do not *discover* God, therefore; we *respond* to God. We become aware of *the address of God* in everything that we meet if we remain open to that address and ready to respond with our whole being. "Meet the world with the fullness of your being and you shall meet Him," writes Buber. "If you wish to learn to believe, love!" (*OJ*, 212 f.).

The eternal Thou is met by every person who addresses God by whatever name, and even by that person who does not believe in God yet addresses "the *Thou* of his life, as a *Thou* that cannot be limited by another." "All God's names are hallowed, for in them He is not merely spoken about, but also spoken to" (*IT*, 75 f.). Our speaking to God, our meeting with God is not mere waiting and openness for the advent of grace. We must go forth to the meeting with God, for here too, as in the I-Thou relationship with our fellows, the relation means being chosen and choosing, suffering and action in one.

To go out to the meeting with the eternal Thou, we need not lay aside the sense world as though it were illusory or go beyond sense-experience. Nor need we have recourse to a world of ideas and values. "The one thing that matters is visible, full acceptance of the present" (*IT*, 78). This does not mean giving up the I, as mystical writings usually suppose, for the I is essential to this as to every relation. What must be given up is the self-asserting instinct that makes a person flee to the possessing of things before the unreliable, perilous world of relation. It is not life in the world that separates us from God but the alienated world of *It*, which experiences and uses. We may know remoteness from God, but we do not know the absence of God, for it is we only who are not always there. In God's response, all the universe is made manifest as language.

In shutting off our awareness of the signs of address, we are shutting off our awareness of the address of God, for the One who speaks in these signs is the "Lord of the Voice," the eternal Thou (*BMM*, 10–15). "To escape responsibility for his life, [every person] turns existence into a system of hideouts" and "enmeshes himself more and more deeply in perversity" (*HMM*, 133). The lie displaces "the undivided seriousness of the human with himself" and destroys the good will and reliability on which our life in common rests (*GE*, 9). Our failure to say what we mean and do what we say "confuses and poisons, again and again and in increasing measure," the situation between oneself and the other person. The perspective in which one sees oneself only as an individual contrasted with other individuals, and not as a genuine person whose transformation helps toward the transformation of the world, contains the fundamental error (*HMM*, 157–59).

> It is a cruelly hazardous enterprise, this becoming a whole. . . . Everything in the nature of inclinations, of indolence, of habits, of fondness for possibilities which has been swashbuckling within us, must be overcome, and overcome, not by elimination, by suppression. . . . Rather must all these mobile or static forces, seized by the soul's rapture, plunge of their own accord, as it were, into the mightiness of decision and dissolve within it. (*GE*, 127)

"Decision" is here both the current decision about the immediate situation that confronts us and through this the decision with the whole being for God.

The Hebrew Bible speaks in terms of the person being created in the image of the imageless God and each person, therefore, having a unique value and a unique created task that no other person has. This notion of "created uniqueness," expanded and developed in Hasidism, was succinctly expressed by Rabbi Nachman of Bratzlav: God never does the same thing twice, and its corollary was aptly formulated by Martin Buber: "Uniqueness is the essential good of man that is given him to unfold" (*HMM*, 110).

Also important to Buber is the biblical concept of *emunah* or trust. *Emunah* is perseverance in a hidden but self-revealing guidance. This guidance does not relieve us of taking and directing our own steps, for it is nothing other than God's making known that He is present. *Emunah* is the realization of our faith in the actual totality of our relationships to God, to our appointed sphere in the world, and to ourselves. "By its very nature trust is substantiation of trust in the fullness of life in spite of the course of the world which is experienced."[6]

Holocaust Theology

Philosophers such as Emil Fackenheim have written as if Buber did not take the Holocaust into account in his later thinking. In this they are profoundly mistaken, as has been shown by Jerry Lawritson in his essay on "Martin Buber and the Shoah,"[7] and by David Forman-Barzilai in his essay "Agonism in Faith: Martin Buber's Eternal Thou after the Holocaust."[8] Buber's approach to the Holocaust, or *Shoah* as it is now called, is best understood in the context of Buber's phrase "the eclipse of God," a terminology that Buber already used in his essay on "Dialogue" in 1928 but that only comes into its own during the time of the Nazis and the years following it.[9] While still in Nazi Germany from 1933 to 1938, Buber reorganized Jewish education as a form of spiritual resistance to the persecution of the Jews and, along with Leo Baeck, helped give the German Jews a sense of Jewish identity and self-respect. Although Buber did not acknowledge the reality of the Holocaust until 1945 or 1946, when he did so he always pointed to this monstrous state-organized crime of inhumanity as so beyond his ability to imagine and take into "inclusion," that he could not hate the Nazis, much less overcome his hatred. "And what am I," he added at the time of receiving the Peace Prize of the German Book Trade in 1963, "that I should here forgive." For this reason, too, Buber rejected ever more vigorously that there could be a redeemed soul in an unredeemed world. In his memorial address for his religious socialist friend Leonhard Ragaz in 1947, Buber cried out: "Standing bound and shackled in the pillory of mankind, we demonstrate with the bloody body of our people the unredeemedness of the world!"[10]

For Levinas, the experience of being Jewish and witnessing the unspeakable horrors of the Holocaust had a profound effect that marked nearly everything he wrote thereafter.[11] At the outbreak of World War II, Levinas was drafted into the French army. He was captured by the Germans in 1940, but because he was a French officer, he escaped being sent to a concentration camp, and spent the rest of the war in a forestry commando unit for Jewish prisoners in Germany. With the exception of his wife and daughter, his family was murdered by the Nazis. His second major work on ethics, *Otherwise Than Being or Beyond Essence* (1974), includes the following dedication:

> To the memory of those who were closest among the six million assassinated by the National Socialists, and of the millions and millions of all confessions and all nations, victims of the same hatred of the other man, the same anti-Semitism.

It is impossible to read these words without being moved by the very personal sentiments they convey. But they also serve as a reminder of the suffering experienced by victims everywhere. What is especially interesting is the way Levinas universalizes the category of "Jew" so that it comes to stand for the persecuted of "all confessions and all nations." The gesture is perhaps open to criticism, attributing as it does a certain exemplarity to Jewish suffering in the very process of extending it to non-Jews, but it also serves as a new interpretation of the Holocaust, which is no longer viewed as a particular historical event that happened to the Jewish people, but rather an event that has a universal significance.

According to Levinas, the Holocaust not only contravenes the fundamental principles of morality, but actually places those principles in question. In an interview he put the point succinctly: "The essential problem is this: Can we speak of morality after Auschwitz? Can we speak of morality after the failure of morality?" (*PM*, 176). Alongside what Kant called "the failure of all philosophical attempts at theodicy," the Holocaust signifies the failure of philosophical attempts at ethics. It shows the speciousness of a "childish" conception of God who metes out rewards to those who are obedient and punishes those who are not, as well as the questionable conception of an ethics entirely based on reason and law. Did not reason altogether fail to become (in Kant's words) "practical" precisely when it most needed to? What the excessive cruelty of the twentieth century has demonstrated perhaps more than anything is the failure of both God and the Enlightenment to keep their promises.

There is more at issue here than simply the impotence of philosophy and its inability to arrest the natural course of violence in recent history. For Levinas it is not merely the inconclusiveness of human reasoning that is to blame for violence, but reason itself, which is not only incapable of stopping the violence, but is shown in important respects to be in complicity with violence. Indeed, it is the totalizing tendency to suppress difference and particularity characteristic of reason and philosophy that is the very definition of violence as construed by Levinas.

Organizational Notes

The present book is composed of four parts. The first is entitled "Dialogue and Difference," and is our way of moderating a relatively unknown "dialogue" between Levinas and Buber in which Levinas responds to Buber's reading of the biblical story of Samuel and Agag (1 Sam 15:33). What is interesting about Levinas's "little" disagreement with Buber's interpretation — beyond the attempt to distance himself from Buber on the question of how to read the Bible — is his using Buber's reading of the story of Samuel and Agag as the occasion to do it. Whereas Buber argues that Saul was right to spare the defeated and defenseless Agag, the sworn enemy of the Israelites, Levinas argues that Samuel was justified in rebuking him for following his conscience instead of the will of God. If there is an irony here, it is that we might have expected Levinas to side with Buber in this particular instance, as Saul's refusal to kill Agag in cold blood appears to result from his following the ethical injunction "Thou shalt not kill" that Levinas claims is the very meaning of the human face. For Levinas, however, the divine order to kill Agag answers the need for *justice*, the same justice for which an event such as the Holocaust cries out, and which he accuses Buber of forgetting on this occasion.

Part 2 is entitled "Ethics and Otherness," and concerns the differences and similarities between Buber's and Levinas's ethical thinking, respectively. In his essay "Buber and Levinas: Philosophical Reflections on an Opposition," Stephan Strasser focuses on the chief philosophical differences between the two, ranging from Buber's belief that God can be "beheld" in everything, a form of representationalism according to Levinas that fails to do justice to God's absolute transcendence, to Buber's description of the I-Thou relation as "reciprocal," which Levinas argues risks reducing it to a "purely spiritual" friendship. Rather than trying to decide which of these two thinkers is "right" here, Strasser is content to let the philosophical opposition between them stand in order to allow a more profound understanding of their work to emerge. Ultimately for Strasser, it is a matter of understanding *both* Buber and Levinas as marking the culmination of two divergent possibilities inherent within the Jewish tradition itself.

Andrew Tallon's essay, "Affection and the Transcendental Dialogical Personalism of Buber and Levinas," argues that Buber and Levinas both share a philosophically developed and nonrepresentational version of affectivity that differs from Western tradition. Affectivity is the very locus of intersubjectivity, according to Tallon, and its respective treatment in the hands of Buber ("between") and Levinas ("proximity") is best understood as belonging to a minor philosophical tradition of the "heart" stretching from Augustine to Pascal.

Robert Bernasconi's contribution is a meticulous study of "the dialogue between thinkers" that occurred between Levinas and Buber. By tracing Levinas's early criticisms of the I-Thou relation, and his subsequent attempt to reveal the ethical "saying" in Buber's "said," Bernasconi attempts to show that the "failure of communication" that often characterized their dialogue is evidence of the nonsynchronism of the saying and the said. To this extent, it should not be construed negatively but positively as the "surplus" of ethical transcendence itself. For Bernasconi, such a surplus underlies what might be called "a Levinasian hermeneutics."

Neve Gordon's "Ethics and the Place of the Other" offers a rejoinder to Levinas's critique of Buber's notion of "reciprocity," which according to Levinas risks reducing the ethical difference between the self and the other. Gordon argues that Levinas's reading of Buber here is open to criticism. Indeed, from Gordon's perspective, Levinasian ethics, which begins with and is founded on the other, does not by itself constitute an instance of Thou-Saying, and can quite easily remain at the level of the I-It. In order for an I-Thou relation to take place, something more is needed than my recognition of the other's independence, which is why, as Buber says, "if all were clothed and well nourished, then the real ethical problem would become wholly visible for the first time."

In the final chapter of this section, Maurice Friedman similarly argues that Levinas's readings of Buber founder due to a failure to understand Buber's philosophy on its own terms. Friedman argues that not only is Buber's situational ethics superior to Levinas's, but also that Buber's ethical thought opens onto a more sophisticated social and political philosophy than Levinas was able to offer. Friedman concludes with an analysis of Buber's and Levinas's divergent readings of the story of Samuel and Agag (see chapters 1 and 2) as a way of illustrating these points further.

Part 3 of the volume, "Religion," discusses Buber's and Levinas's rootedness in the Jewish tradition, as well as their different conceptions of the religious. Ephraim Meir demonstrates how both thinkers highlighted the universal and eminently ethical character in Judaism. However, they greatly differed on various subjects such as prayer, ritual and learning, and had different positions toward the State of Israel.

Michael Fagenblat and Nathan Wolski's essay, "Revelation Here and Beyond: Buber and Levinas on the Bible," explores the thought of Buber and Levinas as it relates specifically to the Hebrew Bible. Both Buber and Levinas call for a return to the Bible, and in so doing illustrate the possibility of a God-oriented worldview that remains entirely grounded in the experience of modernity. Using the Bible as a lens, they suggest that one can trace the similarities and fault lines running through their thought, especially as it pertains to such themes as revelation, interpretation, narrativity, religious experience and historicism.

Robert Gibbs's "Reading Torah: Discontinuity of Tradition" is a detailed examination of Buber's and Levinas's respective reflections on traditional Jewish texts. Arguing that both thinkers share a basic insight that the texts have a surplus of meaning, and have renewable abilities to reveal God to human beings, Gibbs nevertheless goes on to show that they employ quite different hermeneutic approaches, as Levinas interprets the Bible through the writings of the Sages, especially the Talmud, whereas Buber interprets the Bible directly. At the heart of this contrast is a reflection on how these texts still speak to us today — how the discontinuity is maintained and heightened, even as the condition for a text to address us.

Tamra Wright's paper compares Buber's response to the Holocaust with that of Levinas. She looks at the development of Buber's and Levinas's writings on Judaism in the context of Emil Fackenheim's claim that Judaism is "ruptured" by the Holocaust, and of Zachary Braiterman's observation that Jewish writers begin emphasizing antitheodic motifs in Judaism only from the late 1960s onward.

The final essay in this section, Andrew Kelley's "Reciprocity and the Height of God," offers a defense of Buber against Levinas's allegation that the notion of the I-Thou reduces the height from which the other comes, thus threatening to turn God into an equal inasmuch as the other opens something like access to God. Kelley argues that, quite the contrary, Buber's I-Thou not only does not reduce the other to an equal, but as "an address and a turning toward God," it makes transcendence as height possible.

Part 4, entitled "Heidegger, Humanism and the Other Animal," seeks to draw Levinas's and Buber's thinking into the contemporary critical debates surrounding Heideggerian thought, antihumanism and anthropocentrism. Richard Cohen's essay examines the role that Heidegger's fundamental ontology plays in Buber's and Levinas's work. Cohen's analysis reveals that Buber's and Levinas's respective critiques of Heidegger also serve as Buber's and Levinas's respective critiques of each other, with each thinker accusing the other of remaining within the orbit of Heideggerian thought.

In his contribution, Matthew Calarco discusses Buber's and Levinas's retrieval of humanism in the wake of Heidegger's famous critique in the "Letter on 'Humanism.'" Calarco argues that Levinas's "humanism of the other man" ultimately provides a more philosophically fruitful approach to the humanism problematic than does Buber's "believing humanism," while suggesting that the dogmatic anthropocentrism underlying Levinas's humanism needs to be called into question.

Peter Atterton's essay "Face-to-Face with the other Animal?" examines the question of whether Levinasian ethics extends to non-human animals. Comparing Buber's account of the possibility of Thou-saying to nonhuman beings with Levinas's various remarks on animals scattered throughout his writings, Atterton shows that with regard to the animal question, at least, Levinas comes up short.

Finally, despite their diverse interpretations, approaches and goals, the essays compiled in *Levinas and Buber: Dialogue and Difference* have one essential thing in common. They all bear witness to the enduring importance and guiding spirit of the writings of Martin Buber and Emmanuel Levinas — perhaps the most important Jewish philosophers since the twelfth century sage, Maimonides.

Part I

DIALOGUE

ONE

Samuel and Agag

Martin Buber

I once met on a journey a man whom I already knew through an earlier meeting. He was an observant Jew who followed the religious tradition in all the details of his life-pattern. But what was for me essential (as had already become unmistakably clear to me at that first meeting) was that this relationship to tradition had its origin and its constantly renewed confirmation in the relationship of the man to God.

When I now saw him again, it turned out that we fell into a discussion of biblical questions, and indeed not of peripheral questions but central ones, central questions of faith. I do not know exactly any longer in what connection we came to speak of that section of the Book of Samuel in which it is told how Samuel delivered to King Saul the message that his dynastic rule would be taken from him because he had spared the life of the conquered prince of the Amalekites. I reported to my partner in dialogue how dreadful it had already been to me when I was a boy to read this as the message of God (and my heart compelled me to read it over again or at least to think about the fact that this stood written in the Bible). I told him how already at that time it horrified me to read or to remember how the heathen king went up to the prophet with the words on his lips, "Surely the bitterness of death is past," and was hewn to pieces by him. I said to my partner: "I have never been able to believe that this is a message of God. I do not believe it."

With wrinkled forehead and contracted brows, the man sat opposite me and his glance flamed into my eyes. He remained silent, began to speak, became silent again. "So?" he broke forth at last, "so? You do not believe it?" "No," I answered, "I do not believe it." "So? so?" he repeated almost threateningly. "You do not believe it?" And I once again: "No." "What . . . what . . ." — he thrust the words before him one after the other — "What do you believe then?" "I believe," I replied without reflecting, "that Samuel has misunderstood God." And he, again slowly, but more softly than before: "So? You believe that?" And I: "Yes." Then we were both silent. But now something happened the like of which I have rarely seen before or since in this my long life. The angry countenance opposite me became transformed, as if a hand had passed over it soothing it. It lightened, cleared, was now turned toward me bright and clear. "Well," said the man with a positively gentle tender clarity, "I think so too." And again we became silent, for a good while.

There is in the end nothing astonishing in the fact that an observant Jew of this nature, when he has to choose between God and the Bible, chooses God: the God in whom he believes, Him in whom he can believe. And yet, it seemed to me at that time significant and still seems so to me today. The man later came to the land of Israel and here I met him once again, some time before his death. Naturally I regarded him then as the speaker of that word of one time; but in our talk the problem of biblical belief was not touched on. It was, indeed, no longer necessary.

For me, however, in all the time since that early conversation, the question has again and again arisen whether at that time I expressed in the right manner what I meant. And again and again I answered the question in the same way: Yes and No. Yes insofar as it concerns what had been spoken of in that conversation; for there it was right to answer my partner in his language and within the limits of his language in order that the dialogue might not come to naught and that the common insight into one truth at times afforded to two men might fulfill itself, in no matter how limited a way. Insofar as it concerns that, Yes. But No when it concerns both recognizing oneself and making known that man and the human race are inclined to misunderstand God. Man is so created that he can understand, but does not have to understand, what God says to him. God does not abandon the created man to his needs and anxieties; He provides him with the assistance of His word; He speaks to him, He comforts him with His word. But man does not listen with faithful ears to what is spoken to him. Already in hearing he blends together command of heaven and statute of earth, revelation to the existing being and the orientations that he arranges himself. Even the holy scriptures of man are not excluded, not even the Bible. What is involved here is not ultimately the fact that this or that form of biblical historical narrative has misunderstood God; what is involved is the fact that in the work of throats and pens out of which the text of the Old Testament has arisen, misunderstanding has again and again attached itself to understanding, the manufactured has been mixed with the received. We have no objective criterion for the distinction; we have only faith — when we have it. Nothing can make me believe in a God who punishes Saul because he has not murdered his enemy. And yet even today I still cannot read the passage that tells this otherwise than with fear and trembling. But not it alone. Always when I have to translate or to interpret a biblical text, I do so with fear and trembling, in an inescapable tension between the word of God and the words of man.

Translated by Maurice Friedman

Two

On Buber

Emmanuel Levinas

François Poirié — *Speak, if you will, about Martin Buber. I believe you knew him.*

Emmanuel Levinas — Yes, I knew him personally after the war. My interest in the intersubjective relation, my principal theme, is often united with the philosophy of Buber, who distinguished the I-Thou, the relation between persons, from the I-It, the relation of man with things. The relation to the other man is irreducible to the knowledge of an object. Certainly, Buber entered this field of reflection before me. When one has worked, even without knowing it, in a field that has already been prepared by another, one owes allegiance and gratitude to the pioneer. I do not refuse these to Martin Buber, even if in fact it is not by starting out from the Buberian oeuvre that I have been led to a reflection on the alterity of the Other,[1] to which my modest writings are devoted. Gabriel Marcel too came to the same reflection quite independently. I do not know if he recognized Buber's paternity, though he spoke quite openly of parentage. I am therefore very close to the Buberian theses, despite the flash of genius [*éclat de génie*] in his books and the poetic potential of his expression, which is very inspired. His thought is universally known and has exercised a tremendous influence throughout the world. A multifaceted genius, moreover, Buber has devoted to Hasidism — which is altogether strange to me — a considerable oeuvre that all but introduced Hasidism to the European sensibility. He has written tales and novels in which his philosophical thoughts are also expressed.

I read somewhat late his great book *I and Thou*, a fundamental book in which the interpersonal relation is distinguished from the subject-object relation in a very convincing and brilliant manner, and also with a great deal of finesse. The main thing [*la grande chose*] that separates us — or the minor thing [*la petite chose*] (when one speaks of someone to whom one draws near, one often says: "In minor things, there are some differences between us") — the principal thing [*la chose principale*] separating us is what I call the asymmetry of the I-Thou relation. For Buber, the relationship between the I and the Thou is directly lived as reciprocity. My point of departure is Dostoyevsky and his phrase [. . .]:[2] "We are all culpable for everything and for everyone before everyone, and I [*moi*] more than the others."[3] The feeling that the I [*Je*] owes everything to the Thou [*Tu*], and that its responsibility for the Other is gratitude, that the other has always — and *by right* [*de droit*] — a right [*un droit*] over Me [*Moi*], indeed, everything I have said [. . .] about this "I" ("*je*") submitted to obligation, this "I" commanded in the face of the Other — with the double structure of human misery and the word of God — all that represents perhaps a theme that is fundamentally [*foncièrement*] different from that which Buber tackles.

I do not wish to develop this point further; I intend to reedit soon a text on my relationship with Buber. I believe I have been able to call attention to several points of difference between us. But the central thing that determines the difference between my way of speaking and Buber's is the theme of asymmetry. I have read Buber then with a great deal of respect and attention, but I have not reached the point of agreeing with him.

I will tell you about something I read recently that really astonished me, a text of Buber's relative to his biography. There is an encounter with an old, very pious Jew, who poses a question to Buber relative to 1 Samuel 15:33, where the prophet commands King Saul to efface from the map and from History the kingdom of the Amalekites, who in the biblical and Talmudic tradition are the incarnation of radical evil. Were not the cowardly Amalekites the first to attack the Israelites coming out of Egypt, slaves who had only just been freed? We are not discussing either history, or historicity. The meaning of biblical hyperbole is to be found in the proper context, whatever may be the distance between the verses! There is in Deuteronomy 25:12[4] the following: "When the Eternal, your God, will have rid you of all your enemies round about the land that he gives you . . . you will efface the memory of the Amalekites from under heaven." It belongs to man delivered from evil to deliver evil the final blow. Saul did not accomplish his mission. He did not know how to efface. He spares Agag, the Amalekite, and brings back the spoils, the best things of the Amalekite troops. There is a scene where the prophet Samuel calls Saul to account. Dialogue: "What is this bleating of sheep that fills my ears and this lowing of oxen?" "It is for the Eternal, your God." "The Eternal does not like holocausts; he likes his voice to be obeyed. Bring me Agag." Samuel kills him on the spot. Cruelty of Samuel, and yet the son of the most tenderhearted woman in the world, son of Anne.

The question is posed to Buber: How could he do that? Buber's reply: The prophet did not understand what God commanded him to do. Without doubt, Buber thought that his conscience instructed him on the will of God better than the books! And yet why has he not read in 1 Samuel 15:33 the speech of the prophet: "As your [Agag's] sword has left mothers bereaved, so shall your mother be bereaved among women"? I have not always agreed with Buber, I have told you that. I continue to think that without extreme attention given to the Book of books, one cannot listen to one's conscience. Buber, in this instance, did not think of Auschwitz.

Translated by Peter Atterton

Part II

ETHICS

THREE

Buber and Levinas

Philosophical Reflections on an Opposition

Stephan Strasser

Between Martin Buber and Emmanuel Levinas there reigns — despite the high esteem in which Buber held Levinas and the honor that Levinas accorded Buber — an opposition. And one has to encounter all the fundamental causes of this contrast with philosophical wonder. A superficial observation already leads us to posit numerous parallels. Both thinkers are sympathetic to a humanism that is nourished out of the religious sources of Judaism, and, insofar as this Judaism is rooted in its Hebrew past, one can rightly speak of a "Hebrew humanism."[1] It is further evident that both men strive for a renewal and deepening of religious life. Buber expresses a basic thought of Levinas when he speaks of an "eclipsed Transcendence" (*EG*, 127) in our time. A further striking agreement is that speech stands at the center of both philosophers. This is not so much a concern about language as a constituted system of signs as it is about "the word that is spoken" (*KM*, 106–20). Buber and Levinas see in dialogue the word that turns to a Thou, the "primal deed" of the spirit (*IT*, 143).

In addition to such parallels that immediately meet the eye, various individual details at first glance also seem to be parallels but on closer examination prove not to be. Most significantly, both thinkers reject the one-sided prizing of knowledge and of the power that rests on knowing. Buber does this in his well-known doctrine of the two basic words "I-Thou" and "I-It." The sphere of "I-It," for Buber, is the world of objectifying experience and conscious using. Levinas proceeds more exactly: he distinguishes within speech between "saying" that is turned toward the other and the thematizing "said."

The fundamental tendency appears to be the same in both thinkers — even in their negative consequences they appear to have farreaching agreement. Realism as well as idealism leads to an overemphasis of objective knowledge and the concepts that derive from it. Whether "the I is contained in the world" or "the world in the I" makes little difference, remarks Buber. In both cases the human being is separated from "the series of images" that appear to him or her. He remains alone, and this causes him to shudder (*IT*, 121). Levinas rejects realism and idealism in the same way is evident in his whole work. — At first glance, one cannot successfully oppose the two philosophers in the sphere of ethics, Buber's statements that "love is responsibility of an I for a You" (*IT*, 66) and "responsibility which does not respond to a word is a metaphor of morality" (*BMM*, 17) could have stemmed from Levinas. When Buber praises Plato because he recognizes that "the Good towers above being in dignity and power," (*EG*, 102) when he stresses the ethical irreplaceability of the Single One, "the single one and not the individual," (*EG*, chap. 4) then we can imagine that we are reading Levinas.

When one weighs all of this, one asks oneself with renewed wonder how to explain the oppositions. Two things are evident for those who consider themselves philosophical. First of all: one can only speak of an opposition where there is a common basis. The common ground for both thinkers may be vaguely indicated through the slogans Judaism, religiousness, sociality, speech, humanism. On the other hand, where there is much in common, different principles step forth with seemingly distinctive sharpness. To track these divergences, one must not remain immersed in the details. A synthetic grasp of both spiritual personalities and their works is necessary. Only then is it possible to piece together the occurrences, actions and words into a meaningful whole.

I

What lies before us then is to seek the primal causes of the opposition in the *historical situation*. Levinas stems from a family in which talmudic piety and scholarship were cultivated. He confessed to this tradition of Judaism again in his later years; indeed he credited it with decisive significance. To a question of how the voice of Israel is to be perceived, Levinas solemnly responds before a gathering of Muslims, Christians and Jews, "The Judaism with a historical reality — Judaism, neither more nor less — is rabbinic" (*DF*, 13). Alongside this, he warns explicitly against numinous religiousness. "The numinous or the Sacred envelops and transports man beyond his powers and wishes, but a true liberty takes offense at this uncontrollable surplus" (*DF*, 13–4). Now it was precisely that — in the original Greek meaning of the word — "enthusiasm" of Hasidism that captivated the boy and later the man Martin Buber. In his *Tales of the Hasidim*, Buber ever again portrays a zaddik who, seized by a divine superior force, is carried beyond his personal ability and will. One does not have to have a scholarly knowledge of Jewish history to know that a tense relationship has ruled for centuries between the representatives of the talmudic-rabbinical tradition and pietistic Hasidim. Something of this tension is evident in the address given by Levinas for a celebration of Buber in which he emphasized that the study of the Bible without knowledge of the Hebrew language and without consideration of talmudic commentaries is like contemplating a landscape without the depth dimension (*PMB*, 51).

In addition to this opposition, which is rooted in centuries-old tradition, there is also the powerful *difference in the personal destinies* of both men. Hans Kohn reports of the 14-year-old Martin Buber, "He surrendered himself in youthful fashion to be open to all influences, a literary and aesthetic enjoyment of the cultural goods that he encountered in the Austrian and that means the Viennese form."[2] Comprehensive knowledge of the fields of history, literature, comparative study of religion, foreign languages, cultural anthropology and sociology is in part the fruit of those years of study. The reader of Buber's writings enjoys that superior (and therefore never obtrusive) erudition. He forgets the price that the young Buber had to pay for this: nor does he set before himself the danger of uprooting and alienation. "Soon after I left his house [the house of his grandfather], the whirl of the age took me in," Buber himself described it. "Until my twentieth year, and in small measure even beyond then, my spirit was in steady and multiple movement, in an alternation of tension and release, determined by manifold influences, taking ever new shape, but without center and without growing substance" (*HMM*, 56 f.). Entering the Zionist movement did not mean for the young Buber a nationalist confession. It was rather a "renewed taking root" (*HMM*, 56). His new connection with Judaism was later strengthened and made firm by taking hold of the Hasidic life-spirit. Buber could sum up in two phrases what drew him to this religious movement: "genuine community and genuine leadership" (*HMM*, 56).

The longing for real rootedness, for genuine relationship, for "a helper in spirit" (*HMM*, 55) is probably characteristic of a large segment of Buber's life way. Seeking a parallel in Levinas's sketchy descriptions of his life, one comes on only one gloomy, highly suggestive statement: "It [my biography] is dominated by the presentiment and the memory of the Nazi horror" (*DF*, 291). In other words, when Levinas thinks of "community," he thinks of a totalitarian collectivity that organizes actions of conquest, suppression and extermination. He associates the word "leadership" with the dictatorial commanding force over the apparatus of power that seizes everything. Is it surprising that there where the destinies are so different the ways of thinking issue into different spiritual landscapes? Is it not comprehensible that the first concern of Levinas's thought was directed to laying bare and criticizing the philosophical presuppositions of totalitarianism?

II

Historical and biographical comparisons of this sort have limited validity. If one tries to use them as a "method," they prove insufficient. They remain clinging to the surface, telling us nothing of the way the thinker has taken on himself the "rigor of thought." A *philosophical* analysis of the more important thought motifs is essential. Only on the ground of such an analysis can we win insight into the contrast between the philosopher Buber and the philosopher Levinas.

Now is it surprising to discover that the real opposition is not to be found there where Levinas supposed it was? When he criticizes Buber's philosophy — which he does repeatedly and with great frankness — he makes again and again the same reproach: *the I-Thou relationship*, as described by Buber, *shows throughout a formal character*. Levinas bases his critique chiefly on two arguments. In the first place, for Buber without doubt, every existing being can become a Thou. This is just as possible for subhuman reality as for its human contemporaries and the realm of the *geistigen Wesenheiten* [those entities the meeting with which, according to *I and Thou*, enables us to create art]. Levinas concludes from this that in speaking the primal word "I-Thou" all determination of content is left out. Merely the form of the relationship justifies speaking that primal word.

Levinas derives a second argument from the — actually ambiguous — statement of Buber's that: "the innate You is realized in the You we encounter: that this, comprehended as a being we confront and accepted as exclusive, can finally be addressed with the basic word, has its ground in the *a priori* of relation (*IT*, 78–9)". The technical term "a priori" belongs, as is well known, to the language of criticism; Immanuel Kant speaks of an inborn *a priori*. To follow him, in the case of an *a priori* knowledge, the possibility of knowledge is spontaneous, active, indeed, given by law. We can think of the following programmatic statement of Kant:

> In respect of the faculties of the soul generally, regarded as higher faculties, i.e., as faculties containing an autonomy, understanding is the one that contains the constitutive *a priori* principles for the faculty of cognition (the theoretical knowledge of nature). The feeling pleasure and displeasure is provided for by the judgment. . . . For the faculty of desire there is reason.[3]

In Buber's context does this now mean that the I stands autonomously over against the Thou? That it "constitutes" a presupposition of the Thou? That its *a priori* principles for this inborn activity are inborn?

Nothing warrants the conclusion that Buber wants to say anything of the sort. The explanation for his critically pleasing terminology is simple enough. The comparison with Freud leaps to mind. The historical Sigmund Freud, as is well known, used a naturalistic terminology to express knowledge that stood in sharpest contradiction to the naturalism of his age. He drew upon the turns of speech of the scientists and doctors with whom he entered into dialogue. Something similar must be said of Buber. The first unwieldy writing down of *I and Thou* took place, according to Buber's own statement, in the fall of 1919. One who knows the intellectual climate of philosophy in Germany and Austria before and during the First World War, and knows how strongly it was influenced by neo-Kantianism, will not be surprised that the developing philosopher Buber occasionally employed critical vocabulary that did not fit his own inclinations.

The reproach of "formalism" remains. But here too one can ask oneself whether this expression is to be understood in the spirit of Kant. Does it really mean "what our own faculty of knowledge (sensible impressions serving merely as the occasion) supplies from itself"?[4] Again, this stands in contradiction to Buber's whole philosophical tendency. But how can one then explain that all existing beings, when they are addressed in a certain basic attitude, can be transformed into a Thou?

In his "History of the Dialogical Principle," Buber stresses the fact that he had come to the basic concept of *I and Thou* in the course of his occupation with Hasidism (*W*, 297). How does Buber comprehend the leitmotifs of Hasidism? "God can be beheld in each thing and reached through every pure deed," he wrote. "But this insight is in no way to be equated with the worldview of pantheism. For the Hasidic teaching the whole world is only a word out of God's mouth; and nonetheless the least thing in the world is worthy that God reveals himself to the human beings who truly seek Him" (*HMM*, 49).[5] This agrees fully with the basic thoughts that Buber expresses at the beginning of *I and Thou*:

> In every sphere, through everything that becomes present to us, we gaze toward the train of the eternal You; in each we perceive a breath of

it; in every You we address the eternal You, in every sphere according to its manner. (*IT*, 57)

There can be no talk of formalism here, but one could certainly talk of the createdness of all existing beings, the "*créaturalité*" that also plays a decisive role in Levinas's philosophy. However, Buber's creatureliness issues into a *mystical* experience. The living experience of the Thou can be called "mystical" since it does not remain clinging to the objective givenness of the Thou-existing being [*Du-Seiende*] but rather penetrates to the "divine sparks" that arise from its creatureliness (*HMM*, 49).

III

One misunderstanding has been put out of the way. Has the opposition between Buber and Levinas disappeared at the same time? In no way. Rather, only after this clarification have the real oppositions come to light. For Buber the mystical life experience never leads to the soul of the mystic being fused with or extinguished in the divine light. Levinas acknowledges that the dialogical principle is faithful to the tradition of the specifically Jewish mystic (*PMB*, 49). Yet Buber makes statements without qualification such as "God can be *beheld* in every thing" [italics added]. Beyond that, indeed, in his Hasidic chronicle-novel *For the Sake of Heaven*, the zaddik Jacob Yitzhak of Pshysha expresses a thought that is clearly Buber's own: "How beautiful it is, Isaiah, to know at the same time that all images are nothing before Him and yet we are permitted to speak of Him in image" (*W*, 1083). Nietzsche's saying "God is dead" means, if we follow Buber, nothing other than "that the image-making power of the human heart has the appearance of the Absolute" (*EG*, 119). This is connected with a philosophical-religious conviction that Buber formulates in his interpretation of Hasidism. It is not true, he insists, that according to his perception of Hasidism the rift between God and the world is closed. "It is not closed but bridged over, and certainly with the paradoxical instruction to man that he never again set foot on the invisible bridge and thereby make it real" (*PMB*, 736).

Here the genuine oppositions come to light. They can be summed up in the sentence: *Levinas thinks that Buber does not hold the transcendence of God to be sufficiently radical.* It is not possible to compose for oneself images of the transcendent. The God of which Levinas speaks is no existing being, whose greatness can be measured. It is also no noumenon that conceals itself behind a veil of smoke of the phenomena. All of this has a very simple ground: *God is not a being.* Since God is not a being, there are no real existing bridges that can be built to Him. Levinas asks, "Is transcendence a thought that ventures beyond being or an approach beyond thought which speech ventures to utter, and whose trace and modality it retains?" (*CPP*, 62).

This question is rhetorical for Levinas. And the death of God that Nietzsche proclaims is concerned; it is, in the perspective of Levinas, a revolutionary event. No one remains unaffected. The task that the theistic philosopher of religion must set for himself in this spiritual situation is awesome: "After the death of a certain God inhabiting the world behind the scenes," the transcendence is described in words "to which are suited not the nouns designating beings, or the verbs in which their essence resounds" (*OB*, 185).

Levinas sought to master this task in his work *Otherwise Than Being*. There he only hints that in the place of the "manifestation" of the "trace" of God's steps, and in the place of the "vision" and the "image," the "inspiration," in the place of the existing being that is named "divine," there comes the good that — according to Buber's own words — "towers above being in worth and power."

A second opposition between the two philosophers is connected with this first and far-reaching opposition: it concerns the *symmetrical relationship between the I and the Thou.* "We shall direct our main criticism to the reciprocity of the *I-Thou* relation" (*PN*, 32), Levinas emphasizes from the beginning. It is well known that the concept of "reciprocity" or "mutuality" plays a decisive role for Buber. But this must cause us to reflect. For a reciprocal relationship can be established "from the outside"; it is thematizable, objectifiable. A third person can be included in the totality of its realm of power. For Levinas, the peculiarity of the relationship of me to you consists in that only I know it; and I know it in that I accomplish it. It distinguishes itself thereby from all other relationships between existing beings. But then the relationship is not reciprocal, for the Thou fundamentally cannot step in the place of the I (*PN*, 32).

To this comes Buber's emphasis that the reciprocity or reciprocal "inclusion" is *conscious*; the theme becomes the object of knowledge. But this is not just, philosophically speaking, the ground of the "sublime melancholy of our lot," about which Buber grieves, "that every You must become an It in our world" (*IT*, 68)? Levinas characterizes the consequence of Buber's position as follows: "in the end everything is said in terms of knowledge, and the *I-It* corrodes the *I-Thou*" (*PN*, 34). — In the framework of the wholly other vision of Levinas, I am directed to the Thou in a "pre-original" manner, i.e., before all knowledge, before the arising of the stream of consciousness, before the "cogito" of Descartes and Husserl. In this neither chosen nor willed direction to the other my creatureliness reveals itself; and in another — perhaps mystical — manner it does not reveal itself.

Even for *ethics*, Levinas's emphasis on interpersonal asymmetry has its consequences. Let us remember Buber's saying that love is the responsibility of an I for a Thou. Levinas declares himself to be in agreement with this position. But he asks further: on what does this responsibility rest? Biblically speaking, why is Cain actually the keeper of his brother Abel? If the Thou were an exact mirror of the I, then the deeply felt necessity for the Thou to spring into the breach would be in question. Levinas, in consequence, seems to hold the Thou whose guardianship is entrusted to me to be more essential than the I. Employing a biblical expression, one could say: the Thou steps before me in the form of the stranger, the widow, the orphan. The ethics that Levinas espouses begins above all with the consciousness of this essential inequality (*PN*, 32). Negatively speaking, his ethics cannot be coupled with reciprocity and mutuality.

Levinas criticizes something else in Buber's philosophy: "the recurrence of . . . themes of an angelic spiritualism" (*PN*, 33). In *Totality and Infinity*, Levinas even speaks of an "disdainful spiritualism" (*TI*, 69). How is this to be explained? Levinas is, of course, no Marxist. In his works, however, he takes Marxist philosophy seriously. He borrows from the doctrine of Karl Marx *one* thesis that one might formulate in the following manner: every concrete relationship of human being to human being has an economic dimension. Conversely, it follows that every relationship in which that dimension plays no role is not a concrete human one, but an "angelic" one. This conviction has its effect on his conception of the essence of the dialogue between human being and human being. Is a dialogue conceivable without the other concerning me, without care for the others, without "solicitude?," asks Levinas. Has not Buber one-sidedly moved the pure spiritual relationship between friends into the center of his consideration?

This aspect of Levinas's criticism gave rise to an exchange of letters between the two philosophers. One who has no access to the "comradeship of the human creature" will also, even with the most intensively exercised material care for the other, be in no position "to say a true Thou," Buber opines (*PMB*, 273). Levinas replies in a rather belligerent tone. The matter comes to a head in his rectification that he never thought that the mechanical act of nourishing and clothing would lead to a relationship with the other. But certainly once saying Thou is "separated from this giving, even if it is established between strangers, it is a 'purely spiritual,' ethereal friendship" (*PN*, 38).

Added to these social-philosophical judgments there comes in Levinas the consideration of the role of one's own body. The saying of the Thou always traverses my body, including the organs of speech that make possible the saying, the hands that are able to present, and the things that I can give. In short, the other is essentially one of whom I take care, he is "always the poor and destitute (and at the same time my master)." Therefore — this refrain returns again and again — the relationship to the other is essentially asymmetrical (*PN*, 38).

One further opposition is not put into words by Levinas but plays significant background role. It concerns the essence of the monotheistic revelation. Buber considers the religions of the world as a historian; that is, he also seeks to understand them genetically. The history of their formation presents itself to him as a continuous evolution.

The essay on "The Teaching of the Tao" (*W*, 1021–51) could be adduced as *one* example of many. In it Buber describes the continuous process that leads from the nature myths of the primitives to the exalted teachings of Lao-tze, Jesus and the Buddha. His historical-anthropological manner of seeing, however, is not confined to religious-philosophical investigations. Buber also holds the religions as justified from a pastoral and religious standpoint.

> When we desire to lead men to God, we must not simply overthrow their idols. In each of these images we must seek to discover what divine quality he who carved it sought, in spite of everything, to delineate. Then tenderly and prudently we must help him to find the way to that quality.[6]

These words, which Buber again put into the mouth of the "Holy Jew" Jacob Yitzhak of Pshysha, are the expression of a "religious liberalism" that is wholly foreign to Levinas. For him the revelation of monotheism is a one-time happening of super-historical significance. In the light of this event, all magical practices, myths, and mystery cults of the past and the present are transformed into simple heathenism. According to Levinas, monotheism in the form of Judaism has once for all time demagicized the world, and no one should seek to escape this holy sobriety.

> This then is the eternal seduction of paganism, beyond the infantilism of idolatry, which long ago was surpassed: *The Sacred filtering into the world* — Judaism is perhaps no more than the negation of all that. To destroy the sacred groves — we understand now the purity of this apparent vandalism. (*DF*, 232)

One can call the spiritual attitude that speaks out of Levinas's words one-sided, unpsychological, unpedagogical — one cannot gainsay it inner greatness.[7]

IV

At the end of our comparison (which does not claim completeness), one more clarifying word. What strivings they must have undergone. Shall we demonstrate that Levinas is "right" and Buber "wrong"?

Or do we want to assert the opposite? It goes without saying that both lie far from us. Comparative analyses can merely serve to reach a deeper understanding of both philosophers. Perhaps it is evident from these comparisons that Levinas and Buber, despite the great deal that they actually have in common, and despite many words that ring similarly in both of them, represent *opposite types*. Levinas is a direct descendant of those ancient Israelites who, barely after coming to power in their land, cut off the heads of the arrestingly beautiful Roman-Hellenistic statues of gods. The arresting beauty was in their eyes a fountain of temptation. Those who looked at them were in danger of forgetting the holy, the invisible God of Israel. Perhaps one should go further and say with Theodor de Boer[8] that Levinas is of the stock of the prophets who hold before the people unwelcome truths, who announce to kings their moral failures, who demolish the images of false gods, make a laughing stock of magicians. Buber is the harmonious human being who unifies science and law into "teach-ing," but who also understands the art of presenting the teaching in an attractive, living, and fascinating manner. He stands open to all *"geistigen Wesenheiten"* simply because he possesses the power to sub-ordinate them all to an inner law. He gives his teaching shape not only in his work but also in his life. In this sense one can call Buber a "wise person." — The greatly learned, the *wise teacher* and the *prophet*. Is it still not permissible to suggest that they represent the summits of two possibilities that have dwelled within the Jewish people for millennia?

Translated by Maurice Friedman

FOUR

Affection and the Transcendental Dialogical Personalism of Buber and Levinas

Andrew Tallon

What can we say, now more than a century since his birth, is Martin Buber's most important philosophical contribution? Should we take him seriously at all? Is it all poetry and mysticism, evocation with no follow-through? Despite widespread use of "I-Thou" jargon in psychology, philosophy, theology and elsewhere, Buber cannot be held responsible for those who reduce his thought to "pop" religion or psychology. Though everybody talks I-Thou, dialogical philosophy itself has about as much distinct identity in many individuals' minds as existentialism.

In one sense, Buber can be credited with starting a major revolution in philosophy, while in another sense he has been a disappointment because he failed to complete what he started. In these pages, I will walk the narrow ridge between superficial introduction and detailed technical study. By comparing and contrasting it with the work of Emmanuel Levinas, and by circling several times around the topics of intentionality, intersubjectivity and the "between" (*"Zwischen"*), I will suggest just how profound Buber's program really is, why he deserves to be placed at the heart of philosophy today, and how we might go about helping that happen.

I

Buber is taken very seriously in Continental Europe[1] because the dialogical principle is considered a major challenge to the dominant (and sterile, especially for knowledge of persons) theory of intentionality, namely, Husserlian representational intentionality. It is also the best hope of overcoming the very impasse that Husserl met in his ultimately solipsistic and idealistic attempt, still influenced by Brentano, to reduce all intentionality to representations.[2]

By the seemingly simple, but radically revolutionary, move of relocating the locus or "space" of the event of meaning from inside one's head, to the realm of the between, Buber cut the Gordian knot of psychologism and of all rationalism and intellectualism.[3] By denying that life, meeting, meaning, knowing and loving take place in individual consciousnesses as mental states, Buber stated negatively what his program left unfinished positively, that is, the how and the meaning of this between itself. There is no doubt the most important tasks he bequeathed to us are to establish the meaning of the between (as access to the meaning of human being), to understand how it is constituted, and then to turn this all to action in the building of community.[4]

II

The complexity of this most basic of all human questions, the nature and meaning of persons, receives both its infinite complexity as well as its solution in the deeper truth that persons emerge only with the advent of the other, as Levinas says, in the event of persons meeting, in relation, communion, the between. Thus, one of the points Buber makes, a point shared by those phenomenologists whose understanding of intentionality is that it is existential and transcendent rather than immanent, is that no amount of introspection can yield objective truth as though the meaning of human being were an interior datum of consciousness in mind's presence to itself.[5] Rather, the experience of what will become meanings and values precedes thought and freedom, cognition and choice, intellect and will, reason and contract, and so forth. We are already co-constituting the between before we know it. We are in it before it is in us; we bathe in meaning like fish in water. Let us stay with this point for a moment.

Phenomenologists of embodiment,[6] anthropological sociologists, and others who are equally concerned with language (verbal and non-verbal), meaning, dialogue and communication, have long held that space, time, motion, and so forth, *already* make sense to us, already have meaning *prior* to any cognitive or volitional "bestowal" of meaning by a transcendental ego, by any "intentionality" (if by that term is meant a one-sided constituting of a world as bearing meaning).[7]

Second, once we recognize that meaning and value, truth and worth, precede cognitive and affective consciousnesses at the experiential level — that knowledge is always late, as Levinas puts it — the next step becomes the task of understanding how and why this happens. It is one thing to declare and assert that the between is the locus of meaning and value — and to go on repeating it, after Buber — but quite another to figure out what possibly can be understood by claiming that this obviously "empty" space between us here is the bearer of our meaning, is filled and charged with meaning, is something metaphysically real. We "natural born positivists," empirically biased, need a lot of hyperbole, exaggeration and emphasis, it seems, before we begin even to suspect what Buber and Levinas might mean when they say that relations are real, as real as hard, physical objects. We tend to relegate the network of relations called the between to the realm of merely mental entities, psychic projections at best. We tend to balk at invoking an image such as magnetic lines of force — invisible, intangible, without color, smell or taste, yet as real as any physical force we know. But think of the "force field" two persons generate in heated discussion or intimate copresence (so patent to others), or of the tension in the air we can "cut with a knife," or of the "vibes" of resonance (or dissonance) between two friends (or enemies). Is this "meeting of minds" all in our minds? Still another example is Gabriel Marcel's famous description of charm, an event never reducible to one person but always *between* them. No one is charming to all.

Despite the pedestrian level of such examples — or perhaps because of it — explanation remains elusive. Assertions abound, while satisfactory theoretical constructs are wanting. A theory that can adequately account for self-transcendence that is always already going on, showing both its necessity and possibility, is required before dialogue becomes intelligible. Theory would do this by showing the transcendental *a priori* conditions of such necessity and possibility, explicating the process of mutual self-transcendences: *the dialogical must become transcendental.*

But before there can be an adequate theory there must be an adequate description. Buber's "between" broke through a false description of human existence and opened up the way toward an expanded theory of intentionality.[8]

Because of the different characteristics of visual space (in contrast with, for example, acoustic space or tactile space), a visual thought, or a characterization of thought dependent upon vision, predictably affects one's perceptions of and relations with persons.[9] Buber's dialogical philosophy, with Levinas in tow, broke the back of vision bias and implicitly challenged at the same time the dominance of representational intentionality based upon it. Implicitly, vision, visual space, and the characteristics of light and vision, lead to the notion of horizon in Husserl's intentionality, and to the type of theoretical representationalism and intellectualism that goes with it (while neglecting other kinds of intentionality, especially affective).[10] Kohák, for one, traces the intellectualist and representationalist tendency in Husserl back to his teacher Brentano:

> Intellectualism, too, has a rigorous meaning, delineated by Brentano's conviction that *acts of conation and affectivity — willing and feeling — are reducible to acts of cognition — knowing.* Husserl repeats this in the assertion that acts of willing and feeling contain a "kernel" of knowing. In effect, *intellectualism in the strict sense posits knowing as the normative relation between the subject and his world, reducing willing and feeling to variations of knowing.*[11]

And as Levinas has forcefully pointed out, the ultimately totalitarian nature of thought, ignoring the trace of the Infinite that we experience even in our own consciousness, derives from the dominance of the visual.[12]

It is important to avoid confusion here by mixing the metaphysical and phenomenological. Intentionality, as universally verified experience, is phenomenological. To state its meaning and significance, to explain it, to dig for its root, however, is to do hermeneutics or metaphysics (or ontology, according to some uses of the term). Buber, in other words, cannot be interpreted as denying all intentionality, or intentionality as such, but only Husserlian reductive, representational, non- or anti-dialogical intentionality. If Buber's own statements sometimes seem to contradict this interpretation, it is because he was not always solicitous in matters of accurate research.[13]

III

There are two great tasks, each with several parts, for those who work toward the proximate and remote goals of the program Buber and Levinas set for us. There is the task of completing the phenomenology. Involved is the correct understanding of intentionality, including a turning to the arts, humanities and sciences for that part of the phenomenology they are "doing for us." Then there is the task of making explicit the metaphysics implicit in the whole, something neither Buber nor any of the philosophers of dialogue did. As Strasser has noted:

> We find here a fundamental deficiency in the enterprise. Even Michael Theunissen, a passionate protagonist of the dialogists, sees himself forced to address a serious reproach to them at the end of a series of studies of numerous dialogical authors. These thinkers, he remarks, limit themselves to showing that certain phenomena *de facto* do occur, but they fail to examine their ontological relevance . . . the ontological significance of the dialogical event remains unclarified.[14]

To accomplish the first task, then, we must open the meaning of phenomenology, not despite Husserl but through him, by reading him positively and constructively (Husserl as humanist, as Kohák would say) rather than narrowly and too critically, allowing both a transformed meaning for intentionality and a turning toward the arts, humanities and sciences as real sources.

I submit that it is the underlying (or "overarching," as Levinas would prefer to say) metaphysics of the essence of the human as finite spirit in the tradition from Aristotle to Kant, from Hegel to Karl Rahner, that makes possible an understanding of intentionality as existential, i.e., intersubjective, transcendental, personalist, dialogical.[15] Again, intentionality must be understood not as an act immanent to the ego, necessarily objectifying, reducible to representations, but as essentially self-transcendent. Strasser concurs: "intentionality is nothing but my conscious entering into relationship with something or someone . . . we do not look upon intentionality as the expression of an impersonal or anonymous transcendental dynamism but, rather, as the expression of a primordial ontic desire for a bond with the other."[16] Of course, this is but an echo of the protest of Heidegger, Sartre and Merleau-Ponty against the transcendental idealism of Husserl, the same immanent intentionality that Buber and Levinas, challenged in complementary ways, and to which they offered alternatives.

Finite human being, therefore, is necessarily turned toward the other, dynamically open and, by its very nature, exterior. It is thus best known, felt, experienced and lived, not in an "intentional analysis of contents of cognitive consciousness," but in the face of the other, in culture, media, institutions, history, the arts and sciences, and all the "othernesses" in and by which finite spirit makes and finds itself. What Aristotle meant by the soul's never thinking without an image (*De Anima* 3: 7 [431a16]), what Aquinas meant by the conversion to phantasm (*Summa Theologiae*, 1: q. 84, a. 7), and what Hegel said, in so many ways and places, about a necessary relation to other as condition for a self, whether as consciousness, history, culture, etc. — all these are but cognitive expressions of finite spirit's radical general relation to otherness, not limited to cognition.

Once intentionality is recognized as something involving our whole finite being and not just cognition, then it immediately opens to include embodiment. This is because intentionality is but the emanation of finite spirit in its self-becoming, embodiment being its first "othering," and thus includes affection and volition as the other two irreducibly distinct ways of intending the other.[17] From his earliest works, Sartre clearly understood intentionality to be broader than cognition or representation.[18] Recall, for example, the interesting section on affective intentionality in *The Psychology of Imagination*, and the claim that "feelings have special intentionalities; they represent one way — among others — of self-*transcendence.*" Sartre's *The Emotions: Outline of a Theory*, which reveals so much of Heidegger's influence, shows how deeply affectivity is identified with being human. There are passages in *Being and Nothingness* that make the same point.[19] This "extension" of the range of intentionality, especially into the affective response, has made all the difference to the phenomenology and metaphysics of the interpersonal.

How should we sort out and organize the distinctions between the three forms of intentionality: affection, cognition and volition? One useful way to order one's thinking about intentionality is to follow Dietrich von Hildebrand, who, having distinguished two general forms of intentionality, cognition and responses, distinguishes three responses: theoretical (such as conviction and doubt), affective (love and joy), and volitional (free acts).[20] Von Hildebrand argues that, unlike a mere state (e.g., fatigue, which is static and without conscious reference to an object) or a teleological trend (e.g., hunger or thirst, which though dynamic are drives in nature), an intentional act is characterized by its dynamic "aboutness," or subject-object betweenness. What von Hildebrand points out so well is the further distinction between cognitive acts (e.g., perception, imagination, memory, etc.) characterized by receptivity and responses (e.g., giving or making) characterized by spontaneity. In cognition, the content is on the side of the object (I am not red; the object is), while in response, it is on the side of the subject (I am full of joy, maybe overflowing into the between). Then come the three kinds of responses already mentioned: *theoretical* (conviction, doubt, expectation); *volitional* (willing, directed toward possible); and *affective* (love, hatred, joy, sorrow, fear, etc.). Unlike volitional response, which is one dimensional, affectivity involves the whole person. Moreover, unlike the will, it is not free, not produced by fiat. Von Hilderbrand has more to say, but the essential point is that different responses are distinguished by the words said to a person (or object), the affective response being a felt resonance, not restricted to cognition or will, but from the heart of the person.

In what remains of this brief overview of what Buber says to us today, I will focus on affectivity; its description and meaning will necessarily mean turning again to Levinas. Affectivity is our best access to the "between."

Affectivity begins with the discovery that our bodies are already intentional, prior to an intending mind or deciding will. In *The Structure of Behavior*, Merleau-Ponty says: "representative consciousness is only one of the forms of consciousness," and in *Phenomenology of Perception*, he speaks of getting back before knowledge, prior to thematization, which means getting to action, feeling, and will as original. There are simply too many places on body, motion, and space to cite. Especially relevant in this context, however, is the following note: "Husserl's originality lies . . . in the discovery, beneath the intentionality of representations, of a deeper intentionality, which others have called existence." Merleau-Ponty is not far from embracing Buber's "between" when he accuses philosophers who profess an immanentist, nonexistential intentionality of having a visual bias: "In visual experience . . . we can . . . flatter ourselves that we constitute the world, because it presents us with a spectacle spread out before us at a distance. . . . As the subject of touch . . . I cannot forget . . . that it is through my body that I go to the world, and tactile experience occurs 'ahead' of me, and is not centered in me."[21]

"Space speaks" and "time talks" to embodied spirit, to use Edward T. Hall's expression.[22] Motion, nearness, touch, and the infinity of the nonverbal, including culture, media, institutions, already communicate, say something to us, and, in fact "mean" something in the deepest sense.[23] The familiar enough phenomenon of our machines running our lives became especially important when we created the electronic media — extensions of those very senses that are already intentional, existential, and meaningful. Electronic media are readily and unconsciously identified with perception because they are communication, not merely transportation. And it is precisely because of the immediacy of modern electronic media, moving at the speed of light, that communication can no longer be understood according to the model of transportation, as though we still "carried messages," "delivered the news," and so forth. We find ourselves molded and manipulated by these "immediate media," even more than by cars, buildings, credit cards, and fast food, because embodiment, as sensibility, is essentially an extension or emanation of "something" already essentially intentional, namely, finite spirit. Meaning is in media because media are materialized extensions of our senses, which are themselves embodied spirit. We can study ethical, interpersonal space as language, study culture as meaning, institutions as communication, study embodiment as intentional, and so forth, because of these are but the materializations of a spirit that is itself already intentional. Intentionality is *possible* because we are *spirit*, and *necessary* because we are *finite* spirit. Embodiment, space and time (and history, culture, architecture, theatre and so forth) are the ways finite spirit uses to overcome and remedy (mediate) its finitude.

Levinas's particular way of working this out is to locate meaning not so much in Buber's "between" as in the sensibility that makes the between. Sensibility is already the preconceptual experience of meaning because it refers to the other, which is precisely what meaning is (sense as *sens*: directedness to the other).

Johannes Heinrichs is informative here.[24] The idea is that the between, as the event of meaning, precedes I and Thou, self and other, who are only subsequently distinguished. This ties in with both Strasser's three moments of preintentional, intentional, and meta-intentional, and his description of passion and feeling (affectivity in general) as a being taken captive ("captivated") by the other. This in turn is consonant with expressions dear to Levinas, such as being responsible for the other, hostage of the other, persecuted by the other, etc., all of which suggest a passivity like that of passion (sensibility in the grip of the other).

Human sensibility, understood as prior to the distinction between cognition and appetition (or perception and affection), is a spiritual act, i.e., finite spirit's submission to the other (Levinas's sensibility as the subjection of subjectivity). So affectivity is the best concept to pursue in carrying out a description and interpretation of Buber's "between" and in unlocking the difficult writings of the other great philosopher of the interpersonal, Levinas. Better than perception, than purely cognitive or volitional responses — which, though genuinely intentional, existential, and transcendent, are not felt between, as affectivity is felt — the affective response, symbolized by the heart, contains the greatest potential for revealing the essentially human.

Heart stands for the unity of spirit and matter, soul and body, intellect and phantasm, will and passion, prior to distinction that is subsequently made between them. Rahner aptly calls heart an *Urwort*:

> Heart as a total-human primordial word . . . denotes the core of the
> human person which is original and inmost with respect to everything
> else in the human person . . . at which therefore man is originally and
> wholly related to other persons and above all also to God. Attitudes of
> a person towards others . . . exhibit a plurality. In this plurality of atti-
> tudes there exists a unity of form which merges the attitudes of the
> person into one structured, unified whole. . . . Heart is the original,
> formative unity of the attitudes of a person . . . a core of existence . . . a
> common, inmost central point which combines them all and impresses
> on them their ultimate meaning.[25]

Above the animal, beneath the angelic and divine, affectivity gives us the best access to the human embodied spirit. The concept of heart has come down to us today, through Augustine's *cor inquietum* and Pascal's *logique du coeur*, to mean both our felt rootedness in the matter of embodiment[26] and the absolute transcendence of the spirit to the infinite.[27] This will perhaps come as a surprise only to one who does not understand intentionality as self-transcendence, as the mark of finitude in the human spirit, requiring radical openness to and dependence on otherness, which is already the most perfect single concept for human existence in the Bible. Affectivity is the event of otherness in a way no other response is. In no other instance of lived experience (*le vécu*) is the self so well shown to be incapable of auto-generation, to be radically dependent on otherness, and thus on the "between." True access to Buber and to the fulfillment of his program of the "between" is necessary for a correct understanding of Levinas, because Levinas's philosophy of the other gives a happy alternative to the totalitarianism of the self that he so vigorously opposes. The radical passivity of Levinas's self (subjectivity as hostage, etc.) emerges only with the advent of the other, with the face of the other drawing near me. This nearness (*proximité*) is, of course, not an intentionality, not a mental "state" or activity, but a meaning and value precognitively and prevoluntarily experienced as *between* us affectively. Neither one of us in isolation can cognitively and voluntarily constitute nearness or the between, nor is the answer is to be found in the extreme opposite of the activity of constitution (intentionality in Husserl's narrower sense), total passivity, but in the passivity *of an agent*, thus in an *ethical* passivity (patience, suffering, etc.), in response, in responsibility.

Levinas's nonrepresentational phenomenology aims at a subjectivity that is prior to an origin, before any beginning (as *an-arche*), prior to cognition with its totalizing tendency and volition with its freedom. This subjectivity is *felt as affectivity*, a subjectivity, therefore, which is secondary to the other, who is primary. Even though affectivity is treated as my feeling of myself, my ownness or mineness (*Jemeinigkeit* and paragraph nine of Heidegger's *Being and Time* comes to mind), the very essence of all affectivity, as of all meaning and sensibility, depends on *otherness*. Thus one's own body is first an other, an ambiguous bridge between the self as being and the self as having. This ambiguous midpoint that is embodiment, radiating "ecstatically" and existentially toward otherness through sensibility, is *between* selfness and otherness. If to mean is to be for the other, and sense is being for the other, then as sense my meaning is to be for the other. The implication is that as spirit I am for myself, but as *finite* spirit I am for myself only by being for the other.

Levinas notes that the experience of *Jemeinigkeit* is ultimately dialogical in that my affective response in encountering others is my responsibility for them, felt *as* mine in that no one can substitute for me, take *my* place, be me. It is also worth noting that the event or experience is described as the other-*near*-me, and not "in" me (which would suggest idealism and a reductive, constituting consciousness). Nor is the other merely "with" me (one thinks of Marcel's use of categories in their full personal strength). This nearness or proximity (Levinas's *proximité* evokes the *prochain*, as the English "nearness" evokes the "neighbor," the nearby) is felt ethically as the other addressing me. My *felt* meaning is to-be-for-the-other, responsibility. Levinas's proximity is Buber's between, ethically experienced and construed.

Strasser's *Phenomenology of Feeling* also offers access to understanding Levinas's sensibility (affectivity) as being subject to (responsible to and for) the other. Sensibility as affectivity is that very aspect of the person by which he or she who is finite spirit tries to overcome finitude. Though spirit *as such* is self-presence, *finite* spirit becomes self-presence only through others, through the self-absence of one's own embodiment (first otherness) by which he or she mediates all subsequent alterities (who and which he or she needs to know and love in order to become fully whom he or she is). Thus, because all finite self-presence is first self-absence — which means all self-presence is first presence-to-other — the experience of the self is the *feeling* of the self (recall Marcel). But if the very same "organ" of self-feeling is the "organ" of otherness, then before thought and freedom (as spirit) the self is "othered." Levinas is thus correct. I am touched, addressed by the other before I know it (cognition), before I agree to it by any contract (volition), that is, through my embodiment (sensibility, affectivity).

Note, however, that this original affectedness by otherness, seemingly the most original truth about human nature, is itself but the *first* otherness (that is, the embodiment in space and time) of an original, genuine, inalienable, and untotalizable spirit, albeit finite, deficient, created and thus dependent. This is important to emphasize because it prevents the extreme interpretations of Buber and Levinas that lead to loss of self due to too much hyperbole about the primacy of the other, of community, and so forth. It must be said that Levinas himself does not help matters on occasion when he practically equates self and subjectivity as embodiment, sensibility, affectivity, etc., thus opening himself up to a "totalitarianism by the other." One need only read

Strasser's *Phenomenology of Feeling* to be struck by the similarities between his descriptions of passion, feeling, and emotion, and Levinas's descriptions of subjectivity as sensibility and affectivity.[28] Consider the following passages from Strasser:

> Mankind for millennia has conceived of an emotional event as something which "overtakes" us, "overpowers" us, "takes possession of" us, and so forth. Without exception, the words, *passio, affectus, Leidenschaft, hartstocht,* passion indicate this . . . something happens to someone.

> . . . Processes . . . take place in me, near me, with me . . . to which I cannot apply the notion of action. They are indeed not "occurrences" in the world of things. The objective category of "occurrence" is here as inapplicable as the subjective category of "action." The processes of which I speak occupy an in-between position: They have a quasi-objective character and they have their origin in me — though not directly — as quasi-objective processes. They escape from me in my implication with other beings; from me, the one who is attracted, claimed, gripped, stirred, overpowered and so forth by other beings. Hence the impression of passivity which these processes cause . . . I cannot be apprehended at my own discretion; I am dependent upon other beings and other persons for this. (81–82; 150)

Addressing himself precisely to the question of the extremes, which he calls Logos and Pathos, Strasser says:

> simple juxtaposition would, indeed, be equivalent to a perpetual state of total war between Logos and Pathos. I-centered self-governance would stand over against passionate devotion to what is foreign; goal-consciously directed action against automatic discharge; universal apprehension of Being against emotionally distorted apprehension of the situation. (155) . . . The higher rank of the Logos consists in its capacity for a universal view of Being, its being the origin of free acts and of the transcendental positing of goals. The subordination of the pathic performances results from their blindness to Being, their receptivity, their abandonment to what is other, foreign, exterior. (155; 157)

Here we recognize the terms of the dilemma: neither Logos, nor Pathos; neither alone, nor dominant, yet — and this gives the clue — in the wake of the failure of Logos, in the wake of the Holocaust, how tempting to turn to Pathos, in hope.

If I were asked now to explain better the meaning of affection and the affective response, since it has emerged as the chief concept of this study and is, moreover, the bond between Buber and Levinas, I would have recourse to two further ideals, mysticism and connaturality, both kept in bounds by attention to the concept of response. If Buber and Levinas teach us nothing else, they insist that we steer between the Scylla of Pathos or total passivity (to which, I admit, so many of Levinas's hyperboles can lead), and the Charybdis of total action and power that ends up in an egology tending toward solipsism and idealism. It is the personal other whose presence I feel, who speaks, who forbids my totalizing her in a way mere things mutely allow. Presence to this other, whom I meet, is not a constitution by my creative ego at all: I am first passive, not active, first and foremost creature, not creator. The very heart of creaturehood, quite the opposite of the creator, who is spontaneity and generativity, is affectivity.

The only way I have been able to avoid the two extremes is to understand affectivity as a response. It might seem more correct to say affectivity is a capacity, disposition, and ability to respond, but to say so would be to identify the moment of my being-affected-by, prior to my response to such affection. Thus to feel oneself, in lived experience, a subject is precisely to be affected first (this moment is the one Levinas emphasizes almost exclusively) by the other, by nearness, before thought or volition, before rationality and freedom, and second to respond to this being-affected. Finally comes the will, the "executor of the heart," to ratify (or veto) the affective response in the moment of rational freedom, after which comes the deed.

Judging from the literature on mysticism,[29] there is a virtual consensus that felt presence is also the essential minimum requirement for genuine mystical experience. It alone is necessary and sufficient before and without visions, locutions, and so forth; and this felt presence is not thought, not produced by will, but radically dependent upon otherness, essentially a passive affection, a being-touched.

What hints are there in this person-to-person event, which, because of its purity, directness, immediacy and simplicity, can perhaps offer a paradigm, the bottom line, as it were, of the between? Perhaps the nonnecessity of thought and will — and indeed their total inability to constitute mystical experience — points to their derivativeness. Perhaps a dulling of this most general and elemental "sense of the other" or "presence of the other" is traceable to our too ready specification of the other by means of the external senses and reason. Thus something like a "personal *a priori*" — presence to a person *who*, unlike perception of a nature (*what* one is), is irreducible to such *what*ness — precedes all subsequent dualisms and specifications.[30] In other words, before you can say, for example, why you trust someone, before you can specify how you even recognize someone whom you in fact easily *do* recognize (to use Polanyi's example), there has occurred a felt response to the other. Later perhaps, if questioned, you could sort out perceptions, memories, thoughts, convictions, doubts, will acts, etc. This last consideration leads to the other idea, connaturality.

What Jacques Maritain (interpreting Thomas Aquinas) calls affective connaturality is a whole group of attunements and affinities (congenialities, consonances), each of which is intentional, other-directed for its meaning, and thus operative not "in" us but *between* us.[31] Moreover, as affective as well as connatural, the operation is *ut natura*, that is, prior to reflection and will. Now there is a long and valid tradition — call it the heart tradition — summed up in this doctrine, and it is repeated in every age, sometimes with loss, sometimes with gain. I think that tradition is quite relevant to what Buber, Levinas, and many others offer as correctives to the usual ways of knowing and being in relation. While acknowledging variations, without trying to be complete or historical — and omitting what would be pedantic documentation — the following list of names and ideas are part of that tradition.

Beyond the biblical meaning of "to know someone" as intimacy, and the many passages referring to knowledge through love,[32] there are Origen's five "spiritual senses," "heart" in Augustine and Pascal, the "heart" language of Rahner and Strasser, Newman's illative sense, Blondel's action, Scheler's sympathy, Bergson's two sources, von Hügel's mystical (intuitive-emotional) element, Rémy Kwant's (after F. J. J. Buytendijk) encounter and the primacy of person-knowledge,

Kant's practical reason, August Brunner's *compréhension*, Polanyi's personal (and subsidiary) knowledge, Sartre's emotion, Jaspers's illumination of existence (*Existenzerhellung*), Macmurray's "form of the personal," Ricoeur's "thymic," Husserl's *Lebenswelt*, Merleau-Ponty's existence and the body-subject, Marcel's *présence*, Buber's between and dialogue, and Levinas's nonrepresentational intentionality, nearness, etc. Related also are Ebner's dialogue, Heidegger's mood (*Stimmung*) as intentional (or perhaps quasi-intentional, since a mood intends a horizon without an object), Nédoncelle's reciprocity of consciousness and collegiality, Poole's ethical (and philosophical) space, Kierkegaard's indirect communication and second immediacy, the notion of lived experience (*le vécu*) in Merleau-Ponty and in the later Sartre, and the primacy of the other (Theunissen). Even the distrust of reason in Cartesian doubt and Kantian critique point beyond naive "thing-knowledge" of the world or self-knowledge. Persons cannot be known as things nor can the self be known directly and immediately at all. As one whose being is from the other, so is my becoming from the other.

This *mélange* blurs many distinctions. It shows, however, that in many ways others have been a part of this unfinished program of Buber's before it had a name. In conclusion, while the thoughts above are multifaceted in the extreme, they are unified by a simple principle: Buber and Levinas complement one another in the reinstatement of intentionality as affectivity, which is located in the between as a shared field of consciousness. Thus, access is given to the meaning of Buber's "between" while Levinas's philosophy of the other escapes the extreme passivity of a totalitarianism by the other. Without this correction, we end up so adverse to the "playing God" of an idealism constituting the world that we espouse an abject subject, "playing the non-god" (the creature) to such a passive extreme as to be incapable of the ethical responsibility commanded in the face of the other.

FIVE

"Failure of Communication" as a Surplus
Dialogue and Lack of Dialogue between Buber and Levinas

Robert Bernasconi

Strife among thinkers is the "lovers' quarrel" concerning the matter itself.
— Martin Heidegger, "Letter on 'Humanism' "

The proximity between Martin Buber and Emmanuel Levinas which is so striking to the external observer was not always so apparent to Buber and Levinas themselves. Levinas was initially preoccupied with differentiating or separating his own position from that of Buber. But having established the points of difference, he found himself then able to reread Buber in another way. Although Levinas continued to focus on many of the same issues in his treatment of Buber, his approach — his way of relating — appeared to undergo a transformation. The present essay surveys Levinas's numerous studies of Buber, and in particular compares an essay predating *Totality and Infinity* with another postdating *Otherwise Than Being or Beyond Essence* in order to explore both the continuity and change not simply in Levinas's understanding of what Buber wrote, but also in the way in which Levinas approached Buber. The relation between Buber and Levinas has already given rise to a few studies,[1] but these commentaries predate Levinas's most recent discussions of Buber and so are unable to take account of essays that introduce a new stage in Levinas's relation with Buber. Levinas's recent essays on Buber are important not only for an understanding of the relation of these two thinkers, but also because they serve as a valuable introduction to the question of what might provisionally be called "a Levinasian hermeneutics."

THE QUESTION OF RELATION IN BUBER

Heidegger wrote that "we are not in a position — or if we are, then only rarely and just barely — to experience purely in its own terms a relation that obtains between two things, two beings. We immediately conceive the relation in terms of the things which in the given instance are related."[2] It could be said that Buber in *I and Thou* takes up the task of thinking the relation qua relation. One of the characteristics of the I-Thou relation is that it cannot be reduced to the terms related, the relata. Indeed, whenever the terms related are preeminent, the I-It already dominates.[3]

The crucial sentence for this interpretation of Buber runs, "In the beginning is the relation" (*IT*, 69/*DP*, 22). The sentence can be understood to express both the priority of the I-Thou over the I-It and the priority within the I-Thou of the relation over the relata. Buber offered two models or parallels for thinking the I-thou as a "genuine original unity" in this sense (*IT*, 70/*DP*, 22). The first is that of primitive peoples among whom, Buber suggested, the basic word I-Thou is spoken in a natural, unformed or preformed (*vorgestaltlich*) manner prior to any self-recognition of an I (*IT*, 73/*DP*, 26). By contrast, the I-It presupposes a self-recognition such as takes place in the detachment (*Ablösung*) of the I. Buber conceded that the primitive man affords only brief glimpses into the temporal sequence of the basic words I-Thou and I-It and is anyway only a metaphor for what he calls "primal man." He suggested that "more complete information" is given in the child (*IT*, 76/*DP*, 28). Indeed, Buber went back beyond the child to the pure, natural association of prenatal life, where he found evidence of the originality not so much of the relation as such as of the "longing for relation." But it would seem that prenatal life is also appealed to only as a metaphor for "the womb of the great mother — the undifferentiated preformed primal world" (*IT*, 76/*DP*, 28–29). In any case, "In the beginning is the relation" does not refer to the I-Thou — which is how the sentence has often been understood — but to this longing for relation. "In the beginning is the relation — as the category of being, as readiness, as a form that reaches out to be filled, as a model of the soul; the *a priori* of relation; *the innate Thou*" (*IT*, 78/*DP*, 31).

The question of the genetic order of the I-Thou and I-It is a complex one, as Buber himself indicated when he wrote that "the genesis of the thing is a late product that develops out of the split of the primal encounters, out of the separation of the associated partners — as does the genesis of the I" (*IT*, 78/*DP*, 31). The "primal encounters" (*Urelebnisse*) are not to be understood as the I-Thou and the I-It, but rather as "the vital primal words I-acting-Thou and Thou-acting-I" (*IT*, 73/*DP*, 25). The I-Thou is a return to what is primal, rather than the primal itself. In the beginning is not so much the *relation* itself as the *a priori* of relation. There follows from this beginning the splitting of the "primal encounters," giving rise both to the thing and to the I. But the I *is* only in the I-It and the I-Thou and is not the same I in both. The issue could only be pursued in a lengthy commentary on Buber's text, but these details are surely sufficient to disturb the standard picture of Buber. Furthermore, if the "innate Thou" appears to serve as a principle which lends priority to the I-Thou, it should be recalled that Buber also acknowledged a rival principle which accounts for "a progressive increase of the It-world" (*IT*, 87/*DP*, 39). He expressed it in the sentence, "every Thou must become an It" (*IT*, 68/*DP*, 20). The formulation is carefully phrased to suggest that the I-Thou retains a residue of priority and that the I-It is only supplementary in its effect. But the I-Thou and the I-It both arise from the "relation" which is in the beginning and which is itself not the I-Thou.

I have focused on the interpretation of Buber's phrase "in the beginning is the relation" because it assumed so much importance in Levinas's reading of Buber. It is possible to find in Levinas what might at first appear to be a parallel formulation. He wrote in *Totality and Infinity* that "the priority of the orientation over the terms that are placed in it (and which cannot arise without this orientation) summarizes the present work" (*TI*, 215/*TeI*, 190). Similarly, Levinas's frequent references to the "relation without relation" might seem to be doing the same work of freeing the relation from being thought in terms of the relata. But the crucial word here is "orientation." My relation with the Other is a relation of transcendence such that the dimension of height is always in favor of the Other by virtue of my responsibility for him or her. Levinas would be cautious about assigning priority to the relation as such, because it might suggest something like a dissolution of the terms in the relation. On his account the Other is absolute within the relation, which is to say absolved from it. Similarly, my responsibility for the Other *separates* me from the relation. Indeed, it was with reference to this notion of separation that Levinas introduced the phrase "relation without relation" (*TI*, 60/*TeI*, 52, and *TI*, 295/*TeI*, 271). These notions of *separation* and *orientation* govern Levinas's relation to Buber.

LEVINAS'S INITIAL RESPONSE TO BUBER

Writing in 1964, Derrida in the essay "Violence and Metaphysics" touched on the question of Levinas's relation to Buber. In the course of a discussion of alterity he observed how having opposed the magisterial height of the *Vous* to the intimate reciprocity of the I-Thou, Levinas appeared to move in the 1963 essay "The Trace of the Other" to a philosophy of the *ille* or of the third person. Then, in a footnote, having summarized in three points Levinas's response to Buber's account of the I-thou relation, Derrida proceeded to question whether Buber would recognize himself in Levinas's interpretation. I take up this question in the next section, but here I shall concentrate on Levinas's response to Buber as he formulated it between 1946 and 1961, using Derrida's summary as a starting point.

The basis for Derrida's summary was Levinas's brief remarks on the I-Thou relation which punctuate *Totality and Infinity* (1961) and the even briefer comments to be found in the earlier works *Time and the Other* (1948) and *Existence and Existents* (1947). Derrida observed that Levinas reproached the I-Thou relationship "(1) for being reciprocal and symmetrical, thus committing violence against height, and especially against separateness, and secretiveness; (2) for being formal, capable of 'uniting man to things, as much as Man to man;' (3) for preferring preference, the 'private relationship,' the 'clandestine nature' of the couple which is 'self-sufficient and forgetful of the universe.'" And by way of explanation, particularly of this last point, Derrida offered this comment: "For there is also in Levinas's thought, despite his protests against neutrality, a summoning of the third party, the universal witness, the face of the world which keeps us from the 'disdainful spiritualism' of the I-Thou" (*WD*, 314, n. 37/*ED*, 156, n. 1). Derrida thereby touched on the place of *le tiers*, the third, in Levinas's discussion of the face to face and the fact that Levinas characterized as "complacent" and "a dual egoism" the relationship between lovers which excludes the third party (*TI*, 265–66/*TeI*, 242–44). That the third — and thus the whole of humanity — looks at me in the eyes of the Other is what secures in Levinas's thinking the passage from the Other to the Others, the passage from ethics to justice, from inequality in favor of the Other to equality (*TI*, 213/*TeI*, 188). Levinas specified that this original inequality of asymmetry in favor of the Other is not visible to the third (*TI*, 251/*TeI*, 229) as a kind of external observer. And yet it is this notion of *le tiers*, and also that of *la troisième personne*, which contributed to the development in Levinas of a conception of illeity as "a way of concerning me without entering into conjunction with me" (*OB*, 12/*AQE*, 15); an "infinity and divine transcendence, other than the alterity of the Other" (*APB*, 132) — God as trace, not just of the other, but of the others (*OT*, 46/*EDE*, 202). Derrida was well advised not to distinguish too quickly two (or more) concepts of the *third* in an effort to resolve the ambiguity occasioned by this extraordinary collection of themes around this single word, but it is a topic which extends well beyond the present essay and I shall touch on it later only in so far as it concerns the relation between Buber and Levinas.

Already in *Time and the Other*, his first extended discussion of the relation to the Other, Levinas was at pains to distance his account from Buber's. On the very last page Levinas explicitly distinguished his own use of the phrase "I-Thou" (*moi-toi*) from that of Buber on the grounds that Buber underestimated "the ineluctable character of isolated subjectivity" (*TO*, 94/*TA*, 89). Much of what Levinas said to distinguish his account from the philosophies of communion that may be found in Plato or the Heideggerian *Miteinandersein* clearly does not apply to the relation Buber describes in *I and Thou*. Buber's I-Thou relation is not readily characterized as a "we" established through participation in a third term. But it is the distance that arises precisely in respect of the Other's proximity, the duality within proximity, which served as Levinas's focus and differentiated the relation he sought to describe from that which preoccupied Buber. Buber is already characterized as a thinker of reciprocity, according to the terms of the first of Derrida's three points. Both in *Time and the Other* and in *Existence and Existents* (where Buber is not mentioned by name) Levinas offered as his own example of the relation with the other the case of so-called "failure of communication" in love where the absence of the other is something positive — the other's presence as other — and not a deficiency (*TO*, 94/*TA*, 89 and *EE*, 95/*DEE*, 163). Whether the other is stronger or weaker, the other for Levinas is what I am not: "intersubjective space is initially asymmetrical." The references to the poor, the widow, the orphan and the stranger that dominate *Totality and Infinity* are already to be found here — alongside references to the enemy and the powerful one (*EE*, 95/*DEE*, 163).

Although Levinas's treatment of Buber in *Totality and Infinity* (1961) is dispersed throughout the book, there is no difficulty in ascertaining the basis for Derrida's summary. Levinas remained convinced that Buber understood the Thou primarily as partner and friend and thus gave primacy to a relationship of reciprocity, in contrast with his own emphasis on the irreversibility of the relation (*TI*, 68/*TeI*, 40). Alongside it stood a second claim that Buber formalized the I-Thou so that it covered not only the relation between human beings, but also man's relation to things. How well these two claims go together — the claim that Buber understood the I-Thou on the model of friendship and yet at the same time presented it as a "formalism which does not determine any concrete structure" — is an open question. But perhaps the difficulty seems less acute when one observes that Levinas in making this second point was not saying, as he would later, that a formalism cannot account for an ethics.[4] Rather, the point was that Buber was in no position to account for economy, the search for happiness, the representation of things "except as an aberration, a fall, or a sickness" (*TI*, 68–69/*TeI*, 40). These, of course, were precisely the topics with which the second section of *Totality and Infinity* was concerned. The question therefore was not whether Buber lacked a concrete model, so much as whether his distinction between the I-Thou and the I-It was a rich enough tool. The point was not unlike Rosenzweig's complaint on reading the galleys of *I and Thou* that Buber had had to press all authentic life, including the "authentic It," into the I-Thou.[5]

Finally, Levinas charged the "I-Thou" relation with being self-sufficient and forgetful of the universe. The passage appeared early in the section on "The Other and the Others" that focused on the third party. Buber was not mentioned by name at this specific point, but the reference seems unmistakable. "Language as the presence of the face does not invite complicity with the preferred being, the self-sufficient 'I-Thou' forgetful of the universe; in its frankness it refuses the clandestineness of love, where it loses its frankness and meaning and turns into laughter or cooing" (*TI*, 213/*TeI*, 187–88).

It might seem that the same point had already been made by Levinas earlier in the book in his statement that the Other as interlocutor was properly speaking not a thou (*tu*), but a you (*vous*) who challenges my freedom (*TI*, 101/*TeI*, 75). And yet Levinas's use of the *vous* for the relation with the Other as height did not mean that he thereby reserved the *tu* or even the *je-tu* to refer to Buber. To attribute such a terminological decision to Levinas would give rise to a dilemma. In the passage at issue where the I-Thou was referred to as self-sufficient, it appeared to be identified with the clandestineness of love. And yet Levinas wrote in the section on "The Phenomenology of Eros" that "love . . . grasps nothing, issues in no concept, does not *issue*, has neither the subject-object structure nor the me-thou (*moi-toi*) structure" (*TI*, 261/*TeI*, 238). If Levinas meant here by "me-thou" the I-Thou relation of Buber, then the point would be that love could not be given a place within either of the alternatives which for Buber were exhaustive. And Levinas went on to say that "Love does not simply lead, by a more detoured or more direct way, toward the Thou. It is bent on another direction than that wherein one encounters the Thou" (*TI*, 264/*TeI*, 242). Here the use of the word "encounters" (*rencontre*) would again seem to suggest that Buber was still meant. But the I-Thou of Buber could not be meant both in the section "The Other and the Others" and the section on eros. The confusion arises because Levinas's language was not established terminology but thinking that was undergoing transformation, a problem no doubt enhanced by the fact that the book was written over a period of years.

Another example of this ambiguity is given in the very same paragraph in which Levinas referred to the I-Thou as "self-sufficient." He also said there that "The *Thou* is posited in front of a *we*." In context this "thou" who "commands me as a Master" must be identified with what was called earlier in the book the *vous* of height, but it could not also be the Thou of the self-sufficient I-Thou. In sum, it is simply not clear that Levinas did charge Buber's I-Thou relation with being self-sufficient. Even though Levinas wrote that "the I-Thou in which Buber sees the category of interhuman relationship is the relation not with the interlocutor but with feminine alterity" (*TI*, 155/*TeI*, 129), the charge of self-sufficiency could have been directed against the clandestineness of love and not the I-Thou of Buber. It is significant that in "The Phenomenology of Eros" Levinas drew a distinction between love and friendship (*TI*, 266/*TeI*, 244), and it is in terms of friendship, not love, that Levinas presents Buber's I-Thou elsewhere.[6]

LEVINAS'S FIRST ESSAY ON BUBER AND BUBER'S RESPONSE

I noted earlier that in "Violence and Metaphysics" Derrida expressed some doubt as to whether Buber would recognize himself in Levinas's interpretation, thereby suggesting, though only in the briefest out-line, the possibility that Levinas might have offered a more sympa-thetic reading of Buber.

> Others will determine, perhaps, whether Buber would recognize him-self in this interpretation. It can already be noted in passing that Buber seems to have foreseen these reservations. Did he not specify that the I-Thou relationship was neither referential nor exclusive in that it is previous to all empirical and eventual modifications? Founded by the absolute I-thou, which turns us toward God, it opens up, on the con-trary, the possibility of every relationship to Others. Understood in its original authenticity, it is neither detour nor diversion. Like many of the contradictions which have been used to embarrass Buber, this one yields, as the *Postscript to I and Thou* tells us, "to a superior level of judgment" and to "the paradoxical description of God as the absolute Person." (*WD*, 134 n. 37/*ED*, 156 n. 1)

Derrida continued the quotation from Buber: "It is as the absolute person that God enters into the direct relationship to us. . . . The man who turns toward him need not turn his back on any other I-Thou relationship: quite legitimately he brings them all to God and allows them to become transfigured 'in the face of God'" (*IT*, 182/*DP*, 135).[7]

There is some curiosity in finding Derrida, albeit in 1964, appar-ently according a special privilege to whether an author recognizes himself in an interpretation of his works. Did Levinas recognize him-self when he read Derrida's interpretation and would it have posed a problem for Derrida's reading had he not done so? Did not Derrida himself in the same place insist on the difference between Levinas's "intentions" and his "philosophical discourse" (*WD*, 151/*ED*, 224)? Leaving that aside, it is in fact possible to give an exact answer to the question of whether Buber could have recognized himself in Levinas's interpretation of him. At the very time that Derrida was speculating on Buber's likely response to Levinas's treatment of him, Buber pub-lished two sets of replies to questions posed to him by Levinas. The first arose in connection with a volume devoted to Buber in the series "The Library of Living Philosophers." A feature of the series is the reply the articles elicit from the philosopher to whom the volume is dedicated. In his 55-page "Reply to my Critics," Buber made only two brief comments on Levinas's essay "Martin Buber and the Theory of Knowledge."[8] And in fact there are some grounds for believing that Levinas was aware of only one of them, the least interesting.[9] Both comments began by noting that Levinas had misunderstood some crucial point (*PMB*, 697/*MB*, 596; *PMB*, 723/*MB*, 619).

The second response appeared in another volume devoted to the idea of questioning famous philosophers, *Philosophical Interrogations*. There Levinas elicited a more extensive and even less welcoming reply, precisely of the kind Derrida had anticipated. Buber even referred Levinas to the Postscript to *I and Thou*, just as Derrida himself had done. Questioning Levinas's understanding of the concepts of the "between" and the "primal distance" (*Urdistanz*), Buber wrote that "Since Levinas, in the first place, accepts a signification for the two concepts which they do not have in the context of my thought and, in the second, equates with each of them other concepts belonging to totally different spheres of this thought, he makes a direct answer to his questions impossible for me" (*PI*, 27). Buber adopted the role of teacher, contenting himself with "making a few clarifying comments on his objections so far as that fundamental misunderstanding allows." He did not succeed in answering Levinas's objections if that is understood to mean silencing them. They reappeared in later essays. But there was equally no indication that Levinas was unduly disappointed by Buber's replies, as is particularly clear from a memorial article Levinas published on the occasion of Buber's death.[10]

In the final section of Levinas's "Martin Buber and the Theory of Knowledge," Levinas poses three "objections" to Buber. The first focuses on the question of reciprocity, as in Derrida's reconstruction of Levinas's three objections to Buber in *Totality and Infinity*. In his second objection Levinas is concerned that although Buber is preoccupied with distinguishing the I-Thou relation from the I-It, Buber does not appear to attend to the fact that it is only in consciousness that we come to know the between (*Zwischen*) (*PMB*, 149/*NP*, 48). And yet would not this be to refer the I-Thou to the I-It? Levinas's third objection addresses not just Buber but "any epistemology which bases truth on a non-theoretical activity or on existence." Here the whole tendency of recent philosophy as Levinas perceived it was at issue. I shall begin with this third point as it not only serves to explain why the essay takes the course that it does, but at the same time also clarifies the other two objections.

The essay "Martin Buber and the Theory of Knowledge" was in the first instance an attempt to assimilate Buber's account of the I-Thou relation to what Levinas calls "contemporary" philosophical thought. Levinas's presentation of Buber in terms of the problem of knowledge (which he construes as the problem of grasping what is independent so that it maintains its otherness) is questionable because it placed Buber from the outset and without reservation within a philosophical context. Nevertheless it gave Levinas the opportunity to raise the question of separation within a historical framework, a question that in *Totality and Infinity* was posed on the basis of direct description. Ancient ontology was, Levinas said following Plato's *Parmenides*, devoted to the question of how a being subject to error could relate itself to the absolute being without impairing its absolute character. This for Levinas provided the classical formulation of the problem of knowledge. "Modern" (presumably in the sense of Cartesian and post-Cartesian) discussions of the theory of knowledge were marked by the "separation" of the subject. But "contemporary" (Husserlian and post-Husserlian) thought, by contrast, is governed by the rejection of the notion of subject on the grounds that it is an abstraction (*PMB*, 135–36/*NP*, 29–30). It is this development, Levinas suggested, that enabled recent thinking to distinguish knowledge of objects from knowledge of Being, albeit at a high price.[11] For by sacrificing the notion of the subject, contemporary philosophy had deprived itself of the notion of separation, which alone, as he attempted to show in *Totality and Infinity*, made possible "the relation with the detached, absolute exteriority." "Separation opens up between terms that are absolute and yet in relation, that absolve themselves from the relation they maintain, that do not abdicate in it in favor of a totality this relation would sketch out" (*TI*, 220/*TeI*, 195). In *Totality and Infinity*, however, Levinas insisted — following Rosenzweig — that the ontological tradition of Western philosophy has been conceived as a quest for totality. It is clearly not this conception that Levinas had in mind when in "Martin Buber and the Theory of Knowledge" he referred to philosophy as "a rupture of our participation in totality" (*PMB*, 149/ *NP*, 49), so that when philosophy denies separation it denies the impulse which in *Totality and Infinity* is called "metaphysical thought."

The first of Levinas's objections was formulated in terms of the asymmetry of the ethical relation, which is always in favor of the Other. For Levinas a reciprocal relation, such as Buber's I-Thou relation, cannot account for this difference of level. Here, as elsewhere, Levinas did not deny the presence of ethical themes in Buber but rather asked whether he made explicit the ethical structure that belongs to the relation with the Other (*PMB*, 147/*NP*, 46).[12] Levinas at this point referred to a sentence early in *I and Thou* where Buber said that "I become in the Thou; becoming I, I say Thou" (*IT*, 62/*DP*, 15). Levinas's comment was that

> if the I becomes an I in saying Thou, as Buber asserts, I hold the place from my correlate and the I-Thou relation resembles all other relations: as if an outside observer was speaking of the I and of the Thou in the third person. The encounter is formal and is reversible so that it is indifferent whether it is read from left to right or right to left. (*PMB*, 147/*NP*, 47)[13]

The charge of formalism here — and also as it is repeated in *Philosophical Interrogations* (*PI*, 26) and again in an essay of 1968[14] — arose because the asymmetry of the relation disappeared from Buber's account with the loss of separation, as indicated by the phrase referred to by Levinas. Buber, however, challenged this interpretation in his "Replies to my Critics." He complained that Levinas was wrong to infer from his statement that I owe my place to my partner, when it should rather be said that I owe my place to my relation to my partner in that the Thou also does not exist outside of the relation. He denied that the relation was reversible and explained further, "My I — by which here the I of the I-Thou relation is to be understood — I owe to saying Thou, not to the person to whom I say Thou" (*PMB*, 697/ *MB*, 596). Buber appears to have missed Levinas's point, which was concerned with the question of separation or asymmetry. But the aspect of "saying Thou" would serve Levinas later as a basis for developing the ethical structure of the relation to the Other left inexplicit by Buber. There is a sense, therefore, in which the reply offered by Buber that Levinas did not take up would have provided a better basis for dialogue than that which served as the basis for the article "Dialogue avec Martin Buber."

Levinas reformulated the point about reciprocity in the exchange published in *Philosophical Interrogations.* Referring again to the phrase "I become in the Thou," he asked "whether the concept of relation is capable of defining this original structure" (*PI*, 23). Here Buber was again assimilated to the movement of recent philosophical thought, specifically Husserl and Heidegger, where the substantiality and independent reality of the self is denied. Levinas's first concern was to put in question Buber's use of the word "relation" to characterize the basic word I-Thou.[15] Levinas conceded that the question arose only because Buber had conceived the I-Thou as "a relation in which one of the terms remains absolute" (*PI*, 24). Levinas did not want to charge Buber with contradiction: "the apparent contradiction between the absolute and the relative is overcome in the case of social relations." Levinas understood the word "absolute" in the same sense in which he used it in *Totality and Infinity,* where it refers to a relation in which the terms absolve themselves from the relation while remaining absolute within it (*TI*, 64/*TeI*, 35–36). Had Levinas read Buber's 1957 Postscript to *I and Thou* — or indeed had he been more attentive to the third part of *I and Thou* instead of focusing largely, like most readers, on the first part — he might not have gone on to ask whether Buber had been aware of "the logical originality of the relation." Appealing to the notion of an absolute Person, Buber had in the Postscript explicitly embraced the contradictory nature of the relation as arising out of the supracontradictory nature of God. This contradiction is met by the paradoxical designation of God as the absolute Person, that is one that cannot be relativized (*IT*, 181/*DP*, 135).

Levinas explained that his suspicions were aroused by Buber's commitment to the two theses, first, that the I derives its *ipseity* from its confrontation with the Thou and, secondly, that the relation is reciprocal. According to Levinas, this would mean that the terms would be related as objects, each definable in terms of the other and as constituting a totality from which they could not be separated. Levinas knew very well that Buber would deny the appropriateness of the terms "object" and "totality," as indeed he did in his reply (*PI*, 27). Levinas wrote, "If the terms are related in this way, we must infer that it is logically impossible for them not mutually to define one another, because a term which was absolutely *sui generis* would destroy the relation." He was not subscribing to this logic. He was presenting Buber with the consequence of failing — he thought — to specify the inappropriateness of the logic of noncontradiction.

In his response, Buber claimed that, although he did not insist on reciprocity, he regarded asymmetry as only a special case of the I-Thou relation. "The asymmetry that wishes to limit the relation to the relationship to a higher would make it completely one-sided: love would either be unreciprocated by its nature or each of the two lovers must miss the reality of the other" (*PI*, 28). It is necessary to consider whether Levinas's account does have that implication. Certainly Levinas says that "I love fully only if the other loves me" (*TI*, 266/*TeI*, 244). But such assurances are to be regarded as no more final than, for example, Buber's comments about ethics. The issue is, of course, further complicated by Buber's choice of example, which, from a Levinasian standpoint could be said to be a confirmation of Buber's preoccupations. Nevertheless, most significant in this context is the question of the judgment that would confirm a relation as symmetrical. From where might it be posed? For Levinas, I cannot make the comparison between my relation to the Other and the Other's relation to me without absenting myself from the relation and looking at it from the outside. And yet, what is visible from outside is not a relation with the Other at all, but only a synthesis of terms. Buber is not saying only that there should be some reciprocity. His point is surely directed against the idea of a relation that amounts to two asymmetries that are nowhere equalized, so that I relate to the Other as to a height and the Other relates to me in the same way. To insist on reciprocity in this sense is to insist on what Derrida in "Violence and

Metaphysics" called "the transcendental symmetry of two empirical asymmetries" (*WD*, 126/*ED*, 185). Again, if this meant, as Derrida seemed to suggest, that I should recognize myself as other for the other, then Derrida was wrong to say there was no trace of this relationship in Levinas (for example, *TI*, 84/*TeI*, 56).

But were not Buber's remarks governed by an ideal of fusion, of presence, just as his model of dialogue was that of transparent communication? Such models make no sense for a relation conceived in terms of separation, because they can only be posed from a transcendental perspective for which the relation to Otherness is in principle inaccessible. It should not be forgotten that Buber's insistence on reciprocity in the sense of an equal or absolute presence of the lovers to each other had already led Levinas in *Existence and Existents* to introduce the example of so-called "failure of communication" in love where, as I noted earlier, the absence of the other is not a negation or a deficiency, but the other's presence as other.

The course of this discussion in *Philosophical Interrogations* clarifies the relation between the first and second objections in "Martin Buber and the Theory of Knowledge." This second objection is that it is only in consciousness that we come to know the between. It was repeated in *Philosophical Interrogations* when Levinas asked of the meeting between the I and Thou, "How does this *Zwischen* or betweenness where it takes place, the "shock" (*Geschehen*) or "trust" which defines that meeting encroach on the consciousness that is aware of it? How can this unusual relation of the I-Thou be reflected in our conscious awareness when the latter is essentially awareness of an object, without at the same time leading us to suspect that it involves but a moment of consciousness?" (25). The question was again whether the I-Thou relation could be thought except by consciousness, which would be to submit it to the very realm from which it was supposed to be removed. That our knowledge of the I-Thou relation cannot be referred to a secondary act of reflection on an experience or to a consciousness is a constant theme of Levinas's essays on Buber. But what underlay it was the view, most clearly stated in "Martin Buber and the Theory of Knowledge," that Buber's account of the Other fulfilled the ambitions of the theory of knowledge in its ancient classical form. For Buber, only in the I-Thou relation did one succeed in grasping the independent other (*PMB*, 137/*NP*, 34); only there did one enter into community with the totality of being (*PMB*, 138/*NP*, 35). But in consequence Buber offered us a mere union rather than a *synousia*, a social communion (*PI*, 26). That is why Levinas could present Buber's rendering of the I-Thou relation as in some sense a fulfillment of philosophical ambitions, while nevertheless showing how it failed to account for philosophy itself in so far as it was a rupture of the individual with the whole (*PMB*, 149/*NP*, 49).

THE FAILED DIALOGUE MADE GOOD

If the 1958 essay showed Levinas engaged in the task of differentiating his standpoint from that of Buber, the 1978 essay "Martin Buber, Gabriel Marcel and Philosophy" indicated how Levinas came to believe that the dialogue between thinkers is not to be limited to such an exercise alone. This latter essay returned to many of the conclusions arrived at in "Martin Buber and the Theory of Knowledge." So, for example, in both essays Levinas used the notion of intentionality to contrast the basic word "I-Thou" with the subject-object relation. Nor was there anything new in the insistence in the 1978 essay that both Buber and Marcel resorted to the language of Being or ontological language in order to support their descriptions. But the decisive question was now that of the possibility or impossibility of thinking outside or beyond being (*BMP*, 318/*BP*, 508), the very question that had governed Derrida's reading of Levinas in "Violence and Metaphysics."

Another important difference between the two essays was that the question of God, which had been virtually ignored in "Martin Buber and the Theory of Knowledge," now came to play an important role in Levinas's interpretation of Buber. This was not only in conformity with Buber's own insistence in his 1957 Postscript to *I and Thou* that his essential concern in that book had been "the close association of the relation to God with the relation to one's fellow-men" (*IT*, 171/

DP, 122). In 1978, though no doubt too late for Levinas to make use of it in his essay, the text of Buber's 1922 lectures *Religion als Gegenwart*, which served as a draft of *I and Thou*, was published.[16] In these lectures Buber began with the theme of the eternal Thou. Had he persisted, the temptation to offer the kind of anthropological interpretation of *I and Thou* that has tended to dominate the secondary literature would have been diminished. But Levinas's interest in the issue of how the relation to God as the invisible and nongiven takes place in the relation to the other human being as thou (*BMP*, 306/ *BP*, 493–94) is to be understood less with reference to a change of direction in Buber scholarship than to the fact that this issue had become more prominent in Levinas's own thinking, albeit in a way that led him to think of God as He, in explicit contrast to the Thou of Buber and Marcel.[17] Furthermore, the question of how an alliance might be possible between the singularity of the I and the absolute Thou, a question similar to that which dominated Levinas's contribution to the volume *Philosophical Interrogations*, was now dismissed with the remark that Buber had already transcended the perspective from which the question was posed when he took the relation as his starting point: "In the beginning is the relation." And Levinas here acknowledged the importance of language in Buber. "Dialogue functions not as a *synthesis* of the relation, but as its very unfolding (*déploiement*)" (*BMP*, 309/*BP*, 496).

But it was not only that Levinas came finally to a recognition of the importance of the eternal Thou and of dialogue in Buber. On the question of the formalism of the I-Thou relation, which had previously been such a stumbling block, Levinas repeated that it was indeed in some sense formal, but conceded that in Buber it had at the same time an ethical concreteness (*BMP*, 317/*BP*, 506). The response of dialogue already exhibits the responsibility of "the one for the other." Similarly, when Levinas raised once again the question of the reciprocity of the I and the Thou, on this occasion he immediately acknowledged Buber's notion of the between, the *Zwischen* (*BMP*, 307/*BP*, 494). The implication was that the question of the equality of the related terms would no longer arise once attention was paid to the *relation*. So Levinas quoted approvingly Marcel's comment on Buber that "the encounter does not take place in each of the participants, or in a neutral unity encompassing them, but *between* them in the most exact sense, in a dimension accessible to them alone" (*PMB*, 42/*MB*, 37). Later in the essay he would acknowledge specifically that, by virtue of the relation to the eternal Thou, elevation could be found in the midst of reciprocity (*BMP*, 316/*BP*, 506), thereby laying to rest the crucial question of asymmetry. And finally, when he repeated the observation that Buber and Marcel both questioned the primacy of the objectifying act, on this occasion it was no longer to place them among the philosophers of existence. The philosophy of existence retained the priority of truth, whereas these "philosophers of coexistence" maintained a sociality that was "irreducible to knowledge and to truth" (*BMP*, 307/*BP*, 495). There is no doubting that this is a very different assessment from that given in "Martin Buber and the Theory of Knowledge."

In this way Levinas dismissed in just a few sentences the concerns that had preoccupied him in making the first of his three objections in "Martin Buber and the Theory of Knowledge." The 1978 essay was more concerned with Marcel's and Buber's reliance on ontological language, a question that was now taken up in a way more reminiscent of Derrida's discussion of Levinas in "Violence of Metaphysics" than of anything that had appeared in Levinas's previous essays on Buber. The question was whether, having broken with the ontology of objects and substance, Buber and Marcel did not in their descriptions of the encounter hold fast to Being and presence as ultimate referents. The role of presence in Buber's *I and Thou* is pronounced, not surprisingly when one recalls that *Religion as Presence* was the title of the lecture series in which Buber first developed his ideas on the subject at length. Notwithstanding this, Levinas judged Buber the more successful in breaking with ontology, not least because Buber — unlike Marcel — was clear that sociality could not be reduced to an *experience* of sociality.[18]

Levinas at the beginning of the essay contrasted Buber's rendering of the dialogical "relation" with that of Marcel, almost as if he were dealing with two readings of the same text. In spite of "the remarkable community" of their fundamental ideas, Marcel's discussion differentiated itself from Buber's because they came from very different intellectual traditions, even different religions (*BMP*, 305–06/*BP*, 492–93). On these same grounds Levinas would be closer to Buber than he would be to Marcel, and indeed in this essay Marcel seems to serve as something of a foil, as if he was introduced to show the superiority of Buber's formulations. When Marcel asked how it was possible for the I-Thou to transpose itself into the realm of language without degenerating thereby (*PMB*, 45/ *BMP*, 309/*BP*, 497), when he noted that it was impossible to say of the Thou that it was not a thing without reducing it to the status of a thing (*PMB*, 44), he believed that he was drawing on Buber's own statement that only silence leaves the Thou free (*PMB*, 47). "All response binds the Thou into the It-world" (*IT*, 89/*DP*, 42).[19] Levinas, who had earlier characterized the I-Thou as "an understanding without words, an expression in secret" (*TI*, 155/*TeI*, 129), was now in no mood to dismiss the role of dialogue. "Buber eliminates the gnoseological foundation of the encounter. It is a pure dialogue, a pure *alliance* which no common pneumatic *presence* envelops. I am destined for the other not because of our *previous* proximity or our substantial union, but because the Thou is absolutely other" (*BMP*, 312/*BP*, 501).

With this answer to Marcel, Levinas also addressed the second objection that he himself had posed in "Martin Buber and the Theory of Knowledge" about our consciousness of the relation. It is even more explicitly answered when Levinas later in the essay asked if the I-Thou relation joined being only in a secondary and not always legitimate act of reflection. "Does not the ethical relation signify precisely the non-significance of being, even if the theologians, reflecting on it, obstinately persist in rediscovering its meaning in the trace of sociality and interpreting sociality as an experience" (*BMP*, 318/*BP*, 507–08)? At this point it seems that Marcel has been introduced less as a foil for Buber than in order to help Levinas reverse his earlier assessment of *I and Thou*.

Having examined the question of the language of the I-Thou in the context of Marcel's assumption about a more fundamental and silent form of the relation, Levinas then reconsidered the question independently of this assumption. As Levinas posed it, it is the question of whether the immediacy of the I-Thou relation is respected by language as a system of words, language as *said*. The "said" (*le dit*) is to be understood here in distinction from the "saying" (*le dire*), although strictly speaking it is not a "distinction," as the saying and the said are nonsynchronizable. The *said* is a language that "speaks about something and expresses the relation of the speaker to the object of which he speaks, saying what is the case with it" (*BMP*, 315/*BP*, 504). *Saying* says something, says the said, but at the same time says *Thou*. Not that the actual word *Thou* need be said. The *Thou* "is the said of saying as saying" (*BMP*, 315/*BP*, 505). Thus in the I-Thou, language is not the element of degeneration — or perhaps one should say *not that only*. It is also the element of transcendence (*BMP*, 315/*BP*, 504) and "thou-saying" (*dire-toi*) is directed to the invisible, the unknowable, the unthematizable of which one can say nothing (*BMP*, 316/*BP*, 505). Marcel found all language permeated by the "I-It." For Levinas, language is not absorbed irretrievably in the "I-It," but nor can a language of "thou-saying" be separated from it to subsist on its own.

Although Buber in his account of the I-Thou relation remained for the most part bound to ontological language (*BMP*, 314–15/*BP*, 504), Levinas "awoke" in Buber's *said* a *saying* that was absorbed in it, a speaking beyond the language of Being (cf. *OB*, 43/*AQE*, 55). It was a question, in the time-honored phrase, not of understanding Buber better than he understood himself, but of rejoining him and recognizing him as the pioneer (*BMP*, 316/*BP*, 505). And this meant to acknowledge Buber as an ethical thinker. "Surely the immediacy of the I-Thou of which Buber speaks, is not to be found in the negativity of a thought cut off from all recourse to the conceptual systems of the world and of history? Surely it is to be found in the very urgency of my responsibility which precedes all knowing?" (*BMP*, 316/*BP*, 505). Levinas's reading of Buber situated itself — and he used Derrida's word — on the *margin* of Buber's text (*BMP*, 316/*BP*, 505). But it did not stay there very long. Contrary to Levinas's previous reading, "the whole of Buber's work" was to be regarded as "a renewal of ethics" (*BMP*, 317/*BP*, 506).

Levinas also returned to the third of the objections raised in his paper "Martin Buber and the Theory of Knowledge," the question of Buber's relation to the vocation of philosophy. This was now explained, more clearly than had originally been the case, to mean the ability to say "I," as the call to live in a manner other than that of simple submission to the decisions and commands of society, culture, politics and religion (*BMP*, 313/*BP*, 502). The question was whether the dialogical philosophy of Buber could respond to the traditional vocation for philosophy while at the same time contesting the traditional preeminence of ontology, whether the capacity to say "I" could be secured without basing it on the freedom of a consciousness equal to being (*BMP*, 314–15/*BP*, 504). Once again Levinas, now equipped with an ethical reading of Buber, was able to fend off a question that seemed so pressing when he was without such an interpretation. I am I not on the basis of my freedom, but as if I had been elected or chosen (*BMP*, 317/*BP*, 507). *I* cannot divest myself of my ethical responsibility.

Levinas closed the essay by returning to the question of the impossibility of thinking outside or beyond being. One could put the question in this way: When Buber says "all actual life is encounter" (*IT*, 62/*DP*, 15) or when Levinas himself has recourse to the word "dis-inter-estedness" (*dés-intér-essement*) in an attempt to say "the uprooted-ness outside of being" (*BMP*, 318/*BP*, 508) is not the reference to being then ineliminable? Levinas answered the question with another question, the counterquestion of whether the philosophy of dialogue does not show "that it is impossible to encapsulate the encounter with the Other in a theory, as if that encounter was an experience whose meaning reflexion would succeed in recovering" (*BMP*, 320/*BP*, 510). The philosophy of dialogue has brought into focus the ambiguity and enigmatic character of that thinking for which the world and the other person, knowledge and sociality, being and God are bound together, as in Husserl, according to the very structure of the experience of consciousness. With Husserl as his example, Levinas focused on the totalizing tendency of solitary, monadological thinking. For Husserl, the urgent needs of the Other — my neighbor who awaits me when I close my book, put down my pen, and leave my study — mark a return to the *Lebenswelt* and so a renewal of the thread which binds me to life. But in terms of the transcendental phenomenology that Husserl founded, the call of the neighbor merely represents an interruption. Were we pure intellects like the angels, we would be able to work solidly day and night without distraction.

In order to challenge that attitude, Levinas ended his essay with a story from the Talmud. According to this story, when the divine Torah was about to be given to humanity, the angels protested against it being allowed to leave heaven. So an attempt was made to appease the angels. They were reminded that, as they had not been born, they would not die. And because they did not work, eat, have possessions, nor sell them, the Torah did not apply to them. Levinas asks whether the angels were flattered by this answer. Or did they, on the contrary, discover their inferiority to human beings? Humans alone are capable of giving and of being-one-for-the-other. They alone take part in the "divine comedy" above and beyond the understanding of being to which the pure spirits were dedicated (*BMP*, 320/*BP*, 511). In telling this story and in responding to Husserl in the way outlined above, Levinas did not intend an ethical attack on the philosopher's lifestyle, although the ethical connotations of the discussion were relevant. In the context of the essay, Levinas should rather be understood as drawing attention to the character of the saying of transcendence as it takes place within the history of ontology. Thinking has come to be construed as the reduction to solitary consciousness or else as the rediscovery of Being, in Heidegger's sense. Failure to conform to this model is conventionally assessed as the consequence of a lack of resolution, an unwillingness to follow thought through to its final conclusions. If thinking fails to reabsorb the Other in the course of thought's return to itself, then this is regarded as a deficiency, the result of blind passion or the consequence of distraction, "fallenness," in Heidegger's terminology.

The philosophy of dialogue, according to Levinas, challenges this model. The question of whether the angels recognized the superiority of human beings points to the question of whether philosophy can recognize in the human face "a reasonable significance which

Reason does not know" (*BMP*, 320/*BP*, 511). The philosophy of dialogue runs counter to the standard models of thinking and allows us to acknowledge the saying of transcendence as an interruption of ontology.

REFORMULATIONS

"Martin Buber, Gabriel Marcel and Philosophy" could be read as a recantation of the essay "Martin Buber and the Theory of Knowledge," in which case Levinas would be engaged in dialogue with himself as much as with Buber. Other contemporary essays by Levinas on Buber rule out such an interpretation of the relation between the two essays. Levinas did not withdraw the earlier objections, although in some cases they were reformulated.

The essay "Martin Buber, Gabriel Marcel and Philosophy" was followed soon after by "Dialogue," written as a contribution to a German encyclopedia of Christianity.[20] The characterization of Buber to be found there emphasized many of the same points: the multiplicity of consciousnesses was not to be regarded as the result of a fall or ontological catastrophe that befell the One any more than sociality was to be considered as compensation for a lost unity (*OGM*, 143/*DVI*, 219); the originality of the I-Thou is understood to be irreducible to experience or knowledge; the eternal Thou is the Thou *par excellence*, invisible, nonobjectifiable and nonthematizable (*OGM*, 144/*DVI*, 220–21); language is the very event of transcendence (*OGM*, 147/*DVI*, 223); and the relation where the I encounters the Thou is the place and original occasion of the advent of ethics (*OGM*, 148–49/*DVI*, 225).

The essay "Dialogue" marks a development over its predecessors in its application of the notion of an "absolute distance" to the philosophy of dialogue. It is a term Levinas had already introduced in *Totality and Infinity* (for example, *TI*, 143/*TeI*, 116), and it served there to describe the separation between the same and the other. Levinas introduced it in "Dialogue" to acknowledge that Buber had indeed recognized the role of separation. The I and the Thou are said there to be "separated absolutely by the inexpressible secret of their intimacy," and dialogue transcends this distance without suppressing it (*OGM*, 144/*DVI*, 221). "Relation" now has a "*double meaning*" in Levinas's reading of Buber as both "absolute distance" and "immediacy" (*OGM*, 149/*DVI*, 228).

Of the two notions, "immediacy" is the more prominent in Buber's own texts (for instance, *IT*, 62/*DP*, 15). Indeed, when Levinas asked Buber some years earlier in *Philosophical Interrogations* if the reciprocity of the I-Thou relation did not compromise "the absolute distance of the Thou or Other" (*PI*, 26), Buber, as I documented earlier, complained that Levinas had misunderstood him. Buber had understood Levinas to be equating his two concepts of the "between" and "primal distance" and so referred Levinas back to his essay "Urdistanz und Beziehung." It seems that he understood Levinas's *la distance absolue* as an attempt to translate into French his own notion of *Urdistanz*. There was nothing in Levinas's contribution to *Philosophical Interrogations* to justify that interpretation, although it is just possible that it might have been suggested by the essay "Martin Buber and the Theory of Knowledge" where Levinas did refer to the essay "Urdistanz und Beziehung" when construing Buberian man as "the possibility of both distance and relation" (*PMB*, 140/*NP*, 37–38). But Buber's comment should not simply be dismissed as a failure on his part to recognize that Levinas was introducing a concept of his own and not simply translating him into French. Buber specified Levinas's error as a misapplication of the concept of *Urdistanz* to the sphere of the I-Thou relation. The concept of *Urdistanz* is rather an anthropological presupposition for the origination of the duality of the "primary words," of which the I-Thou is one (*PI*, 27). Even if Buber misidentified Levinas's "absolute distance" with his own "primal distance," he was surely correct to recognize a tendency on the part of Levinas — as indeed of many commentators — to confuse the anthropological presuppositions of the I-Thou with the I-Thou itself. This is most clearly apparent in respect of the interpretation of the phrase "In the beginning is the relation." But the difficulty is not confined to Buber's interpreters. It reflects an essential ambiguity that permeates Buber's own texts whenever the question of the relative priority and independence of the I-Thou is raised.

In "Dialogue," Levinas situated this absolute distance less in the failure of one person to know another — a failure of the synthesis that would bring about a coincidence or identity — than in the surplus of the relation. Such a surplus is exhibited, for example, in a gratuitous gift (*OGM*, 147/*DVI*, 224). Levinas also found such a surplus in Buber's notion of grace (*OGM*, 147/*DVI*, 224/*BMP*, 316/*BP*, 505). So when Buber said that "The Thou encounters me by grace — it cannot be found by seeking" (*IT*, 62/*DP*,15) or "Grace concerns us in so far as we proceed toward it and await its presence; it is not our object" (*IT*, 124/*DP*, 77), he acknowledged the Otherness of the Other and the sense in which the relation is one in which I not only address the Other by saying Thou, but also find myself addressed in a manner which is beyond my control.

Levinas's application of the notion of "absolute distance" in his reading of Buber accounted for the lack of an account of separation that in 1958 lay behind many of Levinas's reservations. But had Levinas accomplished this only by a false ecumenism in which the differences were simply concealed and the significant details of their thinking overlooked? At the end of the essay Levinas repeated his charge of reciprocity. Buber sometimes described the I-Thou relation as a harmonious copresence whereby the relation was in this extreme formalization emptied of its heteronomy (*OGM*, 150/*DVI*, 229–30). Levinas thereby upset any presumption that he might himself have come to establish a harmonious copresence with Buber.

This is even more clearly the case in "A propos de Buber: quelques notes," published in 1982. Levinas began this essay by praising Buber for having recognized the ethical relation with the other and having broken thereby with the philosophy of totality. "It is an order fully cognizant of the ethical relation, a relation with an inassimilable and thus, in the proper sense, in-com-prehensible — foreign to knowledge and to possession — alterity of the Other" (*APB*, 128). As always when Levinas is most positive in his assessment of Buber, language is at the forefront of his interpretation of the encounter. "The saying which says *Thou*, be it only implicitly" does so in a manner completely different from that of a thought proceeding dialogically from itself or projecting itself towards an object which it gives itself (*APB*, 127). But Levinas in the remainder of the essay presented a series of notes that returned to the task of clarifying the difference between his own perspective and that of Buber. So, for example, Levinas observed that although he himself regarded justice as derivative, Buber began with the I-Thou which, as reciprocal, was a relation of justice (*APB*, 131). So once again the reciprocity, reversibility and equality of the I-Thou "interpellation" served as a point of contrast with Levinas's own emphasis on the original ethical inequality of a responsibility in which the first person appears not in the nominative but in the accusative (*APB*, 129–30). This raises the question of the extent to which Buber recognized the ethical relation and separated himself from the philosophical tradition.

Yet Levinas seemed less concerned with the possibility that he was giving an apparently contradictory assessment of Buber than with taking the opportunity to rehearse his "objections" or "questions." Did not Buber fail to problematize my identity and unicity, drawing these concepts, not from the correlation of a dialogue where the self is concrete, but according to an "individuation" which is implicitly substantialist (*APB*, 130–31)? Did Buber's own thinking fail to break with the intentionality of consciousness and remain rather in the element of consciousness (*APB*, 131–32)? Was not the very "for-the-Other" of sociality only concrete in a giving of *things*, without which responsibility for the Other would be an ethereal sociality appropriate only to angels? Did not Buber's language, for all its novelty, fail to break with the priority of ontology (*APB*, 133)? These questions were the same as those that had inspired his initial response to Buber. And unlike "Martin Buber, Gabriel Marcel and Philosophy" or "Dialogue," Levinas's concern was not to uncover hidden resources in Buber's text. So, on this occasion, when Levinas juxtaposed his own conception of *illeity* with Buber's notion of God as the eternal Thou, he seemed more concerned to explain how illeity referred to a divine transcendence which nevertheless returns me to the service of my neighbor, than to see how the eternal Thou functions in Buber's text (*APB*, 132).[21]

RE-READING BUBER

When it is said that the question of *separation* and *orientation* (in the sense of asymmetry) governed the dialogue between Buber and Levinas, this should not simply be understood in terms of the way in which Levinas assessed the extent to which Buber recognized this twin aspect of the relation to the Other. At that level, the thematic level, the tension in Levinas's account of Buber remains unaddressed. It remains fundamentally unclear why Levinas was so apparently inconsistent in his assessment, sometimes affirming and sometimes denying that Buber recognized the ethical relation of transcendence, but never affirming or denying unambiguously. In particular, it is unclear why Levinas seemed somehow obliged in "Martin Buber, Gabriel Marcel and Philosophy" to *unsay* the objections of the essay "Martin Buber and the Theory of Knowledge" only to reformulate them later.

Only when it is acknowledged that Levinas came to practice *separation* and *orientation* or *asymmetry* in his reading of Buber is that necessity addressed. In other words, Levinas's relation to Buber took the form of an ethical relation where, on the basis of the separation from Buber that Levinas established in his early discussions, he subsequently came to exercise an orientation in favor of Buber. Which is not to say that that orientation did not in fact predate the objections. The asymmetry in favor of Buber is not a question of Levinas presenting the formula that he "does not have the ridiculous pretension of 'correcting' Buber" (*TI*, 69/*TeI*, 40–41). Rather it is much more a matter of awakening the "saying" of Buber from his said. One could pose the question whether this is not merely to exchange one way of failing to communicate for another. Is not this appeal to a "saying" just a further way of refusing to listen to what is said, much as when one poses objections against a text from a totally different standpoint or when one assimilates a text to one's own standpoint? The answer is that it will probably always seem so from the neutral standpoint of the observer. This is not to dismiss that standpoint insofar as it represents the demand to do *justice* to the text at issue, but — as in Levinas — justice must ultimately be subordinated to ethics as the awakening of saying.

To do justice to both Buber and Levinas it would be necessary, following this reading of Levinas on Buber, to reread Buber himself, not so much to confirm or deny the correctness of Levinas's reading, which would be to pose the question at a level of simplicity that remains divorced from the "dialogue between thinkers." It is more a question of seeing if Buber now reads any differently. In "A propos de Buber" Levinas invited his reader to return to Buber in this way. He said of the questions and objections that he had raised, "It is perhaps not impossible to find a response to them — or even to find in the ideas which determine them a place — in Buber's texts" (*APB*, 129). I shall on this occasion forego accepting this invitation exactly as Levinas conceived it, and content myself instead with an examination of Theunissen's discussion of Buber in his book *The Other*. This does not mean that Theunissen is now to serve as a substitute for Buber. My initial justification for turning to Theunissen in this context is that he offered a more detailed reading of Buber than Levinas, while at the same time acknowledging an agreement with "the general tendency" of Levinas's interpretation as presented in the essay "Martin Buber and the Theory of Knowledge."[22] Although Theunissen ultimately took his reading of Buber in a very different direction from that proposed by Levinas, a number of interesting questions are raised by his account which — particularly in their early development — rejoin themes I have already introduced.

Theunissen explicitly followed Levinas in characterizing Buber's work as an "ontology of the between" (*PMB*, 139/*NP*, 36), and he took as his starting point Levinas's account of the I-Thou as the condition for the I-It. But when he came to focus on the question of how the I-Thou relation can be thought as a "genuine original unity" (*IT*, 70/*DP*, 22), he discovered some of the difficulties that attend this interpretation. Theunissen found that Buber maintained the standpoint of the I in the very displacement of egology, one might almost say *despite himself:* "The I — despite all Buber's assurances to the contrary — assumes precedence over the Thou" (*O* 294/*A*, 281). Theunissen based this claim on the observation that Buber, "regardless of his intention to overcome the supremacy of the I," remained "true to that inner perspective prescribed by the 'mineness' of the I" (*O* 279/*A*, 267). He had in mind, for example, those formulations of Buber which attempted to explicate the becoming of the I. The problem was that although both the I and the Other were said to originate in the encounter, our access to the encounter remained on the part of my I (*O* 285/*A*, 272) or at least must be expressed as such. Theunissen found Buber's formulations "intrinsically ambiguous" (*O* 286/*A*, 273), and attempted a resolution by suggesting that such sentences as "man becomes an I through the Thou" (*IT*, 80/*DP*, 32) and "I become through the Thou; becoming I, I say Thou" (*IT*, 62/*DP*,15) be understood in terms of what he called "reciprocal constitution." This guarded against according priority to the Thou, as if the Thou in some way was the origin of the I. But it still left a question about the meaning of the *necessity* whereby, as Theunissen correctly observed, "in 'my' talk about it" reciprocal constitution appeared "in the shortened perspective of a precedence of the Thou over the I" (*O* 287/*A*, 275).

Theunissen referred it to the methodological orientation toward mineness that leaves me "only in a position to speak about it from my side and not from the other." This methodological precedence of the I gave rise to an ontological precedence of the Thou. But Theunissen treated them as if they somehow cancelled each other out. "The precedence of the Thou over the I . . . is still only the clothing in which the precedence of the between over the I and the Thou manifests itself to me, the one who is met in the meeting." And yet how was the precedence of the between to be established except by a kind of "transcendental symmetry" that, according to Levinas, would inevitably be blind to the ethical orientation of the relation?[23]

In other words, the symmetry was imposed to correct the orientation in favor of the Other. But even so, this only postponed the "trace of the Other" that reemerged later in the form of the relation between, on the one hand, "the precedence of 'being spoken to' over 'speaking to,'" as it arises in concrete experience and, on the other, the act of "speaking to" that secures the precedence of the I and that dominates the conceptual unfolding of the relation (*O* 339/*A*, 324). Buber tended to focus onesidedly on the "thou-saying" where "the initiative goes out from me" (*O* 299/*A*, 286), even to the point of constituting the I (*PMB*, 697). But there was also a place in his thinking for the way, for example, in which we are addressed by the eternal Thou (*IT*, 57/*DP*, 10). The notion of grace to which Levinas drew attention in the essay "Dialogue" was concerned with the way the Other comes to me without my assistance. Hence its role as a "surplus," as Levinas put it. Not simply because, as Buber wrote, "What we have to deal with, what we have to be concerned about, is not the other, but our side" (*IT*, 124/*DP*, 77). But also because grace is a "surplus" over Buber's tendency to dwell on the I saying Thou and which can in no respect be equalized with it in order to establish the between of relation. Even though he was not prepared to abide by the consequences, Theunissen expressed the difficulty well: "speaking to never flows into being spoken to" (*O* 339/*A*, 324). Levinas could perhaps be understood to have already pointed in the direction of this difficulty when in his first objection to Buber in "Martin Buber and the Theory of Knowledge" he wrote, "If the I becomes an I in saying Thou, I hold the place from my correlate and the I-Thou relation resembles all other relations: as if an outside observer was speaking of the I and of the Thou in the third person" (*PMB*, 147/*NP*, 47).

Throughout his reading of Buber, Levinas was clear that Buber's fundamental notion was that of the *between* and that his fundamental thesis was that "In the beginning is the relation." It was this that kept the I-Thou from being conceived as an alliance (*BMP*, 308/*BP*, 496) and secured the primacy of the relation over the relata. Levinas also understood this insistence on the originality of the relation as an indication that the I-Thou relation was conceived as the condition for the I-It.[24] So, for example, Levinas quoted the fourth paragraph of *I and Thou* where Buber used the classic formula for the explication of Husserlian intentionality: "I perceive something. I feel something. I imagine something. I want something. I sense something. I think something. . . . . All this and its like is the basis of the realm of the It." Levinas then commented, "Thus in the measure that the I-Thou relation is distinguished from the I-It relation, the former designates what is not intentional but what for Buber is rather the condition of all intentional relations" (*PMB*, 137/*NP*, 34). The same interpretation was repeated in other essays so that in "A propos de Buber," for example, he wrote that "The basic word I-Thou is in the final analysis the condition of the openness of all language, even of that which announces the relation of pure knowledge expressed by the basic word I-It" (*APB*, 127).

However, in the essay "Dialogue" Levinas addressed this interpretation rather differently. He objected that Buber's descriptions of the dialogue proceed negatively in relation to intentionality and the transcendental structures of consciousness, so putting in question their "philosophical autonomy" (*OGM*, 149/*DVI*, 228). The objection had been presented by Theunissen, who characterized Buber's work as "a purely negative ontology" on the grounds that the "sphere of the between" is presented only in abstraction from the "sphere of subjectivity." Because Buber pursued "his quest for a positive categorial elucidation of the I-Thou relationship in a piecemeal fashion," he was unable to think of the I-It and the I-Thou relationships except in a similar manner — that is to say, "after a model whose ontological basis can only be sustained by the I-It and not only by the I-Thou relationship" (*O* 290/*A*, 276–77). In presenting this objection, Levinas almost certainly had Theunissen in mind, for the phrases he used echoed those to be found in *The Other*. But it is also worth noting that Derrida in "Violence and Metaphysics" had brought a similar objection against Levinas (*WD*, 113/*ED*, 167). Whether directed against Buber or Levinas himself, the point is that a thought that proceeds only negatively is without the philosophical autonomy that both Levinas and the so-called "new thought" of dialogical thinking claimed for themselves. It was in this context that Levinas introduced the idea of the double meaning of relation as both the immediacy of the I-Thou across language and as absolute distance. Furthermore, it is in the concealed — and sometimes unacknowledged — ethical dimension of dialogue that the break with the transcendental model of consciousness is to be found. "Does it not harbor an ethical dimension where the rupture of dialogue with the transcendental models of consciousness appears most radically" (*OGM*, 149/*DVI*, 228)?

It is not that Levinas replaced the objection that Buber speaks of the I-Thou relation from the outside with an acknowledgment of the ethical affirmation made by Buber. It is not a question of whether Buber's is an ethical discourse or an ontological discourse, but of whether Buber's text *harbors* (*recéler*) such a dimension. Levinas is not working with a pair of alternatives in opposition to each other, as Buber is when it is always a case of *either* I-Thou *or* I-It — if it is not undifferentiated as in the beginning.[25] The saying and the said are such that each accompanies, supports and yet subverts the other. It is this that enabled Levinas to say that Buber's account was ontological and yet not ontological but ethical. The parallel with "double reading" as Derrida presents it is clear. Levinas acknowledged what draws Buber's text back into the ontological tradition, and yet at the same time he marked what indicates — to recall the phrases of Derrida's essay "The Ends of Man" — a change of terrain made in a discontinuous and irruptive fashion. But the terms the *saying* and the *said* are not merely ways of designating the two limbs of a double reading. Levinas in reading Buber is, in the first instance, concerned (this is particularly clear in his contribution to *Philosophical Interrogations*) with recalling certain necessities which govern thinking, his own thinking as much as that of Buber. But he also encountered Buber in an ethical relation. His readings of Buber exhibited the asymmetry and separation of such a relation.

But if there is any sense in which I have succeeded in showing that, how could I have done so? Is not this essay a series of observations from the outside that, as such, must be blind to the absolute distance so that it disappears into a synthesis of agreement or opposition? And if saying is the openness of a transcendence that can never be reduced to a said and never made a content, how could it be repeated? Could there ever be a saying of saying?[26] I have tried to resolve these dilemmas in what is perhaps the only way open to me: through the intricate complexity of the *said*. It is when there is a break in the dialogue or when Levinas is forced into the apparent contradiction of a yes-and-no saying that a trace of the saying is perhaps to be found in the said, just as the descriptions in *Totality and Infinity* serve to discover a trace of the infinite in the finite. These characteristics of Levinas's dialogue with Buber are not grounds for dismissing it as unclear, confused or inconsistent, but rather evidence that the encounter was genuine. Levinas can be understood as having offered an exemplary reading, one that, instead of seeking to attain self-definition by means of contrast and criticism, sought to reach out to the other without thought of return. And if Buber and Levinas fell prey to misunderstandings in their communications with each other, we should not be disappointed that they did not exhibit some ideal form of unity achieved through philosophical discourse. For our model of dialogue should also recognize the alterity of the other which shows itself in "the restlessness of the same disturbed by the other" (*OB*, 25/*AQE*, 32) and in the failure to communicate.

SIX

Ethics and the Place of the Other

Neve Gordon

"Nothing could limit the homage due him" — such was Emmanuel Levinas's estimation of Martin Buber (*OS*, 41). The numerous essays Levinas dedicated to the examination of Buber's thought reveal the high esteem in which he held Buber.[1] Yet these essays also demonstrate the profound disagreement between the two thinkers on a number of fundamental issues — a disagreement that has not been sufficiently explored.[2] In the following pages, I shall focus on Levinas's critique of Buber's notion of reciprocity, contrasting it with the prominent place of the "other" in Levinas's thought. Levinas's emphasis on the other contributes notably to contemporary ethical discourse, particularly in a time characterized by increasing intolerance towards the other and the violence that accompanies this intolerance. However, Buber's thought does not lend itself to an ethical relation that commences with the other, or to an ethical relation founded upon the other. Unlike Levinas, Buber believed that "if all were clothed and well nourished, then the real ethical problem would become wholly visible for the first time" (*PMB*, 723).

THE PLACE OF THE OTHER IN LEVINAS'S THOUGHT

In his five essays dealing specifically with Buber, Levinas raises several objections, ranging from Buber's understanding of God and his translation of the Bible, through Buber's notion of reciprocity, to a general claim against an "epistemology which bases truth on a nontheoretical activity or on existence" (*PMB*, 149).[3] As mentioned, I will limit my discussion to the objection regarding reciprocity.

Towards the end of his essay "Martin Buber and the Theory of Knowledge" (See *PMB*, 133–50), Levinas formulates this objection in the following manner: "How are we to preserve the specificity of the intersubjective I-Thou relation without ascribing a strictly ethical import to responsibility, and conversely, how ascribe an ethical meaning to the relation and still maintain the reciprocity on which Buber insists?" (*PMB*, 147).

To better understand Levinas's objection, we must consider his notion that an ethical relation commences from the asymmetry of the interpersonal relationship. The presence of the other's face, Levinas contends, comes from a height that is transcendent to me; it dominates me, yet it does not overwhelm me. Rather, it is precisely the infinity of the other that "summons me to my obligations and judges me" (*TI*, 215). The face posits me as responsible for the image that it presents (e.g., the person who attends to his/her hunger posits me as responsible to feed him/her). The difference between the other and myself is not a difference of properties (tall, strong, and so forth), nor a difference of psychological dispositions (the other's despair does not dominate me). The difference arises from my orientation as a being that is separate from the other. My ego, from which my identity emerges, is founded through my encounter with the infinitude of a separate being, i.e., the other.[4] Human beings are "situated in a 'space' essentially asymmetrical," while the ethical relation between them is based on a heteronomous encounter (*TI*, 216).

It is clear that Levinas rejects the attempt to construct a world from the ego, a tendency that in the past informed the oppression of the colonies by the West, and today is reflected in the economic subjugation of the Third World. Levinas's assertion that the other should not be appropriated by the ego points to the integrity of the other. The emphasis on the other and the prominent place it receives in Levinas's writings reveal the origin of Levinas's assertion that there is an inherent discrepancy between Buber's notion of reciprocity and an ethical relation. In order to judge the accuracy of Levinas's claim, we must examine the place and meaning of reciprocity in Buber's thought. More precisely, how does Levinas describe the I-Thou relation?

"The I-Thou relation," Levinas says, "consists in confronting a being external to oneself, i.e., one which is radically different" (*PMB*, 138). The relation is not informed by an idea of the other, since ideas are appropriated by consciousness, nor is it *about* the other. "The being who is invoked in this relation is ineffable because the I speaks *to* him rather than *of* him and because in the latter case all contact is broken off with the Thou. To speak *to* him is to let him realize his own otherness. The I-Thou relation, therefore, escapes the gravitational field of the I-It in which the externalized object remains imprisoned" (*PMB*, 138). Levinas con-tinues: "Relation is the very essence of the I: whenever the I affirms itself, its affirmation is inconceivable without the presence of the Thou" (*PMB*, 139).

This latter claim requires clarification. If Levinas means that the I of the I-Thou relationship owes its I to *saying* Thou, and not to the person to whom Thou is said, then it seems to me that he is interpreting Buber correctly. If, on the other hand, Levinas understands Buber to be saying that the I is founded by the other, then from Buber's perspective he is mistaken.

BUBER'S NOTION OF PRIMAL DISTANCE

Levinas proceeds to explain that the "meeting" in which this relation occurs creates a *between*, which is not to be considered as a space that exists independent of the I-Thou, but as an opening that is unique to the I and the Thou who enter into the "meeting." The between is reconstituted with each new "meeting." This is not to be understood as if humans constitute reality, but rather that they are the articulation of the "meeting." "Man does not meet, he is the meeting. He is something that *distances* itself and in this distancing the anonymous existence of the world of things affirms itself by various uses we make of it" (*PMB*, 140). Levinas continues, claiming that the "act whereby the I withdraws and thus distances itself from the Thou or 'lets it be,' in Heidegger's terms, is the act which renders a union with it possible" (*PMB*, 141). Levinas's use of "distancing" in this context is foreign to Buber's description, and as such is problematic.

In *Philosophical Interrogations*, Levinas makes a similar claim. He asserts that the Thou reveals itself as an absolute other, "but it does so in a relation which does not imply reciprocity" (*PI*, 24). This claim is later formulated somewhat differently: "Is it not the case that the reciprocity of the I-Thou relation compromises rather than promotes the originality of the I for whom *separation* is essential? Is not the absolute *distance* of the Thou or Other thereby compromised?" (*PI*, 26; italics added). Levinas misreads Buber's philosophy here in two ways. First, and as Buber points out in his answer,[5] Levinas "mistakenly identifies the concept of the between, which belongs to the sphere of the I-Thou relation, with the essentially different concept of *Urdistanz* (primal distance), which provides the anthropological presupposition of the origination of the duality of the 'primary words,' of which the I-Thou relation is one: I-It signifies the lived persistence in the primal distance, I-Thou the movement from it to the relation, which at times, to be sure, establishes itself only as overcoming the given distance between the two beings" (*PI*, 27). In other words, Buber criticizes Levinas for ascribing the notion of primal distance to the I-Thou relation, while in his writings (*KM*) it is attributed to the primordial human relation with the world. Second, Levinas mistakenly conflates reciprocity with symmetry.

Concerning the first mistake, note that Levinas's attempt to introduce distance into the I-Thou relation creates an inconsistency in his own criticism of Buber. On the one hand, he mistakenly reads Buber as if the latter claims that by distancing itself, the I enters into an I-Thou relation because it affirms itself as different from the Thou. Such a reading is firmly connected with Levinas's own idea that an ethical relation is founded upon some kind of distance, or more precisely, asymmetry, that is manifested in the self's orientation as different — as separate from the other. On the other hand, and in conflict with his attempt to introduce the concept of primal distance as the foundation of the I-Thou relation, Levinas also mistakenly criticizes the I-Thou relation for being formal, that is, an essentially symmetrical relation that may be "read indifferently from either side" (*PMB*, 147). Put differently, this relation is one in which difference does not manifest itself.

Buber pointed out that Levinas misunderstood him regarding the idea of primal distance. In his short essay "Distance and Relation,"[6] Buber distinguishes between two movements of which one is the presupposition (*not* the source or the foundation) of the other. The first movement is defined as the "primal setting at a distance," and the second is defined as "entering into relation." Humans, Buber claims, are differentiated from animals through their ability to set the other at a distance. "Only man, as man, gives distance to things which he comes upon in his realm; *he sets them in their independence* as things which from now on continue to exist ready for a function and which he can make wait for him so that on each occasion he may master them again, and bring them into action" (*KM*, 55; italics added). By setting the other at a distance the first movement is satisfied, but that is not to say that a person has entered into an I-Thou relation. Rather, the I-Thou relation has been presupposed, and one can fulfill it only when the other is no longer conceived as a component of one's life — only when one relates to the other as an autonomous self (this will be discussed below). The I-It, as Buber explained in his answer, is the lived persistence in the primal distance, indicating that Levinas's association between the Thou and primal distance was mistaken.[7]

As to Levinas's criticism that the I-Thou relation is formal, Buber replies:

> Levinas cites my statement that through Thou I become I and infers: hence I owe my place to my partner. No; rather the relation to him. Only in the relation is my Thou; outside of the relation between us this Thou does not exist. It is consequently false to say that the meeting is reversible. Neither is my Thou identical with the I of the other, nor his Thou with my I. To the person of the other I owe the fact that I have this Thou; but my I — by which here the I of the I-Thou relationship is to be understood — I owe to saying Thou, not to the person to whom I say Thou. (*PMB*, 697)

As Derrida (*WD*, 314) and Bernasconi[8] have pointed out, following Buber himself (*PI*, 27), Levinas neglected to read the 1957 "Postscript" to *I and Thou* before making his criticism. Buber's response not only defends against Levinas's criticism of formalism (the reversibility of the I and the Thou), but challenges Levinas's notion that Buber's I-Thou relation is always symmetrical.

RECIPROCITY AND FORMALISM

In the "Postscript" Buber tells his readers:

> Everything, from your own experience of looking day after day into the eyes of your "neighbor" who needs you after all but responds with the cold surprise of a stranger, to the melancholy of the holy men who repeatedly offered the great gift in vain — everything tells you that complete mutuality does not inhere in men's life with one another. . . . Yet there are also many I-Thou relationships that by their very nature may never unfold into complete mutuality if they are to remain faithful to their nature. (*IT*, 177–78)[9]

Buber gives three examples of such relationships: the genuine educator and his or her pupil, the psychotherapist and his or her patient, and the spiritual leader and his or her congregation. Thus, Levinas is not only mistaken in his reading of Buber regarding the reversibility of the I and the Thou, but his identification of reciprocity and symmetry is problematic. On this point, Buber answers Levinas, stating that it is "not true that I 'unceasingly affirm' the reciprocity of the relation. On the contrary, I have always had to talk about it with great reservations and qualifications" (*PI*, 27). Buber indeed talks about reciprocity with reservations, but not in the sense that the I-Thou relation is not reciprocal — rather that the mutuality, the giving and receiving, is not symmetrical.[10]

An asymmetrical relation that is essentially reciprocal is perhaps most evident once one considers Buber's discussion of the eternal Thou. Buber describes the relation with the eternal Thou as a relation that can simultaneously be both inclusive and exclusive. One can speak of God's relationship to humans only in a paradox, he asserts, formulating the paradox thus: "How is it possible for man's Thou-relationship to God, which requires our unconditional turning toward God, without any distraction, nevertheless to embrace all the other Thou-relationships of this man and to bring them, as it were, to

God?" (*IT*, 180). God as the "ground and meaning of human existence establishes each time a mutuality of the kind that can obtain only between persons. The concept of personhood is, of course, utterly incapable of describing the nature of God; but it is permitted and necessary to say that God is *also* a person" (*IT*, 181). This is evidently a contradiction, Buber explains, since a person "is by definition an independent individual and yet also relativized by the plurality of other independent individuals; and this, of course, could not be said of God. The contradiction is met by the paradoxical designation of God as the absolute person, that is one that cannot be relativized" (*IT*, 181). Accordingly, the contradiction gives way to a higher insight, namely, that "God carries his absoluteness into his relationship with man. Hence the man who turns toward him need not turn his back on any other I-Thou relationship: quite legitimately he brings them all to God and allows them to become transfigured 'in the countenance of God'" (*IT*, 182). It is indeed mysterious that Levinas attributes symmetrical and formal characteristics to Buber's I-Thou relationship, in light of his teachings concerning God. The I and Thou are certainly not reversible, nor is God considered to be symmetrical to the I.

In "Martin Buber's Thought and Contemporary Judaism" (See *OS*, 4–19), Levinas returns to his claim of formalism, asserting "we remain, with Buber, too often on the level of the purely *formal meeting*, even though he adds the word 'responsibility.' Despite its repetitions, the word seems to lack vigor, and nothing succeeds in making it more specific" (*OS*, 17; italics added).[11] Levinas's criticism of Buber to this extent is odd, for only one paragraph earlier he claims that Buber's "meeting" is unique and that the "irreducibility of the Meeting to any relation with the determinable and the objective, remains Buber's principal contribution to Western thought" (*OS*, 17). How, one may ask, can Levinas legitimately characterize Buber's "meeting" as formal, without content, and for this reason unethical (in the sense that it does not promote responsibility) and at the same time claim that it is unique and irreducible to the objective and the determinable?

The dubious character of Levinas's criticism is accentuated once one compares his characterization of Buber's "meeting" with the manner in which he himself portrays the metaphysical Other in

Totality and Infinity. "The strangeness of the Other," Levinas says, "his irreducibility to the I, to my thoughts and my possessions, is precisely accomplished as a calling into question of my spontaneity, as ethics" (*TI*, 43). The similarity between Buber's "meeting" (both according to the original text and Levinas's first characterization of it) and the metaphysical Other is obvious.[12] Considering both the similarity between the "meeting" and the metaphysical Other, and that Buber had already answered Levinas's charge of formalism a few years earlier, Levinas's criticism of formalism is unwarranted.

From the formalism charge, Levinas moves on to challenge Buber's opposition to Heidegger's notion of solicitude (*Fürsorge*).

> *Fürsorge* as response to an essential destitution accedes to the alterity of the Other. It takes into account that dimension of height and misery through which the very epiphany of others takes place. Misery and poverty are not properties of the Other, but the modes of his or her appearing to me, way of concerning me, and mode of proximity. One may wonder whether clothing the naked and feeding the hungry do not bring us closer to the neighbor than the rarefied atmosphere in which Buber's Meeting sometimes takes place. Saying "Thou" thus passes through my body to the hands that give, beyond the speech organs — which is in a good Biranian tradition and in keeping with the biblical truths. (*OS*, 18)

Levinas is repeating here some of the same objections he made in his two earlier essays. Interestingly, in his "Replies to My Critics," published a few years before, Buber had already addressed what he believed to be the problem of emphasizing *Fürsorge*. Levinas, he says,

> in opposition to me, praises solicitude as the access to the otherness of the other. The truth of experience seems to me to be that he who has this access apart from solicitude will also find it in the solicitude practiced by him — but he who does not have it without this, he may clothe the naked and feed the hungry all day and it will remain difficult for him to say a true Thou. If all were well clothed and well nourished, then the real ethical problem would become wholly visible for the first time. (*PMB*, 723)

Levinas's objection in "Martin Buber's Thought and Contemporary Judaism" is testimony to a lack of dialogue with Buber. Instead of addressing Buber's reply, he is merely repeating what he had already claimed in his earlier essays. Furthermore, the Thou that he uses and puts in quotation marks is surely not a Buberian Thou. Let us ask, however, what Buber means when he says that one may clothe the naked and feed the hungry all day and it will remain difficult for him or her to say a true Thou. The answer to this question will reveal one of the profound differences between the two thinkers.

THE TWO MOVEMENTS

"Man sets things which he uses at a distance," Buber tells his readers, "he gives them into an independence in which function gains duration, he reduces and empowers them to be the bearers of the function. In this way, the first movement of the principle is satisfied, but the second is not" (*KM*, 56). By clothing the naked and feeding the hungry, one has not necessarily moved beyond the movement that sets the other at a distance and gives him or her independence. For Buber, acknowledging the otherness of the other is an insufficient condition for an ethical relation. He stresses that even "within the most closely bound clan there still exist free societies of fishers, free orders of barter, free associations of many kinds, which are built upon acknowledged differences in capacity and inclination. In the most rigid epochs of ancient kingdoms, the family preserved its separate structure, in which despite its authoritative quality, individuals affirmed one another in their manifold nature" (*KM*, 57). The human capacity that acknowledges the other's independence is crucial, Buber believes, for understanding how humans managed to assert lordship over the earth.[13] "Man, as man, sets man at a distance and makes him independent," yet this setting at a distance still does not necessarily disclose an ethics.

For the I-Thou relation to emerge, I need to enter into a relation with the other, where the other is not a component of the independent world situated across from me. Only when I grasp the other as a human being does the other cease "to be a component and is there in his self-being as I am; his being at a distance does not exist merely for me, but it cannot be separated from the fact of my being at a distance for him" (*KM*, 61). The difference between the two movements is that the first movement of setting the other at a distance, as independent, puts human beings into coexistence. I exist alongside the other, I perceive his or her diversity, and I perceive the multiplicity of the world — the widening gap between the rich and the poor, the oppression of the other. I acknowledge this multiplicity as part of my life in this world. I might have perceived, for example, the destitution in Rwanda, Kosovo, Afghanistan, or the Palestinian Occupied Territories and have offered a donation so that food could be sent. But even after I become aware of the oppression that surrounds me, I have not necessarily surpassed the first movement.

The second movement, that which allows me to enter into an I-Thou relation with the other, puts the I and the Thou into a mutual relation. The difference between a coexistence and a mutual relation is that a relation is "fulfilled in a full making present when I think of the other not merely as this very one, but experience, in the particular approximation of the given moment, the experience belonging to him as this very one" (*KM*, 161).

There is a similarity between Buber's view that the mutual relation emerges when I encounter, confront and participate in the experience that belongs to the other, and Levinas's conviction that the other's *attending* calls upon me. For Buber, as I have indicated, the mutual relation occurs once the other becomes a self with me, and this can happen only when I relate to the other's experience in the presence of the other — when I participate in the actuality. Once I encounter being and becoming as that which confronts me, I encounter "always only *one* being and every thing only as a being. What is there reveals itself to [me] only in occurrence, and what occurs there happens to [me] as being. Nothing else is present but this one, but this one cosmically" (*IT*, 83).

For Levinas, the primordial essence of the face's expression does not consist in passing information concerning her or his interior world, like "I am hungry because I did not eat this past week, would you please help me?" (Clearly, according to Buber, passing of information belongs to the I-It attitude). Rather, Levinas claims, "in expression being presents itself; the being that manifests itself attends its manifestation and consequently appeals to me" (*TI*, 200). The other's destitution as a person who is hungry manifests itself via the other's attendance to her or his hunger, and not through the information that she or he passes to me. By attending to the hunger, the other exposes her/himself to my response and my questioning, similar to Buber's I-Thou relation where the I participates in the actuality, in the experience of the other. In Levinas, I do not impose myself on the other, and therefore the other's expression promotes my freedom. The other's attendance to her or his hunger puts me into question: What is *my* obligation toward this person? This question, Levinas claims, demands a response — it demands that I assume responsibility. Nevertheless, it is also crucial to emphasize a difference: While for Levinas ethics begins with the other, for Buber it does not. The question that I have posed still stands. How is it that for Buber, the real ethical problem will become visible once the hungry have been nourished?

THE LACK OF DIALOGUE CONTINUES

In his discussion of Levinas's "Martin Buber, Gabriel Marcel and Philosophy" (OS, 20–39), in "'Failure of Communication' as a Surplus," Robert Bernasconi paints an overly optimistic picture. He names this part of his chapter "The Failed Dialogue Made Good," claiming that Levinas had essentially dismissed his earlier concerns regarding the questions of formalism and reciprocity.[14] On the question of the formalism of the I-Thou relation, Bernasconi asserts, "Levinas repeated that it was indeed in some sense formal, but conceded that in Buber it had at the same time an ethical concreteness." On the question of reciprocity, he claims that Levinas acknowledged Buber's notion of "between," and ultimately assented that "by virtue of the relation to the eternal Thou, elevation could be found in the midst of reciprocity."[15] Bernasconi concludes this discussion by stating that there is no doubt that Levinas's new assessment is very different from his earlier claims.

Levinas does retract some of his former arguments. Particularly worth noting is his perception of responsibility in Buber's thought.

Yet does Levinas adequately portray Buber's philosophy in his later expositions? At the outset of this same essay, Levinas concedes that the I and Thou relation is reciprocity itself. "There is, then, on this view, something resembling an initial equality of status between the addressor and the addressee" (*OS*, 22).[16] Later, he grants that Buber's "meeting" takes place in the between, and that the ultimate meaning of the relation cannot be reduced to truth or knowledge, but should be understood as sociality; thereby he retracts the major criticism that he had posed in "Martin Buber and the Theory of Knowledge."[17] Levinas also claims that Buber's fundamental thesis is that "in the beginning was the relation." Generally speaking, this is a tenable assertion. It is on the fourth and final section of this essay that I wish to focus.

In this section, following an interesting comparison between his own *said* and *saying*, and Buber's I-It and I-Thou, Levinas discusses the crucial issue — the ethical relation. He forewarns the reader that he is "taking a few steps outside Buber," yet he swiftly adds that this move is not in order to "'understand him better than he understood himself,' but to try to apprehend him and recognize him as a pioneer" (*OS*, 34).

In his discussion of the eternal Thou, Levinas asserts that "it is from the relation with the human Thou that Buber glimpses the relation with the Eternal Thou itself — the latter being, in the final analysis, the foundation of the former" (*OS*, 34). The claim that the relationship with the eternal Thou is the *foundation* of the relationship with the human Thou is foreign to Buber's thought. Rather, Buber claims that "God's address to man penetrates the events in all our lives and all the events in the world around us, everything biographical and everything historical, and turns it into instructions, into demands for you and me" (*IT*, 182). Unlike Levinas who describes the relationship with God as a foundation, Buber describes God as penetrating the world. This is not a minor distinction.

Levinas emphatically claims that Buber's entire oeuvre is a renewal of ethics, one that "begins before the exteriority of the *other*, before other people, and as I like to put it, before the face of the other, which engages my responsibility by its human expression, which cannot — without it being changed, immobilized — be held objectively at a distance. An ethics of heteronomy that is not a servitude, but the service of God through the responsibility for the neighbor, in which I am irreplaceable" (*OS*, 35). What happened here to the reciprocity and equality between the one who addresses and the one who is addressed? Both were mentioned at the beginning of Levinas's essay. Bernasconi describes these differing descriptions as dialogue. Yet, where does Levinas find the notion of heteronomy in Buber's thought? Where does Buber intimate that in the face of the exteriority of the other ethics begins? Clearly, one can find these ideas in *Totality and Infinity* and in *Otherwise than Being*, but not in Buber's philosophy. Levinas's attempt to attribute his description of ethics to Buber is even more dubious when one considers Buber's reply offered over 15 years earlier:

> The "asymmetry" is only one of the possibilities of the I-Thou relation, not its rule, just as mutuality in all its gradations cannot be regarded as the rule. Understood in utter seriousness, the asymmetry that wishes to limit the relation to the relationship to a higher would make it completely one sided: love would either be unreciprocated by its nature, or each of the two lovers must miss the reality of the other.
>
> Even as the foundation of an ethic, I cannot acknowledge "asymmetry." I live ethically when I confirm and further my Thou in the right of his existence and the goal of his becoming, in all his otherness. I am not ethically bidden to regard him as superior to me through his otherness. I find, by the way, that our relationship to the domestic animals with whom we live, and even that to the plants in our gardens, is properly included in the lowest ethical building. The Hasidim even see it as beginning with the implements of work. And shall there not perhaps be an ethic for the relationship to oneself? (*PI*, 28)

Buber's answer speaks for itself.

The I-Thou Relation

Examining Levinas's last essay on Buber, *Apropos Martin Buber: Some Notes*, I agree with Bernasconi that in this essay Levinas essentially presents a series of notes that attempt to clarify some of the differences between Buber and himself. I find this short piece refreshing, since in it Levinas no longer attempts to appropriate Buber's ideas to his own philosophy. Here we can probably answer the question I posed earlier in this paper: what does Buber mean when he says that the real ethical problem would be visible only once the other is well clothed and nourished? Although I cannot deal with this issue here, I find Levinas's examples of the hungry, naked, widow and orphan problematic mainly because his philosophy has phenomenological pretensions that cannot hold with such limited type of examples. What happens when I encounter a young man who is well dressed, well fed, and a son of two very fine parents? Can an ethical relation emerge from his face, and in what sense? Let me offer a direction that I believe will underscore one of the fundamental differences between the two thinkers.

In section five of *Apropos Martin Buber*, Levinas contrasts his ethical approach with Buber's. In Buber, he concisely claims, "justice begins within the I-Thou." He distinguishes this notion from his own view in which "the passage from ethical inequality . . . to 'equality between persons' comes from the political order of citizens in a state," and explains that it is "the responsibility for the other that determines the legitimacy for the state, that is, its justice" (*OS*, 45). According to Levinas, the epiphany of the face that appears before me, the manifestation of its infinity, defies my intention to possess it, and invites me to an ethical relation. The depth of infinity that is perceived through the sensible appearance of the face undermines imperialist inclinations that desire to appropriate the other to the same. From this experience, Levinas explains, I realize that I cannot dominate the other in its totality, because its totality is infinite and as such exceeds me and my power (*TI*, 198). Reason, Levinas continues, also emerges from the encounter with the face of the other. The encounter produces the first signification and as such establishes language from which intelligibility emanates. Reason is something we share with the other, while will is considered by Levinas as fundamentally different from the intelligible because it maintains a radical separateness from the other and is irreducible to it (*TI*, 217). Responsibility, which also emerges from the encounter of the other, is perceived by Levinas as a corollary of the intelligible, of reason. Yet, it is responsibility that invites the will into the encounter. Thus, through the encounter with the face both reason and responsibility arise, responsibility invites the will, and in this manner the will opens to reason. Language, which also arises in this moment of encounter with the first signification, allows us to respond to the other, to make the ethical act.

For Buber, as Levinas points out, things are quite different from a phenomenological point of view and from an ethical perspective. Levinas says that for Buber justice begins within the I-Thou. This claim is basically accurate. In *I and Thou*, Buber tells his readers that "whether the institutions of the state become freer and those of the economy more just, that is important, but not for the question concerning actual life . . . for they cannot become free and just on their own." "What is decisive," he continues, "is whether the spirit — the Thou-saying, responding spirit — remains alive and actual" (*IT*, 99). For Buber a just and free society is dependent on the ability to say Thou. Where Thou is said, just institutions will exist. For Levinas justice means feeding the hungry and clothing the naked, whereas for Buber such actions are not necessarily indicative of the ability to say Thou. So, what, according to Buber, is needed in order to say Thou?

There is no prescription of how one could venture into the supreme encounter, Buber says. "Going forth is unteachable in the sense of prescriptions. It can only be indicated — by drawing a circle that excludes everything else. Then the one thing needful becomes visible: the total acceptance of the presence" (*IT*, 126). What, one might ask, does Buber mean, when he says that one must accept presence in order to venture into the encounter? Buber answers: "When we walk our way and encounter a man who comes towards us, walking his way, we know our way only and not his; for his comes to life for us only in the encounter" (*IT*, 124). On one level, this passage can be understood to be saying that if we do not accept the other in his or her presence, and if we project on the other our own preconceptions of what we believe this person *is* before the encounter even occurs, then we have predefined the person as an essence. In this manner, we have related to the other as lacking freedom, thus transforming the person into an object. We have encountered the person as an It.

This account cannot fully answer the query posed — why the ethical question becomes visible once the hungry are well nourished — since, according to Levinas, we encounter the hungry when the other is attending to her or his hunger, i.e., in the presence of the other. The difference begins to be disclosed when Buber says:

> Our concern, our care must be not for the other side but for our own, not for grace but for will. Grace concerns us insofar as we proceed toward it and await its presence; it is not our object. The Thou confronts me. But I enter into a direct relationship to it. Thus the relationship is at once being chosen and choosing, passive and active. For an action of the whole being does away with all partial actions and thus also with all sensations of action . . . and hence it comes to resemble passivity. (*IT*, 124–25)

This passage is telling in many respects, yet at this point I wish to focus on Buber's assertion that in order to enter into an I-Thou relation we must concentrate on ourselves. Buber's suggestion that one begin with oneself does not indicate, that the I in the I-Thou relation is not concerned for the other. On the contrary, one must begin with oneself, but not end with oneself; "to start from oneself, but not to aim at oneself; to comprehend oneself, but not to be preoccupied with oneself" (*WM*, 35). Buber suggests that in dialogue one must be concerned for one's own side; one must focus on the will with which one enters into the relation. He also thinks, as the passage attests, that in the dialogue one cannot handle, needless to say, take over, the other side. Buber considers the other in the I-Thou to be grace, and it is hardly conceivable that one can relate to grace by striving to possess, dominate or appropriate it. The other, as grace, is not an object at our disposal that can be managed or controlled.

We read that in order to relate to the other as grace the I of the I-Thou must *actively* "proceed towards it" and *passively* "await its presence." Thus, the presence of the other arises only if I go forth to meet the other, the grace, the mystery, but this activity is supplemented by my passive anticipation of the other that allows the other to appear in its presence. In this manner, the I does not dominate the other, disempower him or her. Nor is the I disempowered, regulated to the position of merely waiting-for, of totally depending on the other.

The I, Buber assures us, chooses the other, but in order to enter the relation, the I must also be chosen.[18] The relation is reciprocal.

At the end of the passage Buber informs us that an action of one's whole soul does away with all partial actions and in this manner resembles passivity. We understand that the I-Thou relation, from which the ethical arises, can occur only when the partners of the relation relate to each other and themselves as a whole. In the "Postscript" Buber explains what he means by relating with one's whole soul through his description of a relationship between a genuine educator and his or her pupil. We are told that the teacher must know the pupil "not as a mere sum of qualities, aspirations, and inhibitions; he must apprehend him, and affirm him, as a whole. But this he can only do if he encounters him as a partner in a bipolar situation. And to give his influence unity and meaning, he must live through this situation in all its aspects not only from his point of view but also that of his partner. He must practice the kind of realization that I call embracing [*Umfassung*]" (*IT*, 178).

The relationship in which one feeds the hungry and clothes the naked does not require that one relate to the other with one's whole soul. Often I have given money to a beggar on the street without relating to him or her with my whole soul, nor did I relate to the beggar as a partner, nor did I live through the situation from the point of view of the beggar I was encountering. The relationship Levinas describes begins with the other, who calls upon us to care for his or her needs, to assume responsibility for his or her existential condition. But caring for the other's needs does not, according to Buber, necessarily lead to the I-Thou relation, and therefore is an insufficient condition for an ethics. The I-Thou *relation*, and not merely care or even the other as such, can lead us to be ethical, to practice inclusion.

Unlike Buber, Levinas suggests that the other precedes the I, and is the basis of ethics. It remains an enigma who is the other that produces responsibility in the I, and enables the I to become an active human being. As he or she is portrayed in Levinas's writings, the other, on the one hand, is too vague; on the other hand, the widow and

the orphan, the naked and the hungry, are a group that is too confined. Do I have responsibility to any other? Or perhaps, only to the
oppressed? Buber does not have such a problem, since for Buber
ethics does not begin from the other, but from the reciprocal relation
between I and Thou. One begins with oneself, but does not aim at
oneself or is preoccupied with oneself; rather one proceeds towards
the other, awaiting the mystery of the other, awaiting grace.

It is appropriate, I believe, to end with a story. Rabbi Mendel of
Kotzk, Buber tells us, once said to his congregation:

> "What, after all, do I demand of you? Only three things: not to look
> furtively outside yourselves, not to look furtively into others, and not
> to aim at yourselves." That is to say: firstly, everyone should preserve
> and hallow his own soul in its own particularity and in its own place,
> and not envy the particularity and place of others; secondly, everyone
> should respect the secret in the soul of his fellow-man, and not, with
> brazen curiosity, intrude upon it and take advantage of it; and thirdly,
> everyone in his relationship to the world, should be careful not to set
> himself as his aim (*WM*, 39).

SEVEN

Martin Buber and Emmanuel Levinas

An Ethical Query

Maurice Friedman

Juxtaposing Martin Buber and Emmanuel Levinas is irresistible. Both are solidly rooted in Judaism. Both are philosophers who have broken with the central thrust of philosophy from Plato to Heidegger in favor of a radical relation to otherness, alterity. Both are centrally concerned with ethics. Both link the relationship with God with the relationship with our fellow human beings. Both are thinkers who lived, wrote and acted in the present century.

Beyond that, important differences begin to emerge. Although Buber is as much of a *Maskil* (a person concerned with enlightenment) as he is a Hasid, he was open to mysticism and myth in their many forms, and espoused a teaching of Hasidism and Judaism that might be called a concrete mysticism of hallowing the everyday. Levinas, in contrast, is a *mitnagid*, the traditional opponent of the Hasidim. He rejected both mysticism and myth as pagan and polytheistic. Levinas was rooted in the Bible, as he saw it, with the emphasis on its moral injunctions and its laws, and in the Talmud. Buber was rooted in the Hebrew Bible as a covenant between a people and God to make real the kingship of God in history by establishing communities and societies of righteousness, justice and loving-kindness.

From this we turn to the differences in their philosophies. Levinas was a philosopher's philosopher. He constructed a fullscale philosophy and, despite his turning away from both Husserl and Heidegger, many aspects of a phenomenology. At the core of Buber's thought, in contrast, were philosophical insights that he elaborated and illustrated with philosophical consistency. Yet Buber did not construct a systematic philosophy, much less a phenomenology. As Andrew Tallon has put it, Buber initiated a revolution in philosophy in the twentieth century but he did not carry through. In his last commentary on Buber, Levinas wrote:

> That valuation of the dia-logical relation and its phenomenological irreducibility, its fitness to constitute a meaningful order that is auto–nomous and as legitimate as the traditional and privileged *subject-object* correlation in the operation of knowledge — that will remain the unforgettable contribution of Martin Buber's philosophical labors. . . . Nothing could limit the homage due him. Any reflection on the alterity of the other in his or her irreducibility to the objectivity of objects and the being of beings must recognize the new perspective Buber opened — and find encouragement in it (*OS*, 41–42).

Once after I gave a paper on Franz Rosenzweig's critique of Buber's *Ich und Du* at the annual conference of the American Academy of Religion, a distinguished scholar of the history of religion asked me why it was that people now seemed to have turned from Buber to Rosenzweig. My own response to this question is that Rosenzweig offers us a systematic philosophy, whereas Buber does not. The same, I believe, explains in part the recent popularity of Levinas in comparison to Buber, especially among philosophers. If I am right, then it is worth our while to look at what Buber himself said about this in the "Philosophical Accounting" section of his "Replies to My Critics."

> Since I matured to a life from my own experience . . . I have stood under the duty to insert the framework of the decisive experiences that I had . . . into the human inheritance of thought, but not as "my" experiences, rather as an insight valid and important for others and even for other kinds of men. Since, however, I have received no message which might be passed on in such a manner, but have only had the experiences and attained the insights, my communication had to be a philosophical one. It had to relate the unique and particular to the "general," to what is discoverable by every man in his own existence. It had to express what is by its nature incomprehensible in concepts that could be used and communicated (even if at times with difficulties).

More precisely, I had to make an It out of that which was experienced in I-Thou and as I-Thou.

I am convinced that it happened not otherwise with all the philosophers loved and honored by me. Only that after they had completed the transformation, they devoted themselves to the philosophy more deeply and fully than I was able or it was granted to me to do. . . . *Reason . . . may not sacrifice to consistency anything of that reality itself which the experience that has happened commands it to point to.* If the thought remains true to its task, a system will not come out of it, but certainly a connected body of thought more resolved in itself, more transmittable. (*PMB*, 689–90; italics added)

I am convinced that Buber has done just that in his writings on the philosophy of dialogue and on the philosophical anthropology that underlies it.

Buber never commented directly on Levinas's philosophy, although he did respond to Levinas's critique of his own thought. Levinas, in contrast, wrote many commentaries on Buber's thought, not all of them consistent. Even so, Levinas's critiques of Buber might have helped us in comparing their two moral philosophies *if he had understood Buber from within, which he did not.* Instead he either criticized Buber by making him the opposite of his own thought, even when he was not, or he assimilated Buber to his thought even when that meant ignoring the real differences between them.

Quite a number of philosophers have written on Buber and Levinas together. Some have tried to reconcile the two. Others have criticized Buber from the standpoint of Levinas (the worst of which was the author of a book on Ivan Boszormenyi-Nagy and Levinas who, after I had given a lecture on Buber and Levinas, suddenly exclaimed, "Isn't Buber's 'between' empty and shallow!"). Still others have defended Buber against Levinas's critiques by showing them to be misinterpretations of Buber's thought. No one, so far as I know, has focused on the issue of the adequacy of the moral philosophies of each of the two men.

Robert Bernasconi has written an illuminating essay on Buber and Levinas that tries, I would say unsuccessfully, to reconcile the two. To follow Levinas's suggestion and go back and read Buber himself, writes Bernasconi, "would be to pose the question at a level of simplicity that remains divorced from the dialogue itself."[1] That seems to me a strange conception of dialogue. In opposition to this statement of Bernasconi's, Neve Gordon writes, "I believe that it is more becoming to begin by reading Buber without assimilating him to Levinas. Only after one wrestles with Buber's ideas, after one understands his insights, it becomes appropriate, I think, to criticize, expand on and develop his ideas."[2] I am entirely in agreement with Neve Gordon.

The weakest of Levinas's critiques of Buber, although one often repeated, is the charge of "formalism," which Levinas bases on the notion that the I-Thou relation for Buber is reversible and that it has no content. To see it as reversible is to deny the uniqueness and particularity that is at the very heart of the I-Thou relationship. In reply to this charge Buber himself writes:

> It is false . . . to say that the meeting is reversible. Neither is my Thou identical with the I of the other, nor his Thou with my I. To the person of the other I owe the fact that I have this Thou, but my I — by which here the I of the I-Thou relationship is to be understood — I owe to saying Thou, not to the person to whom I say Thou. (*PMB*, 697)

The charge that the I-Thou relationship is lacking in content Buber answered, in the same volume, replying to the Israeli philosopher Nathan Rotenstreich:

> It is for me of the highest importance that the dialogue have a content. Only this content is so much the more important, the more concrete, the more concretizing it is, the more it does justice to the unique, the coming to be, the formed, and is also able to incorporate in it the most spiritual, not metaphorically but in reality, because the spirit seeks the body and lets speech help find it. (*PMB*, 696 ff.)

Levinas's stronger and most insistent critiques of Buber's philosophy are tied up with his own assertion that the relation to the Other must be asymmetrical and that, correspondingly, I must place the Other at a height above me even while, at the same time, I must relate to the other as an orphan, a poor person, someone who hungers — someone who needs something from me, the responsibility for which my very encounter with his or her otherness awakens in me. Here there is, indeed, a real issue between Buber's ethics and that of Levinas. As a corollary of this, Levinas misconceives Buber as calling for an I-Thou relationship that is a sort of elitism of two persons who exclude from their relationship any concern with the plights of other people. Buber's reply to this charge speaks for itself:

> Levinas errs in a strange way when he supposes that I see in the *amitié toute spirituelle* the peak of the I-Thou relation. On the contrary, this relationship seems to me to win its true greatness and powerfulness precisely there where two men without a strong spiritual ground in common, even of very different kinds of spirit, yes of opposite dispositions, still stand over against each other so that each of the two knows and means, recognizes and acknowledges, accepts and confirms the other, even in the severest conflict, as this particular person. In the common situation, even in the common situation of fighting with each other, he holds present to himself the experience side of the other, his living through this situation. This is no friendship, this is only the comradeship of the human creature, a comradeship that has reached fulfillment. No "ether," as Levinas thinks, but the hard human earth, the common in the uncommon. . . . [One who does not have access to the other] may clothe and feed the hungry all day and it will remain difficult for him to say a true Thou.
>
> If all were well clothed and well nourished, then the real ethical problem would become wholly visible for the first time. (*PMB*, 723)

Although Levinas grounds the ethical in externally defined acts, such as feeding the hungry and clothing the naked, he does not adequately articulate the call of the ethical aside from these obvious examples. What is more, Levinas seems afraid that the I-Thou relationship will remain on a purely spiritual plane if it does not explicitly begin with and include these sorts of ethical actions that the Hebrew Bible and the Talmud enjoin.

Levinas has the, for me, curious notion that only if I feel the other as superior to myself — at an infinite height — will I be impelled to act ethically toward the other. He also sees the same person as poor, hungry, widowed or orphaned, and in that sense below. Buber's view is quite different:

> It is not true that I "unceasingly affirm" the reciprocity of the relation. On the contrary, I have always had to talk about it with great reservations and qualifications, which I recently summarized in my Postscript to the

second edition of *I and Thou*. . . .[3] The "asymmetry" is only one of the possibilities of the I-Thou relation, not its rule, just as mutuality in all its gradations cannot be regarded as the rule. Understood in utter seriousness, the asymmetry that wishes to limit the relation to the relationship to a higher would make it completely one-sided: love would either be unreciprocated by its nature or each of the two lovers must miss the reality of the other.

Even as the foundation of an ethic, I cannot acknowledge "asymmetry." I live "ethically" when I confirm and further my Thou in the right of his existence and the goal of his becoming, in all his otherness. I am not ethically bidden to regard and treat him as superior to me through his otherness. I find, by the way [as Levinas, who restricts ethics to the interhuman, emphatically did not], that our relationship to the domestic animals with whom we live and even to the plants in our gardens is properly included as the lowest floor of the ethical building. The Hasidim even sees it as beginning with the implements of work. And shall there not perhaps be an ethic for the relationship to oneself? (*PI*, 27 ff.)

These contrasts between Levinas's "vertical" ethics and Buber's "horizontal" ethics, to coin phrases that neither of these thinkers used, will become still clearer if we look at Buber's autobiographical fragment that tells of his experience with two of his fellow pupils in the Polish gymnasium where he went to school from ages 10 to 18. When Buber was 12 years old, he and his classmates experienced an autumn utterly spoiled by rain. Instead of rushing out to play during the recesses, they had to sit at their benches. At this time, two of the boys undertook to entertain the other boys as mimics, with clown-like agility, trying their best to remain straightfaced to avoid being seen by the master. After a while, however, the game took on a unmistakably sexual character, and now the faces of the two boys looked to Martin like the damned souls being tormented in hell, which his Catholic schoolmates had described to him in the tone of experts. The other boys looked on but said nothing to one another about these occurrences. About two weeks after the game had taken on this character, the master called the young Buber to his office.

"Tell me what you know of what those boys have been doing," the master said with a gentle friendliness that the pupils knew to be an essential part of his nature.

"I know nothing!" Martin screamed.

The master spoke again, as gently as before. "We know you well," he said. "You're a good child — you will help us."

"Help, help whom?" the young Buber wanted to reply. But instead he stared silently at the director. Finally, a great weeping overcame him such as he had never experienced before, and he was led away almost unconscious. Yet a few hours later, when he recalled at home the last look of the master, it was not a gentle, but a frightened, one.

He was kept at home for a few days, and then he returned to school. When he came into the classroom, he found that the bench where the two boys sat remained empty. It remained empty for the rest of the year.

It was many years before Buber could understand the full ethical implications of this event and could formulate the lesson that it taught him: that the true norm commands not our obedience but ourselves. But even at the time that he began to realize what he himself later called the problematic relation between the maxim that addresses everyone and no one and the unique concrete situation that addresses the person in his or her uniqueness (*PMB*, 88–100).

This realization meant the shattering of the security that simple childhood norms of obedience to authority had given him until then. When he wanted to shout, "Help? Help whom?," he was aware, as the master was not, of the suffering of the two boys and of the impossibility of his accepting the bribe as "a good child" who will help in return for betraying them. Most importantly of all, instead of finding security in the "once-and-for-all" of general moral norms, Buber began living with the insecurity and responding to the unique and irreducible situation to which no general categories could do justice. He rejected the norm that came from above, and that split one into an obedient part and one into a rebellious part, in favor of "the true norm" that commands us, that is, addresses us directly in the situation and leaves us to respond with our whole being. The address of the true norm is on the level where the human being is at, where one brings oneself in response to what faces one at that moment. This command cannot demand "obedience" because it does not dictate the form and way in which one should answer. As Buber wrote in "The Question to the Single One," "God tenders me the situation to which I have to answer; but I have not to expect that he should tender me anything of my answer" (*BMM*, 69). The answer Buber sees as coming from the conscience — not the routine "play on the surface" conscience, but "the unknown conscience in the ground of being, which needs to be discovered ever anew. . . . The certainty produced by this conscience is of course only a personal certainty; it is uncertain certainty; but what is here called person is the very person who is addressed and who answers" (*BMM*, 69).

"The idea of responsibility is to be brought back from the province of specialized ethics, of an 'ought' that swings free in the air, into that of lived life. Genuine responsibility exists only where there is real responding." "Responding to what?" Buber asks and answers, "the events of everyday life." We can still avoid responding by wrapping silence around us or stepping aside into the accustomed way. Yet if we venture a stammering answer, we enter into the situation that has at this moment stepped up to us, a situation "whose appearance we did and could not know, for its like has not been" (*BMM*, 16).

Responsibility to Buber means hearing the unreduced claim of each hour in its crudeness and disharmony and answering it out of the depths of one's being. This responsibility does not exclude a person from membership in a group or community, but it means that true membership in a community includes a *boundary* to membership so that no group or person can hinder one's perception of what is spoken or one's answer from the ground of one's being.

The great character, who could awaken responsibility in others, is one who acts from the whole of his or her substance and reacts in accordance with the uniqueness of each situation. S/he responds to the new face that each situation wears despite all similarity to others. The situation "demands nothing of what is past. It demands presence, responsibility, it demands you." The traditional values are useful and suggestive, but one may not for all that move from them to the situation. Rather one must move from the concrete situation to the decision to what is the right direction in this instance.

Responsibility does not mean responding to everything and every-one[4] but to what Buber calls the "signs of address." By "signs of address," Buber does not mean fixed signs that have one universal meaning for all time. This is what characterizes all knowing by rule from the crudest superstition to the highest reaches of gnosis. Rather the true signs of address are unique. They stand in the stream of "happening but once." "Lived life is tested and fulfilled in the stream alone." The signs of address speak to me in my life, but not in such a way that they can be interpreted or translated, explained, or displayed. They are for no information or appeasement. They are inseparable, incomparable, irreducible.

> It is not a *what* at all, it is said into my life; it is no experience that can be remembered independently of the situation, it remains the address of that moment and cannot be isolated, it remains the question of a questioner and will have its answer. (*BMM*, 12)

Buber's situation ethics (*PMB*, 171–200) does not mean that life is reduced to a series of unconnected moments:

> A situation of which we have become aware is never finished with, but we subdue it in the substance of lived life. Only then, true to the moment, do we experience a life that is something other than a sum of moments. We respond to the moment, but at the same time we respond on its behalf, we answer for it. A newly created concrete reality has been laid in our arms; we answer for it, a dog has looked at you, you answer for its glance, a child has clutched your hand, you answer for its touch, a host of men moves about you, you answer for their need. (*BMM*, 17)

Levinas saw the foundation of justice in the fact that a third person exists who must see not only my other but myself as persons worthy of receiving what is due us. This has led Levinas and his followers to the strange notion that Buber founded justice entirely within the I-Thou relationship, and that for Buber there was neither a We nor a larger group or community that needed to be taken into consideration. Actually, for Buber, dialogue and love were what ought to govern the direct relations between human beings, justice the indirect. Not only did Buber explicitly posit an "essential We" alongside the "essential Thou," he also had, as Levinas did not, a fully formed social and political philosophy — a federalistic communal socialism and an important distinction between the "political principle" and the "social principle" such as could never have been envisaged in Levinas's abstract and undeveloped formulations.[5]

Having no inkling of what Buber called "the bestowing side of things" [*das Schenkende in die Dinge*] that comes to meet us when we bend over it with fervor,[6] Levinas thought that Buber's concepts of the I-Thou relation with animals and plants originated in his artistic nature. If this were so, it would weaken the seriousness of Buber's approach to ethics. Actually, no one could have been more serious about ethics than Buber was. A Hasidic tale that Buber included in his collection of *The Tales of the Hasidim* expresses exactly what Levinas teaches when he says that we can discern only the "trace of God" or infinity in the faces of our fellow human beings but that the command that comes to us from the encounter with the other is our truest access to God:

> If someone comes to you and asks your help, you shall not turn him away with pious words, saying: "Have faith and take your troubles to God!" You shall act as if there were no God, as if there were only one person in all the world who could help this man — only yourself.[7]

In a half century of concern with moral philosophy my focus has been on the source of the moral ought. "Why ought I (or We) to do or not do something?" For Levinas the source of the moral ought was clearly the human face — the face that brings with it the infinity that we cannot know directly, the face that places a demand on us prior to all moral reasonings or inculcated values. This demand is an address to which we must respond. It is an unqualified demand that rises from the radical alterity of the other and from the direct knowledge of his or her vulnerability or mortality. From it comes in unmediated form the command to us "Thou shalt not kill."

For Buber, too, the source of the moral ought is found in the unmediated response to what addresses us. Buber's "ontology of the between" is not the totality of *being* that has dominated philosophy from Plato to Sartre. It is the "really real" or what I call the "touchstone of reality." "All real living is meeting."

To that extent we can say that the source of the moral ought for both Buber and Levinas was the meeting between person and person. Yet there are important differences, as Levinas pointed out. Against Heidegger's collectivity of the side by side (*Miteinandersein*), wrote Levinas at the end of *Time and the Other*, one of his first books, "I have tried to oppose the 'I-you' collectivity." But, he immediately pointed out, not in Buber's sense of reciprocity where the ineluctable character of isolated subjectivity is underestimated. It is quite possible that Levinas did not understand the two primal movements of distancing and relating that underlie Buber's I-Thou relationship, or the emphasis on overagainstness that led Buber to define "dialogue" as opening oneself to the otherness of the other as opposed to "monologue" where one relates to the other as a content of one's experience.

Nonetheless, we can discern a real difference here that Levinas emphasized by speaking of an "I-you" relationship rather than an "I-Thou" relationship and by his repeated use of the term "illeity" to refer to transcendental infinity. Buber certainly eschews the sort of fusion of horizons that Hans-Georg Gadamer speaks of. Buber characterized even agreement as a mixing of understanding and misunderstanding, always holding the tension between the two partners in relationship. In his dialogue with Kierkegaard, "The Question to the Single One," moreover, Buber wrote of the necessity of solitude with the strictness of an inner worldly monastery if we do not want to debouch into the infinite. In *I and Thou* too he wrote of the necessity of solitude without making solitude a goal or a way of life. But he did not prescribe to the "I-Thou relationship" [*Ich-Du Beziehung*] an ineluctable character of isolated solitude as Levinas did. I stress this because in a thoroughly situational ethics like Buber's, which accepted the I-Thou relationship in whatever form it took, there are far more ethical possibilities than are envisaged in Levinas's moral philosophy. This is why Buber replied to Levinas, "when all are fed and clothed the real ethical problem will have just begun."

Responding to the accusation of the American philosopher Marvin Fox that he was a moral relativist, Buber argued that there were some ethical commands that he held to be absolute, for example, honor thy father and mother. But he added in his "Replies to My Critics," "anyone who knows in advance what that means in the current situation does not know what he is talking about."

In the first section of his essay "Religion and Ethics," he was quite explicit in his answer to the question of the source of the moral ought. I want to quote a part of this section here:

> We find the ethical in its purity only there where the human person confronts himself with his own potentiality and distinguishes and decides in this confrontation without asking anything other than what is right and what is wrong in this his own situation. The criterion by which this distinction and decision is made may be a traditional one, or it may be one perceived by or revealed to the individual himself. What is important is that the critical flame shoot up ever again out of the depths, first illuminating, then burning and purifying (*EG*, 95).

I cannot set over against this statement of Buber's any passage from the heart of Levinas's philosophy. Yet I think I can throw some, admittedly secondary, light on the approach of Buber and Levinas to the source of the moral ought by presenting Buber's autobiographical fragment "Samuel and Agag" and Levinas's response to it. In this fragment, Buber tells of a reunion on a train with a thoroughly observant religious Jew during which he discussed with him the passage from the Book of Samuel where Saul delivers Agag over to Samuel, the prince of the Amalekites — the people against whom Moses swore eternal enmity and whom Saul had just defeated in battle. Buber told his companion that it horrified him as a child to read how after Agag said to Samuel, "Surely the bitterness of death is past," Samuel "hew" him into pieces. Buber confessed that even now when they were speaking together he could not believe that this was a message of God. His partner's brow contracted angrily and he demanded of Buber, "What do you believe then?" Buber answered, "I believe that Samuel misunderstood God." The angry brow of his companion smoothed, the eyes became positively gentle and radiant, and he said, "I think so, too." God does not abandon the created man to his needs and anxieties, Buber reflected later; he gives him the comfort of his words. "But man does not listen with faithful ears to what is spoken to him." Instead he blends together command of heaven and statute of earth, revelation and orientation. We have no objective criterion to distinguish between what is received and what is manufactured. "We have only faith — when we have it."

> Nothing can make me believe in a God who punishes Saul because he has not murdered his enemy. And yet even today I still cannot read the passage that tells this otherwise than with fear and trembling. But not it alone. Always when I have to translate or to interpret a biblical text, I do so with fear and trembling, in an inescapable tension between the word of God and the words of man. (*PMB*, 33)

In a 1986 interview, Levinas commenting on Buber's "Samuel and Agag," wrote that "Without doubt, Buber thought that his conscience instructed him on the will of God better than the books!" and added: "I continue to think that without extreme attention given to the Book of books, one cannot listen to one's conscience. Buber, in this instance, did not think of Auschwitz."[8]

For Levinas to question Buber's "extreme attention to the Book of books" seems strange in light of the fact that Buber spent a large part of his lifetime, literally up till his final coma, translating the Hebrew Bible into German and revising that translation again and again. Even stranger is Levinas's statement that Buber was not thinking of Auschwitz. "There is not an hour when I do not think of it," Buber once said to me.

Samuel met Agag's face, but in this meeting he heard no command, "Thou shalt not kill" or "Thou shalt not murder," and, Levinas's own repeated statements about the immediate, originary effect on our meeting with the face to the contrary notwithstanding, nor in this particular case did Levinas. Buber was just as familiar as Levinas was with Samuel's statement, "As you have made other mothers childless, so I will make your mother childless." Levinas undoubtedly quoted these words because he wanted to move from the direct meeting between Samuel and Agag to a third personal concept of justice. I am convinced that it is on the same grounds that he reproved Buber for not thinking of the Holocaust. When Levinas asserted, "Buber thought that his conscience instructed him on the will of God better than the books," he relegated Buber's "nothing can make me believe in a God who punishes Saul because he did not murder his enemy" to a wholly inward subjectivity and ignored completely Buber's constant attitude of listening to God's word implicit in his final statement, "Always when I have to translate or interpret a biblical text, I do so with fear and trembling in an inescapable tension between the word of God and the words of man."

It would be tempting to say of Levinas the opposite of what Buber said about his orthodox traveling companion, namely that here when Levinas had to choose between God and the Bible, he chose the Bible. But we cannot do so for the simple reason that Levinas simply identifies God with the biblical text and excludes the possibility that Samuel misunderstood God. But we *can* say that *in this case* Levinas found the source of the moral ought in the tradition, as we know it from the "Book of books," without the critical flame that shoots up from the depths and *not* from the meeting with the Face that he so often proclaimed as the direct source of the moral ought and the indirect source of third personal structures of justice in society.

Levinas was fond of quoting Dostoevsky's statement, "We are all guilty of all and I more than anyone else." I prefer Dostoevsky's statement, "Each is responsible for all." I like even more Abraham Joshua Heschel's statement, "We are not all guilty, we are all responsible." I also like, again in contrast to Levinas, Buber's understanding of existential guilt as something one has taken on oneself as a person in a personal situation, something that injures the order of being that one knows, at some level, to be the foundation of one's own and of all human existence.

Part III

RELIGION

Eight

Buber's and Levinas's Attitudes Toward Judaism

Ephraim Meir

Levinas and Buber have in common a reverence for human life as well as a philosophy of human relationship. They made an enormous contribution to the ethical thought and the religious consciousness of the twentieth century. The differences as well as the common ground between the two creative thinkers are seen in their different views of Judaism. In this article, I first characterize some main differences between them in order better to understand their respective attitudes toward Judaism. Buber developed a Hebrew humanism, and considered Judaism principally as a pioneering way of life in ethical openness. Levinas went beyond humanism, and pointed to concrete elements as the condition for the "ethical life."

SIMILARITY AND DISSIMILARITY

As is well known, Buber presented his dialogical ideas in a nonsystematic way. He refused to be called a philosopher because he thought that philosophical language did not adequately render the idea of dialogical life; he wanted to conduct a conversation. Levinas, too, was aware of the inadequacy of philosophy. However, rather than abandon it, he sought to surprise philosophy by the introduction of several new categories. This and other differences between the two dialogic thinkers permit us to grasp their different approaches to Judaism.[1]

Idealism and the Rupture of Ontology:
Metaphysics of Presence and Metaphysics of Absence

Buber's religious philosophy is based on dialogue and communication. In his *I and You*, he develops the idea that the I is related. The I is more an I in-relation than a separated Cartesian thinking entity. If there is a positive, nonfragmentary attitude to what surrounds it, the I is I-You.[2] It becomes I-It when there is a dichotomy between the subject and the object and a partial approach to things when persons and ideas are situated in time and space.[3] The relating I, with its holistic view, is opposed to an isolated I, who isolates itself from the non-I through its fragmentary view. In the authentic relationship there is presence, mutuality and directness. Buber's account of the relationship is basically an idealistic one, starting from the I and its standpoint. The main time for him is the present, lived in the presence of another person.[4]

In Levinas's work, the same is challenged by the Other in order to leave the same's solipsism and become the one-for-the-other in humble service. The asymmetric relation characterizes humanity in the human being, who leaves his autism and narcissism and opens himself up in responsibility to a transcendent call. The rupture of the totality of the ego, his awakening from the autistic dream by the Other in favor of an I that is "subjected" to the Other is the result of an ana-chronic call. Levinas's metaphysics is not a metaphysics of the present, but of a past that cannot be reconstructed and of a future that cannot be foreseen. The call of the Other is before all time, from eternity, from a timeless time. It metamorphoses the I, prior to choice, projecting it into an unseen future.

The Role of Distance

Whereas in Buber's thinking, the I orients itself toward You, Levinas's Other orients the I. Fundamental in Buber is the orientation of the I with respect to a You. In Levinas's thinking, the orientation of the I is the result of the urgent call of the Other, and of the welcoming of his face. Buber writes on dialogue, unity and mutuality between the I and the You in relation (*Beziehung*) and encounter (*Begegnung*).

Levinas discusses relation in terms of separateness. The "for the Other" comes before any dialogue. I am held hostage by responsibility before freedom, asked to account for things before I am even able to choose. Of course, Buber's *Begegnung* is not a mere attitude; it is an event that happens rather than an idealistic *Beziehung*. As such, it is closer to Levinas's same-Other relationship. Proximity for Levinas is the result of distance, whereas for Buber, distance is the result of a dichotomous, inauthentic attitude. Buber develops a kind of idealist approach to reality in which the intentionality of the I is important. Levinas gives more weight to the totalizing I, which in constant identification reduces every alterity to the same.

Jerusalem and Athens

Another important difference between Buber and Levinas lies in their approaches to knowledge. Buber has the tendency to disqualify systematic thinking as belonging to the I-It domain, which, in almost Manichaean fashion, is separated from the I-You sphere. Levinas, too, regards the problem of knowledge as overly focused upon the self. Nonetheless, he uses Greek to surprise and confront it with a prophetic message that leaves its "trace" in conceptual discourse. Buber thinks knowledge does not elevate us as human beings. Rather, human dignity lies more in relation. Levinas situates knowledge in the perspective of the answering I.

Like Levinas, Buber counters Western thought with the Jewish spirit. They depart where the role of Athens is concerned. Buber did not translate the Jewish tradition into Greek terms. He was too skeptical toward philosophy, which belongs to the domain of the I-It. Hence, he separated Jewish discourse from Greek, using the Greek discourse only because he had no alternative. Levinas, far removed from Leo Strauss or Shadal's antithetical thinking, combined Jewish and Greek thinking.[5] He was convinced that Judaism was not incompatible with rational thought. Maimonides is Levinas's example: the Rambam "masterfully traced" the way "toward the synthesis of the Jewish revelation and Greek thought" (*DF*, 15). Nevertheless, man is more than the rational animal of the Greeks inasmuch as he is made "in the

image of Elohim" (Gen. 1:27). He is thus more than what humanism says about him — he is a creature, God's partner, associated with
Elohim.[6]

The Welcoming I and the Divine

Both Buber and Levinas took as their starting point the related I
who welcomes without interpreting rather than the dominating, con-
trolling and mastering I. They replaced the Cartesian dictum *"cogito
ergo sum"* with *"respondeo ergo sum."* They did not think that the Other
is to be approached first of all by knowledge, but by empathy. In
Buberian terms, it is not the spatio-temporal "orientation" that is important but "realization." Both thinkers emphasized the greatness of
a pure heart.

Their concept of God is not separated from this relating I. For
Buber, the contact with the You leads to contact with the eternal You.
For Levinas, *Illeity* is approachable in the infinity of the demand of the
other person.

Dialogue

Levinas and Buber place *teshuva*, understood as responsibility, at
the center of their thinking. Whereas Buber sees it as the return to the
real I of the I-You, to the whole and united I, Levinas conceives *teshuva*
as the answer to an always exterior Other, before any dialogue. Buber
sees the I in the I-You as constitutive for dialogic reality. Levinas,
by contrast, argues that dialogue is impossible before the preoriginal,
an-archic demand of the Other. Proximity or nonindifference as result
of "love your neighbor as yourself" comes before any dialogue.

PERSPECTIVES ON JUDAISM

Buber's and Levinas's common concerns, as well as the differences
that separate them significantly color their respective visions of Judaism. Buber's Judaism has been given much more attention than
Levinas's.[7] Despite the general supposition that one can understand
Levinas without reading his Jewish essays, his Jewish thinking have

more relevance for his philosophical thinking than one might imagine at first sight?

God and the Concept of God

Buber was convinced that one has to get rid of the concept of God in order to meet Him through the intersubjective encounter. Levinas, on the contrary, did not think one has to free oneself of the concept of God in order to be in contact with Him. He is to be approached in the infinity of the demand of the Other and "comes to mind" in the horizon of the other person's demand.

For Buber, true religiousness lies in relation.[8] God's living presence comes through the presence of a You. The essay "The Question to the Single One" (*BMM*, 40–82) attacks Kierkegaard's notion of the "single one" (*der Einzige*), who develops a relation with God at the expense of the human relation. Buber contrasted "the single one" with the "person" who is living in the presence of others, and consequently in the presence of the eternal You. There is contact with the Infinite only by means of finite beings.

God from Inside or from Outside

It is significant that Buber writes on the everlasting You, and not about "God" or "the Eternal." The human-God relationship is a relationship from below to above. Opposed to this, Levinas writes about the human-God relationship as taking place from above to below. The demand comes from on high. Buber's God is the supreme Presence vis-à-vis the presence of world, human beings, and things of the spirit. Levinas's God leaves His trace as *Illeity* and is always already gone.

Both Buber and Levinas agree that God does not help and intervene. Their God is linked to the interhuman relation. However, whereas Buber thinks that the eternal You is linked to the You of the natural world, of fellow human beings, and of the things of the spirit, Levinas links his nonnuminous *Illeity* rather exclusively to man. For Buber, by saying "You," one catches a glimpse of God. For Levinas, the signifier "God" never reaches the signified even in a remote way.

In his Jewish essays, as in his philosophy, Levinas discusses God in describing the call of the Other, coming from outside. In this way, he preserves the separation between humans and God as well as the transcendent character of God. Buber's approach is totally different. He discusses the I as I-You and through a nondualistic approach of the You, he sees the possibility of being in touch with the eternal Thou. His God comes from inside.

God's Presence and Absence

After the Shoah, Buber had to cope with the idea of God and the problem of evil. In his *Eclipse of God*, published in 1953, he maintained that God's face has been obscured by the deeds of humans. Buber's God was never a magical God. We humans are responsible for His presence.

In Levinas's post-Auschwitz thinking, theodicy is bankrupt after the Shoah (*US*, 156–67). There are no divine interventions; God is to be approached in the infinity of the Other's demand.[9] God manifests Himself in the emptiness of a childish heaven. In such an a-theistic concept, human autonomy is respected and the entire responsibility for what happens is put on the shoulders of the human being. Thus, Levinas's God is always absent, always leaving His trace in the face of the other person.

Buber's God is spoken to — not spoken about. His is a living God, to be met in dialogue, not a philosophical God. Levinas's use of the word "God" is much more demythologized and less personal. The word "God" has a strictly logical function in his philosophical discourse. And though Levinas is not estranged from theological talk about the God of Scripture and the literature of the Sages, he nevertheless translates this ancient discourse about a personal God into the no less ancient, nonmetaphorical, logos.

Creator

Rivka Horwitz[10] has described how, historically speaking, Buber's *I and You* shows the traces of the thinking of Ferdinand Ebner, who developed a Gnostic view on God and did not appreciate God as Creator.[11] As early as December 1921, Buber had read Rosenzweig's *Star of Redemption*. Even earlier, he became acquainted with the writing of Ebner, who was profoundly influenced by Kierkegaard and foremost by the Gospel of St. John. Buber was impressed by Ebner's *Das Wort und die geistigen Realitäten*, which appeared in 1921, and which clearly formulated the dialogical principle of the I in relation with the divine Thou. Ebner's divine Thou remains a-cosmic and exists only in the second person, not as "He."

It was only after *I and You* that Buber accepted the sharp criticism of Rosenzweig, who made his friend aware of the existence of the world of creation, a world beyond the world of I-You. Gradually Buber internalized Rosenzweig's criticism, and accepted God as Creator of the world. One symptom of this change is Buber's later attack on Kierkegaard who fully neglected the aspect of the Creator and the interhuman relation to the You.

Despite this evolution in Buber's thinking, did Buber completely get rid of the Gnostic tendencies that are palpable in his early writings? Isn't there still also in his later work the Gnostic idea that the world stays between God and humans and that, ideally, God stays between humans and the world? Is Buber's dualistic vision blotted out after *I and You*? Later, I will point out that Buber is against institutions that belong purely to the world of I-It. A comparison with Levinas sheds further light on this somewhat utopian Buberian position. Both thinkers stress that the relation with God takes place in the human relationship. According to Levinas, however, one does not have to choose between the world I-You and the world I-It. The ethical relation asks for a concrete engagement in the world. God is related to politics, tribunals, economics — that is, to the world. God has a relation with the world of "It." The material care for the Other is the expression of a "created" I who is aware of his or her own needs and of the needs of the fellow human being. After *I and You*, Buber admitted the relation of God to the world without, however, thinking this idea through to the end. Levinas reminded him of the necessity of thinking this idea to its utmost consequences.

Buber, while fighting against gnosis, remains somehow influenced by it. Nevertheless his question remains relevant: Buber repeatedly showed in his constructive criticism of egoism, personal interests, corruption and petrifaction the necessity for permanent renewal and steady purification of depersonalizing human institution.

Revelation and Teshuva

For Buber, revelation is an ongoing event.[12] It is a formal address — the voice of You sounds.[13] The content of revelation remains undefined; it is a voice without *logos*. Revelation is not conceived as divine content poured into an empty human vessel but is meeting. Perhaps one might even say that meeting is revelation. Buber sees revelation as a gift, as the touch of the other. In contrast to Nietzsche, who claims that "you take, you do not ask who it is that gives,"[14] Buber believes that "as we take, it is of the utmost importance to know that someone is giving. He who takes what is given him, and does not experience it as a gift, is not really receiving; and so the gift turns into theft. But when we do experience the giving, we find out that revelation exists."[15]

For Levinas, too, revelation is not an isolated event that is limited to the revelation at Sinai (*LR*, 190–210). It is the breakup of totality that makes the I a "hostage." Revelation has a concrete and prescriptive content, concisely formulated as "Thou shalt not murder." Revelation, in Levinas's perspective, is also a call for exegesis. The reader participates in the revelation by deciphering, by seeking. The word, which comes from the outside, lives in the person who receives it. Moreover, the divine word is heard by a multiplicity of people and each one of them is necessary to produce all the dimensions of meaning. We will return to Levinas's concept of revelation as a continual process of hermeneutics, as demanding human interpretation. Meanwhile, it is clear that this process and this interpretation are only possible by the bursting open of the "less" that is unable to contain the "more." Revelation is the explosion of the "more within the less," which Descartes called "the idea of Infinity" (*LR*, 208).

Thus, *teshuva* for Buber is different from Levinas's conception of *teshuva*. For Buber, *teshuva* is a "return" to the dialogical kernel, which is at the same time living in the face of God. For Levinas, *teshuva* as "answer" is linked to an ever-external demand, which comes first and to which a concrete answer is secondary.

Grace and Task

For Buber, the encounter (*Begegnung*) is grace. Encounter cannot be sought out; it occurs between (*zwischen*) two human beings. The element of the task in the relationship is less stressed. The Buberian relation remains formal, without specific content or deeds. True, man has to initiate it, but the grace of a real encounter can never be acquired.[16] It is as though Buber is afraid of an activism that closes man within himself and does not lead him to the lofty *Begegnung*.

In Levinas's thought, the task and activity are primordial, because the face of the Other faces the same and ordains him to various acts in being-for-the-other. Grace is concretely expressed in the demand.

Magic

Both Buber and Levinas fulminate against magical conceptions of religiosity. In magic, one manipulates the higher reality in a childish way. To Buber, magic as manipulation and gnosis as mastery through secret knowledge threaten authentic religiosity.

Levinas's antimagical attitude is clearly expressed in his talmudic reading "Toward the Other" (*NTR*, 12–29), where he writes that "my neighbor, my brother, man, infinitely less other than the absolutely other, is in a certain way more other than God: to obtain his forgiveness on the Day of Atonement I must first succeed in appeasing him" (*NTR*, 16). Against magic ritual, which would efface evil, he writes, "the world in which pardon is all-powerful becomes inhuman" (*LR*, 20).

Buber's understanding of Judaism is related to the hearing of the divine voice and to "realization." The people of God have the vocation of realizing unity; they have great experience with it.[17] They collectively hear God's voice turn their fate into a destiny. Magic has to be absent from this destiny. Whereas Buber regards all ritual as potentially magic, Levinas fulminates against a magical perception of the ritual, without abolishing ritual.

Humanism and Beyond

There are Jews who do not accept the idea that Judaism equals humanism. Buber does. Judaism and respect for human beings are for him the same. Jews have to be the pioneers of a dialogical humanity.[18] Buber's Judaism is a believing humanism in which humanism cannot exist without faith, and vice versa (*BH*, 17–22). The real *humanum* is the capacity of meeting with other existing beings. Against Sören Kierkegaard who recognizes only the meeting between humans and God, and against Ludwig Feuerbach, who excludes any transcendent element from the intersubjective relation, Buber sees the I-You relationship as all embracing; it is a relationship with God *and* humans.

Levinas does not seek to separate Judaism and humanism. Yet, the French-Jewish philosopher went beyond humanism and its recognition of the centrality of "man" (*DF*, 277–88). Humanism and Judaism are not entirely congruent for Levinas. There is the non-communicable element in Judaism that is essentially a criticism of what is usually accepted by humanism — a criticism that derives from infinite responsibility. Following in the footsteps of R. Mordechai Chouchani,[19] Levinas wrote that when "Israel" appears in the Talmud, one may read "humanity." Yet, he continues, "Israel signifies a people having received the Law and, consequently, a humanity that has arrived at the fullness of its responsibilities."[20]

Levinas recognizes the crisis of humanism and liberalism in the twentieth century, in the Shoah and other forms of genocide and atrocities. He further points to the problem of a science that calculates the real without always thinking it. He mentions a philosophy (Heidegger) that subordinates the human to anonymous Being, a politics and administration that do not suppress exploitation or war, and a socialism that becomes bureaucratic. In the light of all these deviations, Levinas pleads for a singularity that combines freedom and law, and keeps a distance from history and its successes. He criticizes the belles-lettres in which noble principles are lost in rhetoric. He distances himself from the violence of revolutionaries, and sees the possibility of a Jewish rebellion, or patience, without resentment and without becoming persecutor. He mistrusts the innocence of natural movements. Levinas denounces in a certain Jewish education complacency and pathetic ideology; he also opposes the defense of a "moral order." What is at stake in Judaism is the very possibility of a freedom inscribed on the tablets of stone, the reservation with respect to the illusions of happiness, in the solitary ecstasy of drugs or otherwise.

Levinas stresses more than Buber the particularity of Judaism (*DF*, 282), though without separation from non-Jews. Judaism is in permanent association with other human beings. However, he maintains that Jewish values are more than the echo of the surrounding civilization. Judaism has to do with limits placed on the interiorization of principles of conduct and with the necessity that inspirations become gestures and rituals (*DF*, 288). Most succinctly, he says, "the meaning of humanity is not exhausted by the humanists" (*DF*, 281). Levinas was far from being a liberal Jew. He was committed to Halakhic life. Against Buber, who was not interested in Rabbinic Judaism at all, Levinas liked the Rabbinic tradition and loved to reflect on the wisdom of the Sages in his talmudic lectures. This tradition, frequently against the mainstream, cannot be subsumed under an abstract universalism.

He shows the relevance and actuality of this tradition, which points to the Infinite by way of concrete, finite means.

Though Levinas, following his teacher Chouchani, talks about Israel as humanity, there is something in his writings that presents a Jewish task to non-Jews. Israel represents a kind of criticism of the world. The concrete Israel stands for humanity that has reached its maturity. Levinas also emphasizes the pioneering role of Israel; he recognizes its specific function, which nevertheless remains totally universal. Levinas emphasizes religiosity before religion, and is allergic to any kind of mission or conversion.

The World in Need of Judaism

In Levinas's talmudic lecture "As Old as the World?" (*NTR*, 70–88), Judaism is perceived as necessary to the world. The world is in need of justice and truth, exemplified in the institution and acts of the Sanhedrin. And what is asked from the Sanhedrin is asked from Israel as a whole. In Israel, there is a harmony between the order of love and the absolute and universal spirit, where the people show their faces to each other. Justice and love are intertwined.

In Levinas's thought, the message of Jerusalem is more than Hellenistic humanism, more than what can be learned from Greece about humankind. The excellence of Israel lies in its teaching of what is possible for human beings. Accused from the beginning,[21] Israel is an awareness of responsibilities.

The condition for justice lies in *mitzvot.* Jacob-Israel, bearing the clothes of his brother (Gen. 27:27), is already "for the others." He takes upon himself the responsibility of others. Israel lives freedom as fraternity and responsibility for sins that we do not commit. Here, Levinas uses his difficult and provocative terminology of responsibility, hostage, and persecution in order to show that the place of Israel is relative to an absolute place — the Place, *ha-Maqom* (*NTR*, 87–88).

Institutionalized Judaism, Halakha, Ritual and Prayer

Buber is extremely critical of institutions, especially religious ones. His is a religiousness that combined humanism with a way of life inspired by the Bible and Hasidism. In this religiousness, where presence to the You, and so to the everlasting You, is central, ritual is problematic. It precludes the immediacy of God's presence. Buber felt that institutionalization of relations depersonalizes.

Pamela Vermes goes so far as to write that Buber was "averse to religion."[22] In the end, religions as particular systems would have to disappear. He opposes religion to religiosity, the real kernel of all religions. Buber inherits the term religiosity from his teacher Georg Simmel, defining it as the attitude that does not need to be expressed in ritual and observances, and which is a function of social life.[23] Religiosity is the relationship to God, distinguished from religion with its dogmas and ritual prescriptions, which reduces religiosity to a conditional universe.[24] Thus, for example, Buber wrote extensively on Hasidism without committing himself to the Hasidic way of life. He is a modern man, linked to the tradition but free of its shackles. He shows the deeper layers of the Jewish tradition, without considering the different *mitzvoth* and ritual prescriptions as divinely promulgated.

Levinas, on the contrary, sees religious observances and rituals as expressions of authentic emotions and feelings that in the course of time became gestures, externalizing inner attitudes. For him, the ritual law is necessary. *Halakha* is a "severe discipline" that "tends towards justice." It belongs to "acting" before reflection — a stumbling block for philosophy. Levinas refers to the Jewish response to revelation on Mount Sinai, "We will do and we will listen," as the preparation for a life worth living. Ritual for him is necessary in Judaism. The Day of Atonement, for instance, is as important as a fixed day in the calendar. Forgiveness as "the freeing of the guilty soul" requires such a fixed day in order to enable the work of repentance to take place every day (*NTR*, 15–16).

Levinas stresses the importance of a singularity beyond universality. Torah is a correction of what is generally accepted in our modern world but which can become corrupted when made absolute, as is clear in the case of freedom. Freedom is a high value; yet when made absolute, it is corrected by a freedom (*herut*) engraved (*harut*) on the tablets of the Law.

Buber's Judaism is inspired by the Hassidic intention (*qavvanah*). Levinas's Judaism is much more cognitive insofar as study tradition-ally occupies a prominent role in it. For Buber (*BH*, 115–16), each religion is an exile. Only the redemption of the world liberates from exile. The historical religions tend to become ends in themselves. With-out self-criticism, they distance themselves from revelation, which is at their origin, and thus "obscure the face of God." Religions do not have a monopoly on God; they are the house of man and not the house of God on earth. Buber further suggests that the "religious need" of today is for the most part a human need for religion (*BH*, 123). The authentic life is outside institutionalized religion. Faith can-not be formalized.[25] Levinas sees the continuity between religiosity and religion. Buber and Levinas meet again when they both stress that religious life does not bring security. On the contrary, it is a life that constitutes a breach in the naive feeling of safety and demands of the human being to become an answerable being.

Buber does not like *Halakhic* Judaism, afraid as he is of object-ivization and neutral codification (WMB, 38). His attitude is not Law-less; he thinks that the true community, the fulfillment of the covenant with God could not be realized by the "observance of pre-scribed forms."[26] In his eyes, Judaism comes before the Law. The Law is addressed to the soul that cannot be understood outside of this Law. But the soul is not the Law: "The teaching of Judaism comes from Sinai; it is Moses' teaching. But the soul of Judaism is pre-Sinaitic" (*IW*, 28–29). For Levinas, who was humbly committed to *Halakhic* life, the acceptance of the Law is inherent in the Jewish faith. He would never talk about a "pre-Sinaitic" Jewish soul. The ritual prac-tice is a necessity because Judaism is not merely something in the heart of humanity. Ritual life is expressed; it orients us toward devo-tion to the Other. Nonetheless, Levinas understands that many great souls leave the gray routine of synagogal life because they are "in love with the absolute" and actively concerned with things of primordial social and political importance (*DF*, 272).

In sharp contrast to Buber, Levinas perceives the original note of Judaism in the harmony achieved between goodness and legalism: the two principles are interdependent. He admires the people capable of daily ritual. The Law, which is not a yoke, has a joy that nourishes religious life (*DF*, 19). Levinas considers prayer to be the human act of blessing God in living a life for the Other. This does not replace traditional prayer. On the contrary, prayer conditions ethical life. Pray-ing for the nonsuffering of the I is valid, if it is a prayer to God who suffers in the suffering of man (*LR*, 233–34). Buber did not believe in ritual or in fixed prayer. He did not attend services. All this was for him not a direct encounter with the divine Thou.

The Place of Strategic Rationality

Levinas and Buber both consider ethics, and therefore also the relation to God, as something deeper or higher than "practical rea-son." Ethics engages the entire person. It is, in Dilthey's terms, not an understanding, a "*verstehen*," even less an explaining, "*erklären*." The ethical attitude, the realization of values through openness to the non-

I, makes the world more human. Beyond this common ground, an insurmountable gap separates both thinkers. Buber's and Levinas's different attitudes toward ritual commandments, but also their differences with respect to religious or state institutions, are grounded in a more fundamental difference between them. A detailed account of this profound difference will allow a better understanding of their different positions toward Judaism.

In Buber's theory, symmetrical communication is the only authentic relation, whereas strategic rationality belongs to the sphere of the inauthentic, to the domain of the I-It. In Levinas's philosophy, by contrast, strategic rationality has great weight as demanded and controlled by ethics. Vittorio Hösle describes the dialectical relation between strategic rationality and communication.[27] He writes that it is a widespread theory that strategic rationality is responsible for the evil in the world, and that one expects from communication a solution for the very problem. It is as though something is moral when it is communicated and not hidden, and as though strategic rationality beyond the mere "*Sollen*" is not needed to minimize evil in the world. According to Hösle, it is our duty to work on institutions that minimize humanity's problematic natural state and reduce the strategic attitude to economic, political and scientific concurrency. Institutions are necessary for combating evil. The evil of the natural state cannot be vanquished without strategic rationality. But this rationality is not enough; confidence, a common normative concern, is needed.

By the standards of this theory, Levinas seems more realistic. He pays attention to institutions and the inner life, keeping in mind that institutions are limited by what Hösle calls "a common normative concern," or by what Levinas himself calls "the ethical Saying." Buber, on the other hand, does not trust institutions as much as he does the inner life. Buber separates the I-You from the I-It, where one knows, compares and controls. Levinas, wrote about the State, courts, army, police, etc., that are not separable from the high ethical demand that both requires institutions and criticizes them. Buber described the peaceful quiet mind, the oriented relating I. In Levinas's metaphysics, the Other "ordains" the I, whose answer has to take into account the noise of our manifold activities. And yet, in criticizing Buber for not having placed a strong enough emphasis on the conjunction of the I-You and I-It, how one does bypass his prophetic criticism of the institutions of Israel? Is his accent on the prophet rather than on the priest not a healthy correction of structures that ipso facto tend to eternalize themselves at the expense of dialogical, living reality?

Zionism and Israeli Politics

Buber was critical of Israeli politics. Made aware of the pathology of nationalistic chauvinism by his friend Gustav Landauer, he was allergic to nationalism in the form of collective egoism. He thought that states are built in blood and tears, and as many Jews of that time, he did not think that a Jewish State had to be established. Social units like the kibbutz could be linked in a federation and form a greater society.[28] He wanted to live in understanding with Arab neighbors and had a dovish standpoint in the Jewish-Arab dispute. Already at the Twelfth Zionist Congress in Karlsbad (1921), Buber had pleaded for Arabs and Jews in Palestine to unite their life interests. Unlike the majority in Israel, he defended a binational state in the movement *Ichud* (formerly *Berit Shalom*), founded with people such as Henrietta Szold, Moshe Smilansky, Jehuda L. Magnes and Ernst Simon. He feared, as did the prophet Samuel, that the nation of Israel would become like all other nations, and felt confident that Zionism is, finally, the teaching and realization of righteousness.

Buber conceived Zionism as the embodiment of Jewish Renaissance. Buber's socialist, cultural Zionism, influenced by Ahad Ha'Am, hardly matched the practical, nationalistic approach of the movement. Although in 1901 he became editor of the Zionist periodical *Die Welt*, his Zionism was much more spiritual than political. Buber proclaimed that the renewal of Judaism and the renewal of the world were one. Judaism has had its creative periods in which Judaism is renewed: first of all, there were the prophets, and then the Essenes, early Christians, Hasidim and, finally, the Zionist pioneers.[29]

Levinas more than Buber saw the importance of the state, be it the French Republic or the Jewish State. The Jewish State makes possible the renaissance of Jewish culture as a profoundly human phenomenon, and a source for positive opposition. What occurs in Israel could have an effect on the Diaspora. Levinas expected a lot from Jewish studies in Israel, which could rediscover the actuality of the ancient wisdom. Like Buber, he believed that Israel is more than another nationalism. It is first of all the possibility of realizing the prophetic message and of renewing Jewish life. The State of Israel should avoid "reasons of State" in order to constitute its "Jewish" character. In discussing the episode of the explorers of the Land through the Talmudic Tractate Sota (34b–35a), Levinas shows us our own anxieties in the fear of the explorers (*NTR*, 51–69). Is the Promised Land allowed? Do we have the right to conquer the magnificent buildings of others? Is this not colonialism? Is Jewish history not like any other history? Do even an absolutely moral people have the right to conquest? One has to take these questions seriously. And yet, the revolt of the explorers is the crisis of atheism, worse than the crisis of the Golden Calf, which was still religious. Perhaps, Levinas adds, also the explorers also "caught a glimpse of *sabras*" and feared the end of the Jewish people. Nevertheless, the explorers were severely punished. Levinas warns against the absolute pacifists, against these people with an "egalitarian conscience" who "denounced as antidemocratic the wisdom that excluded from freedom the murderers of freedom." He further opposes those who say: "We are one hundred million strong to crush you." To the Jewish people, the date of the exile is fixed before that of the conquest. They live in a country that vomits up its unjust inhabitants.

Levinas and Buber shares the longing for a just community in the land of Israel. They do not agree with the saying that "man is a wolf to other man," as Hobbes taught in his reduction of reason to reckoning. They conjoin ethics and politics.[30]

Jewish Education

Buber was concerned with Jewish studies, participating in Rosenzweig's *Freies jüdisches Lehrhaus* in Frankfurt. In 1933, he became head of the *Lehrhaus*. He also was director of the Central Office for Jewish Adult Education, the *Mittelstelle für jüdische Erwachsenenbildung*, created for Jews who were prohibited from attending German educational institutions. After his emigration to Israel, Buber became one of the founders of the College for Adult Education Teachers, *Bet ha-Midrash le-more 'am,* which trained immigrant teachers.

Concerned over the need to translate Jewish sources into modern languages, Levinas also thought Jewish studies should play a critical role in Israel. After World War II, René Cassin, president of the Alliance Israélite Universelle asked him to become director of the *Ecole Normale Israelite Orientale,* a Jewish high school and seminar for teachers. Levinas accepted and remained there for about 30 years. He worried about the assimilation of the young generation of Jewish Moroccan immigrants, and tried to offer them both openness to the world and a firm engagement with the traditional Judaism they inherited from their parents.

Levinas and Buber were both university professors. Levinas loved the prestige and elitism of the Academy, without neglecting the discipline and the joy of learning Talmud. Buber preferred the less formal structure of the *Lehrhaus* and occasional conversations and lectures outside the University, which seemed to him a more fitting framework to convey his dialogical teaching.

Judaism, Christianity and Messianism

Levinas as well as Buber writes on what unites Jews and Christians, and on what separates them. Levinas stresses the symbiosis of the twin religions and wrote about the Judeo-Christian friendship,[31] yet he also indicates essential divergences as regards the finality of the human. Buber is more concerned with Christianity than Levinas. In his *Two Types of Faith,* he distinguishes between *emunah,* belief *"in"* God, and *pistis,* belief *"that"* God exists. Community creates *emunah,* whereas *pistis* causes community. The second type of faith is that of an individual who came to faith through *metanoia,* a mental act. The first type of faith is that of a community that lives in *teshuva,* in return to real life. In his description of both types of faith, which are linked to each other and nevertheless different, Buber is much influenced by Rosenzweig's theory, exposed clearly in the third part of the *Star.* He sees the possibility of a true relationship between Christians and

Jews. Religions may be associated with each other and clarify what can be done to bring redemption nearer (*BH*, 115–16). Exclusivity is forbidden.

Levinas seems to be more concerned with highlighting Israel's specificity, which gets lost in the New Testament. He is more concerned with Israel's "difficult wisdom concerned with truths that correlate to virtues" (*DF*, 275) than in binding Judaism and Christianity together, although he has warm words for the Jewish-Christian symbiosis. Several times, he points to the problem of interiorization. He quotes Rabbi Johanan in the name of Rabbi Jose ben Kisma (Sanhedrin 103b): "Of great importance is the mouthful of food." The Other's hunger limits the rights of the I by putting its spontaneity into question: "there is no bad materialism other than our own" (*DF*, xiv). Judaism has to do with more than "inner life." It is related to doing, not to a spiritualized purity; it is a discussion about what is pure and what is impure. Above all, it is related to the realization of purity in everyday life. True, much of Jewish life takes place in Christian space and time, yet in the Christian milieu Jewish life maintains its concrete specificity, its discipline of acts, of *mitzvot*.[32]

In 1902, Buber read Albert Schweitzer's book on the Eucharist that put Jesus in relation with the mysteries of Judaism (*BH*, 65). Buber linked Christianity to Judaism in his *On Judaism* and later in his *Two Types of Faith*. In *On Judaism*, he maintains that original Christianity is Judaism. And also in *Two Types of Faith*, the teaching of Jesus manifests the authentic Jewish principle (*OJ*, 12). Jesus is seen by Buber as "my big brother," having an important place in the faith of Israel.[33] According to Bernard Dupuy, however, with time, Buber becomes more and more critical of Christianity.[34] Indeed, Buber associates Christianity with *pistis*, with a Paulinian-Gnostic dichotomy of matter and spirit, and with a faith that lacks demands and realization. He severely criticizes the position of Kierkegaard and his "suspension of the ethical." Ultimately, Israel remained for Buber distinct from Christianity in that Israel links redemption to the accomplishment of creation and does not see that history is accomplished in a Messiah who has already come.

Messianism is common to Judaism and Christianity. Levinas, like Buber, regards Messianism not as a one-person phenomenon, but as a task given to everyone. In Levinas's words: "Messianism is . . . not the certainty of the coming of a man who stops History" (*DF*, 90). In the thinking of Buber[35] and Levinas, the Messiah is popularized, actually present in the suffering human being, suffering for the suffering of the Other. Each human person has the possibility to be animated by Messianism, to become a suffering servant about whom the prophet Isaiah spoke.

Levinas comments on Sanhedrin 98b–99a and the words of Rabbi Nahman, who says: "If the Messiah is of those living [today], it might be one like myself" (*DF*, 88). Rabbi Nahman, according to Levinas says: "The Messiah is Myself; to be Myself is to be the Messiah" (*DF*, 89). In this conception, the Messiah is "the just man who suffers, who has taken on the suffering of others." All persons are destined to be the Messiah by not evading the burden imposed by the Other. Every possible relationship between God and humanity is subordinated to the striving for a just society, which is considered an eminently religious act. This striving is a state of mind, "normally called Jewish Messianism" (*DF*, 21).

Bible and Talmud

One of the great differences between Buber and Levinas is that Buber concentrates on the study of the Bible, whereas Levinas reads the Bible through the eyes of the sages who succeeded in reading the spirit in the letters. Levinas could not think about Jewish singularity without the Talmud. Between 1957 and 1975, he regularly delivered talmudic lectures within the framework of the yearly colloquia of the Jewish French-speaking intellectuals. On Shabbat, he combined some lines of the *parashat ha-shavu'a* (the weekly Torah portion) with the commentary of Rachi and a fitting talmudic passage.

Without trying to give an indepth analysis of his talmudic lectures, let us merely note that Levinas combines his lectures of the ancient texts written in Babylonia with thoughts on the Western tradition and its foundations. As expected, he does not see here a contrast between

Judaism and universality; The Other in these texts is the cultural horizon that was so often forgotten in the West. He talks about Heidegger when commenting on a talmudic text concerned with pardon, about modern war when talking about "fire damage," about totalizing thought ("temptation of temptation") when discussing the meaning of the reception of the Torah on Mount Sinai, and about modern economy when discussing a text on "sorcery." Here the new explains the old, and vice versa. Levinas attempts to translate aggadic talmudic discourse into modern language (*NTR*, 39), using Talmud to debate and clarify modern problems.[36] In Levinas's lectures, the Jewish sages and European culture communicate. He sees his own subjective interpretation as necessary for the revelation to which the text bears witness; in the words of Annette Aronowicz, "the prominence of his own subjectivity in the text is not incidental to his hermeneutic but crucial" (*NTR*, xvi). More than Buber, Levinas sees the possibilities of Jewish hermeneutics and highlights the dissemination in the text, the multiple interpretations by the different interpreters and in different interpreting communities. The text refers to other texts, and functions in a context: text becomes pre-text for active interpretation. The texts signify infinitely, differently in different times. The reader is actively involved in the production of meaning; he becomes a scribe himself (*LR*, 190–210).[37] Reading the pages of texts, the reader comes in contact with the Good beyond Being. In contrast to Buber, Levinas stresses the necessity of the oral Law as the way in which the text inspires discussion and a multitude of readings. The Saying — which prototypically comes to expression in the biblical said — has to be re-said today, as it was exemplarily re-said in talmudic times.

Buber does not concentrate on the oral Law. He studied and translated the Bible, and adopted biblical criticism as well as the unity of the Bible.[38] Nevertheless, he was not considered by the professional exegetes to be one of them because his aim was not so much the reconstruction of history as the hearing of the voice of the supreme Presence. He restores to the Bible its spoken character (*Gesprochenheit*), and wants the reader to become a listener.[39] With Rosenzweig, he undertook in 1925 a German translation of the Bible, which was only completed by Buber in 1961. The two translators followed the Hebrew sentence structure and rhythm, and wanted to be close to Hebrew words, sounds and sentences. They created a kind of palimpsest. They wanted to surprise German with Hebrew culture, not to Germanize Hebrew.

The differences between Levinas and Buber may be enormous. Yet, is Levinas's attempt to confront the Talmud with the modern problematic of Europe all that different from Buber's (and Rosenzweig's) confrontation of the German language with original Hebrew text? Do not both prefer the actual message of the ancient biblical words to the sophisticated elaboration of the historico-philological approach of the biblical texts?

Both thinkers are great translators, Buber publishing a German translation of the Bible and Levinas making the teaching in the literature of the sages relevant and actual. In his annual lectures, Levinas analyzes the said in order to make audible the Saying, i.e., the ethical demand of the other human. This ethical demand as the ultimate hermeneutic horizon is revelation. The said of this Saying is revelatory and points to what cannot be said exhaustively because the demand is infinite. "Revelation" in his interpretation is the epiphany of the face. Levinas also interprets classical Jewish terms, and translates them into "Greek." So, for instance, "prophetic speech" becomes the call of the Other. It is a call for "holiness," for responsibility and respect. Traditional terms such as "God" or "election" in his Jewish writings, also appear in his philosophy. "God" who does not "appear," is linked to the infinity of the demand of the Other. The "Elected" are those who are called by the Other and designated to become individual, i.e., encumbered with an infinite responsibility that cannot be escaped.

While Levinas approaches the Bible and philosophy through the Talmud and "Jewish" eyes, Buber too appreciates Jewish exegesis, not in the form of Halakhic discussions, but in the form of the Midrashic approach of the Bible. Above all he emphasizes the direct contact with humankind, illustrated in the Bible. This direct contact requires neither the mediation of prayer nor the mediation of biblical or talmudic texts. In translating and commenting on the Bible as the common heritage of Jews and Christians, Buber, like Levinas, reaches out to a non-Jewish public.

Romantic Enthusiasm and Lithuanian Sobriety

It is well known that Buber made the evolution from a mystical thinker to a religious existentialist for whom the realization of a true community is imperative. Such a true community he found in Hasidism, by which he was profoundly influenced. He was an inspiring person and an enthusiastic teacher. Levinas, an exponent of the demanding, intellectual, Lithuanian Judaism, disliked mystical moods and advocated lucidity and realism. He was distrustful of forms of life that testify to spiritual drunkenness. Weren't the two eldest sons of the high priest Aaron punished because they entered into the Tabernacle with "unholy fire" (*'esh zarah*), with unrestrained exaltation (Lev. 10:1)?

We already mentioned that real life for Buber is meeting. In the words of *Daniel*, it is "realization" (not "orientation"), or, in the words of *I and You*, I-You, knowing about the between (*Zwischen*), not I-It. The relation starts from the genuine, whole I in an immediate approach to the You. In the meeting, the I becomes I. The I, getting rid of its self-sufficiency, transcends itself in the relation. Levinas is interested less in the becoming of the I and more in the rights of the other person. The Other transcends the I and ruptures its totalizing tendencies. At the heart of Levinas's thinking, the I has no choice: it is "subjected" to the judgment of the Other. The Buberian I meets the absolute or eternal You in the meeting with a personal You. The Levinasian self is surprised by the ab-solute, which is the meaning of "holiness." The self is called by the always separated Other. Consequently, Levinas's thinking is much more heteronomous than is Buber's.

Whereas Buber wants an empathic, immediate, spontaneous relation with the You, leading to the presence of the eternal You, Levinas remains skeptical of enthusiasm (*DF*, 14–16). He is suspicious of spontaneity, which he equates with the common charm of wild beasts and young children. It is the figure of the Pharisee who brings humanity for Levinas (*DF*, 27–29). The Pharisee, absent in modern Judaism, brings great peace by waging a war of reasons, devoid of anger and envy. He does not live from inspiring grace, but his is a paradise in which joy is created from suffering. Levinas's paradigm of the Jew is the one who takes part in the permanent dialogue between wise men, whose obedience is sovereignty and whose "austere tenderness" brings them into contact with the ever-exterior God. The Jewish singularity "beyond the pathetic" is linked to the exteriorization and even the ritualizing of inner feelings.

Thus, Buber highlighted empathy; Levinas's discourse flees from enthusiasm and favors cognition. Further, in *I and You*, Buber writes about love and about the human being who dwells in God's love. Love is between I and You; Hasidism is the love of creature.[40] Levinas is hesitant to use the word "love," which has an erotic connotation, and prefers the word holiness, in Hebrew "*qedusha*," which means etymologically "separation."

Buber and Levinas both highlighted in Judaism elements that remain important in our own day. Buber calls for a permanently renewed, dialogical lifestyle, of which Jews are pioneers. His prophetic criticism of the establishment remains highly relevant. On the other side, Levinas sees in Judaism an "extreme humanism of a God who demands much of man," a way of life governed by the Law (*DF*, 26). Both thinkers are far from a "pious" or a "dogmatic" Judaism, and define Judaism not in parochial terms but in terms of an engagement with the world at large. They convey, different messages — a sublime message of empathy that creates real meetings and a dignifying message of intellectual sobriety that testifies to inspired rationality. Buber teaches that relation is impossible without the right, inner intentionality of the I, and Levinas taught that the conditions for relation lie in the exterior call of the Other, as well as in the expression of the listening I. It is my opinion that these different emphases are what ultimately color their respective reflections on Judaism.

NINE

Revelation Here and Beyond

Buber and Levinas on the Bible

Michael Fagenblat & Nathan Wolski

Buber and Levinas equally regard the Bible as a moral and spiritual wellspring of both Jewish and Western civilization, and agree that the modern reader has much to learn by turning back to the Hebrew Bible for instruction.[1] For both thinkers, the Bible is the book in whose light we see and judge our social and historical condition, but it is also foremost *Torah*, meaning "teaching." What is it that the Bible teaches? According to Buber and Levinas, the Bible teaches of the possibility of the meaning of God in the social and historical life of human beings. Following Franz Rosenzweig, the central interest of the Bible for Buber and Levinas is not its status as dogma but its testimony to a religious possibility that modern life often fails to perceive.[2] They turn to the Hebrew Bible as a way of illustrating the possibility of a God-oriented worldview that remains entirely grounded in the experience of modernity.

However, Buber and Levinas understand the possibility to which the Bible points in distinct, indeed rival ways, all the more interesting given that both thinkers made similar appeals for a modern return to the Bible. Before exploring their respective views about what the Bible teaches and how it should be approached, we will consider why both Buber and Levinas urged the modern reader to return to the Bible. In so doing, we hope to understand better their critical engagement with major trends in modern scholarship.

I

Buber diagnosed modern life as being set adrift amid the impersonal forces of history, and thus direly lacking an ultimate orientation.
He turned to the Bible as a way of giving historicized consciousness a
sense of personal destiny and meaning. He argued that only a personal experience of revelation could provide a human life with an
ultimate sense of purpose, of moving from a determined condition
toward a meaningful future:

> The man of today knows of no beginning. As far as he is concerned,
> history ripples toward him from some prehistorical cosmic age. He knows
> of no end; history sweeps him on into a posthistorical cosmic age. What
> a violent and foolish episode this time between the prehistorical and
> the posthistorical has become! Man no longer recognizes an origin or
> goal because he no longer wants to recognize the midpoint. Creation
> and redemption are true only on the premise that revelation is a present
> experience. Man of today resists the Scriptures because he cannot en-
> dure revelation. To endure revelation is to endure this moment full of
> possible decisions, to respond to and be responsible for every moment.
> (*IW*, 95)

Buber suggests that the Bible is of paramount relevance today because
it situates the modern within a redemptive narrative that gives teleological significance to an otherwise futile passage through historical
time. Buber's appeal to an experience of revelation and his commitment to "the premise that revelation is a present experience" are heavily
grounded in Dilthey's concept of *Erlebnis*, which involves a re-situation of that which merely occurs to a person within the "meaningful
whole" of existence.[3] This re-situation transforms happenings into
events and behavior into action, a transformation that, according to
Buber, alone allows one "to respond to and be responsible for every
moment."

For Buber, the experience of revelation does the work of resituating
meaning. It takes the modern person out of his or her "violent and
foolish" indeterminate historical condition and offers a new, purpose-
ful vision of the past and future. Revelation, then, is not some bygone
occurrence that hangs over the present like a shadow extending from

days of yore; it is an ever-present possibility for each person that re-
deems time and gives meaning to personal and historical narratives.
"The Jewish Bible," Buber writes,

> does not set a past event as a midpoint between origin and goal. It
> interposes a movable, circling midpoint which cannot be pinned tc any
> set time, for it is through the words of the Bible that I the reader, the
> hearer, catch the voice that from its earliest beginnings has been speak-
> ing in the direction of the goal. The midpoint is this mortal and yet
> immortal moment of mine. Creation is the origin; redemption the goal.
> But revelation is not a fixed, dated point poised between the two. The
> revelation at Sinai in not this midpoint itself, but the perceiving of it,
> and such perception is possible at any time. (*IW*, 94)

The modern is thus urged to undergo the *Erlebnis* of revelation in
order to resituate what merely happens within "the true history of the
world": "that is to say, of the history according to which the world has
an origin and a goal. The Jewish Bible demands that the individual fit
his own life into this true history, so that 'I' may find my own origin in
the origin of the world, and my own goal in the goal of the world"
(*IW*, 94).

It is important to point out that by situating the "I" within the
biblical narrative of creation and redemption, Buber appeals to a solidarity that includes the whole world. Buber's coconception of the
Bible as the origin from which Jewish national sentiment springs does
not compromise this appeal to solidarity with the whole of creation.
On the contrary, it anticipates an important view in contemporary
moral and political discussions that promotes the use of "thick" par-
ticularistic narratives that are compatible with "thinner" values apply-
ing to all people or beings.[4] In highlighting a personal and national
metanarrative to the Bible, Buber had in mind both the autonomy
and dignity of the Jewish people among the nations of the world and
the moral vocation of this people within the ultimate narrative of human solidarity (*IW*, 240–44).

In a certain sense Buber's articulation of the experience of revelation as "possible at any time" recalls the traditional Jewish view of the

calendrical cycle of ritual life that draws history into *its* orbit, and thus never comes undone in the face of historical events. Levinas likewise turns to the Bible for the way in which it urges us to see history and life within an ahistorical cycle that reflects a higher moral order. However, for Levinas it is more definitely liturgical life rather than the personal or national narrative that frames the step beyond the violence and arbitrariness of history. He turns to the ritualized time of Jewish liturgical life in order to view history from an external vantage that nonetheless retains the materiality of historical experience. Ritual time is precisely not a view *sub specie aeternitatis*; it is embodied, particular, narrated, and lived through with others. Ritual time thus bears a rich materiality that maintains an integrity of meaning in the face of the brute force of history. It provides a way of transcending "profane history" by weaving everyday life with the "holy history" of another story and another moral order.[5]

Thus, in his most important essay on the Bible, Levinas cites the *locus classicus*, the *haggadah* of Passover, which extols the primacy of liturgical time over historical consciousness. The virtue of liturgical life practices is that they do not succumb to the reductionisms of positivistic history, nor do they rarefy meaning through the abstractions of metaphor or allegory, nor do they lapse into the biases of myth.[6] In praise of liturgical time and life practices, Levinas writes:

> At once commemoration of Holy History and a continuation of the events commemorated, the practices are, through *interpretation*, reinserted into the texture of those events. . . . In this way the narrative loses its archeological character. . . . Celebration becomes actualization, a personal reenactment of the past. . . . To belong to a book as one belongs to one's history! This explains how, in the name of the Book and in the perspective opened up by it, an historical act can be accomplished as a ritual gesture. . . . It is situated beyond the space in which any philology can unsettle it. (*OS*, 128–29; modified translation)

Like Buber, Levinas sees belonging to the Bible as a way of recontextualising one's concrete narrative. But this affinity makes it all the more important to stipulate their different reasons for venerating the Bible. Buber's move to the metatime of the Bible resituates the modern Jew within a story that provides personal and national purpose that has a clear political horizon, namely, the establishment and moral renaissance of a Jewish State. Thus, Buber's critique of historicism by way of an *Erlebnis* of revelation, while resembling a major traditional move toward ahistorical liturgical time, in fact marks an essential rupture with tradition since the re-situation it makes is on the plane of history rather than on ritual. Levinas, writing after the establishment of Israel, turns to the Bible for a more traditional modeling of an ahistorical narrative with embodied, normative content. By attending to the normative transcendence that the Bible brings to bear on the here and now, Levinas offers moderns who are captivated by history a material way of living in the interstices of history, within and beyond one's historical horizons. Levinas thus calls on the modern Jewish reader to turn to the Bible owing to the liturgical time it demands (of the rabbinic-interpretative community). The time of liturgy frees one from the time of history even as it is lived within a historical community.

Moreover, if, for Buber, the Bible promises an *Erlebnis* of revelation, for Levinas the Bible makes an impossible promise that no "religious experience" could ever fulfill. Indeed if the revelation of Buber's Bible is ever-present, "possible at any time," then Levinas's Bible is never present, promising what is precisely impossible to assimilate within the limits of the here and now. For Levinas, the Bible, by way of the rabbinic commentaries, demands that one cross from one's own time, where one's needs condition all that one does, to its liturgical time where one's service attests to a value relative to the needs of the Other. He suggests that: "a work is possible only in patience, which, pushed to the limit, means for the agent to renounce being the contemporary of its outcome, to act without entering into the Promised Land. . . . To renounce being the contemporary of the triumph of one's work is to envisage this triumph in a *time without me*, to aim at this world below without me, to aim at a time beyond the horizons of my time, in an eschatology without hope for oneself, or in a liberation from my time."[7] Here the promise of the Bible is strictly defined in terms of a future beyond the reach of the present. Later, Levinas casts the idea of the biblical demand in terms of an immemorial past, but this shift reflects a farreaching and complicated move in Levinas's understanding of the self that we cannot detail here.

Whether it is for the sake of a better future or owing to the obligations of an immemorial past, for Levinas the Bible signifies an order of service and goodness that can never be realized in the present. Accordingly, Buber's idea of experiencing the revelation of the Bible is anathema to Levinas's understanding of its normative significance. In place of experience, Levinas posits the separation of two times embodying two orders of meaning that are never quite synchronized, and therefore prevent responsibility from coming to rest. His account of the Bible focuses on its prophecy of the Good or its commandment toward the Good, and these are orders of revelation that can never be integrated into experience because they come from, and point to, the other rather than the self. He thus gives up on the idea that the right spiritual or moral experience might redeem one from one's "moral disequilibrium" and characterizes revelation in terms of commandments rather than experience: "the revealed is welcomed in the form of obedience" (*BV*, 146). For Levinas, then, the idea of revelation refers to a normative order that stands outside reflection and experience; it constitutes the one who responds to it as commanded, as morally elected. Like the Israelites at the foot of Mount Sinai who say "we will do and we will hear" (Exodus 24:7), the stance of revelation inverts the usual order of intentional action by acceding to obligations before their logic has been apprehended.[8] To this structural-constitutive dimension of revelation, Levinas adds the mediated aspect of normative life that is given expression through the interpretive activity of a community. The idea of revelation as standing outside reason and experience expresses radical, ungrounded trust or faith (in Hebrew these are one word) in goodness, but it also places revelation outside the sphere of critical discourse, and is thus a dogmatic gesture. Accordingly, Levinas invests the interpretive community with the discursive task of mediating revelation. However, interpretation too is not to be characterized by experience; it is exegesis, inspiration, dialogue, and practice rather than *Erlebnis*. We will have more to say of this exegetical order of revelation below. For now, the point to consider is that whereas Buber's recourse to revelation invests personal experience with the task of realizing the promises of the Bible, Levinas, who is more suspicious of the value of experience, turns to the idea of biblical revelation as a vision, a commandment and a practice of interpretation.

II

Buber and Levinas also differ in their sense of what is of crucial importance in the Bible. For Buber, the Bible testifies to "the remembrance and the expectation of a concrete situation: the encounter of God and men" (*IW*, 14). "The theme of the Bible is the encounter between a group of people and the Lord of the World in the course of history, the sequence of events occurring on earth. Either openly or by implication, the stories are reports of encounters" (*IW*, 89). Buber's focus on the concrete situation, the encounter or the event as emblematic of many biblical narratives, is hard to dispute, and indeed has been a key progenitor of the fecund "Bible as literature" movement. So, too, is his claim that dialogue is the privileged mode of presenting this encounter. Robert Alter, one of Buber's most original and proficient successors, claims that "spoken language is the substratum of everything human and divine that transpires in the Bible."[9] Indeed, Buber goes so far as to say that the Bible is essentially "a dialogue between God and his creature" (*IW*, 16). As such, it presents "the foreshadowing of dialogical man, of the man who commits his whole being to God's dialogue with the world" (*IW*, 131). With this focus in mind, Buber produced his outstanding readings of the Bible, especially the story of Exodus and the prophets, which draw out the significance of the historical, dialogical experience, while avoiding historical reductionism, as detailed in section four.

This only goes to highlight the peculiarity of Levinas's approach to Bible studies, which is virtually the inverse of Buber's. Although Levinas also regards the Bible as central to Western civilization, his references to it are motivated by what are at once more traditional and more modern — even postmodern — concerns. The postmodern motivations are theological; they constitute a response to modern philosophy's critique of religion, and lead Levinas to figure God without reference to presence.[10] Separating God from presence requires Levinas to reject the language of encounter, event, and dialogue and, by implication, to invoke an entirely different Bible from the one Buber admires. For Levinas, it is not the presence of God through speech that is significant but the Bible's stature as Scripture, "its essence as Book, that is, by its very writing, signifying precisely prescription" (*ITN*, 58). Levinas's desire to accommodate a radical critique of traditional positive theology leads him to envisage a Bible that privileges writing over speech, the trace of God in place of divine presence, the study of the Bible over its emulation, and, above all, its prescriptive rather than descriptive significance (*ITN*, 58–59). Though Levinas's writings increasingly risk naming God, he does so by employing a hypernegative theology that interrupts the language of experience and narration rather than confirms it.[11] As a result, he never approaches the Bible as "narrative theology," as Buber does.[12]

For the same reason, instead of offering sustained readings of biblical stories, which is the great strength of Buber's approach, Levinas illustrates his argument by using biblical fragments and talmudic interpretations of the Bible to reflect his conception of what a divinely revealed Book might do.[13] Scripture, for Levinas, is essentially inscription and prescription; it is significant for it testifies to a God who commands irrespective of "spiritual needs." On the basis of its essentially inscribed and prescribed character Levinas argues that revelation is interpretation rather than manifestation. Again, this distances him from experiential and narrative theology while exalting God as the normative center of social life. Such interpretative life sees God as its ultimate normative orientation and yet eschews all contact with the divine. Accordingly, for Levinas, God appears in the Bible only to command, and the Bible is of fundamental significance because it marks the interruption of command and commentary in human life. Prescription and commentary fill the space left behind by God's departure from modernity.

Another way of casting the difference between Levinas and Buber on the Bible is to consider an alternative faultline that each endorses, that between the Hasidim and their impassive, bookish opponents, the Mitnagdim. Buber, who first introduced the grassroots pietistic movement of Hasidism to the non-Jewish world, extols the popular mystical emphasis on immediacy, encounter, community, and even ecstasy. For his part, Levinas, in keeping with his Lithuanian origins, assumes the side of the Mitnagdim, the traditional opponents of popular mysticism, by characterizing the Bible as a book of liturgical and practical *mitzvoth* (commandments) gleaned through talmudic exegesis. To Buber's veneration of "the life of man . . . lived in the face of the mystery of God" (*IW*, 22), Levinas might have offered this trenchant critique:

> The numinous or the sacred wraps and transports humans beyond their power and will. But true freedom takes offence at these uncontrollable excesses. The numinous annuls the relationships between persons by making beings participate, albeit ecstatically, in a drama that is not willed by them, in an order in which they dissolve. This somehow sacramental power of the divine is seen in Judaism as an insult to human freedom and as contradicting human education, which remains *an action on a free being*. Not that liberty is an end in itself, but it does remain the condition for any value one may attain. The Sacred that wraps me up and transports me is violence. (*DF*, 14)

Ironically, for all Levinas's avoidance of the numinous, it is clearly Buber who addresses a Bible closer to the *pshat*, the literalness of the text. Levinas's unease with divine presence is clearly not reflected in much of the Bible, which combines accounts of God's immanence and various manifestations even as it introduces the idea of an invisible God. And yet concern for a literal reading of the Bible is a rather late development in Jewish hermeneutics, having first preoccupied the great rabbinic exegetes of the eleventh century.[14]

Thus, in another ironic twist, Buber's closer fidelity to the literalness of the Bible marks a rupture with most traditional Jewish approaches to Scripture, while Levinas, who is motivated by postmodern theological concerns, invents a Bible that in some ways more closely resembles the Jewish Written Torah. This is less than surprising in context. Buber's interest in the Bible converged with his national-political aspirations for a Jewish return to the biblical homeland and a renaissance of Jewish national life outside the horizons of rabbinic, and especially *hallachic*, Judaism. His emphasis on the unmediated experience of reading and emulating the Bible reflects not only a concern for the literal concrete religiosity of the Bible, but also disregard for the politically disenfranchised rabbinic tradition of biblical exegesis. Levinas, for his part, is motivated not only by a postmodern theological sensibility, but equally by the conviction that a Jewish reading of the Bible cannot avoid the mediation of traditional commentaries. Like the talmudic rabbis before him, Levinas depicts contact with God as an exegetical and normative affair rather than an experiential one.[15] This explains how Buber's literalism plays itself out untraditionally whereas Levinas's construction of the Bible in terms of the normative significance of divine absence recalls the more traditional affirmation of revelation as exegesis and commentary.

Here we might mention one other irony. Buber's claim that the Bible depicts a dialogical religious anthropology can be met with the counterclaim that the Bible usually presents a series of divine dictations to which the people of the Bible are subject. In contrast, Levinas makes the point that it is the Talmud, even more than the Bible, that institutes dialogical textuality (*OS*, 130). To be sure, God only rarely intervenes in this religious dialogue, but for thousands of pages spanning hundreds of years, the Talmud records the debates of the rabbis as they discuss, interpret and dispute each other in light of the Bible.[16]

All the same, Levinas's postmodern traditionalism deviates in one crucial respect from the tradition it recalls. For if Buber risks reducing the Bible to the one grand theme of the dialogical encounter, Levinas falls prey to a more unlikely essentialism when he claims, for example, that "the entire Torah, in its minute descriptions, is concentrated in the 'Thou shalt not kill' that the face of the other signifies" (*ITN*, 111). While there is reason to laud the moral innovations introduced by certain aspects of the Bible, it is entirely misleading to depict the

Bible as coming to teach one essential moral lesson.[17] More worrisome still is the implication that the Bible reveals the essence of morality. This view ignores the many instances in the Bible of divinely sanctioned normative instruction of what most of us today would clearly regard as patent examples of immorality. Falling back on the idea that judging these instances requires the mediation of commentary provides little or no help, for we cannot turn to the talmudic commentaries as readily as Levinas might like for examples of the idea that revelation commands responsibility for the other. The most pertinent example is perhaps the rabbis' interpretation of the foremost biblical "Other," the stranger who lives among you. Instead of reading the Bible literally as it refers to the non-Israelite who dwells among the people of Israel in their ancient land (*ger toshav*), the rabbis interpreted "stranger" (*ger*) in much narrower national or familial terms to mean convert (*ger tsedek*), and thus excluded the real other, the stranger.[18] The twofold idea, then, that the Bible presents one moral teaching that accords with Levinas's ethics of the other, and that instances where this moral teaching seems problematic can be redeemed by talmudic interpretation, must be taken with a grain of salt. It is better to claim, as Levinas himself does on occasion, that what is significant about the idea of revelation is not its ethical content (even if in important ways some of our dearest moral sensibilities are instituted by the Bible), but its modeling of a heteronomous, normative teaching that demands interpretation and practice and that therefore has the effect of disciplining, rather than announcing, one's ethical responsibilities for the other.[19]

Buber and Levinas present us with two competing paradigms for a hermeneutics and pedagogy of the Bible. We have seen, however, that at issue is much more than a theory or a method of reading. Rather, their disagreement on the essence and function of the Bible reflects their divergent views on, among other things, the nature of revelation, the significance of religious experience, and the meaning and mode of being Jewish. However perhaps the two greatest points of conflict expressed in their different views on the Bible are the role of community and tradition in mediating personal, religious experience, and the implications of historicity for religious life. It is to these last two points of conflict that we now turn.

III

The difference between Levinas and Buber regarding the significance of the Bible — the former prizing its prescriptivism, the latter its value as dialogical encounter — plays itself out also at the level of community and tradition. For Buber, the Bible's immediate availability is not only possible, but indeed desirable, since such an encounter breathes new life into the stale commentaries on commentaries that obscure the biblical saga. Buber's Bible addresses the person as an individual and as a national, appealing to his or her sense of personal and historical destiny. In a sense, Levinas goes further as he seems to endorse a radically singular and even subjective approach to the Bible:

> The Revelation as calling to the unique within me is the significance particular to the signifying of the Revelation. It is as if the multiplicity of persons — Is not this the very meaning of the personal? — were the condition for the plenitude of "absolute truth"; as if every person, through his uniqueness, were the guarantee of the revelation of a unique aspect of truth, and some of its points would never have been revealed if some people had been absent from mankind. . . . [T]he multiplicity of the irreducible people is necessary to the dimensions of meaning; the multiple meanings are multiple people. (*BV*, 133–34)

Levinas is clearly commending the plurality of interpretations. However, we have seen that what makes his approach distinct is that he gives singularity a normative rather than a narrative or hermeneutic spin. For Levinas, then, the significance of the Bible is that it both prescribes action, thereby generating a sense of personal responsibility, and also multiplies meaning, thereby enabling a sense of social and interpretative plurality. To be sure, the interpretative register runs the "risk of subjectivism," as Levinas notes (*BV*, 136).

On this point, perhaps the difference between Levinas and Buber is not so great, since both in effect appeal to the uniqueness of a personal response to the Bible. For Levinas, however, the risk of unbridled individualism is negotiated by "a necessary reference of the subjective to the historical continuity of the reading, and by the tradition of commentaries that cannot be ignored under the pretext that inspirations come to you directly from the text" (*BV*, 135). As Tamra Wright suggests, "the community of readers provides some protection from subjectivism."[20] However, this solution has its own problems. For restricting interpretation by insisting on the mediation of the community of readers is in fact an elitist, if not hegemonic, gesture. It amounts to suggesting that interpretative individuation is garnered only by those individuals who are able to stamp their influence on the community of readers (Rashi, Maharal, R. Chaim of Volozhin, the talmudic sages, etc.). Thus it is only *"if some people had been absent from mankind"* that the revelation would be lacking. One might be tempted to conclude that the remaining readers, by failing to add to the multiplicity of reading, fail to attest to the plenitude of revelation. That criticism cannot be directed at Buber, whose guard against subjectivism does not refer to the tradition of commentary, and who in fact embraces an acutely personal experience of reading.

It is therefore fortunate that Levinas offers a second, less elitist way of accommodating the plurality of interpretations. He does this by reverting to practice as the fence that keeps interpretative plurality in play (*BV*, 139–41). Levinas suggests that Jewish practice, *hallakah*, provides a way of unifying the community of readers without restricting the individuality and multiplicity of readings. Indeed, it is a remarkable fact that Jewish life has accommodated a vast and contradictory set of interpretations while achieving unity through normative practices.[21] This too, however, is an extremely traditional gesture that is worth both celebrating and critically appraising. On the one hand, it is true that a practical, *halakhic* unity admits a striking plurality of an array of meanings that are often incongruous. This practical, noncreedal approach to Scripture makes room for singularity while avoiding anarchy. It accepts radical individualism at the level of understanding while containing it within an organized set of communal practices. On the other hand, this gesture too has a certain exclusiveness and authoritarianism inherently built into it. For these practices unify readers of

Scripture only to the extent that they divide Jews from non-Jews, and divide Jews of one "denomination" from Jews of another. Moreover, the authorities (*poskim*) who determine the communal practices are subject to historical and psychological factors (not to mention political and polemical ones), while their decisions govern the life practices of the various individuals within the community. The unity achieved through practice comes at the cost of other values that some of Levinas's contemporary readers will not readily forfeit. Levinas's proposal, characteristically, is thus both postmodern and traditional, and, to some extent, suffers from the conflicting values it tries to assume. His pluralism reaches a limit when the bounds of community are underscored (between non-Jews and Jews, or between different "types" of Jews),[22] and his invocation of singularity risks being suppressed by his appeal to canonicity as a check on subjectivism. We should note, however, that these are not Levinas's problems alone; they are part and parcel of the complexity of modern Jewish life.

For his part, Buber rejected the mediating role of commentary and, for all his proclamations about the utmost relevance of the Bible, rejected the idea of determining life practices through exegesis. Nevertheless, his individualism has its own protective mechanisms. In particular, Buber appeals to a deeper concern for the *pshat*, the literalness of the text, in order to guard against radical subjectivism. Like Levinas, Buber also wants to avoid the reductionism usually associated with historicism. But most interesting about his attempt to avoid reductionism is his use of historical methods. It is to this that we now turn.

IV

We have suggested that Levinas's postmodern approach paradoxically aligns him with traditional Jewish attitudes to the Bible, especially when it comes to the key role he ascribes to traditional commentaries, the interpretative community, and regulatory normative practices. The great strength of Buber's sophisticated method of reading the Bible and Levinas's interpretive limitations come to the fore when one compares their respective attitudes to critical exegesis and, more generally, to historiography. While both thinkers understood themselves as "postcritical," their attitudes to the critical-historical approach to Scripture attest fundamentally different stances. Buber's, several biblical commentaries combined his dialogical method with the best of contemporary scholarly research. His major works of biblical commentary — *Moses* (1946), *The Prophetic Faith* (1949), and *The Kingship of God* (1967) — represent, in Gershom Scholem's words, a "downright strikingly rich and seemingly ostentatious discussion of scholarly literature."[23] The richness of Buber's commentaries speaks for itself; their seemingly ostentatious character comes, we would like to suggest, from their use of historiography to promote an entirely different end from merely critical or historical insights. For Buber, the historical method was a way of uncovering the phenomenology of biblical religion, which he considered to be supremely relevant to the religious phenomenology of his day. His use of historical methods, therefore, has as its goal the understanding and articulation of the possibility of a living religiosity that is both near to God and true to its modern context. This, to say the least, subverts the original intentions of the authors of the documentary hypothesis. Moreover, while Christian scholars caught on to the fecund possibilities of this critical approach soon after its inception, Buber's use of historiographic methods introduced a new possibility to Jewish scholars, who are even today indebted to this attitudinal shift, if not to his historical claims. Whereas Levinas remained convinced that biblical criticism is "a listening that is incapable of perceiving the divine resonance of the Word" (*OS*, 126), Buber sought to use the critical-historical method to arrive at "the original nucleus" of historical events, and thereby "become acquainted with the meeting between . . . [a] people and a vast historical happening that overwhelmed it."[24]

As we have already seen, for Buber, the Bible is paradigmatic of the dialogical encounter between Creator and Creature in the course of history. He remained firm in his conviction that the Bible does not describe inner spiritual experiences, and ought not be read allegorically. Rather, the Bible records a "verbal trace" of "actual events" (*IW*, 97–98). While far from naively accepting the documentary hypothesis, Buber took on board the critical school's central tenet, namely, that the Bible is the work of many hands over many centuries. Indeed the critical hermeneutic that Buber employs in his readings takes as its point of departure an understanding of the multiple historical layers found in the biblical text. In *Moses*, he spells out what he takes to be the task of the biblical commentator:

> a threefold critical task which, difficult as it may be, nevertheless seems in some degree to be capable of accomplishment. It is necessary to draw a distinction between saga produced near the historical occurrences, the character of which is enthusiastic report, and saga which is further away from the historical event, and which derives from the tendency to complete and round off what is already given. . . . Finally, it is also necessary to penetrate to the historical nucleus of the saga as far as possible . . . we are entitled to hope for the ascertaining of genuine historical outlines . . . the saga element too, in so far as it is characterized by closeness to history, is historically important, being a document of the reception of *what befell in the minds of those whom it befell.* Yet we may go further; what was added later is also of importance for us. Even the men who round off and supplement do what they do not arbitrarily but *under the sustained urge of the primeval impulse.*[25]

As the emphasized phrases indicate, while Buber was somewhat interested in postfactum textual additions, his primary interest lay in uncovering the original "nucleus" of the orally preserved tradition. Thus, in his commentary to the Song of Deborah in *The Prophetic Faith*, he speaks of "a genuine historical song, that is to say a spontaneous poetical outbreak of the heart of man, who having taken part in a mighty historical event is now impelled to master it in rhythmical form, to grasp, to express, to transmit it" (*PF*, 8). And when writing about Miriam's Song at the Sea, he asserts that it "can have been born only of the situation itself."[26] To be sure, Buber was not seeking to get at "what really happened," but he was seeking to get as close as possible to historical, spiritual events — "in their footsteps so to say" — and to "recover much of the manner in which the participating people experienced those events" (*PF*, 14, 16).

In this sense, Buber's phenomenological hermeneutic of biblical religious life differs radically from Levinas's interpretative practices.

Levinas has little or no interest in uncovering, let alone approaching, "the historical event." He neither wants to understand "what really happened," nor for that matter to empathize with those whom the Bible records as having experienced the event. What is crucial for Levinas is not the historical event, but the teachings borne by the receiving community through the work of "inspired interpretation," to borrow James Kugel's felicitous phrase.²⁷ For Levinas, then, historiography is beside the point, for it grasps the text at the profane level of its composition rather than on the plane of inspiration to which it appeals.

> Scripture has a mode of being distinct from that of pure matter available to the grammarian's analysis. A being such that the history preceding writing counts less than the lessons following it; such that inspiration is measured by what it has inspired; such that a break is produced in the synchronic system of signs circulating within immanence so that, under cover of the first signified, other significations begin to make themselves heard, calling for a new Saying, an interpretation: these are some of the traits of an ontology that the scientific thematization of the text cannot but miss. (*OS*, 127)²⁸

For Levinas then, the literal meaning of the text, the historical background of the events portrayed, and the experiences described in the Bible are of secondary significance to the living tradition of commentary that these texts inspire. Like Rosenzweig before him, Levinas also sees a fundamental opposition between the critical-historical gaze and the endeavor to receive the Torah as teaching.²⁹

In many of his Jewish writings, Levinas cautions against the dangers and banalities of critical-historical readings. In his commentary to the first Mishnah in Perek Helek in Sanhedrin (BT 99a) — "Among those who have no share in the world to come, there is . . . he who says . . . the Torah is not from heaven" — Levinas makes the following observation: "Idolatry would be the reduction of these sources to the histories and anecdotes lived by the individuals of the past, instead of sensing in them the prophecy of persons and the genius of a people, and hearing in them the birth of a message for all and the voice of God in its extreme straightness through the appearance of the tortuous paths it takes" (*ITN*, 65). Levinas finds in the Gemarah's discussion of this Mishnah a criticism of "the historian who, in the voice of Moses, hears only an everyday, private discourse, and who is content to reduce the meaning of a biblical verse to its hither side — the circumstances, dictated by events, leading to its coming to mind; content to seek in the logical configurations themselves in which the verse is developed nothing but the trace of I know not what social or ideological condition of non-narrative historical analysis" (*ITN*, 65).

Yet for all his distrust of a critical-historical approach to Scripture, Levinas nevertheless sees one advantage in the reading strategies of the scientific school, namely, the possibility for more sophisticated notions of revelation to be developed in response to the challenge posed by critical exegesis. It is perhaps in the face of this challenge that Levinas himself is inspired throughout many of his Jewish writings to conceive of more subtle understandings of revelation than those modeled on positivist assumptions. Discussing the implausibility of traditional notions of revelation, Levinas contends that "Perhaps it [critical exegesis] signifies no more than the end of a simplistic conception of inspiration, the 'death' of a god lingering in the 'hinterworlds,' and . . . still acting as a force among forces" (*OS*, 126). While maintaining a traditional commitment to the exteriority, heteronomy, unity and transcendence of revelation, Levinas goes on to demystify the notion of revelation so that it accords with modern or postmodern horizons of understanding. What might such a notion of revelation suggest? One way Levinas answers the challenge of critical exegesis is by offering a humanized model of revelation that makes no recourse to positivism. This model proposes a continuum between the inspired human word and the revealed Word.

Establishing a continuum between the human and the divine word leads Levinas, not to reduce revelation to a set of merely historical forces, but to elevate human speech to a prophetic level that pierces history. Historiography and natural sciences do not reduce revelation to immanence but show that human expression, which rises above contingency, is of a revealed order:

Is the human word not the very modality of the manifestation and resonance of the Word? Is not humanity, in its multi-personal plurality, the very locus of interrogation and response, the essential dimension of interpretation, in which the prophetic essence of the Revelation becomes the lived experience of a life? . . . And whatever may be the vicissitudes and divisions and traces of "histories" that the historian's eye discerns in the contributing elements of inspiration, the confluence into a unique, coherent message of the many human meanderings of prophecy and rabbinic discussions — is not that confluence as miraculous, as supernatural, as a common origin of sources? (*BV*, 64)[30]

Levinas is here making two arguments. First, he is suggesting that a human being's expression is continuous with that of the divine word. Second, he is arguing that the confluence of a certain set of such expressions is sufficient to count for a revealed tradition, or, in traditional parlance, can be legitimately ascribed to Sinai. If critical exegesis highlights the different voices in the Bible, this only goes to show, says Levinas, the extraordinary if not divine character of the inspired word and the miraculous, even if contingent, confluence of such prophetic expressions.

By developing a sufficiently sophisticated modern theology, Levinas thus neutralizes the potential threat of biblical criticism. Unfortunately, Levinas never developed this idea of a postcritical Scriptural hermeneutic beyond these cursory and at times elliptical remarks. Nevertheless, these reflections define the task for the postcritical religious thinker, namely, to keep the Torah in heaven while holding fast to the human trajectories of the inspired word.[31] One might even wonder if it was not Martin Buber's unique combination of critical exegesis and dialogical philosophy that first exemplified this work among Jewish critics. In this light, clearly it is Buber who more fully realizes the task of postcritical biblical commentary.

Perhaps more than any other Jewish modern, Levinas powerfully and eloquently articulates some of the dangers confronting the contemporary Bible reader. He reminds us of the need to find a way of receiving the Torah as teaching rather than neutralizing it through the leveling gaze of the historian. "The Torah is transcendent and from heaven by its demands that clash, in the final analysis, with the

pure ontology of the world" (*ITN*, 61). That said, it is equally necessary to caution against what might be taken to be a Levinasian return
to a precritical religious consciousness. "Persons and communities who
are crossing the deserts of Crisis [of modern historiography] unaffected
by it — and who keep the Inheritance whole and intact — reassure
our overly subtle minds. Their credo is closed to history, science and
the infinite resources of Metaphor — but open to the high virtues and
most mysterious secrets of Proximity" (*OS*, 126–27). Are we to understand Levinas to be suggesting that we should turn our back to
history, science, and metaphor in order to preserve what he calls the
"authenticity" of the tradition? How would we then understand the
meaning of the "critical" in Levinas's self-professed "postcritical"
hermeneutic?

Levinas's view can imply a degree of ahistoricism that makes inte-
grating historiography difficult. In this respect at least, his position
seems very far from other postcritical exegetes who, agreeing with
Levinas, assume "that there are dimensions of scriptural meaning which
are disclosed to us only by way of the hermeneutical practices of believing communities and believing traditions of Jews and Christians,"
and yet make the additional assumption, "in the spirit of post-
Spinozistic criticism, that these dimensions may be clarified through
the disciplined practice of philological, historical, and textual/rhetorical
criticism."[32] We agree with this twofold task outlined by Peter Ochs,
and think that the attempt to separate the register of history entirely
from that of revelation risks rendering the Bible irrelevant and dividing religious life and tradition from "everything else we know to be
true," as Emil Fackenheim warns against.[33] If the main virtue of
Levinas's biblical hermeneutic is in circumscribing the limits of historiography, that virtue must be coordinated with the invaluable and
inevitable enterprise of biblical criticism. Indeed, besides developing
a modern theory of revelation that would neutralize the threat of
the historian, it must be clearly stated that historiography offers the
best known way of clarifying the text of the Bible, and detailing its
multifaceted theological revolutions. Works such as Yehezkel Kaufmann's *The Religion of Israel*, Moshe Weinfeld's *Deuteronomy and the*

Deuteronomic School, Moshe Greenberg's *Studies in the Bible and Jewish Thought*, and Israel Knohl's *The Sanctuary of Silence*, to mention but four available in English, demonstrate how biblical criticism can serve the Bible-centered community as much as threaten it.

V

Buber and Levinas, like Rosenzweig before them, propose original hermeneutic strategies for the modern reader to encounter the Bible. Both Buber and Levinas are working with challenges that are pointedly modern. Buber, who formulated his thoughts in the early part of the twentieth century, conceived of a Bible that rises to the challenge of historical criticism, that answers the demands for national identity, and that affirms religious experience in its most immediate and communal expression. Levinas, writing a generation later, proposed a Bible that takes atheism and divine absence even more seriously, that affirms practical over reflective consciousness, and that makes experience dependent on obligation and commentary rather than the other way round. In some sense, the differences between them reflect different understandings of modernity. Though both seek a demythologized phenomenology of religion and a demythologized Bible, they move in divergent directions on account of the distance between each one's rival myth. This distance leads them to develop alternative exegetical strategies through which to view and understand the Bible. We who follow them are situated between their different takes on modernity — we prize history *and* tradition — and thus neither way taken alone is entirely adequate to our situation.

The fact that that we have made no attempt here to reconcile the disparity between Buber and Levinas reflects our conviction that both hold indispensable keys to modern Jewish life, and can readily serve as models for (and no doubt have parallels in) other religious traditions. Buber is correct to insist on the unavoidable encounter with historiography, and in particular with biblical criticism, as he is right in utilizing this field for its contemporary theological and phenomenological relevance. Levinas has responded precisely to this task by developing a postcritical account of revelation, though from this he proposed for the most part an ahistorical position. Levinas's model ought to be developed along the lines that Buber tried to do. What is needed is both a theological matrix for understanding the place of the Bible in a distinctly modern context *and* a way of reading the Bible that tackles rather than suspends its richly nuanced historical density. The work has already been started, though the critics and the theologians tend to keep their distance. Reading Buber and Levinas alerts us to the dangers of maintaining this distance, and promises a way of reading the Bible that does justice to contemporary historical and religious concerns.

TEN

Reading Torah
The Discontinuity of Tradition

Robert Gibbs

One of the most basic agreements between Levinas and Buber is a shared insight that what happens in the action of language, in the performance of signification or in the facing of another, is the origin of meaning. The pragmatic dimension of our relations to others, the way a sign relates to the ones who signify, who "use" the sign, governs the interpretation not only of discourse and of language, but more of thought and, beyond that, of ethics and of social relations. Buber's distinction between the I-It and the I-Thou articulates the way that the address to another differs from any description of the world. Levinas interprets the face as my exposure to the other as my teacher, as the shattering of images in the moment of being addressed. These are central insights into the pragmatic claims of others, claims that engender language, thought and action.

Still more interesting, for both Buber and Levinas this claim about the act of signifying centers on the experience of reading, on the interpretation of texts, and ultimately, on reading the Bible. This biblical orientation is manifest in Buber's works, and is central to the appeal and wide reception of Buber's works. Those works were welcomed not only for their cadence or style, but much more for their ability to call us back to the Bible. For Levinas, the matter is more implicit. His major work, *Totality and Infinity*, had only a smattering of explicit references to the Bible, although the refrain about justice for the stranger, the widow, the orphan, the poor, resounds in the work. In later work, including his various volumes of Jewish writings, Levinas has been much more forthcoming on the role of the Bible in his thought, and more importantly, on the biblical orientation of his views of language and ethics.

While the thinking of both men finds its origin in and orientation from the Bible, how to read the Bible opens a significant space between the two. Indeed, that gap provides a kind of scale for thinking through the way that words work, and the ways that meaning arises. I will focus on one key difference: Buber requires a direct reading of the Bible and Levinas requires a reading through the Talmud and Midrash. That there is a contrast is relatively obvious: both in literary form (Buber's many works on biblical texts and figures, Levinas's many readings of talmudic texts and diverse writings about the rabbinic reading of the Bible), and in their explicit account of what is required in reading the Bible. There is even a polemic from Levinas against Buber's choice.[1] The historical influences that lead to this contrast is in itself interesting and worthy of pursuit: Levinas's Lithuanian enlightenment (*Haskalah*) background and commitment to the rationalist schools of interpretation (*Mitnaggidic*), and Buber's commitment to his sympathetic and even existentialist interpretation of pietistic practices (*Hasidic*). But this essay focuses on philosophical rather than historical differences; modes of reasoning, the temporality of texts and their reading, and the role of discontinuity in a tradition. These are themes I wish to explore.

Both Buber and Levinas seem to require a face-to-face interaction for the orienting moment of ethics and of human existence. Many have accepted Derrida's critical questioning of Levinas's privilege of speaking over writing, and Buber's I-Thou seemed, in principle, to exclude the written text as an ossified moment, firmly located in the I-It. However, several scholars have radically contested and transformed these readings of both thinkers, and showing that both philosophers are, in fact, textual reasoners, who hold that the orienting relations of ethics occur in reading as well as in listening. The work of Steve Kepnes, Dan Avnon, Jill Robbins and Richard Cohen, as well as my own writings on Levinas, transforms our understanding of the place of reading and of texts in the philosophies of Buber and Levinas.[2] Buber focuses our attention on the work of art and the latency of I-thou relations within it; Levinas, on the excess of meaning in the written word, meaning, for Levinas, as more than an author intends the definition of the infinite as a thought that contains more than a thinker can think. In both cases, it is not the text as artifact that is central, but the text as read — the practices of reading are the ways that ethics and meaning arise from texts. And so by looking to their explicit interpretations and explorations of ways of reading, we can determine how texts, and biblical texts especially, orient the thought of the two philosophers. It is not a question of looking for a slogan or watchword ("widow and orphan"), nor of looking for a theme (creation or revelation), but rather of turning to the Bible to learn how we think and how we use language.

Commentary on passages from the works of the two thinkers follows.[3] I have examined the need for commentary at considerable length in my recent book, *Why Ethics? Signs of Responsibilities.* But in one sentence, I would say that the responsibility in reading is to hold open the openings of the text before me, and in this way take responsibilities for the others' written words. In the final section I will have occasion to explore briefly what it means to read these thinkers so closely.

BUBER AND HEARING THE VOICE

Buber enjoined Rosenzweig to produce a new translation of the Bible into German in 1925. Together, although Rosenzweig was utterly bedridden with ALS, they managed to translate almost one third of the Bible before Rosenzweig died in 1929. Buber revised and completed the translation (1963). It is a remarkable translation. Most strikingly, Buber and Rosenzweig chose to produce a German translation of the Hebrew text to be read aloud. They focused on the breathing, the sound, the rhythm and auditory aspects of the Hebrew Bible. The result was a shockingly unfamiliar German translation. This was not a chance effect, but at the very core of what both strove to accomplish. Why?[4]

While they agreed on method, Buber had a somewhat different interpretation of the problem and its solution than Rosenzweig. For Buber, the crisis for modern people is many layered because the Bible does not speak to them. The Bible has become too familiar, but beneath there is a deeper crisis — for the modern person looks for and fails to find a religious teaching in the Bible. The modern interpretation of religion, according to Buber, is voluntaristic, indeed, self-centered. We include religion as one sphere of activity and of meaning, and then go looking in the Bible for instruction, or at least, for something meaningful, and in the process we do not doubt our own authority to make from disparate spheres our selves. Thus we fail to understand what religion, or better, relation to God should be, and living under that illusion, we *also* overlook the Bible as a source for that misconceived religion. Thus, even were we to think the Bible fascinating and rich, we would still be looking to it only for doctrine, or for experiences, as a resource for developing ourselves. But the Bible is neither a resource for doctrine nor a religious book.

The Bible has a much greater destiny for us — and to turn toward it is to be turned to a new mode of relationship, to a new teaching, to a new way to become a self, to a new kind of thinking and a new kind of language. Consider this opening of a memorial essay by Buber in honor of Rosenzweig:

> 1.a) The special duty for a renewing transmission of Scripture, which woke in the present and led to our undertaking, resulted from the discovery that the times had largely transformed Scripture into a palimpsest. The original Scriptural traits, the original meanings and words, had been overlaid by a ready conceptuality, of partly theological, partly literary descent. What people today ordinarily read when they open "the Book" is so unlike the attentive speaking that is registered there, that we might reasonably prefer a shoulder-shrugging rejection of it, on the part of those who "just don't know what to do with it" to such a sham reception of the text.[5]

Like a paleographer, Buber sets his task as unpeeling the overlay and rediscovering the original text, below the palimpsest. Both literary and theological interpretations have rendered the text altogether too familiar — we know what it says because we have been educated theologically.

But beyond unfamiliarity, there is a deeper issue — that the text speaks and speaks to me. The passage continues:

> 1.b) This applies, moreover, not only to reading in translation but also to reading in the original; the Hebrew sounds themselves have lost their immediacy for a reader who is no longer a listener; they are suffused by a voiceless, theologically and literarily determined rhetoric, and are compelled by that rhetoric to speak not the spirit that attained its voice in them but a compromise among the spiritualities of two thousand years. The Hebrew Bible itself is read as a translation — as a bad translation, as a translation into a smoothed-over conceptual language, in what is apparently well known but in reality is only commonplace.

The crisis, then, is not the language itself, but its being covered over by layers of interpretation. Even Hebrew words will not sound, will not call to a listener, because of the tradition of reading. Buber does not spare the theological tradition here, but thinks that it, too, has silenced the original voice of Hebrew. Perhaps this is the key insight from an essay that seeks to explain why and how he and Rosenzweig translated the Bible — even in Hebrew the Bible is hidden in a "translation" ("a bad translation"); the letters on the page are not enough, nor is the trope in the synagogue. The problem, familiar to us from hermeneutic theory, is the loss of voice, where what is commonplace and obvious has substituted for the true call of the voice in the text. The implication is that even for a Hebrew reading audience, the Bible needs a new translation, a new awakening. Hence for Buber, the crisis is for all modern people and is not about the limited access to Hebrew language, but the relation that is no longer sought, in the Bible or elsewhere.

> 1.c) Scripture asks for a reverent intimacy with its meaning and its sensory concreteness; but that has been replaced by a mix of uncomprehending respect and unaware familiarity. This pseudo-Bible is the object to the shoulder-shrugging dismissal noted above; and its

relation to the real Bible resembles the relation of the "murdered" "God" of our time — that is the commonplace vague concept of God — to the actual God.

It is the concreteness (the *Sinnlichkeit*) that has been compromised. For both Levinas and Buber, the meeting with another person has a sensory specificity, a relation to a specific other in nearness that formal or abstract relations betray. Meaning arises in a concrete, "existential," relation to another person. But the Bible also calls us to a kind of intimacy, of nearness, in which meaning arises in the concreteness of the language — especially in the breathing and sounding of the words. Hebrew excels in its concreteness: language is called *tongue*, presence before another is *to the other's face*, and so Buber named the I-you relation, for instance, with the personal pronouns — as though thought can best achieve its meaning by remaining near to concrete language and to the speakers and listeners.[6] For Buber, the Bible depends on just that sort of engagement with language for its meaning. The pseudo-Bible is just another conceptual (or emotional) construct, and is perhaps something at which one should properly merely shrug one's shoulders. Not a yoke or relationship, but rather something that does not sit upon one, that in no way invests one in responsibility — the already understood Bible does not function as Bible at all. Most significantly for Buber, the pseudo-Bible is like our commonplace concept of God — the one that we have murdered and must learn to live without. But the real Bible is then like the actual God (indispensable, and deeply unfamiliar).

Buber claims that a new translation will allow us to hear something new from the Bible, and that to hear anew is also to disrupt our commonplaces. The claim for the renewed Bible is not that it will be a book with better concepts, but rather that it will displace our familiar and vague expectations of religion. More, it will offer us a new access to meaning, a meaning that is rich in its relation to the concrete relation of speaking with others. How our own specificity, our own time, relates to this commonplace Bible, indeed, the place of history in interpreting not only the Bible and its message, but, meaning and signification in general will be considered below.

Throughout Buber's work translating and interpreting the Bible, his constant concern is to negotiate with and distinguish himself from the biblical historians, the academic "critical" and "scientific" interpreters of the history of both the biblical text and people of biblical times. When Buber begins to speak about the renewal of biblical voices, of displacing the commonplaces, we might naturally think that his goal is to recover the original context and meaning of biblical texts — a historian's interest in the past as past. Alternatively, when this renewal is portrayed theologically, we might think that he is trying to recover biblical religion, in line with some fundamentalists who seek to return us to the Temple cult and the religion of priests and prophets (and perhaps even kings). But Buber is keenly aware of his own location and ours — a location in a modern era where new challenges, distinct from those of biblical times, beset us. The historical gap is one of the most significant features of the new translation, and it intends to alter the present through an encounter with the past text.

One of the most anthologized and cited texts from this period is Buber's "People Today and the Jewish Bible," and in the full version, that essay ends with a stirring coda:

> 2.a) It is not a matter of a "return to the Bible." It is a matter of the resumption of a genuinely biblical, unified life with our whole time-enmeshed being, with the whole weight of our belated many-sidedness weighing on our souls, and with the incomprehensible material of this historical hour at present without reduction. It is a matter of holding our own responsibly and dialogically in our current situations, in an openness to belief that is true to the Bible.[7]

It is not the original reader that we emulate or aspire to become, but ourselves as new readers, ourselves as called to a new way of living biblically. Academic biblical scholars are looking for the past, a past that does not speak to us. For them, as Rosenzweig commented, the Bible is filled with things — dead things. But the Bible as Word speaks to today.

Interestingly, Buber also does not support a "return to the Bible" — as though what we will hear is merely the same old message, as though what was said at that time is not a matter of temporality and history at all, but purer, basic, eternal biblical truths. For Buber this is neither possible nor desirable. Instead, the needs of the hour, the specific sense of "today" are paramount, and the speech of the Bible is precisely an address to us today. The historical gap is met by staying where we are, facing our own situation, our own time, but also reaching back to the Bible, to its message — which is not a doctrine for Buber, but that which offers instruction on unifying our lives, opening ourselves to the world, responding to our situation. It can teach us how, or perhaps why much more than it can teach us what. The essay concludes:

> 2.b) Do we mean a book? We mean the voice. Do we mean that people should learn to read it? We mean that people should learn to hear it. There is no other going back but the turning around that turns us about our own axis until we reach, not an earlier stretch of our path, but the path on which we can hear the voice! We want to go straight through to the spokenness, to the becoming spoken, of the word.

The text is not something to read, to learn. This scripture speaks, calls, singles us out and challenges us now. Buber and Rosenzweig translated the Bible with attention to the breathing and the speaking of the text. They set the page visually in a way that prompts the reader to hear the text, to read it out loud. Reading as calling, as out loud, *Kriat Torah* — the more basic meaning of the Hebrew word for reading. But the call calls us to our own stretch of path, to our day and not to the distant past. The primacy of hearing, of paying attention, of finding oneself called — these are the cornerstones of Buber's interpretation of language and of meaning. And the text, through Buber's renewing translation, can get to the spokenness of the word. It opposes the writtenness, or perhaps the notion of the written as static, as contained by the eye grasped by the hand and by the mind. The call accentuates the passivity, and the words are both "literally" heard, but more important they are becoming spoken — we learn how to read in order to hear, to feel the call bear upon us as a yoke upon our shoulders that we cannot simply shrug off with indifference. The text does not contain a doctrine but is like a script for performance, and the performing is not merely intoning the words but is an attending, awakening our need to respond. Whether Buber and Rosenzweig succeeded, or perhaps how well they succeeded, is a difficult and important question, but for our purposes, the interpretation of both the biblical text as a script and the call it makes to us today are key insights.

LEVINAS AND READING THROUGH THE RABBIS

Levinas's interpretations of the Bible occur in diverse contexts. The following passage about the task of translation comes from a talmudic reading ("The Pact" from *Beyond the Verse*) and addresses the question of how we might think biblically. Here again, is an emblematic view of the task of Jewish thinking.

> 3.a) This passage from the Hebrew to the universality that I call Greek is thus very remarkable. It is the formula *ba'er hetev*, "very distinctly," recommending the clarity and the distinctness of Scripture, that sets to signifying complete translatability. The freeing and universalizing, therefore must be continued.[8]

Levinas is commenting on a text from the talmudic tractate *Sotah*, which itself describes a series of covenantal meetings at which the Jewish people accept the Torah and its rewards and punishments. The talmudic text is a commentary on the Mishnah, a text edited around 200 CE, and it includes the description that after one such covenantal agreement, "They wrote thereon all the words of the Torah in seventy languages, as it is written "very distinctly" [*ba'er hetev*]" (Sotah 6:5). That *very distinctly* refers to a passage in Deuteronomy, where this particular event has just been described in a set of commandments: "and you shall write on the stones all the words of this Torah very distinctly" (Deut. 27:8).

Levinas is interpreting a shift from biblical to rabbinic text (a shift marking a gap of at least 700 years), from a prescription in the imperative to a recounting in the past tense. Aside from the tense and the loss of the demonstrative pronoun (*this* Torah), the great change is the description of writing it in 70 languages ("tongues"). Levinas, writing 1,800 years later, collapses this translation into all the languages of the world (for that is what 70 tongues represent to the rabbis), into one main translation project, into Greek. Scripture's clarity and concreteness is what makes it translatable, even into the universalizing and more abstract language of philosophy, into a discourse for everyone. The rabbis' opening up of the biblical text to a range of discourses in all the world's language is transformed by Levinas into an emblem of a philosophical task: the translation and freeing of the biblical text into the wider world, into an intellectual world that disavows Judaism.

> 3.b) We have not yet finished translating the Bible. The Septuagint is incomplete. More, we have not finished translating the Talmud. We have barely begun. And for the Talmud, we must say that the task is delicate. A heritage that until now has been reserved for oral teaching passes, perhaps too quickly, into foreign languages and loses in the new forms its unusual bearing.

With Rosenzweig and Buber, Levinas holds we have not finished translating the Bible. It is not merely a question of a new French or English version, but rather of bringing the voice of the Bible into our culture, of making it audible and so opening philosophy to the biblical voice and message. Hence the Greek translation of the Hebrew Bible, the Septuagint, is incomplete — not the text itself but the task of using the Bible to transform philosophical discourse. And we have barely begun translating the Talmud. Levinas does not mean the German and the various English translations, but rather that we have not shown philosophy how to think talmudically. Just as Rosenzweig and Buber were aware of the risks in translating the Bible, Levinas is concerned about this talmudic project. The problem is that the teaching tradition, where vocality and the dynamics of interaction are central, can yield philosophemes, concepts, and principles in translation and lose its distinctive kind of concreteness.

Nonetheless, much of Levinas's work is in translating, both, in his yearly talmudic readings and more generally in his transformation of philosophy with talmudic thinking. If Buber is committed to translating the Bible and its message, then Levinas is committed to a translation of the Talmud. This rich contrast, opens a subtle and complex relation between the two philosophers.

The question is how to move from the Bible to the present. For Levinas, the traditions of Jewish readings, centering on the rabbis, is the key. Buber's "reader of today" reads the text directly, and experiences an ancient voice calling now. The existential reading of the Bible addresses us, and shows us that we are called, but it also bypasses the specifically Jewish route through the sages' readings. In 1957, when speaking before the very first Colloquium of French Speaking Jewish Intellectuals, Levinas negotiated the relation of history and of the today somewhat differently.

> 4.a) I would add a word for the *Midrash*. Revelation is not only a dicta-
> tion from God at a given moment. It may be a revelation through time
> and, if one admits that, the *Midrash* is indispensable. It consists of go-
> ing toward the ancient texts in the light of the secular Jewish experi-
> ence. We go to the *Midrash* because we think that Jewish experience is
> an authentic experience. Judaism has always affirmed the existence of
> an oral law. The text must be able to provide assistance to the plastic
> image that it becomes, and that is unable, as Plato said, to provide this
> assistance to itself. It requires the living interpretation of the *Midrash*.[9]

Levinas recognizes that revelation continues into today, and indeed, continues throughout time. It is not the production of the biblical text, nor is it limited to a one-time-only event at Sinai. The possibility for revelation to continue is remarkable, but unlike Buber, Levinas holds that the Midrash is indispensable. The biblical text depends on a living oral law, an ongoing tradition of hearing, the voice of another person and the voice coming from reading the text. Levinas recognizes that Jewish experience is precisely a record of hearing the call from the Bible. The interaction that Buber aims for in his translation is a contemporary version of the Midrash, and the Midrash is an ongoing record of this engagement, this listening. Just as Buber and Rosenzweig claimed that the Bible was the record of encounters, Levinas now claims that the Midrash is the enlivening, the record of listening to those recorded encounters, which are then encounters again.

> 4.b) To read, through the Midrash, is not at all to falsify. On the con-
> trary it is to read from today, but this today exists only if one has passed

through history and as a function of all that that history has already wished to find there.

Levinas, then, defends the Midrash. Unlike the theological common-places of Buber's writings, it is not a falsification, not a covering that separates us and prevents us hearing the Bible. Of course, the Bible must be read from today. Here Levinas, consciously or not, echoes Buber. Levinas is no antiquarian, trying to find out how to read the Bible from its own historical context. But what is today? Today depends on passing through a history, a history of reading. Today is not a discrete moment with no history. Rather, today is constituted by history. And the today of reading or listening includes past listenings. History, despite what one might have thought, is important for Levinas when we understand history to be the Midrash, that is the traditions of readings, of hearing the call of revelation, the call from the other. Jewish experience is the hearings, the interpretations of Scripture, without which we cannot understand the Bible.

The conflict with Buber on this matter comes into focus specifically in several essays and interviews. In the essay "Martin Buber's Thought and Contemporary Judaism," Levinas presents Buber's biblical herme-neutics and largely praises Buber's work at biblical translation. But he also contests Buber's choice of listening directly, of omitting or simply jumping over the rabbinic interpretation of Scripture.

> 5.a) Buber reverts to the Hebrew text without recourse to the rabbinic literature that represents precisely the way that this text had been read through creative Jewish history. The Talmudic or rabbinic method of reading — when I say "rabbinic" I am always thinking of the rabbis of the Talmud — could be defined (I think that this will perhaps be new to a part of the public that I find here) by a permanent interiorization of the letter, without achieving that interiorization by abstraction; an attempt that consists, at once of interiorizing and preserving completely the contents of Scripture in drawing teaching from its contradictions themselves.[10]

In marking what for Levinas is Buber's abandonment of Jewish history, Levinas offers us a rich and difficult definition of rabbinic reading. The minimal condition is to preserve all of the contents of the text, and that means holding onto the letter of the text. The specificity of the words, the juxtapositions, and so forth — that for which Buber and Rosenzweig created the specific acoustic texture of Scripture — are not to be compromised. But that "literal-mindedness" is then linked to an interiorization, and the production of concepts. Not by philosophical abstraction, but by some other paths of thought, the rabbinic interpretation yields a learning, a teaching that is received for each person. This is what Kierkegaard called reduplication, and what Buber calls hearing the voice. The sense of the inner here is linked precisely to the external, to the letters, to the contents of the text, and yet it also indicates conscious reception. This particular linkage of letter and message is in close harmony with what Buber claimed to attempt, but it also is a useful image for the rhetoric of both thinkers' philosophical reflections. The challenge in thinking about the face or nearness is that we require both concrete specificity and interiorized (philosophical?) reception. Whatever relation this might have to other thinkers (Levinas mentions Heidegger in this context; Herder, Vico, and J. L. Austin are also worth consideration), the striking claim is that this particular linking is the characteristic of rabbinic interpretation.[11]

> 5.b) The ritual law itself will reveal its interior meaning. It is a method that ultimately has a view of Judaism more dramatic than what the West assumes, but which is proven by the centuries of spiritual life and hangs less on the particular religious experience that Buber contributes. It is undeniable that Buber reads the Bible as if he alone has the entire Holy spirit. That particular experience of each is without a doubt required by the history of faith, but tradition shall not fade away before it. It is the union of that personal experience and that tradition that permits the Hebrew Bible to preserve its full meaning.

Levinas's text continues by claiming that even details about animal sacrifice and mixtures in grains and fabrics can provide interior meaning. Indeed, the Midrashic collection that comments on Leviticus (a text saturated with ritual laws) is one of the great documents of Jewish theology (*Leviticus Rabbah*). That the tradition is proven is merely an empirical claim. What distinguishes the Jewish tradition here, for Levinas, is a kind of *drama*. The West assumes, on the contrary, that

Judaism is basically static, that biblical religion continues in more or less the same manner — that tradition is a repetition of an established original insight. It can then come as a shock to find out that living Jews — in Europe, North America, or Israel — do not follow either the practices or accept the theological vision articulated in the Bible. That new interiorization that the rabbis provided did not abandon the Hebrew text but did renew it, often with dramatic reversals.

More importantly here is a challenge to Buber's notion of experience, an experience that calls to each individually, directly from the Bible. In a rather irascible comment, Levinas asserts that Buber reads as if the Holy Spirit rested on him alone. The insult is meant to imply that Buber regards his reading as gifted, as somehow indebted to a revelatory gift of spirit, and that because he is translating and reading the whole Scripture, then he must be able to hear each verse. The irony of this insult is that Buber heard it with Rosenzweig. His is a dialogical revelation, from the text to two readers reading for each other and with each other. Even more importantly, Buber claims that today's reader is called upon to find the voice in each verse, to make it all come alive. Even Levinas cannot contest that and admits that faith requires an interiorization that is a revelation to particular readers in their own times. What Buber lacks, says Levinas, is the tradition of past readers, who also were able to renew specific parts. Thus for the verses that don't seem to call us, we can rely on a tradition of different readings, of moments when other Jewish readers found what was alive in the text, and calling them. By relying on their listening, we can renew not only what speaks to time but learn to renew what seems not to speak to us at all.

LEVINAS AND DISCONTINUITY IN TRADITION

Thus both Buber and Levinas are interested in the today, in our own reading and listening. But Levinas's today includes a relation to the history of interpretation. The Jewish tradition at first glance seems only a treasure trove of earlier readings, of testimonies to hearing the call of the biblical text. History is unlike the image of a continuous stream, a repetition of repetitions of the biblical message, the sort of accretions that with Buber we might well jump over — for sameness would rule in this epoch of reading. If the context of the readers changes, but the message remains the same — then why not go back to the original message?

The answer lies first in recognizing that a history of interpretations (or at least for the Jewish tradition, but I would hazard for others as well) is marked by discontinuities, not simply by breaks that have somehow to be gotten over. On the contrary, the discontinuities are positive. They allow the stabilized letters to produce new and different interiorizations (readings). To mark that discontinuity requires that later stages criticize and confront what is inadequate in the earlier stages. With radical change, we are allowed, even called, to return to the earlier texts, but through the later ones. Sometimes we applaud the breaks, sometimes we wonder if still something more lies back in the earlier strata. Levinas's notion of the drama of Jewish tradition hinted at this insight. Secondly, because the canon holds diverse materials and even mismatched repetitions, it is not hard to discover contradictions in the text (consider the differences in the two versions of the Ten Commandments or the two creation narratives). Here the obligation to interpret is obvious, and in Levinas's account, rabbinic interpretation acknowledges the contradictions, even as it creatively finds ways of resolving what the text left unsolved.

However, there is a still richer sense of the discontinuity, centering on offensive texts. Very early on in the sequence of Colloquia of French Speaking Jewish Intellectuals, Levinas offered an interpretation of Rosenzweig ("Between Two Worlds"), and in the original volume from the conference there is a heated debate following the talk. Many of those intellectuals were shocked that Levinas seemed to defend Rosenzweig's interpretation of Judaism as living beyond politics and outside of history. Others were angry that the Jews were restricted to religious Jews, and that Judaism seemed to dominate all other kinds of Jewish thought and practice. Robert Misrahi attacked both, accusing Rosenzweig of racism and contesting the religious concept of being Jewish.

Levinas's response is itself angry and sharp:

> 6.a) But I would also like to say a couple of words about the references
> of Mr. Robert Misrahi to the biblical texts. That has a bearing that
> surpasses our particular problem. Judaism only reads the Bible through
> the Talmud. The Talmud, that is the fact of thinking the Bible not by
> bits and pieces, but globally. Each page of the Talmud thinks all of the
> Bible at once.[12]

Misrahi had cited some general sense that in Genesis [*sic*] there are
passages where God makes a contract with the Jewish people about
how they are to occupy a country, following God's commandments.
Before Levinas discusses that text, he emphasizes that Judaism reads
only through the Talmud and that talmudic reading offers a global
view of the biblical message: that is, it offers a wider access and application of biblical commandments and thought. Like the translation
into all the languages of the world, the talmudic interpretation dis-
plays the widest reach of biblical thought. Levinas continues:

> 6.b) You pulled out an isolated text that scandalizes you; the Bible
> doesn't know love since it presents it as a contract, since it asks for it
> under a threat. Believe me, the text that you cite is not unique and is
> not the most scandalous. One could find worse, I assure you.

He summarizes Misrahi's own summary claim: the relation of God
and the Jews is not love because it depends on a threat from God.
Levinas points out that this "text" is isolated — not bound up with all
the other texts of the Bible. Levinas does not defend the Bible or this
"text." On the contrary, he accepts that it offends us (and indeed may
well have offended other Jews, in the past). There are, Levinas promises, much worse texts in the Bible. The Bible is not a nice book (not
a book for children — if we have limited children's books to books
where the message is always nice and safe). The Bible, as Buber wrote,
is a book whose commonplace reading obscures its own character,
and part of that character is offensive texts.

At this point, Misrahi interjects:

> 6c) I said contract, but I thought blackmail.

He actually did not mean merely to say that a contract is not love, but
rather that blackmail ("if you don't conquer and occupy the way I

require, I will harm you") is the true tenor of the biblical text. Levinas's comment about having even worse texts to offer has allowed Misrahi a chance to strengthen his objection. But Levinas then continues and explains the place of these scandalous texts:

> 6.d) We Jews, we refuse a reading of the texts separated from their spirit or having lost their precision in translation. Through the Talmud we would grasp this spirit beyond the letter. We maintain that the primary evidence is that the Torah is a law of absolute goodness and justice. As a result, the particular texts must be treated in the light of what is essential and not the inverse.

Here Levinas has still sharper hesitations about translation (a trope that he comes to use more in the later 1960s), because the concreteness that Buber had praised provides limited insight. Levinas's presupposition is that the overarching message of the Torah is good and just — and thus allows us to criticize texts which fall short. We do not read the Bible from the worst and most offensive texts, but recognize the inadequacy of those texts from the central principles of goodness and justice. The prophets criticize the community and especially the rulers, for instance, and we learn from them the nature of critique and the extra-ordinary demands of justice. This is not a blank check of endorsement but rather an interpretative position that recognizes that the scandalous texts are juxtaposed with ones that proclaim a radical goodness. We hear the voice that disgusts us in the context of the voice that calls us to justice.

> 6.e) To interpret three lines of Plato with rigour, you study Greek for ten years, and to discuss the Bible thirty minutes is enough for you. That is not enough. Excuse me. I know that it is not good taste to return to the classics; but truly, this time, one cannot do otherwise.

Levinas is not finished, however. He scolds Misrahi. Any fool can find a "bad" passage of the Bible, but to read, to listen to the biblical voices, requires attention and study. Why do intellectuals, the people of today, neglect the serious study of the Bible, which for Levinas, of course, also means the Talmud?

6.f) The Jew is the one who does not touch the Bible directly, but through the tradition from the outset, not from piety, but from necessity. It is the tradition that gives meanings to those obscure, closed texts, which are more scandalous sometimes than you think, and the tradition that restores order.

Finally, Levinas returns to the obscure and the scandalous texts, as well as those that are closed — the ones that don't call to us today. The respect we have for the tradition is not because we are pious, but because the biblical text is both confusing and dangerous. In rabbinic parlance, to touch the Torah is to make one's hands impure. Not touching the Bible directly means not reading it, without the intermediary of rabbinic interpretation. The rabbis did not abandon the intransigent texts in the Bible. They did not pretend they were pretty and nice, but they did struggle with them, in their obscurity, contradictoriness, and even offensiveness. One has only to read narratives of violence, commands of conquest and genocide, technical legal matters regarding infidelity, and so on, to find those horrifying texts. But Levinas recognizes that the sages were also horrified, also aware of the scandal. They accentuate certain aspects of justice, of goodness, and of the messianic future. They criticize by interpreting and renew both the best and the worst by confronting what is offensive. This discontinuity between the sages and the biblical text energizes the Jewish tradition, and Levinas criticizes Buber in specific for failing to confront and engage the text as the Sages did.[13] Rabbinic reading confronts and responds to texts that don't fit, texts to which we object. Misrahi thinks that one bad text is reason to abandon the Bible, or, at least, that we should skip over that text. Levinas counters that confronting that text is our precise task in learning how to read and respond.

The tradition, then, opens up chasms and reversals — and preserves the biblical message. The rabbinic texts retain both high and low points via the literal text, but accentuate their own role in interpreting and in finding the text's call to them. And so on with later strata — each one revalues the previous strata, discovering new moments of revelation and new scandals. Levinas's reading also confronts not only the rabbinic texts that fit his claims, but also the ones that scandalize him. Because of the loyalty to the text and to the renewal of the message, the tradition has proven itself through Jewish history. By reading the rabbis, we learn not only what the Bible meant then, but we learn how to renew and confront the text for today.

BUBER AND THE HISTORY OF RELIGION

While Levinas argues that our thinking is made complex precisely by the discontinuities the tradition requires of us, Buber offers a parallel and complex interpretation of the biblical text, as one that bears within it the revaluing of earlier texts and practices. In a series of large works emerging out of the translation project, Buber offered historical reinterpretations of the Bible, focusing on the emergence of the messianic dimension of Judaism. Levinas insisted on reading the Bible through the rabbis, but ignored the growing and challenging historical scholarship on the rabbis and their work. Buber, on the other hand, engaged in close struggle and negotiation with the historians of the Bible. His struggle was not to establish an historical account of the events that the Bible narrates (e.g., Did Moses live?), nor a historical account of the literary sources with which the Bible is constructed (the relation of the Elohist [E] to the Priestly [P] texts). To the former, Buber responds with a theory of the saga. A saga originates in events, but those events in their sheer historicity are inaccessible. The text points to an event, but does not reach all the way to that event. He argues that the attempt to date and decompose the biblical text into literary sources, will not give us enough insight either into the religious development of the biblical religion, or, into the role of the redactor (whom Buber and Rosenzweig agreed to call *R*, with the delightful pun that that is also *rabbenu*, our teacher).

Instead, for Buber the historical task is in the history of religion, which is the sequence (even development) of religious practices and concepts.

> 7.a) It is possible to render a content that is spiritually historical and especially a history of religion's content. Here it is not a matter of the authenticity of an external event. We merely inquire whether in the

period under discussion the religious act or position, the religious relation under discussion, was extant. This question can only be decided by
the inner media of history of religion. What here we have to compare
are the earlier or later stages of religious development; we have to make
clear whether it is possible to understand the narrative historically.[14]

The task in reading the Bible, then, is not to determine the authenticity of the external event but the reality of the religious relation. Literary source analysis does not dig deeply enough into the relations to
which the text bears witness. A reading that is willing to listen to different kinds of relations, to find in each a testimony and not merely a
political agenda, a testimony to the interactive dynamic — that reading will also be able to renew the texts today. It is not enough to say
that the Bible is a simple unity to which we must attune ourselves.
Rather the Bible itself has different strata, and those strata reverse and
confront each other. The listening we must do is to hear the diversity
of the message, and, in Buber's argument, hear to understand a narrative of these strata of religious relations.

> 7.b) The intuitively scientific method, that is the method that seeks
> after the witness of a founding *concreteness* at the basis of an evidence,
> here nears it by methods advancing to the embodied fact. Obviously,
> by this we do not experience the course of an historic occurrence, but
> we do experience that in a definite age, in a definite tribe or people, one
> of our insights in the strong sense of a unique relationship of a believer
> to that in which he believes, actually appeared as unique to that desig-
> nated stage, a relationship which incarnates itself in an actual event
> [*Ereignis*], which continues actually to operate.

Once more we see an insistence on concreteness. Closely parallel to
Levinas's claims about rabbinic reading, Buber's reading attends to
the embodied facts, to a testimony that rests in a concreteness. But
that concreteness is not the external objective reality, it is rather the
event of a lived relationship. Whatever did happen to the biblical characters, we can see in the text the witness of those for whom those
characters were evidence of certain kinds of relations with God. The
biblical texts reveal that specific communities understood the narrated
events as significant for them, as constituting real relations for the
narrating community. The past event retains its actuality in the testi-

mony that offers a renewal of these relations. In history of religions, we locate the moment of the testimony of relation — which is not identical to the moment of the literary source, and certainly not that of the narrated events.

Buber, however, understands the biblical text to bear witness to failed relations as much as to achieved ones. Indeed, the discontinuity that characterizes the different strata of biblical texts is the record of relations that fell apart, and the displacement from one strata to the next is of great moment for Buber. Thus shifting from a history of external events (conquests and exiles) and even from one of literary sources (a theo-political history of sorts), Buber arrives at a history of religion's history — but it is not a continuous or triumphal history. Rather, it is quite clearly the history of failure. In a programmatic essay on biblical leadership from 1933, Buber defines the history he finds in the Bible.

> 8) For this is what the Bible understands as history: a dialogue in which [humanity] is addressed and refuses [*versagt*] and in refusing always rises up again and tries to answer; the history of God's disappointments, but a history of disappointments, which is a way, so that the way, the way of the people, the way of human beings, yes the way of God, His way through humanity leads from disappointment to disappointment, beyond all of them. I say there are five basic forms of these successive stages of this dialogue.[15]

In the context of dialogue, we have utter breakdown. God calls, addresses human leaders, and they do not respond. The basic terms of call and hearing are confronted by this *Versagen*, this failure that is a kind of un-saying, refusal to join the conversation. Each of these different modes of relation (of different strata of relations of leadership) collapses as a disappointment. So when we attend, when we hear the voice that calls in the biblical text, it also comes with its disappointment, its failed relation. The idea of a way here is a way that runs through the unanswered calls, and to listen to the voice, the renewal of the text, is precisely a confrontation with the strata of failures.

The history we can tell, then, is of the different testimonies, and how they themselves (whatever the events narrated portend, whatever the circumstances in which the literary source was formed) stratify into distinguishable kinds of disappointed theological relations. Historiography, in this history of religions mode, is a way through the failed relations, calling us to not fail to respond, to not refuse in our time. What is required is a much more careful and engaged kind of historiography than anything we find in Levinas. Buber recognizes the discontinuities in the traditions that were held together in the biblical canon. But he thinks that we today can learn to hear the call better by distinguishing those strata and changes.

Thus while Buber does abandon the rabbinic readings, and constitutes the today in marked discontinuity from the last two thousand years of Jewish history, he explores the discontinuities that continue through the rabbinic period. When he engages the hundreds of years of biblical texts, he proves himself a much more engaged and serious historian than Levinas, with as profound a task as Levinas can muster: to renew the biblical message for today, by exploring its testimony to failures and its discontinuity, its change and self-conscious reinterpretation in the formation of the biblical text. He claimed that much of what we call Midrash can already be found in the Bible.

READING AMONG THE PHILOSOPHERS

If one theme is clear, it is the one with which we began, that listening to the voice of the Torah is fundamentally a different kind of relationship than we normally expect from the Bible or indeed from any text. Moreover, the message, the call we receive, is linked to the concreteness of the text with its specific narrated events. This centrality of concreteness in thinking and in ethics arises for both Levinas and Buber in relation to the Bible. However, both in the biblical text and in the subsequent Jewish tradition, there have been strata of readings, testimonies of hearing the call, and those diverse testimonies also have their own concreteness. Thus our today, in which we need to renew these texts to hear the voice, arises in relation to these sequences leading up to and beyond the biblical canon. The philosophers' call to unify those sequences — whether through Buber's mantra-like insistence on the unity of the Bible or Levinas's emphasis on a history of

Jewish experience — signifies much about the plurality, self-criticism and even reversals that punctuate the bodies of texts. The contradictions, the refusals, and even the offense of some of the texts must be faced, not abolished, leading to better and stronger texts. In the realm of pure ideas, all contradiction is overcome and abandoned, but in the ethics of relations, the concreteness of others constitutes plurality that is not overcome.

While Buber understood the space of a call *before* God, and Levinas understood space as a relation to God *through* the Talmud, we have taken our stand *among* the philosophers. We have learned to think and to listen for the voice of the call among the thought of others, others who themselves have hearkened and attended by rereading Jewish sources. In this respect we are very close to the work of the Swiss Jewish thinker, Hermann Levin Goldschmidt. Goldschmidt was a follower of Hermann Cohen, Buber and Rosenzweig, and he often wrote about biblical texts in ways that resemble Buber's. But regularly in his writings Goldschmidt chose to gain access to biblical sources not through the rabbis, but through the philosophers and other Jewish thinkers who drew their thought from the Jewish sources.[16] Through these readings, he found a philosophical message in the Jewish sources — in ways similar to Levinas's reading of the translation into seventy languages. His situation is not as a metathinker, reflecting upon their work from above, but rather someone who takes his stand *among* them. They are the place from which he thinks the messianic future.

I do not want to blunt the criticism that Levinas made of Buber, for I, too, believe that it is time for a translation of the Talmud. In my own work, especially in *Why Ethics? Signs of Responsibilities*, I create a new kind of text, a talmudic text, in which I interpret passages from diverse philosophers. If Levinas calls us to think talmudically as philosophers, and to understand that our way to the Bible is through the strata of Jewish tradition, then Buber shows us the patience and the rigor of the serious historical project examining the religious relations that produced the Bible. But even here, in this short essay, we can see that the discontinuity between Buber and Levinas itself is a source, a kind of testimony to the task of renewing thought, to renewing reading and ethics. Working closely with the writings of both philosophers has not only defined their opposition more clearly but helps us grasp what our relation to past tradition can and should be. Reading among philosophers can itself be a path that maintains the concreteness of the texts and teaches us to listen anew to the call.

ELEVEN

Beyond the "Eclipse of God"

The *Shoah* in the Jewish Thought of Buber and Levinas

Tamra Wright

INTRODUCTION: POST-HOLOCAUST JEWISH THOUGHT

Post-Holocaust Jewish thought, perhaps surprisingly, is generally seen as a phenomenon that begins not in the 1940s or 1950s, but in the 1960s.[1] The great Jewish theologians of the earlier part of the twentieth century, including the Orthodox thinker Joseph Soloveitchik, the conservative theologian Abraham Joshua Heschel, the founder of the Reconstructionist movement, Mordecai Kaplan, and Martin Buber, all made only "haphazard and oblique reference to the Holocaust immediately after the war," according to Zachary Braiterman (*GAA*, 6–7). Certainly nothing was published in English in the 1950s and early 1960s that is comparable to the book-length studies of post-Holocaust Jewish theology published by such figures as Emil Fackenheim, Eliezer Berkovits and Richard Rubenstein.

Why did post-Holocaust theology emerge only a full two decades after the end of the war? Psychologists have focused on two explanations of this phenomenon: firstly, that the experience was still too raw for discussion, and secondly, that the emphasis after the war was on rebuilding, both in the newly founded State of Israel and in the Diaspora. Braiterman suggests another explanation: thinkers in the 1940s and 1950s lacked the vocabulary to talk about the event.

Discursive factors explain this relative silence better than psychologism. Buber, Heschel, Soloveitchik, and Kaplan lacked a widespread discourse with which to discuss the Holocaust. A flurry of memoirs, literature, film, and scholarship would begin to chronicle the Holocaust in graphic detail. Such texts disseminated a vocabulary, a body of knowledge without which one could only have referred to the Holocaust in passing and general terms. . . . Without a significantly developed discourse, there was simply no language with which to talk about the Holocaust, no pastiche of image, figure, phrase, slogan, narrative, and reflection with which to rivet the religious imagination. (*GAA*, 7)

Braiterman sees Richard Rubenstein, who espoused a Jewish "death of God theology," as having "practically invented . . . de novo" post-Holocaust theology in 1966, with the publication of *After Auschwitz*.[2] For Braiterman, the distinction between modern and post-Holocaust Jewish thought centers on the question of theodicy. Modern twentieth century thinkers, including Heschel and Soloveitchik, as well as Buber, continue to espouse theodicy in various forms, whereas the discourses of post-Holocaust/postmodern thinkers are marked by recurrent "antitheodic" motifs. Braiterman uses the term theodicy in a broad sense, to include not only justifications of God despite the presence of evil in the world, but also a religious attitude of acceptance. Antitheodicy, on the other hand, means "any religious response to the problem of evil whose proponents refuse to justify, explain, or accept as somehow meaningful the relationship between God and suffering" (*GAA*, 31).

Braiterman's assessment of Buber, as indicated above, is that he failed to move beyond the theodic stance of modern Jewish theology. According to Braiterman's own understanding of the discursive factors which explain the belatedness of truly post-Holocaust discourse, this observation cannot be understood as a criticism: Buber was simply writing too soon to formulate an antitheodic, post-Holocaust position.

Fackenheim, too, despite his acknowledged indebtedness to Buber, sees Buber as having failed to formulate an adequate response to the *Shoah*. It is interesting to note, however, that Fackenheim himself did not come to a "post-Holocaust" position until after Buber's death. In the 1950s, his theological approach recognized neither the "radical evil" of the Holocaust, nor the possibility that Judaism could ever be successfully challenged by an empirical event. Fackenheim's own case adds weight to his observation that for most of the outstanding Christian and Jewish thinkers of his generation, the 1940s and 1950s were still "too soon" for radical responses.

Fackenheim argues that the Holocaust is a *novum* in human history, which "ruptures" Christian, Jewish and philosophical thought.[3] This rupture has profound implications for the interpretation of Jewish texts. According to Fackenheim, our hermeneutic situation is radically altered by the Holocaust. An abyss separates our "here and now" from the "then and there" of both the Bible and its rabbinic interpreters.[4]

The remainder of this essay is devoted to a comparison of Buber's response to the Holocaust with that of Levinas. I will focus on two related issues: Braiterman's observation of the preponderance of antitheodic motifs in post-Holocaust thought, and Fackenheim's view that the hallmark of such thought is discontinuity, the recognition of a radical rupture with the past. What is the balance between theodicy and antitheodicy in Buber's and Levinas's Jewish writings, and to what extent do their writings evince a "ruptured" Judaism?

BUBER: THE ECLIPSE OF GOD AND NARRATIVE THEOLOGY

Unlike Fackenheim and some of his fellow North American Jewish thinkers, including Richard Rubenstein and Eliezer Berkovits, neither Buber nor Levinas wrote lengthy works focusing explicitly on the possibility of Jewish faith after the Holocaust. Scholars looking to evaluate Buber's response to the *Shoah* have often started with his *Eclipse of God*, based on lectures given in 1951 and published in 1952. However, as both Braiterman and Steven Kepnes have noted, Buber's earlier work *The Prophetic Faith*, composed during the 1940s, reveals more of his own response to suffering than does the analysis of twentieth century philosophy and religion in *Eclipse of God* (*TAT*, 63).

The Prophetic Faith forms part of Buber's extensive corpus of biblical translation and commentary. As Kepnes has demonstrated, Buber's approach to the Bible is founded on his I-Thou philosophy, but also transcends it. On the one hand, his narrative biblical theology can be seen as the result of an I-Thou encounter between Buber and the Bible, and themes from Buber's dialogical philosophy certainly appear in his biblical writings. On the other hand, Buber's biblical theology cannot be reduced to an exemplification or justification for his philosophy of I-Thou. In particular, Buber described the underpinnings of his biblical theology not in terms of his philosophy of dialogue, but by drawing on the notions of creation, revelation and redemption as articulated in Rosenzweig's theology.

> What Buber's encounter with . . . the Bible did for him and what he hoped it would do for modern readers was to introduce a sense of "tense" and "tension" into the present of everyday life. When we are conscious of the significance of the creation of the world in the past and the redemption of the world in the future our present moment becomes charged by awareness of the past and future. (*TAT*, 122)

In his biblical writings, Buber attempted to extend the Jewish reader's personal memory and temporal sense, so that the past of the Jewish people became absorbed into personal memory, and the messianic future became part of his personal vision. Arguably, this integration of communal and personal memory has always been one of the main goals of Jewish education. Indeed, according to *Halakha* (Jewish law), every Jew is obligated to achieve this fusion of personal and communal memory at least once a year: on the first night of Passover Jews must tell the story of the Exodus from Egypt and attempt to see themselves as though they personally had been redeemed from slavery (Mishna, *Pesachim*, ch. 10). As Fackenheim has noted, this tradition of retelling also means that the formative "root experiences" of Jewish history are accessible to later generations.[5]

For Buber, however, the *seder* ritual of Passover night does not provide the only context through which an individual can gain access to the Jewish common memory. Hermeneutics provides a different route: one need only open the biblical text and approach it in the mode of I-Thou (*TAT*, 190, n. 26). By doing so, not only does the individual rejoin the collective memory, but the Bible can speak to the reader's contemporary concerns. Kepnes offers a detailed explanation of how Buber sees the ability of the Bible to speak to readers of any generation. One of the most important general points in this discussion is that for Buber, the Bible has a unifying theme, which is clearly relevant in all generations. In his 1906 essay "The Man of Today and the Jewish Bible," Buber identifies this theme: the Bible is concerned with "the encounter between a group of people and the Lord of the world in the course of history." The different genres of biblical text are variations on this theme: "Either openly or by implication, the stories are reports of encounters. The songs lament the denial of the grace of encounter, plead that it may be repeated, or give thanks because it has been vouchsafed. The prophecies summon man who has gone astray to turn, to return to the region where the encounter took place, promising him that the torn bond shall once more be made whole."[6] Thus for Buber, the God of the Bible (like the "Eternal Thou" of *I and Thou*) is a God of personal encounter, not the God of doctrinal belief systems. The biblical stories, songs and prophecies, far from being outdated relics of an ancient past, are concerned with what is and ought to be a very contemporary concern: how can the torn bond with God be mended?

In *The Prophetic Faith*, Buber traces the changing nature of the relationship between God and Israel, emphasizing the intimacy of God with the patriarchs and with Moses, as well as examining the distancing that occurs at other times, such as when the Israelites sin by worshipping the golden calf (Ex. 32). Buber sees the covenant between God and the Israelites in the wilderness as the paradigm of an ideal relationship between God and human beings. The Israelites are commanded to form "a kingdom of priests, a holy nation" (Ex. 19:6) in which God, as their only king, is central to public life and all members of the community are equal. But the golden calf episode is just one in a series of instances when the people fail to live up to their obligations, and thus distance themselves from God. The role of Moses and the subsequent prophets is to try to overcome this distance by bringing the people back to the true service of God. According to Buber, the seeds of Jewish Messianism can be found in the prophecies of Amos, Hosea and Isaiah, who envision a future return to the nomadic faith of the past. Isaiah prophesies that a descendant of the house of David will establish a "real, political kingship" (*PF*, 140) over Israel; and, according to Buber, this is "not a prediction but an offer": the Messiah will come when the people have made a decision to return to God (*PF*, 144).

Buber's emphasis on the role of human decision in bringing the Messiah is clearly "theodic" in Braiterman's terminology, and does not address the issues raised by the Holocaust. However, in the final chapter of *The Prophetic Faith*, entitled "The God of the Sufferers," Buber discusses the suffering of the innocent. He again discusses Messianism, but this time the figure of the Messiah is not the descendant of the house of David who figures in the Immanuel prophecies of Isaiah (7:14–7; 8:5–10). Instead, this Messiah is the "suffering Messiah" of Deutero-Isaiah, a figure Buber interprets as the community of Israel rather than as an individual. Buber also draws on the book of Job and the Psalms to develop the theme of innocent suffering. Although he does not explicitly link these biblical images to the victims of the Holocaust, it is reasonable to conclude, following Kepnes, that "*The Prophetic Faith* ended with exile, suffering, and the radical separation of God and humanity to give expression to the radical separation or 'eclipse of God' caused by the Holocaust" (*TAT*, 136).

Braiterman concurs with this assessment, but argues that even this last section of *The Prophetic Faith* remains theodic. Buber's reading of the book of Job does not emphasize the antitheodic moment of protest, but the eventual reestablishment of Job's relationship with God. He explains, "Buber wrote: Job knows that the friends, who side with God, do not contend for the true God. He has recognized before this the true God as the near and intimate God. Now he only experiences Him through suffering and contradiction, but even in this way he does experience God [*PF*, 192]. In this view, the book of Job is less about the suffering of an innocent man than about the conditions underlying religious encounter. According to Buber, Job's tale narrates the man of suffering, who by his suffering attained the vision of God [*PF*, 197]" (*GAA*, 64).

For Braiterman, Buber's reading of Job remains theodic because although Buber recognized the reality of Job's suffering, "he attributed meaningful, cathartic significance to it." Similarly, the "suffering servant" in the final chapter of *The Prophetic Faith* is "a messianic figure patiently awaiting ultimate redress" (*GAA*, 64).

Braiterman argues that Buber's critique of modern life in *Eclipse of God* "formed a practically seamless outgrowth" from his earlier biblical exegesis, including *The Prophetic Faith* (*GAA*, 64). The phrase "eclipse of God" may sound like it was devised specifically to describe the silence of God at Auschwitz, but in fact Buber applied it to the entire twentieth century, which he saw as a time of spiritual and moral eclipse. Indeed, the concluding chapter of *Eclipse of God* repeats the diagnosis of the "sickness of the age" that had been offered in *I and Thou*: the ever-increasing preponderance of I-It over I-Thou:

> In our age the I-It relation, gigantically swollen, has usurped, practically uncontested, the mastery and the rule. The I of this relation, an I that possesses all, makes all, succeeds with all, this I that is unable to say Thou, unable to meet a being essentially, is the lord of the hour. This selfhood that has become omnipotent, with all the It around it, can naturally acknowledge neither God nor any genuine absolute which manifests itself to men as of nonhuman origin. It steps in between and shuts off from us the light of heaven. (*EG*, 166–67)

Buber, however, did not end the book on a despairing note. As Fackenheim observed,[7] the impermanence of an eclipse means that even a total one is, in a sense, a hopeful image — an eclipse does not last forever: "The eclipse of the light of God is no extinction; even tomorrow that which has stepped in between may give way" (*EG*, 167).

If *Eclipse of God* ends on an unmistakable note of hope, Buber's 1952 essay "The Dialogue Between Heaven and Earth" reaches a more disturbing conclusion. As Kepnes has noted, this essay, which explicitly addresses the post-Holocaust situation, explores the same three figures of innocent suffering as did the final chapter of *The Prophetic Faith*: Job, the Psalmist and the Suffering Servant. In "Dialogue Between Heaven and Earth," the discussion of Job follows on from harrowing questions:

How is life with God still possible in a time in which there is an Auschwitz? The estrangement has become too cruel, the hiddenness too deep. Can one still "believe" in a God who allowed those things to happen, but how can one still speak to Him? Can one still hear His word? Can one still, as an individual and as a people, enter at all into a dialogical relationship with Him? Dare we recommend to the survivors of Auschwitz, the Job of the gas chambers: "Give thanks unto the Lord, for He is good; for His mercy endureth forever"?[8]

As Fackenheim has pointed out, Buber's question about the possibility of divine-human speech after the Holocaust is never really answered. The question, however, has far-reaching consequences for Buber's dialogical philosophy, since "the centre of Buber's thought is dialogical speech" and, moreover, it is "divine-human speech that confers meaning on all speech."[9] Fackenheim's concerns point to an important issue that lies beyond the scope of the present inquiry: Is any I-thou relation possible in an age in which relation to the Eternal Thou is precluded by the "eclipse" of God?

Buber raises his questions about divine-human speech on the penultimate page of the essay. He then returns to the biblical Job:

> But how about Job himself? He not only laments, but he charges . . . that the judge of all the earth acts against justice. And he receives an answer from God. But what God says to him does not answer the charge; it does not even touch upon it. The true answer that Job receives is God's appearance only. . . . Nothing is explained, nothing adjusted; wrong has not become right, nor cruelty kindness. Nothing has happened but that man again hears God's address (*OJ*, 224–25).

This paragraph suggests that Buber's Job, or Buber himself, is not satisfied with the answer he receives and this impression is strengthened by the subsequent, concluding section:

> And we?
> We — by this is meant all those who have not got over what happened and will not get over it. Do we stand overcome before the hidden face of God like the tragic hero of the Greeks before faceless fate? No, rather *even now we contend, we too, with God*, even with Him, the Lord of Being, whom we once chose for our Lord. We do not put up with earthly being, we struggle for its redemption, and struggling we appeal

to the help of the Lord, who is again still a hiding one. In such a state we await His voice, whether it comes out of the storm or out of a stillness that follows it. Though His coming appearance resembles no earlier one, we shall recognize again our cruel and merciful Lord.[10]

In this essay, Job is not simply the man of faith who awaits the return of God, but the brave believer who (like Abraham) argues with God, and who protests rather than simply lamenting. And God, for His part, is recognized as being both merciful and cruel. Nevertheless, despite the way in which Buber uses Job "to unleash an untypical tide of disappointed anger with God's hiding," Buber still "appealed to the help of God and awaited God's voice" (*GAA*, 67).

Buber, in other words, never abandoned the biblical conceptual framework. He saw contemporary Jewish life as a continuation of the dialectic of biblical Israel — the alternation of distance and nearness between God and the Jewish people. The metaphor of an "eclipse of God" seems less radical when seen in the context of this alternation.

Although Buber's writings offer no solution to the theological problems raised by the *Shoah*, they do go some way to showing how a person can maintain faith while awaiting the end of the eclipse of God. As Kepnes points out, the most powerful source of consolation in the Hebrew Bible are the Psalms. Buber's 1952 book *Good and Evil* includes interpretations of Psalms 1, 12, 14, 73 and 82, all of which relate to the theme of innocent suffering. Buber does not claim to find complete and satisfying answers to the problem of evil in these Psalms, but he suggests that sufferers can achieve a renewal of faith and hope and some consolation for their suffering through the process of reading them. Reciting Psalms at times of trouble is an ancient Jewish custom, and Buber himself turned to the Psalms for comfort throughout his life, particularly when he endured separation from his mother as a young boy following the divorce of his parents (*TAT*, 140).

Buber understands the power of reading Psalms as dependent on an "existential exegesis," by which he seems to mean that the reader's own life experience is seen "in and through the psalmist's narrative" (*TAT*, 142). As Kepnes explains, this experience involves the movement of a narrative from the common memory of Judaism to the interpreter's personal memory. It is an interpretive experience that happens in and through a life experience. In the morning I read the Psalm and it appears as a beautiful but strange and austere expression of an unhappy man. In the afternoon I lose a lifelong friend and suddenly the psalmist's words ring through my head again is if they were my own. It is an experience described by one of the psalmists as 'deep calls to deep.' [Ps. 42:6] (*TAT*, 142)

Whereas Fackenheim criticizes Buber for not making the breakthrough to a radically new post-Holocaust philosophy, Kepnes presents Buber's work as a resource for the faithful. From the 1906 essay "The Man of Today and the Jewish Bible," through the development of Buber's dialogical philosophy to his late writings, Buber consistently presented the Bible as a text that can speak to contemporary readers, provided that they approach it in an open, I-Thou mode. Moreover, contrary to Fackenheim, Buber's understanding of the central theme of the Bible — "the encounter between a group of people and the Lord of the world in the course of history" — is that, the text will be relevant and accessible to readers in every generation. The apparent absence of God in any particular historical era does not render the Bible irrelevant or a closed book, but, on the contrary, makes the reading of both the narratives of divine-human encounter and the lamentations of the absence of such encounter more poignant.

"Loving the Torah More than God": Levinas's Response to the *Shoah*

As suggested earlier, one of the key factors that has to be considered when comparing the impact of the *Shoah* on Levinas and Buber is simple chronology. By 1940, Buber was a mature thinker whose philosophical outlook was well established. Levinas, by contrast, was still 20 years away from publication of his first major work (*Totality and Infinity*) and subsequent appointment to a university post. Indeed, Levinas himself wrote that his entire intellectual biography was dominated by "the presentiment and the memory of the Nazi horror" (*DF*, 291). Like Buber, however, Levinas did not write any lengthy works explicitly and exclusively concerned with the challenges to Judaism raised by the Holocaust.

One of the most valuable sources for insight into Levinas's under-standing of post-Holocaust Judaism is the essay "To Love the Torah More than God," which was first delivered as a radio address in 1955. Like much of Buber's writing on Judaism, Levinas's essay takes the form of commentary on a text. In this case, however, the text is not a biblical book, but a secular work of literature, a story entitled "Yossel Rakover Speaks to God."[11]

The story, by Zvi Kolitz, is written in the form of a monologue conveying the final thoughts of one of the last survivors of the Warsaw Ghetto Uprising. The monologue has a complicated textual history and was sometimes mistaken for an authentic historical document. Levinas, however, clearly understood it to be a work of fiction, al-though he refers to it as a "beautiful and true text, true as only fiction can be" in which "every one of us who survived recognizes his own life in astonishment" (*DF*, 142).

The narrator of the monologue, Yossel Rakover, is an Orthodox Jew, scion of a Hasidic family, of which he is the last surviving mem-ber. Overwhelmed by his experiences, he has come to the recognition that if any God exists, it is one who has withdrawn from the world. In so doing, Yossel says, God has "handed men over to their savage instincts . . . and since these instincts rule the world, it is natural that those who preserve a sense of divinity and purity are the first victims of this rule" (*DF*, 143). Rather than inferring God's nonexistence from His absence, Yossel Rakover continues to believe in God. As the monologue develops, it becomes clear that this belief is not based on blind faith. Paradoxically, his experience of the absence of God is lived as revelation. The inhumanity he has witnessed makes him more ap-preciative of the ethical principles of the Torah, thus intensifying his pride in being Jewish and his commitment to Judaism. Through this strong identification with the Torah, he experiences an intimacy with the otherwise distant God. "Now I know that you really are my God," he says, "for you could not be the God of those whose acts represent the most horrible expression of an absence of God" (*DF*, 144). This intimacy with the Divine in no way diminishes the centrality of the Torah, however. Echoing an expression of the Talmud, Yossel exclaims,

"I love Him but I love His Torah even more and even if I were disappointed by Him and downtrodden, I would nevertheless observe His Torah" (*DF*, 144). This exclamation is the source of Levinas's title, and will be discussed in greater detail below.

Levinas's commentary considers the meaning of the suffering of the innocent. He acknowledges that the simplest and perhaps sanest answer would be to say that such suffering proves that God does not exist. However, Levinas insists that this is an adequate answer only if the conception of God we begin with amounts to a "strange magician," a "rather primitive God who awards prizes, imposes sanctions, or pardons mistakes, and who, in His goodness, treats people like perpetual children." An "adult's God," Levinas writes, "reveals Himself precisely in the emptiness of the child's heaven. That is the moment when God withdraws Himself from the world and hides His face" (*DF*, 143).

Yossel succeeds in maintaining faith in God in spite of his experience of radical evil. Levinas stresses that there is nothing mystical or blind about this faith. The divine-human relationship, he asserts, is one mediated by a teaching, by the Torah. Since God does not reveal himself through any terrestrial authority, faith in Him can only rest on the inner evidence and value of a teaching. The Jews' faith is "based on the internal evidence of the morality conveyed by the Torah" (*DF*, 143).

Levinas identifies Yossel's exclamation ("I love Him, But I love His Torah even more . . . and even if I had been disappointed by Him . . . I would nonetheless observe the precepts of the Torah") as the high point of the monologue, which "echoes the whole Talmud."[12] The significance of this last phrase must not escape us. Levinas is not simply pointing out that the monologue is alluding to a talmudic story, the culmination of which is God's exclamation "So should it be that they would forsake me but keep my Torah" (Jer. Hag. 1:7).[13] Rather, Levinas is claiming that Yossel's cry represents the essential teaching of rabbinic Judaism ("the entire Talmud").

Yossel's exclamation has two related components. The first, echoing perhaps Job's "though He may kill me yet I hope in Him" (Job 13:15), is a defiant commitment to love God, whatever may happen, however unjust the sufferings that may have befallen him. The second component is an affirmation that the Torah is somehow more important than God Himself. Levinas is sensitive to both components, and to the fact that the religiosity expressed in this stance is "heroic" (*DF*, 145). But it is the second aspect that Levinas repeatedly stresses in his writings on Judaism.

In the context of a comparison of Buber and Levinas, it is particularly important to realize that when Levinas refers to "Judaism," he generally does not mean all historical manifestations of Jewish religious thought and practice. Specifically, Levinas is interested neither in Hasidism nor in Kabbalah (mysticism). The Judaism Levinas writes about is the Judaism of the Talmud and of the *yeshivot* (talmudic academies). As Hilary Putnam has pointed out, "Levinas's Judaism manifests a 'Lithuanian' distrust of the charismatic." Levinas was born in Kovno, Lithuania, a city that, like the more famous Vilna, was for many years the home of great academies of Talmud study. Putnam somewhat understates the case when he explains that Lithuanian Jews "were famous for their insistence on rigorous argument, and their contempt for the enthusiastic and charismatic religiosity associated with Hassidism."[14]

Levinas, in any case, frequently indicates his association of "Judaism" with the Talmud and, more generally, with rational interpretation. "Judaism," he writes in "Revelation in the Jewish Tradition," certainly "is" the Bible, but the Bible as "read through the Talmud" (*LR*, 197). Whereas Fackenheim argues that after the Holocaust our hermeneutic situation vis-à-vis the Bible is radically altered, Levinas does not see a problem. He acknowledges that there is a lack of continuity between the world of the Bible and our own. However, he attributes this lack of continuity not to the *Shoah* per se, but to "modernity" characterized as "lack of faith." More importantly for our purposes, Levinas insists that the Talmud is not separated from modernity in the same way. The Talmud, "despite its antiquity and precisely because of the continuity of talmudic study, belongs, as paradoxical as it may seem, to the modern history of Judaism. A dialogue between the two establishes itself directly" (*NTR*, 6). Hence for Levinas, modern Jews do have access the Bible, provided that they approach it via the Talmud and the rabbinic commentaries.

On this point, Levinas also differs significantly from Buber. Fackenheim's insistence on reading the "naked text" of the Bible without immediate recourse to rabbinic commentaries was learned from Buber. In his 1968 article "Martin Buber's Thought and Contemporary Judaism," Levinas criticizes Buber for adopting this stance, writing that "Buber reverts to the Hebrew text without availing himself of the rabbinic literature that is precisely what constitutes the way that text has been read throughout creative Jewish history. . . . *It is undeniable that Buber reads the Bible as if he possessed the entire Holy Spirit all by himself.* The particular experience of each individual is doubtless required for the history of the faith, but tradition must not fade away before it. It is the union of personal experience with tradition that allows the Hebrew Bible to retain its full meaning."[15] This disagreement between Buber and Levinas over the authority of rabbinic interpretation is, of course, linked to their different views of Jewish law as well. Levinas, as an Orthodox thinker, upholds the importance of *Halakha*, whereas Buber embraced an antinomian approach to Judaism. This difference, important though it is, lies beyond the scope of the present essay.

The difference between Levinas and Fackenheim on the issue of biblical hermeneutics is, however, essential to our enquiry. Levinas's equation of "loving the Torah more than God" with a talmudic, rather than a specifically post-Holocaust, approach to Judaism shows that, unlike Fackenheim, he did not see Judaism as "ruptured" by the Holocaust. On the contrary, the thrust of "Loving the Torah More than God" seems to be that the task of the faithful Jew in a post-Holocaust world is the same as it has always been in postbiblical times, namely, to remain faithful to the Torah, despite the apparent absence of God from the world. Nowhere in the essay does Levinas suggest that the situation of Yossel Rakover or of the generation he represents requires a radically new approach to Judaism.

Levinas's view of rabbinic Judaism as an "adult faith" based on love of the Torah is echoed by David Hartman in *A Living Covenant*.

Hartman notes that biblical faith was profoundly challenged by historical events during the rabbinic period, including, but not limited to, the destruction of the Temple. The Bible generally presents a strongly theodic worldview: God intervenes directly in human history; rewards and punishments operate both on the level of the individual and that of the collective (e.g., the nation); and, most importantly, rewards and punishments are wholly this-worldly. Hartman writes:

> The God of Sinai does not merely hand over responsibility for the *mitzvoth* [commandments] to Israel and then decide to take His leave. He also commits Himself to permanent involvement in the history of the community, promising magnificent rewards for observance of the *mitzvot* and threatening terrible punishments for transgressions against them. Long and dramatic lists of those promises and threats are given in Leviticus and Deuteronomy. (*LC*, 184)

During the rabbinic period, however, there were many instances in which the rabbis acknowledged that collective rewards and punishments did not seem to be operative in the world. Idolatrous nations prospered; and it was difficult to correlate the worldly success of Israel with its fidelity, or lack of fidelity, to the Torah at any given period. On an individual level, the rabbis observed a similar lack of clear correlation between deeds and deserts. Various strategies were therefore adopted to afford an understanding of the workings of Providence. As Hartman makes clear, a variety of different approaches were put forth by different talmudic sages. It is therefore not possible to present a single, unified "talmudic" response to suffering (or indeed, to almost any issue).

A common feature of many of the responses was a distancing of God from history. One strategy is to rethink the notion of reward and punishment for individuals, so that it applies not in this world but in an afterlife.[16] On the collective level, the midrash suggests that the lack of divine intervention in history can itself be understood as a sign of God's power. Both Hartman and Fackenheim cite the following talmudic passage:

Rabbi Joshua ben Levi said: Why are they called men of the Great Assembly? Because they restored the crown of the divine attributes to its ancient completeness. Moses had come and said: 'the great, the might, and the awesome God [Deut. 10:17]. Then Jeremiah came and said: 'Aliens are frolicking in His temple; where then are His awesome deeds?' Hence he omitted the 'awesome' [Jer. 32:18]. Daniel came and said: 'Aliens are enslaving His sons; where are His mighty deeds?' Hence he omitted the word 'mighty' [Dan. 9:4]. But [the men of the Great Assembly] came and said: 'On the contrary, therein lies His mighty deeds that He suppresses His wrath, that He extends long-suffering to the wicked. Therein lie His awesome powers, for but for fear of Him, how could [our] one nation persist among the nations? [*Yoma* 69b] (*LC*, 216–17)

As Hartman explains, "The men of the Great Assembly . . . were able to recognize the might and awesomeness of God in His ability to restrain Himself and not wrathfully strike down the oppressors of Israel." He also notes that this reinterpretation of divine power also affected the rabbinic understanding of human morality.

The Mishnah quotes Ben Zoma as saying: "Who is mighty? He who subdues his [base] instinct, as it is said: 'He that is slow to anger is better than the mighty, and he that rules over his spirit [is mightier] than he that captures a city' [Prov. 16:33]" (Avot 4:1). The heroic virtue of human self-control and restraint despite provocation parallels divine forbearance toward the wicked. Inner discipline is the source of power and strength. (*LC*, 217)

In general terms, Hartman's exposition highlights a rabbinic approach that allowed the rabbis and their followers to remain faithful to the covenant even when the biblical promises were only partially fulfilled, if at all. Hartman describes this transition from biblical to talmudic theology in terms that echo Levinas's description of an "adult religion" in *Difficult Freedom*.

If one can transcend picturing God exclusively as an overprotective parent, by viewing His love also in terms of a restraint that encourages human responsibility, then one can establish a covenantal understanding of God's relationship to history that is grounded in a mature feeling of autonomy rather than in childhood dependency. A childlike spiritual personality needs to believe in a God Who immediately crushes sinners and the enemies of Israel. Only a more mature appreciation of the intrinsic significance of the Torah could enable the community to affirm commitment to a God Who manifests his power by giving sinners time to repent and by giving Israel's enemies time to bring about their own ruin. This process of maturation allowed the spirit of the Sinai covenant to continue to grow even when the power of God was not visibly triumphant in human history. (*LC*, 221)

According to Hartman, such a mature covenantal spirituality is represented by a passage from the evening prayer, which equates God's love for Israel with His giving of the Torah rather than His protection of the people:

> With everlasting love hast Thou loved the house of Israel Thy people. Thou hast taught us thy Torah, its commandments, statues, and ordinances. Therefore, Lord our God, for all time when we lie down and when we rise up we will speak of what Thou hast ordained, rejoicing with fervour in learning the words of Thy Torah and Thy commandments. For they are our life and the length of our days, and on them we will meditate by day and night. (*LC*, 221)

"Loving the Torah more than God," then, does not present a distinctively post-Holocaust understanding of Judaism, but an approach that is continuous with the rabbinic emphasis on Torah and *mitzvoth* (commandments) as mediators of the relationship between God and human beings.

In Levinas's 1982 essay "Useless Suffering," however, there are indications that the *Shoah*, and the other twentieth century massacres, call for a new approach to both religion and morality. Levinas's critique of theodicy begins with a discussion of its underlying intention — to make suffering bearable. He both condemns theodicy as morally scandalous and acknowledges it as a persistent human temptation. Levinas does not understand theodicy narrowly, as a type of religious answer to the problem of evil, but as any ideology that sees suffering as necessary for, or insignificant in comparison to, some overriding greater "Good."

Levinas's phenomenological account of suffering emphasizes its intrinsic meaninglessness: "the least one can say about suffering is that in its phenomenality, intrinsically, it is 'useless,' 'for nothing'" (*US*, 161–62). However, theodicies, both religious and secular, have sought to make suffering bearable by finding meaning in it, through reference to a metaphysical order.

> This is a kingdom of transcendent ends, willed by a benevolent wisdom, by the absolute goodness of a God who is in some way defined by this super-natural goodness; or a widespread, invisible goodness in Nature and History, where it would command the paths which are, to be sure, painful, but which lead to the Good. Pain is henceforth meaningful, subordinated in one way or another to the metaphysical finality envisaged by faith or by a belief in progress. (*US*, 160)

Significantly for our purposes, Levinas acknowledges both a general theological form of theodicy as explaining suffering through reference to sin, and a specifically Jewish form, which sees "the drama of the Diaspora" as a reflection of "the sins of Israel." "The wicked conduct of ancestors, still non-expiated by the sufferings of exile, would explain to the exiles themselves the duration and the harshness of this exile" (*US*, 161).

Levinas insists, however, that theodicy has — and must — come to an end. He does not present a theoretical critique but instead argues that the refusal of theodicy is the necessary response to the human suffering witnessed in the twentieth century. He cites the familiar inventory of human slaughter and genocide, from World War I to Auschwitz and Cambodia, and argues that the suffering of the innocent in the twentieth century has led to a revolution in contemporary consciousness, writing, "Perhaps the most revolutionary fact of our twentieth century consciousness . . . is that of the destruction of all balance between the explicit and implicit theodicy of Western thought and the forms which suffering and its evil take in the very unfolding of this century." (*US*, 161). Theodicy is destroyed not by the simple numerical weight of victims, but by the diabolical qualities signified by the names Hitler, Stalin, Gulag, Cambodia and, paradigmatically for Levinas, Auschwitz. Under these regimes, suffering and evil were deliberately imposed, in a way that was completely detached from any ethics or rational limits. For Levinas, "the disproportion between suffering and every theodicy was shown at Auschwitz with a glaring, obvious clarity" (*US*, 162).

The recognition of the failure of theodicy is not simply theoretical. Rather, what is revealed is an ethical awareness that the justification of the suffering of the other is morally scandalous: "But does not this end of theodicy, which obtrudes itself in the face of this century's inordinate distress, at the same time in a more general way reveal the unjustifiable character of suffering in the other person, the scandal which would occur by my justifying my neighbour's suffering?. . . For an ethical sensibility — confirming itself, in the inhumanity of our time, against this inhumanity — the justification of the neighbour's pain is certainly the source of all immorality" (*US*, 162). Here Levinas seems to isolate what it is that makes theodicy morally repugnant — the act of justifying the suffering of the other. Since, according to Levinasian ethics, the self is inescapably and infinitely responsible for the other, theodicy in this sense would amount to a dereliction of duty, a refusal of my responsibility.

Levinas takes the analysis further, however, and argues that the philosophical problem posed by the suffering of the innocent in the twentieth century "concerns the meaning that religiosity and the human morality of goodness can still retain after the end of theodicy" (*US*, 163). Similar questions are raised by Levinas in the introduction to *Totality and Infinity* ("are we not duped by morality?" (*TI*, 21) and in the interview "The Paradox of Morality."[17] In the latter context, Levinas explicitly links the question about the status of morality to both Jewishness and the Holocaust: "If there is an explicitly Jewish moment in my thought, it is the reference to Auschwitz, where God let the Nazis do what they wanted. Consequently, what remains? Either this means that there is no reason for morality and hence it can be concluded that everyone should act like the Nazis, or the moral law maintains its authority. . . . The essential problem is: can we speak of an absolute commandment after Auschwitz? Can we speak of morality after the failure of morality?" (*PM*, 175–76).

The answer that Levinas presents in "Useless Suffering" takes the form of a commentary on Fackenheim's notion of a 614th

commandment: "Jews are forbidden to hand Hitler posthumous vic-
tories."[18] Levinas glosses the 614th commandment as follows:

> To renounce after Auschwitz this God absent from Auschwitz — no
> longer to assure the continuation of Israel — would amount to finishing
> the criminal enterprise of National-Socialism, which aimed at the anni-
> hilation of Israel and the forgetting of the ethical message of the Bible,
> which Judaism bears, and whose multi-millennial history is concretely
> prolonged by Israel's existence as a people. For if God was absent in the
> extermination camps, the devil was very obviously present in them.
> From whence, for Emil Fackenheim, comes the obligation for Jews to
> live and remain Jews, in order not to be made the accomplices of a
> diabolical project. (*US*, 163–64)

The emphasis on the role of Israel as bearers of the ethical message of
the Bible is perhaps more representative of Levinas's view of Judaism
than of Fackenheim's approach. However, what is most important for
our purposes is the use Levinas makes of a structure of resistance that
he sees in Fackenheim's work. Levinas finds in the 614th commandment not just a Jewish response to the Jewish crisis of faith, but a way
for humanity to respond to the inhuman events of the twentieth century. Fackenheim sees the Jewish people as facing a choice between
allowing evil to flourish or remaining faithful to Judaism, in spite of
the absence of God. Levinas presents contemporary humanity as
facing a similar choice between abandoning the world to useless suffering or accepting the self's responsibility for the suffering of the
other — even after the "failure of morality." He then asks, "At the
end of the twentieth century and after the useless and unjustifiable
pain which is exposed and displayed therein without any shadow of a
consoling theodicy, are we not all pledged — like the Jewish people to
their faithfulness — to the second term of this alternative?" (*US*, 164).

Significantly, Levinas stresses that a form of religion based on something like the 614th commandment and its secular analogue in the
sphere of morality are new religious and moral modalities. He writes
that "this is a new modality in the faith of today, and also in our moral
certainties, a modality quite essential to the modernity which is dawn-
ing" (*US*, 164).

Similarly, in the 1987 interview cited above, Levinas acknowledges that traditional religious faith has been dependent on theodicy, specifically the notions of reward and punishment, writing that:

> Before the twentieth century, all religion begins with the promise. It begins with the "Happy End." It is the promise of heaven. Well then, doesn't a phenomenon like Auschwitz invite you, on the contrary, to think the moral law independently of the Happy End? That is the question. I would even ask whether we are not faced with an order that one cannot preach. Does one have the right to preach to the other a piety without reward? That is what I ask myself. It is easier to tell myself to believe without promise than it is to ask it of the other. That is the idea of asymmetry. I can demand of myself that which I cannot demand of the other. (*PM*, 176)

Levinas's comments on the *Shoah* in the three texts we have considered fit fairly easily into the chronological schema outlined by Braiterman and Fackenheim. Although "To Love the Torah More than God" is certainly not a theodic text, neither is it strongly antitheodic. More significantly, the emphasis in the 1955 essay is not on the discontinuity between pre- and post-Holocaust Judaism, but on continuity. Yossel Rakover's approach to the Torah is presented as an essentially "talmudic" attitude, emphasizing commitment to the Torah over the individual's relationship with God. "Useless Suffering" (1982), by contrast, is both strongly antitheodic (by virtue of its sustained critique of theodicy) and an expression of a self-consciously "new modality" of religious faith. Significantly, given Braiterman's emphasis on the discursive history of post-Holocaust thought, both "Loving the Torah More than God," and large parts of "Useless Suffering" are in fact commentaries on literary or philosophical treatments of the Holocaust.

In "Useless Suffering" Levinas is clearly in general agreement with Fackenheim's view that both philosophy and Judaism need to be radically rethought after the *Shoah*. With regard to philosophy, this is hardly a new development, as Levinas had already critiqued the "violence" of Western philosophy in *Totality and Infinity*. It does, however, represent a departure from the earlier stress on the continuity of Judaism in "Loving The Torah More than God."

Where Levinas differs definitively from Fackenheim, even in his later works, is in his approach to hermeneutics. The essay "Revelation in the Jewish Tradition," in which Levinas argues, as we saw above, that the Bible is accessible to contemporary readers through rabbinic interpretation, was written in the 1970s. Moreover, the talmudic commentaries and essays on Judaism that Levinas wrote in the last decades of his life show the same underlying hermeneutic stance: the Talmud, and through it the Bible, yields its meaning to contemporary readers. We have already seen that a central notion of Buber's biblical hermeneutics is that the theme of encounter with the Eternal Thou makes the text accessible to all generations. Levinas, similarly, uncovers a universal theme in the Talmud: it extracts from the written Torah "ethical meaning as the ultimate intelligibility of the human and even of the cosmic" (*NTR*, 93).

CONCLUSION: BIBLICAL, TALMUDIC AND POST-HOLOCAUST JUDAISM

Following Braiterman's work, the significant differences between Levinas and Buber that were outlined above can be explained, in part, through chronology. Buber did not live long enough to be part of the movement of post-Holocaust thinkers who sought radically new understandings of Judaism. Had Buber done so and been exposed to the Holocaust discourse that became established in the 1970s, his thought might have developed along more strongly antitheodic lines. The questions he raised in "Dialogue Between Heaven and Earth" might eventually have led to the recognition that Judaism was indeed ruptured by the *Shoah*, and that the I-thou relation needed to be rethought to take account of the "eclipse" of God. Levinas, notably, did develop a strongly antitheodic position in the 1970s.

However, such a transformation in Buber's thought is not the only possibility. The differences between Buber and Levinas can be partially accounted for by the fact that Buber was continuously involved with the "naked" text of the Bible, whereas in Levinas's approach, the Bible and Jewish faith are seen through the prism of rabbinic thought. Buber might never have abandoned a biblical worldview that focuses on the longed-for encounter with God. As Kepnes has shown, Buber's work is a rich resource for the contemporary believer who seeks hope and consolation whilst patiently awaiting the end of the eclipse. Levinas offers an even more difficult Judaism. Moving beyond the "adult faith" that Hartman sees as characterizing rabbinic Judaism, Levinas's latest writings present the possibility of a faithfulness to the Torah — and to the ethical — without the consoling promise of a "Happy End."

TWELVE

Reciprocity and the Height of God

A Defense of Buber Against Levinas

Andrew Kelley

There is a strong similarity between Martin Buber's notion of the I-Thou relation and Emmanuel Levinas's philosophy of respect for the other. Levinas recognizes this similarity and, as a result, Buber's name continually appears in books and articles written throughout the course of Levinas's career.[1] Both thinkers stress the social or ethical aspect of religion. Showing the influence of Hasidism on his thought, Buber claims that to "love God truly, one must first love man."[2] Levinas, who has been influenced greatly by Jewish thought, also views the human relation with God as a social relation. Thus, we see him proclaim that "the dimension of the divine opens forth from the human face. A relation with the Transcendent . . . is a social relation. . . . There can be no "knowledge" of God separated from the relationship with man. The Other is the very locus of metaphysical truth, and is indispensable for my relationship with God" (*TI*, 78/*TeI*, 50). His main criticism of Buber stems from the supposed aspect of "reciprocity" involved in the I-Thou relation. Regarding his own philosophy concerning the relation with the other, Levinas writes that, "the other is . . . the manifestation of the height in which God is revealed" (*TI*, 79/*TeI*, 51). As a result, the true relation between the I and the other (and, thus, God) should be *asymmetrical* because the other comes to me from a dimension of height. Hence, Levinas worries that Buber's I-Thou relation would reduce the height from which God comes to us and thus turn God into an equal, that is, into a partner or a friend.

This essay shows that Buber's philosophy obviates Levinas's criticism. The I-Thou relation does not destroy the height from which God comes.

WHAT DOES "RECIPROCITY" MEAN AND WHY DOES LEVINAS REPROACH BUBER?

In a criticism of Levinas's *Totality and Infinity*, Derrida nicely sums up Levinas's chief worry about Buber's I-Thou relation: "Levinas in substance reproaches the I-Thou relationship for being reciprocal and symmetrical, thus committing violence against height" (*WD*, 314–15). Both Levinas and Buber write from the standpoint of the "I." For Levinas, there is something about the other — the person opposite — that I cannot grasp. This alterity of the other calls my being into question. It informs me of my freedom and also of my responsibility toward other humans. Speech, for Levinas, issues from the height of the other: "For language can be spoken only if the interlocutor is the commencement of discourse . . . if he is not on the same plane as myself" (*TI*, 101/*TeI*, 75). Furthermore, Levinas doubts if the I can be taught by the other unless the other approaches the I from a dimension of height (*PMB*, 145). Finally, and most important of all, it is the height of the other which calls my existence into question (*TI*, 171/*TeI*, 145). If the height of the other is destroyed, then what or who can call me to responsibility? "The other is . . . the manifestation of the height in which God is revealed" (*TI*, 79/*TeI*, 51).

In a reciprocal or symmetrical relation, another being relates to me in the same manner as I relate to it (*TI*, 36/*TeI*, 6). That is, a reciprocal relation would be a situation in which both terms of the relation are equal (*TI*, 170/*TeI*, 145). Hence, Levinas wonders "if *thou-saying* does not place the other in a reciprocal relation, and if this reciprocity is primordial" (*TI*, 68/*TeI*, 40). Most grave, for Levinas, is that Buber's I-Thou relation destroys the height from which the other comes. "The interlocutor is not a Thou, he is a 'You' [*'Vous'*]" (*TI*, 101/*TeI*, 75). Because of this "destruction" of height, Levinas holds that the "I-Thou . . . does not enable us to account for . . . a life other than friendship" (*TI*, 68–9/*TeI*, 40). He only sees the I-Thou relation as the apogee of "spiritual friendship" (*PMB*, 145). In the end, if "discourse is discourse with God and not with equals" (*TI*, 297/*TeI*, 273), then Buber has reduced God to an equal.

BUBER'S "REPLY"

According to Buber, there are two possible ways that I can interact with the world. I can either utter "I-It," or I can speak the primary word "I-Thou." "I-Thou" can only be spoken with the whole being, whereas "I-It" can never be uttered with the whole being (*IT*, 54/*W*, 79). When I speak the latter word, I consider what faces me as an It, as an object. Conversely, when I say "I-Thou," I do not consider the other as an object. Instead, I take a stand in relation to the other (*IT*, 55/*W*, 80).

The word "I-It" intimates a metaphysics in which the world is only considered as having a subject-object structure. I have some "thing" — an It — as my object. Furthermore, "It" can just as easily be replaced with the terms "He" or "She" when I regard people as objects (*IT*, 53/*W*, 79). The I-It "relation" does not occur *between* me and my object; it occurs *within* me because the relation is wholly dependent upon my action. When I pronounce this word, I situate myself and my object in space and time. Thus, if I perceive something, sense something, feel something, etc., the relation is an I-It relation. Experience and the accumulation of knowledge belong to the world of It (*IT*, 54–56/*W*, 79–81).

However, Buber does not wholly disdain the I-It relation. In order to nourish myself, to survive, I must live in the world of It. The world of the statesman or the economist would collapse if it were considered solely in terms of Thou (*IT*, 96/*W*, 109). Likewise, all "Thous" that are pronounced inevitably become "Its." As soon as the I-Thou relation is worked out or reflected upon, it becomes an I-It relation. The opposite is also possible. An It may always become a Thou but only if I address it as Thou (*IT*, 69, 84/*W*, 89, 100–01).

The other pole of human existence, the I-Thou, becomes less prevalent as I develop the ability to experience (*IT*, 84/*W*, 100–01).

Buber recognizes the importance of the It-world: "without *It* a human being cannot live. But he whoever lives only with that is not a human being" (*IT*, 85/*W*, 101). Life is passed between the two poles of the It-world and the Thou-world. No person can live at either extremity. However, it is possible to live more under the influence of one or the other (*IT*, 114/*W*, 122).

Whereas the I-It relation is characterized by what happens *in* me, the I-Thou relation takes place *between* I and Thou (*IT*, 56/*W*, 81). In speaking such a word, I no longer dominate a "thing." Instead, I take my stand in relation to a Thou. While every It, He and She, is bounded by other Its, Hes, and Shes, the Thou is not bounded by anything. In fact, "Thou" is not a "thing" (*IT*, 55/*W*, 80). In saying "I-Thou," I do not experience the other *as* a person for to do so would be to make the other into an It. Nor does "Thou" refer to the person to whom one says "Thou." "Thou" is simply an utterance that indicates that I am turning to another person and addressing this person. This is true relation. In addressing the one who confronts me with the word "Thou," I have not reduced him or her to a thought that is part of me, to an object.

I *know* the other who faces me as a He or a She, and I first approach the other as an It, because this is the only way that I can "know" or recognize the other as other. However, as soon as I say "Thou" to Him or Her, the other no longer is an object for me. I now stand in relation to Thou. Buber refers to his notion of the I-Thou not as friendship, but as comradeship (*PMB*, 723/*KM*, 75). In friendship, I can approach the other out of selfish need, whereas in comradeship, I approach the other for the sake of relation. Because the relation is a meeting, because it does not happen in me, but rather *between* me and the other, it no longer has the structure of a subject that contains its object in a moment of thought. The relation between I and Thou is in no way a communion, coexistence, or interaction as Levinas might be inclined to believe, but a meeting. "Meaning is not found in one or both of the partners, it is found only in their dialogue, in this 'between' which they both live together" (*KM*, 75). Buber emphasizes that the I-Thou relation takes place neither in me, nor in the other, but rather *between* I and Thou. He writes that the I-Thou relation does not already exist in speech; rather it creates or begets speech (*IT*, 57/*W*, 81). The act of uttering the sound "Thou" "with one's vocal chords does not by any means entail speaking the uncanny basic word [I-Thou]" (*IT*, 85/*W*, 101). Buber considers most discourse to be a speaking *at*, instead of a speaking *to*, someone. Discourse in our day and age aims at no one except the speaker's own ego; it is conversation, idle talk, or "technical dialogue aimed at objective understanding" (*KM*, 78/ *BMM*, 3, 19). "True" speech does not need to involve any sounds or gestures (*BMM*, 3). "Genuine dialogue" means turning toward the other person, while at the same time recognizing — accepting — the otherness of that person (*KM*, 79, 85).

Buber stresses the element of "meeting" that the I-Thou relation entails. Dialogue — Thou-saying — is a response to a call. "In our life and experience," Buber asserts, "we are addressed" (*BMM*, 92). The response to these signs of address is neither a gesture nor an utterance arising out of one's mouth. Such responses would serve only to banish the one who addresses me to the world of It. The true response is a turning toward the other who addresses me.

Two questions must still be answered: (1) to what extent is Buber's I-Thou relation a reciprocal relation, and (2) to what extent do Buber's writings obviate Levinas's criticisms? One of Levinas's deepest concerns about any type of reciprocal relation, as Derrida shows, is that such a relation destroys the height of the other.

The I-Thou relation, however, is not a reciprocal relation. Speaking the primary word "I-Thou" does not destroy the height from which the other approaches, that is, the other's alterity. Reflection, the action that constitutes the I-It relation, occurs when I withdraw from accepting another person in his particularity, or when the I lets the other exist as part of myself. As soon as I stop addressing the other, as soon as I begin to reflect upon the other, I reduce the other to an object within the world of It (*BMM*, 23–24). In speaking the Thou, that is, in turning to the person and addressing him or her, I do not consider the other only insofar as the other fits into my conceptual framework. I allow the other to be as he or she really is. It is in this way that speaking — or addressing another — does not destroy the height of the other. "Genuine conversation, and therefore every actual fulfillment of relation between men, means acceptance of otherness" (*KM* 69). What Buber emphasizes about the relation, as opposed to Levinas, is that it takes place between me and the Thou to whom I am addressing myself; the relation does not happen *in* me. "Spirit," Buber tells his reader, "is not in the I, but between I and You [Thou]" (*IT*, 89/*W*, 103).

Likewise, it will be remembered that the Thou cannot be bounded by anything, or else it would then be an object, a thing. A person cannot calculate the sum of Yous [Thous], as one can calculate a sum of individuals, because "the sum of You and You and You never yields anything but You again" (*IT*, 96/*W*, 109). "Thou" simply indicates the initiative of turning toward and addressing another. As a result, there could never be a sum of Thous, for how could a "turning toward" be quantified or objectified?

This act of addressing the other reveals the role that God plays in Buber's conception of interhuman relations. For Buber, God cannot be inferred in anything, nor is God found by seeking (*IT*, 128–9/*W*, 132). "God" Buber declares, "may only be addressed" (*IT*, 124/*W*, 128). Buber equates what he terms the "eternal Thou" with God. He writes: "Every single You [Thou] is a glimpse of [the eternal You]. Through every single You the basic word addresses the eternal You" (*IT*, 123/*W*, 128). This does not mean that in every human there is a part of God; God can only be addressed. Every time I turn and address another person — or even an animal — I am, by the very action of addressing, necessarily turned toward and addressing God, the eternal Thou. In fact, in the introduction to his translation of *I and Thou*, Ronald Gregor Smith states that, although Buber himself never used the word "transcendence," his writings on human interaction and its relation to God point toward a transcendence drawn into the world. Yet, Buber wants to "transcend" this duality of infinite and finite, because he does not want to make God into the "wholly Other," into something that has no effect in the everyday world. For this reason, he stresses that inasmuch as God is wholly Other, God is wholly present

(*IT*, 127/*W*, 131). The "dialectical theology" from which he tries to distance himself only views God as a radical alterity, not as something mundane and interacting in the human sphere (*PMB*, 712). Buber distinguishes his notion of the infinite from any mathematical definition of infinity.

Buber also makes it clear in *I and Thou* and in a later essay entitled "What is Common to All" that the I-Thou should not be equated with any type of mystical unity with God, such as Spinoza may be proposing with his concept of the intellectual love of God (*IT*, 131–32/*W*, 134). Furthermore, the "I" is not to be raised to the level of God or a deity, such as proponents of certain strains of "existentialism" might suggest (*IT*, 132/*W*, 134). The eternal Thou is only something that one addresses and not something that one "knows." Buber writes that, "by its very nature the eternal You [Thou] . . . cannot be placed within measure and limit, not even within the measure of the immeasurable and the limit of the unlimited . . . it cannot be grasped as a sum of qualities, not even as an infinite sum" (*IT*, 160/*W*, 154). In turning toward another person and addressing him or her, I respect his or her alterity and I also address God. Accordingly, in addressing God, I neither turn God into an object of thought, nor into a friend or partner who stands on equal footing with me.

CONCLUSION

In Buber's notion of the I-Thou relation is not a reciprocal relation. The word "Thou" merely indicates the initiative on the part of an I of turning toward and addressing that which confronts the I. In speaking "Thou," the I does not reduce the other to an object, that is, an It. Hence, one allows the other to be as it is. More importantly, the action of speaking "Thou" is also an address and a turning toward God. In so doing, the I has not reduced God to an equal, as Levinas fears.

Part IV

HEIDEGGER, HUMANISM AND THE OTHER ANIMAL

THIRTEEN

Buber and Levinas — and Heidegger

Richard A. Cohen

The Levinas-Buber relation is a deep and instructive relationship.[1] Martin Buber is senior and far better known. His book, *I and Thou*, first published in 1923, was immediately and widely recognized as an important spiritual work and quickly translated into many languages, including Japanese. Buber is himself a recognizable figure, the bearded Jewish sage said to resemble a biblical prophet (even though, as Levinas once remarked, we have no photographs of the biblical prophets). Emmanuel Levinas, on the other hand, while a philosopher of the first rank, is never likely to be popular or well known. Although his many books and collections of articles have been translated into English, his name still often draws a blank — and this is almost as true within the academic community and the Jewish community as it is for the public at large.

What makes grasping the differences dividing Levinas and Buber of special importance, beyond the intrinsic value of gaining a sharp understanding of their thought separately and in conjunction, is the fundamental role that the ontological thought of Martin Heidegger plays for both of them. Both Buber and Levinas are critics of Heidegger. In an interesting twist of thought, however, their respective critiques of Heidegger serve, at the same time, as their critiques of one another. Buber accuses Levinas of being Heideggerian, and Levinas accuses Buber of the very same allegiance. Because for both thinkers these accusations are damning, their critiques of one another hinge in an important sense on the validity and depth of their respective critiques of Heidegger. The central thesis of the present essay is that it is Levinas — and not Buber — who fully critiques Heidegger. Levinas's critique of Heidegger is thus also a critique of Buber for unwittingly remaining within the orbit of Heidegger's thought.

BUBER ON LEVINAS AND ON HEIDEGGER

1957 Afterword to I and Thou

Although Buber wrote hardly anything directly about Levinas's thought, at a conceptual level, beyond explicit texts with proper names, he did respond rather directly to at least one of Levinas's central criticisms. He did this in the short Afterword of 1957 that he appended to the second edition of *I and Thou*. There Buber defended and focused on the topic — the reciprocity of the I-Thou relation — that is perhaps the central bone of contention in Levinas's 1958 article, "Martin Buber and the Theory of Knowledge."

Several Shorter Works

In this 1957 Afterword, Buber also indicates that "several shorter works" published after *I and Thou* function "to clarify the crucial vision by means of examples, to elaborate it by refuting objections, and to criticize views to which I owed something important but which had missed the central significance of the close association of the relation to God with the relation to one's fellow-men, which is my most essential concern" (*IT*, 171). These shorter writings are found in *Between Man and Man*. Here, as we shall see, the role of Heidegger becomes central. The "several shorter writings" of Buber are important, because they further develop and defend the central theses of *I and Thou* and because Levinas refers to them in his criticisms of Buber. But they are important also because in them Buber invokes and criticizes certain Heideggerian conceptions that play a key role not only in his own philosophy but also in his debate with Levinas. Opposition to Heidegger is important to Levinas's 1958 article on Buber and to all of Levinas's philosophy, and it is important as well, from Buber's perspective, in understanding Buber's short 1963 and 1967 responses to Levinas.

"What is Man?"

One of Buber's most important criticisms of Heidegger, one to which Levinas often refers in his 1958 article on Buber, is contained in Buber's 1938 inaugural course of lectures as Professor of Social Philosophy at the Hebrew University of Jerusalem. These lectures were delivered shortly after Buber fled a hostile Nazi Germany. Among his many distinctions as a thinker, Buber has the honor of being one of the earliest and most trenchant critics of Heidegger. Buber's 1938 lecture on Heidegger appeared in English translation in 1965, in a monograph entitled *"What is Man?"* (*BMM*, 118–205).

"Religion and Modern Thinking"

The second and briefer of Buber's criticisms of Heidegger came shortly after the war, that is to say, shortly after the Holocaust. They were also delivered as lectures, but this time presented at several American universities (Yale, Princeton, Columbia, Chicago and others) in November and December of 1951. This series of lectures was critical of what for Buber were the inadequacies of the philosophical stances of a variety of thinkers — Kant, Kierkegaard, Nietzsche, Sartre and Carl Jung — in relation to religion. One of these lectures, entitled "Religion and Modern Thinking" (*EG*, 63–92), presents an extended criticism of Heidegger. For the most part, however, these 1951 lectures reproduce Buber's earlier criticisms of 1938.

HEIDEGGER

It is unfortunate that Heidegger wrote no response to either Buber or Levinas, though he certainly had ample opportunity — and legitimate reasons — to do so. Nevertheless, this void does not hamper our aims. The concern of the present essay lies not in texts and proper names but rather with thought, in this case with Heidegger's original and central contribution to philosophy, namely, the "ontological difference," the *Seinsfrage*, the question of being. It is important to grasp the unity of Heidegger's central question and position in order to see how and to what extent it influenced, positively or negatively, both Buber and Levinas. While we cannot assume that the reader is intimately familiar with Heidegger's work, neither can we divert a great deal of attention to elaborate introductions. Like Buber and Levinas, this essay will draw from Heidegger's 1927 magnum opus, the "fundamental ontology" of *Being and Time*. It will also follow the "turn" (*Kehre*) of his ontology from its early orientation, found in *Being and Time*, which moved from beings — more particularly *Dasein* — to being, to its later and more original orientation, found in Heidegger's writings on language, poetry and thought, from being to beings.

BUBER AND HEIDEGGER, AND LEVINAS

As just noted, Buber gave two lectures critical of Heidegger, one before the war in 1938 and one after the war in 1951. In the earlier lecture, Buber considers Heidegger in relation to philosophical anthropology. Heidegger's philosophy is reviewed as part of a series of lectures published under the title "What is Man?" This publication is one of the "shorter works," as Buber says in his 1957 afterword to *I and Thou*, produced to "clarify the crucial vision" of *I and Thou*. It is an instance of Buber's desire "to criticize views to which I owed some-thing important but which had missed the central significance of the close association of the relation to God with the relation to one's fellow-men, which is my most essential concern" (*IT*, 172). It contains three criticisms of Heidegger; we will focus especially on the third that concerns Heidegger's notion of "solicitude," a notion that was critical in the exchange between Buber and Levinas in 1963 (*PN*, 33). The later lecture of 1951 is also critical of Heidegger. It locates his thought as one of three inadequate ways of approaching religion in modern thinking, the other two being Sartre's existentialism and Karl Jung's psychology. Because the later lecture is less developed and less relevant to our concerns, I will turn to it first, but briefly.

A second reason for considering Buber's postwar criticism of Heidegger first is that, with the exception of the adulatory cult of Heideggerians emanating from Jean Beaufret in Paris, certain historical reasons for criticizing Heidegger and his thought were glaringly obvious in the postwar, post-Holocaust context. Heidegger was a member of the Nazi party from 1933 to 1945. After the war and until the end of his days, he never apologized or rendered a convincing moral justification for his behavior. The obvious criticism, then, is that Heidegger's thought — like Heidegger himself — was somehow too deeply embedded in history to have been able to recognize and to judge from a responsible critical distance the horrors of the Nazi terror. In his 1951 lecture, Buber states: "Heidegger creates a concept of a rebirth of God out of the thought of truth which falls into the enticing nets of historical time" (*EG*, 78). Such is Buber's basic criticism, namely, that Heideggerian thought — *Denken* — lacks an adequate notion of transcendence or the divine to be able to properly judge history. The notion of "resolution," which engages *Dasein* authentically in its temporality and history according to *Being and Time*, leads no further than to an embrace of personal "fate" (*Schicksal*) within the overriding context of a social-historical "destiny" (*Geschick*)[2] — even if that social-historical destiny and that fate are Nazi! The historical or "epochal" ontological difference, the source and provider of whole worlds of meaning, is all too apparently incapable of differentiating between right and wrong.

When Buber uses the expression "a rebirth of God out of the thought of truth," he is referring to Heidegger's reading of Hölderlin's claim that ours is a time of "indigence." According to Heidegger's reading, this claim means that ours is "the time of the gods who have fled and of the God who is coming" (cited in *EG*, 72). Because his particular interest is in the most basic "I-Thou," the "I-Thou" with God, Buber interrogates Heidegger's thought to discover what this phrase, "the God who is coming," can mean. For Buber, speech faithful to the divine must be "a testimony to that which I call the dialogical principle" (*EG*, 76). This is not what Buber hears in Heidegger.

Instead — and Buber invokes Heidegger's infamous "Rectoral address of May, 1933, along with a manifesto delivered to students dated November 3rd of the same year" — "here history no longer stands, as in all believing times, under divine judgment, but it itself, the unappealable, assigns to the Coming One his way" (*EG*, 77). Heidegger is guilty of having "allied his thought, the thought of being, . . . to the hour as no other philosopher has done," and in doing so he must, as he did, "succumb to the fate of the hour" (*EG*, 77). The dark syllogism is clear: Heidegger has so bound his thought to the truth of being, and the truth of being to history, that when the critical hour came to judge history rather than to embrace it, Heidegger embraced it along with the "sinister leading personality of the then current history" (*EG*, 77), i.e., Hitler, whose name, by this circumlocution, Buber refuses to enunciate. This is what Buber meant when he said that "Heidegger creates a concept of a rebirth of God out of the thought of truth that falls into the enticing nets of historical time." No doubt Levinas would agree fully with Buber on this critical point.

Beyond the basic argument, that Heidegger's ontology falls into an uncritical historicism and the polemics that follow from it, the earlier lecture of 1938 explores why Heidegger embraces truth as a function of being rather than of dialogue so that he loses the capacity to judge history rather than to be swept along by it, and hence falls prey to the dark path of evil.

1938 Lecture

In this lecture, as I have indicated, Buber presents three criticisms of Heidegger, examined briefly below. The third, Buber's criticism of solicitude in Heidegger, will return in the Levinas-Buber confrontation.

a) *Dialogical Relation More Real than Heideggerian Self-Relation.* Buber's first — and primary — criticism of Heidegger is that "fundamental ontology" is neither fundamental nor in contact with the fullness of the real. Contrary to Heidegger's intention, his fundamental ontology is both narrow and abstract, representing only a limited or simple part, a fragment or aspect of being rather than the complex whole of what is genuinely real and meaningful. According to Buber's critical explication:

> Fundamental ontology does not have to do with man in his actual manifold complexity but solely with existence in itself, which manifests itself through man. . . . Heidegger abstracts from the reality of human life the categories which originate and are valid in the relation of the individual to what is not himself [death], and applies them to "existence" in the narrower sense, that is, to the relation of the individual to his own being. . . . Heidegger's modified categories disclose a curious partial sphere of life, not a piece of the whole real life as it is actually lived. (*WM*, 163–65)

Levinas criticizes Buber's fundamental philosophical commitment to ontology rather than to ethics. Quite clearly, Buber's critique of Heidegger is not based on a critique of ontology as such, but rather on a different version of ontology. For Buber, what is wrong with Heidegger's ontology has nothing to do with the fundamental status of ontological notions such as "reality," "actuality," and "being," but rather with the narrowness, and hence the abstractness, of Heidegger's characterizations of these ontological notions. Buber's primary point is not directed against ontology as such, but rather lies in the positive and ontological claim that dialogue serves as a better basis for ontology than what Heidegger takes for its foundation, namely, Dasein's care for existence and resolute engagement in historical-epochal being. Buber has no argument, therefore, over the fundamental status of ontology as the final arbiter of all things. Rather, his challenge to Heidegger is an argument over which ontology is best suited for that status.

Buber rejects Heidegger's attempt to restrict Dasein to existence. For Buber "original guilt" derives precisely — and in direct contrast to Heidegger — not from a lack of resoluteness, not in an essential failure to be able to recover one's own ground in being, but rather "in remaining with oneself" (*WM*, 166). That is, for Buber true being lies in the being of dialogue rather than in Heidegger's self-referential being, even when the latter includes not only the effort at self-recovery but takes that effort into its social and historical context. Thus for Buber the "call of conscience" that in Heidegger is a call from being to Dasein's being, is in reality a call from the other as encountered in Thou-saying. Buber writes: "'Where were you?' *That* is the cry of conscience. It is not my existence which calls to me, but the being which is not I" (*WM*, 166).

But this persisting commitment to ontology, characterizing the alterity of the Thou as "the being which is not I," and the self's Thou-saying as an accomplishment of the self's "whole being," is also the ground of Levinas's critique of Buber. Levinas found Buber's recognition of the primacy of a nonepistemological relation to otherness praiseworthy. What he finds most praiseworthy is when Buber speaks of this relation as person-to-person encounter. But for Buber person-to-person encounter is but one instance, and not the privileged instance (despite what we have seen above), of nonepistemological relation. Levinas takes issue with Buber's failure to recognize both the proper structure and the radical consequences of giving primacy to a non-epistemological relation. Buber fails to appreciate that the only relation capable of escaping epistemology, including the hermeneutic epistemology of Heidegger's "fundamental ontology," is ethical intersubjectivity. Buber does not recognize the radical consequences of a grounding of thought in intersubjectivity because, Buber's interpretation of intersubjectivity in terms of the reciprocity of the "I-Thou" is a continuation of, rather than a break with, ontological thought. Dialogical thought, then, would be a "full" rather than a "partial" ontology, to cite Buber's own words. Levinas argues that Buber does not realize that intersubjectivity cannot be properly interpreted within the confines and according to the standards of ontology.

b) *Transcendence of Dialogue versus Solitude of Dasein.* Buber's second criticism hinges on the question of solitude and transcendence. Buber contrasts the self-enclosure of Heidegger's "monological" thinking with the transcendence or "absolute" of his own "dialogical" thinking. The problem with Heidegger's thought, based on its narrowness and abstractness, is that it improperly grasps the transcendence that appears only within the "I-Thou" of dialogue. Thus Heidegger's Dasein, despite its attachment to the whole of historical being, remains "solitary."

> Heidegger's "existence" is monological. And monologue may certainly disguise itself ingeniously for a while as dialogue, one unknown layer after the other of the human self may certainly answer the inner address, so that man makes ever fresh discoveries and can suppose that he is really experiencing a "calling" and a "hearing"; but the hour of stark, final solitude comes when the dumbness of being becomes insuperable and the ontological categories no longer want to be applied to reality. . . . Heidegger's man stands before himself and nothing else, and — since in the last resort one cannot stand before oneself — he stands in his anxiety and dread before nothing. (*WM*, 168–72)

Levinas, too, criticizes Heidegger's philosophy of being for its inability — even in the essential being-in-the-world of Dasein, as well as in its appreciation for the "ontological difference" — to surpass the category of *Jemeinigkeit* or "ownness." Levinas contends, however, that Buber's alternative, what he calls "dialogue," is itself unable to escape the solitude, monologue, *Jemeinigkeit*, or "*closed system*" (*WM*, 171), that plagues Heideggerian thought. Dialogue, too, according to Buber's own account, becomes a relationship of being with itself.

c) *Essence versus Solicitude*. Buber's third criticism of Heidegger, in subsection five (and to some extent in the next two subsections) of "The Doctrine of Heidegger," has to do with the latter's notion of care or solicitude.

> For the relation of solicitude which is all he [Heidegger] considers cannot *as such* be an essential relation with the life of another, but only one man's solicitous help in relation with another man's lack and need of it. Such a relation can share in essential life only when it derives its significance from being the effect of a relation which is essential in itself. . . . In its essence solicitude does not come from mere co-existence with others, as Heidegger thinks, but from essential, direct, whole relations between man and man. . . . It is from these direct relations, I say, which have an essential part in building up the substance of life, that the element of solicitude incidentally arises, extending after that,

beyond the essential relations, into the merely social and institutional. In man's existence with man it is not solicitude, but the essential relation, which is primal. (*BMM*, 170–01)

Here Buber rejects solicitude as merely a secondary gloss on the more "primal" or "essential" encounter.

Ironically, Levinas's later criticism of solicitude is really an echo of Buber's original criticism of Heidegger found here. I say "ironically" because Levinas in "Martin Buber and the Theory of Knowledge" appears to defend Heidegger's notion of solicitude against Buber's critique. In fact, Levinas's point is not so much to defend Heidegger, as Buber seems to have thought, as to attack Buber.

> Buber rises in violent opposition to Heidegger's notion of *Fürsorge* — or care given to others — which would be, for the German philosopher, the true access to others. It is not, surely, to Heidegger that one should turn for instruction in the love of man or social justice. But *Fürsorge*, as response to essential destitution, is a mode of access to the otherness of the Other. It does justice to that dimension of height and of human distress, by which (far more than by *Umfassung*) the Relation is characterized. . . . Is dialogue possible without *Fürsorge*? If I criticize Buber for extending the *I-Thou* to things, it is not because he seems to be animistic in relation to nature; it is rather that he seems too much the *artiste* in his relation to people. (*PN*, 33)

Levinas is not defending Heidegger's notion of *Fürsorge* as such. Levinas is even more aware than Buber that its ultimate context is ontological rather than ethical. Rather, contra Buber, Levinas is saying that in the notion of Dasein's solicitude one can at least see a break with theoretical and practical reason instigated by an ethical inter-subjectivity (even if Heidegger does not ultimately understand it this way) rather than via the allegedly deeper embrace (*Umfassung*) of Buber's "essential" relation, which by Buber's own account is not bound to intersubjectivity and hence is not bound to ethics. In other words, Levinas *uses* Heidegger's notion of Dasein's solicitude to the extent that it is an ethical notion (notwithstanding the use to which Heidegger puts it) to oppose Buber's notion of "essential" relation, which is ultimately not an ethical relation. Thus Levinas *also* rejects both Buber's "essential" relation and Heidegger's "ontological difference" by insisting that the transcendence proper to the origin of signification is ethical and not ontological.

It is interesting to note, because it confirms Levinas's criticism of Buber, that in this same discussion of solicitude in Heidegger, Buber links his notion of "essential" relation to reciprocity or mutuality. Against Heideggerian solicitude Buber writes, "In *mere* solicitude man remains essentially with himself, even if he is moved with extreme pity; in action and help he inclines toward the other, but the barriers of his own being are not thereby breached; he makes his assistance, not his self, accessible to the other; nor does he expect any real mutuality, in fact he probably shuns it; he "is concerned with the other," but he is not anxious for the other to be concerned with him" (*BMM*, 170). Levinas would be the first to agree with Buber that the flaw in Heidegger's notion of solicitude lies in the irrefragable immanence of Dasein, in fact that "the barriers of his own being are not thereby breached." Nonetheless, while for Buber the issue and the alternative lies in the grace of reciprocal encounter, "for the other to be concerned with him," for Levinas the alternative lies rather in a more radical one-way being "toward the other" without any consideration of return, mutuality or reward. The ethical subject for Levinas is ethical precisely because its deepest self occurs as responsibility for-the-other before it is in any way for-itself, and certainly, therefore, also before any concern or anxiety regarding the other's concern for the self. Therefore Levinas criticizes Buber for precisely what Buber criticizes in Heidegger: "Heidegger's self is *a closed system*" (*BMM*, 171). Heidegger's closed system includes all of being-in-the-world, and Buber's includes the holistic embrace of essential relation, but both remain closed off to the genuine transcendence deriving from the moral priority of the "height and destitution" of the other.

d) *Society: Communion versus Justice.* In his 1938 essay "What is Man?" Buber writes:

> But is there on this level something corresponding to the essential *Thou* in relation to the multitude of men, or is Heidegger here finally right?

What corresponds to the essential *Thou* on the level of self-being, in relation to a host of men, I call the essential *We*.

The person who is the object of my mere solicitude is not a *Thou* but a *He* or a *She* [i.e, objectified being, "It" world]. The nameless, faceless crowd in which I am entangled is not a *We* but the "one" [Heidegger's *das Man*]. But as there is a *Thou* so there is a *We*. (*BMM*, 175)

The special character of the *We* is shown in the essential relation existing or arising temporarily between its members; that is, in an ontic directness holding sway within the *We* which is the decisive pre-supposition of the *I-Thou* relation (*BMM*, 175–76).

A full treatment of the topic of sociality and justice in Buber and Levinas goes far beyond the limitations of the present paper. Even a discussion of Buber's position vis-à-vis law, a central and complicated topic much discussed in the secondary literature, is not possible here. What is clear, however, is the parallel which exists for Buber between the primal relation of I-Thou in contrast to the I-It, and the I-We relation which is built on the I-Thou and which is for Buber the primal social relation. The I-We relation is an *extension* of the I-Thou relation, perhaps even a *projection* of it: "But as there is a *Thou* so there is a *We*."

Because Buber elaborated his idea of the "We" in terms of "utopia," we turn to his book of 1949, *Paths in Utopia*. To extend or project the I-Thou onto society seems a peculiar because an essential feature of the "I-Thou" is precisely its intimacy, that is to say, its inwardness, an experience of the "between" reserved exclusively for the two partners of the primal relation. Here lies Levinas's basic criticism: the "I-Thou" relation, by its very nature, cannot be projected socially. So how does Buber do it or claim to do it? "Community," Buber writes, "is the inner disposition or constitution of a life in common."[3] In "What is Man?", written 11 years earlier, he had already said, along the same lines: "The special character of the *We* is shown in the essential relation existing, or arising temporarily, between its members; that is, in the holding sway within the *We* of an ontic directness which is the decisive presupposition of the *I-Thou* relation. . . . Only men who are capable of truly saying *Thou* to one another can truly say *We* with one another"

(*BMM*, 175–6). In *Paths in Utopia* he writes, "A real community need not consist of people who are perpetually together, but it must consist of people who, precisely because they are comrades, have mutual access to one another and are ready for one another."[4]

So, like the intimate dyad of primal encounter, the community of the "We" is not only immediate and fundamental (socially), it is characterized as a relation of immanence, wholeness, mutuality and grace. It is "utopian" insofar as it represents only for some the "real community," the future for all, and as such is the social version of the primal relation existing sporadically between two in the I-Thou, against the backdrop of a world dominated by I-It relations.

It might seem overly clever to say of Buber's notion of utopia that it is utopian in precisely the sense that he faults Marx, that is to say, unreal, impossible, romantic fantasy, but there would be a kernel of truth to it. Just as the embrace of encounter happens by chance, by "grace," so too does the We of genuine social relations. Moreover, there is an additional problem: Buber shows no way to get from encounter to community. Each is self-contained and accidental. "Community," he writes in *Paths in Utopia*, "should not be made into a principle; it too, should always satisfy a situation rather than an abstraction. The realization of community, like the realization of any idea, cannot occur once and for all time; always it must be the moment's answer to the moment's question, and nothing more."[5] Just as anything that disrupts the moment of the "I-Thou" is an "I-It," anything that interferes with the "moment" of the "We" is no less extraneous and no less a loss of the between of the community. Thus, when Buber attempts to describe positively the community of the We, he resorts to the same poetic language that he had earlier used to point to the primal encounter of I and Thou. Both are based in experiences which Buber admits are "rare" and for which he can claim little more than that they have the seal of "wholeness" or "being" (*BMM*, 176). In both cases, Arno Munster detects the residues of Buber's early partiality for Hasidic enthusiasm and oriental mysticisms.[6] Another scholar credits Buber's "enthusiasm" to the infiuence of his reading of Nietzsche, while Levinas sees its genuine forebear in Bergson's notion of duration.⁷ One might also think of Charles Peguy's notion of "mystique" in this regard. Regardless of its source, it is clear that Buber's "We" is intended as a community of *Gemeinschaft* in contrast to what he takes to be abstract sociality of *Gesellschaft*.⁸ Nonetheless, his specific analysis, qua social theory, ends in a vagueness equivalent to abstractness of the latter, suggesting little more than a romantic, even mythological account of social being.

Levinas also speaks of "utopia" with regard to social being, but his is an account of justice, justice based in and derived from the morality of the face-to-face. Here "utopia," literally "no place," refers to the incomplete status — the ongoing task — of the justice demanded by morality. Insofar as a just world has not yet been established, and our world is thus an "unredeemed" world, a *u-topos*, no more important program is demanded by morality itself, and justice remains humanity's deepest and most pressing ideal. Its "place" is the future, the yet to come (*a-venir*: "to-come," and *avenir*, "future"). It is not a reality but an ideality. Still, it is neither an idea nor a fantasy, but the concrete day to day project of establishing exact measures and weights, fair courts, democratic polities, secure rights (speech, assembly, religion, press, etc.), equitable and universal distribution of food, clothing, shelter, health care, and the like. Of utopia and justice, Levinas writes: "Utopia, transcendence. Inspired by love of one's fellowman, reasonable justice is bound by legal strictures and cannot equal the kindness that solicits and inspires it."⁹

While justice does not presently "equal the kindness that solicits and inspires it," its aim is to set up a world in which such an equivalence can occur, a world in which justice and charity, justice and kindness, that is to say, social justice and the morality of the face-to-face, are in harmony with one another. Justice, then, has a source and a guide: the moral transcendence of the other. Its aim to create a world where morality is everywhere and at all times actual. Such, is the "utopian" or "messianic" structure of justice and history from Levinas's fundamental ethics.

The difference that divides Levinas and Buber, then, is the same difference, ultimately, that divides Levinas and Heidegger, and unites,

paradoxically, Buber and Heidegger. For Levinas goodness is fundamental; the good grounds the real. For Buber and Heidegger, in
contrast — each in his own way, to be sure — being is fundamental.
What Buber upholds in both the I-Thou and the We is the fleeting
presence of a wholeness of *being*. In contrast to the I-It, whether the
objectification of the other who faces or the social objectification of
Gesellschaft, both of which produce mere "fragmentation," the
experience or "embrace" of the "between" of "essential" relation
presents being in its wholeness. The ground for Buber, as for
Heidegger, remains ontological: a relation to being, a relation of being.
What Buber calls the "problem of ethics" is in truth the problem of
being, the problem of attaining wholeness of being. For Levinas, in
contrast, in both the morality of the face-to-face and in the social call
to justice, what is most important lies in a transcendence "otherwise
than being and beyond essence" — an ethical metaphysics.

FOURTEEN

The Retrieval of Humanism in Buber and Levinas

Matthew Calarco

Few thoughts could appear more outmoded today than those that attempt to recover humanism. As Nietzsche suggests, we find ourselves in an age in which we have become "tired of man," an age characterized above all by "modesty" regarding the self-knowledge and self-consciousness that has traditionally served as the hallmark of Western man.[1] What else could a retrieval of humanism signify except a naive denial of this exhaustion, and an exaggerated confidence in the dignity and uniqueness of human knowledge? Those who have such confidence do not belong to our time.[2] Critical works by the hermeneutists of suspicion (Nietzsche, Freud and Marx), along with Continental antihumanists (Althusser, Foucault, Lyotard and Lacan, to name only the most prominent) have disabused us of any facile pretensions to the distinctiveness and dignity of human modes of knowing.

Given the exhaustion of the humanist program, we are faced with a critical question. Should Buber's and Levinas's respective efforts to recover humanism be read as further instances of the outmoded and rearguard neohumanist response to the discourse of antihumanism? Or should their writings be interpreted as enacting a critical, deconstructive retrieval of humanism, beyond the closure of classical humanism? The primary task of this essay is to argue for the latter thesis. In particular, I shall argue that Buber's "believing humanism" and Levinas's "humanism of the other man," insofar as they seek to locate the essence of the human *outside* the realm of consciousness

250

and knowledge, should be read as productive and original (though not wholly unproblematic) responses to the crisis of humanism in our age. Indeed, both Buber's and Levinas's humanism serve as examples of how the critique of humanism in Continental thought does not necessarily lead to the annihilation of "man," but rather opens up the possibility for a new and more fecund understanding of what it means to be human. In both cases, the recovery of humanism inaugurates a new determination of the fundamental mode of being-human as *being-in-relation*.

HEIDEGGER'S CRITIQUE OF METAPHYSICAL HUMANISM

Before examining the motifs of relation and humanism in Buber and Levinas, it is useful to recall the basic theses of Heidegger's critical reflections on humanism because both Buber and Levinas situate their recovery of humanism over and against Heidegger.

For many readers, Heidegger's texts on humanism belong to a genealogy of theoretical *anti*-humanism.[3] The displacement of man from the center of beings, the shift in emphasis from human Dasein to the thought of Being, the rejection of the concept of "humanism" as a path for thought — these and related themes in Heidegger's work seem to point toward a unqualified rejection of humanism and its theoretical foundations. However, while there is much in Heidegger's texts to support such a reading, there is another, less perceptible, stratum running throughout his work that suggests his relation to humanism is far more ambiguous and complicated. A close reading of texts such as "Letter on 'Humanism,'" "Plato's Doctrine of Truth," the Nietzsche lectures from 1941, and other writings from this period reveals that Heidegger's critical remarks on humanism are directed less at humanism per se than at a particular *concept* and *history* of humanism, specifically the humanism that belongs to the Western metaphysical tradition. The dominant thrust of Heidegger's thinking in these works discloses the inner logic at work in the establishment and closure of metaphysics. Humanism itself comes under criticism only insofar as its classical forms mask the possibility of such an inquiry.

Consequently, when Heidegger suggests that "thinking" (the name given to what occurs at the limits of Western metaphysics) should risk rejecting "humanism" as a guiding concept,[4] this rejection should be understood alongside his rejection of other fundamental concepts of metaphysics, for example, "ethics." Such labels and divisions are rejected because they presuppose an interpretation not only of the meaning of Being (the central question of *Being and Time*), but also an answer to the question of the truth of Being. Given these simple and basic questions concerning Dasein's relation to Being, terms like "the human" and "ethics" only serve to weigh thought down with unnecessary metaphysical baggage.

But even as he rejects such labels as "humanism" and "ethics," Heidegger's work remains fundamentally concerned with the "object" that constitutes the focus of humanism and ethics, namely, the human. It is this underlying concern that accounts for Heidegger's repeated contention that his work should not be read as culminating in nihilism or a simple rejection of all ethics.[5] Likewise, despite his sustained critique of anthropocentrism and the modern technological rationality of Western humanity, Heidegger's thinking never abandons the human in favor of an "impersonal" Being. Quite the opposite is the case. As Heidegger himself acknowledges, his thinking remains humanist *in the extreme*, even despite the explicit disavowal of the label "humanist."[6]

The chief lesson to draw from Heidegger's delimitation of the essential complicity between metaphysics and all previous humanisms (Roman, Christian, Marxist and existentialist) is not that it is necessary to forgo any and all forms of humanism. It is true that Heidegger himself abandoned the term since he believed it was too laden with metaphysics; but this should not be taken to imply that *all* subsequent attempts to recover humanism are somehow naively metaphysical and pre-Heideggerian. What needs to be retained from Heidegger's analysis, rather, is the insight that *any effort to recover humanism must attend to its reliance on metaphysical thinking*. A humanism that addresses anew the question of the relation between the human and the Being of beings is no longer uncritically metaphysical, and thus serves as one means of responding positively to Heidegger's critique of *metaphysical* humanism. The reading of Buber and Levinas to which we now turn will attempt to demonstrate that their respective recoveries of humanism constitute just such a productive response.

BUBER'S "BELIEVING HUMANISM"

In his 1963 speech entitled "Believing Humanism," Buber seeks to identify his own version of humanism with Erasmus's Renaissance humanism. According to Buber, he and Erasmus share a common *concept* of humanism: a "believing humanism," as opposed to a secular, or faithless, version. While one might suspect that this conjunction of humanism and faith is precisely what Heidegger would criticize as being onto-theological, and thus classically metaphysical, such a humanism departs from this tradition in several important ways. To begin with, Buber's believing humanism is actually much closer to a preontological or "vulgar" understanding of *humanitas*, against which second century Roman essayist Aulus Gellius rails in his *Noctes Atticae*:

> Those who have spoken Latin and have used the language correctly do not give the word *humanitas* the meaning which it is commonly thought to have, namely, what the Greeks call *philanthropia*, signifying a kind of friendly spirit and good feeling towards all men without distinction; but they gave to *humanitas* about the force of the Greek *paideia*: that is, what we call *eruditonem institutionemque in bonos artes*, or "education and training in the liberal arts." Those who earnestly desire and seek after these are most highly humanized. For the pursuit of this kind of knowledge, and the training given by it, have been granted to man above all the animals, and for that reason it is termed *humanitas*, or "humanity."[7]

In contrast to Gellius's attempt to define and delimit the proper significance of *humanitas* in terms of *paideia*, Buber insists on something much closer to the common or philanthropic sense of the term.[8] For Buber, what renders the human being "most highly humanized" is not an "education and training in the liberal arts," but rather a joining of one's humanity with a certain ethics and faith, i.e., with a respect for the Other who is outside one's own scope of knowing.

Even though Buber and Erasmus share a believing humanism, they differ significantly in determining what is unique to the human. Indeed, as Buber suggests, it is precisely the contemporary effort to define the essence of the human with "sufficient exactness" that separates more recent humanists from their Renaissance forefathers. With respect to this modern trend, Buber distinguishes two dominant currents, only one of which leads toward a believing humanism. The first approach is the one taken by post-Kantian German philosophers, among whom Buber includes Hegel and Heidegger. Both of these thinkers, albeit in radically different ways, define the human as the sole and unique entity in all of Being in which Being as such is brought to consciousness. The preeminent function of man thus becomes "reflexion, the reflection on oneself through which . . . [man] ever again accomplishes the reflection of *Being* on itself" (*BH*, 118). Buber reads this act of reflection as a substantival reflex wherein the self is turned or thrown back on itself. What the self encounters in this reflexive and reflective movement is a de-worlded and formal concept of Being, the very concept of Being that serves as the foundation for all metaphysics. But if one defines the uniqueness of man as stemming from a relation to Being by way of self-consciousness, i.e., in terms of the conditions of possibility for metaphysics or cognition as such, then clearly the possibility of a *believing* humanism is foreclosed a priori. As Buber conceives it, faith demands a turn away from the knowing self closed in on itself, outward toward a relation *beyond knowledge* with others. Wherever the essence of the human is grounded in this latter conception of faith, it comes into direct conflict with the Hegelian-Heideggerian determination of being-human.

Thus, in order to unearth the foundations of a *believing* humanism, Buber argues that one must take leave of the Hegelian-Heideggerian approach to defining the uniqueness of the human. He does not, however, return to a site that is pre-Hegelian or pre-Heideggerian. Instead, Buber begins from *within* the Hegelian-Heideggerian horizon — a horizon in which sociality and relation are understood as fundamental aspects of being-human (Hegelian *Gemeinschaft* and Heideggerian *Mitsein*) — in order to extend and deepen the thought of relation begun there. Buber's critical advance over both Hegel and Heidegger lies in his determination of the essence of man *wholly* from within this site of relation. Relation, as Buber understands it, is not one fundamental mode of being-human among others (such as being-rational, being-linguistic, or being-self-aware); it is rather the principal and unique characteristic of human essence. In Buber's words, "what is central to [being-human] is not the relation of the human person to himself. . . . What is central, rather, is the relation of man to all existing beings" (*BH*, 119).[9]

Although, as this passage indicates, the relational aspect of human existence opens us to encounters with nonhuman beings, Buber problematically restricts the *opening up*, or *possibility*, of relation to human beings alone. Such a restriction occurs in the name of determining human essence with the "sufficient exactness" characteristic of contemporary humanism. Elaborating on the essential distinction between human and all other nonhuman beings, Buber writes:

> What appears here as the *humanum*, as the great superiority of man before all other living beings known to us, is his capacity "of his own accord," hence not like the animals out of the compulsion of his needs and wants but out of the overflow of his existence, to come into direct contact with everything that he bodily or spiritually meets — to address it with lips and heart or even with the heart alone. (*BH*, 119)

I will have occasion below to return to this issue, but it will suffice for the present moment to underscore the point that the human capacity for "address" or relation here denotes for Buber the simultaneous condition for any sort of ethical regard for other beings. The human being that of his or her "own accord" meets and engages with other beings is the only sort of entity that can encounter other beings as irreducible to the self and self-knowing. When other beings are approached solely as a means of meeting one's own "needs and wants," the independence of the other remains altogether unrecognized, and ethical regard beyond knowledge is impossible.

The Buberian determination of the essence of being-human as being-in-relation thus issues a challenge to any form of humanism that figures human essence in terms of a cognitive relation to other beings. Buber's version of humanism calls into question both classical forms of metaphysical humanism (in which the uniqueness of human beings lies in certain cognitive capacities such as *logos, ratio,* or *Wille*) and the post-metaphysical varieties (in which human uniqueness is characterized in terms of self-reflection on Being) that he locates in the Hegelian-Heideggerian tradition. To locate the uniqueness of being-human solely in the realm of knowledge, whether such knowing takes the form of *ratio* or a reflection on the Being of beings, is, according to Buber, to miss another, more fundamental relation that humans can have with other beings. Throughout his work, he characterizes this relation that exceeds cognition in various terms, including the "Thou-saying" and "Meeting."[10]

Inasmuch as the essence of the human is found on the other side of cognition, reuniting humanism with the faith requisite of a "believing humanism" is of decisive importance for Buber. Buber's believing humanism is not just another example of classical onto-theology, but is in many ways much closer to the faith of what we would today call "post-theological" theology. It is a faith prior to any revealed religion, a humanism that locates in relation — or rather *in the very opening of relation* — nothing but the site of a radical faith and nonknowing. There is no dogma that can be retrieved from this site and it is precisely this impossibility that accounts for Buber's religious liberalism.[11]

Despite the critical potential of Buber's "believing humanism" as a means of retrieving humanism from its fate at the hands of antihumanist critics, the accent Buber places on *voluntarism* in his description of human relation and meeting remains problematic in his thought. Indeed, this very aspect threatens to undermine Buber's attempt to exceed the closure of metaphysical humanism outlined by Heidegger. On Heidegger's account, the metaphysical tradition inaugurated by Plato's interpretation of the essence of truth culminates in the voluntarism of a "technological rationality" wherein all beings are reduced to mere "objects" for a dominating "subject." The paradoxical consequence of the metaphysical tradition is that, at the very point at which human civilization reaches a position of near total domination and power over all beings, it simultaneously and paradoxically finds itself on the brink of becoming nihilistic, decadent and "inhuman."[12] Buber is also concerned with this inhuman consequence of contemporary technology, and offers believing humanism as a "counterforce."

> Now one might object to my use of the attribute "modern" that precisely in our time very little of such a believing humanism is to be discerned. And, in fact, it will appear that today more than ever a type of man predominates who prefers to observe and make use of the beings whom he encounters on his life way instead of turning soul and deed toward them. . . . I mean the crisis of the human race which threatens it with extinction. I mean the technology that has become leaderless, the unlimited mastery of the means that no longer have to answer to any ends; I mean the voluntary enslavement of man in the service of the split atom. In the growing, still plastic generation more and more men are aware of what is preparing itself there; their day-by-day increasing awareness, the knowledge of the crisis, summons in them the only counterforce that can succeed in elevating ends again. . . . It is this counterforce that I call the new believing humanism. (*BH*, 121)

Arguably the very effort on the part of the self to "turn soul and deed" toward an encounter with other beings remains inextricably linked to a metaphysics of subjectivity and self-presence, the very metaphysics that undergirds the technological crisis that both Buber and Heidegger seek to overcome. Both the decision to turn *toward* and to turn *away* from other beings originates from within the self-conscious I rather than from the Other. In order to develop a humanism that is able to push beyond this voluntaristic and intellectualist limit, it is necessary to rethink the subject as being *always already* turned toward other beings, as ex-posed and in-clined *prior* to any decision on the part of the self. Beginning from this site, Buber's notion of a subject who turns "soul and deed" toward other beings is understood as an affirmation of an initial exposure and inclination toward those very beings. Although there are elements of this thought in Buber's work, Levinas's writings on humanism, to which we shall now turn, presented this conception in far more elaborate and rigorous detail.

SUBJECTIVITY AND HUMANISM IN LEVINAS

In the essays "Humanism and Anarchy" (1968) and "No Identity" (1970) (included in *Humanisme de l'autre homme* [1972]), Levinas develops his version of a "humanism of the other man" in response to the antihumanism prevalent in French thought in the late 1960s. Throughout these two essays, Levinas accepts the basic arguments of modern antihumanism. Advances in the social sciences, certain trends in Heideggerian and post-Heideggerian thought, as well as the horrifying realities of countless wars and dead bodies have rendered tragicomic the notion that the human being of Western metaphysics is the privileged point of reference, or telos, of the universe (*CPP*, 127). Modern antihumanism attests to this displacement and ex-centering of the human from the comfort, safety and integrity of self-presence by demonstrating the priority of language and structures in the constitution of subjectivity (anthropology), the primacy of the unconscious in the ego (psychoanalysis), and the primordiality of Dasein's finite ek-sistence or transcendence over and against the human's self-presence (Heidegger). Since Levinas acknowledges the obvious significance of these advances, there is no question of going back to a philosophy *before* antihumanism in order to find a ground for his own humanism. Rather, in *Humanisme de l'autre homme*, Levinas posits his thought of humanism in the form of a critical *question* to modern antihumanism.[13]

According to Levinas, the various forms of antihumanism all contest the primacy of the inward world of the subject (*CPP*, 144). Prior to and more basic than our human persevering in our own being and self-presence, an openness to otherness at the very heart of subjectivity renders self-presence secondary and compromised. This openness can be understood, Levinas suggests in three ways: 1) the "openness of every object to all others, in the unity of the universe" (*CPP*, 145), that is, the interaction or community of substances in the Third Analogy of experience in Kant's *Critique of Pure Reason* (A 211–15/B 256–62; see esp. A 211/B 257–8); (2) The openness of Dasein's ek-static mode of being and its ek-sistence in the openness of Being, or what Heidegger often refers to as an openness to the call of Being;

(3) openness in the more radical sense that Levinas seeks to locate at the core of the subject, a "denuding of the skin exposed to wounds and outrage" (*CPP*, 146). This characterization of the openness or subjectivity of the subject — exposed in sensibility to the persecution of the other, interminably troubled in bad conscience, radically passive beyond mere receptivity, suffering and vulnerable — is something that can only be thought after or following antihumanism. In other words, before the subject can be determined as radically passive, there must be a critique of the autarchical ego, secure in its own self-presence. Modern antihumanism helps to accomplish this critique. But the antihumanist critique only makes possible the thought of the subject as radical passivity; it does not itself pursue this thought of the subjectivity of the subject proper to the saying of responsibility. As Levinas writes in *Otherwise Than Being or Beyond Essence*:

> Modern antihumanism, which denies the primacy that the human person, free and an end in itself [*la personne humaine, libre but d'elle même*], would have for the signification of being, is true over and beyond the reasons it gives itself. It clears the place for subjectivity positing itself in abnegation, in sacrifice, in a substitution which precedes the will.[14]

Levinas poses his more primordial notion of the subjectivity of the subject to antihumanism in the form of a skeptical question. In a memorable passage from the last lines of "Humanism and Anarchy," Levinas suggests that "Modern antihumanism is perhaps not right in not finding in man, lost in history and in order, the trace of this pre-historical and an-archical saying" (*CPP*, 139). What Levinas's guarded critique implies is that antihumanism has perhaps overlooked the diachronic time of the saying of responsibility in which the subject as sensible is exposed to alterity beyond consciousness — in short, antihumanism has perhaps ("perhaps," for there is no possibility of certainty, knowledge or proof here) missed the moment of ethics. To argue, as antihumanism does, that structures (psychological, cultural, symbolic, linguistic, etc.) constitute subjectivity does not answer the question of what a subject must be in order to be open to structures as such. Levinas's answer to this question is that the subjectivity of the subject, its openness to the Other, is perhaps located in the "diachronic" time of bad conscience, sensibility and radical passivity — all of these ethical terms serving as different names for a time and entity that is "otherwise than being." This understanding of subjectivity can only be offered as a skeptical question to antihumanism inasmuch as the time of ethical subjectivity escapes consciousness and knowledge. The call of the Other, and the subject's openness to this call, are structured in such a way that any statement about them in synchronic language is an "abuse of language," a betrayal of the "saying" by the "said," an attempt to render the unknowable known and present.[15]

CONCLUSION

If we wish to speak of humanism today in a manner that does not fall back simply within the closure of metaphysical humanism, Levinas's conception of human subjectivity as outlined here is one of the few viable starting points. Although Buber's believing humanism gestures toward a similar thought, it nevertheless risks uncritically repeating a thought of subjective agency that can easily be subsumed within the Heideggerian delimitation of metaphysical humanism. Levinas's humanism, on the other hand, attenuates this risk inasmuch as it begins from within the space of the post-Heideggerian, antihumanist critique of subjective agency. By taking up a critical relation to the subject and freedom, Levinas does not sacrifice agency altogether, but rather reinterprets the subject's freedom as a "gift" or "investiture" deriving from the Other. This displaced conception of freedom, where my freedom and my decision to turn toward or away from Others is not wholly of my own making, is perhaps what marks the most promising starting point for any humanism that seeks to be post- or non-metaphysical.

In bringing this essay to a conclusion, I want to address briefly a lingering question that haunts any discussion of a postmetaphysical retrieval of humanism: If we grant that the metaphysical foundations of humanism (the definition of man as *animal rationale*, and the determination of the Being of beings as objective presence) no longer offer us a tenable point of departure for developing a thought of humanism, and if we further decide to follow Buber and Levinas in grounding postmetaphysical humanism in radical faith and exposed subjectivity, can we be certain that the thought we are developing is still a humanism? In other words, can the Buberian notion of faith and the Levinasian notion of subjectivity, these "structures of ex-appropriation," as we might call them, be limited to human beings alone? Can the obligations that are contracted in the site of exposure be said to originate only from other human beings?[16] These questions cannot be avoided if the critical retrieval of humanism begun by Buber and Levinas is to avoid repeating the anthropocentrism of the metaphysical humanism it seeks to overcome.

FIFTEEN

Face-to-Face with the Other Animal?

Peter Atterton

I am human, and nothing human is alien to me.
— Terence, *The Self-Tormentor*

What's outside we only know from the animal's face.
— Rilke, *Duino Elegies*

It is perhaps no exaggeration to say that the inclusion (*Umfassung*) (*IT*, 178) of nature within the I-Thou relation has been the biggest obstacle to the reception of Buber's thought. Levinas is one critic for whom the possibility of Thou-saying (*Du-Sagen*) to nonhuman beings constitutes a retreat from the fundamental insight of *I and Thou*, which consists in distinguishing between the interpersonal I-Thou relation and the impersonal I-It relation to things known objectively and scientifically. To speak of an I-Thou with anything other than the human undermines what for Levinas is "Buber's fundamental contribution to the theory of knowledge" (*PN*, 23). It implies that Thou-saying is capable of almost any content, and thus is something purely "formal" (*PN*, 29).

This criticism of Buber, which first appeared in "Martin Buber and the Theory of Knowledge" (1958), was repeated three years later in Levinas's magnum opus, *Totality and Infinity* (*TI*, 68), and there is no indication that Levinas ever regarded it as misplaced, despite Buber's various replies to his critics (*PMB*, 697, and *PI*, 28). In the following study, I shall not take sides in the meeting — or mismeeting (*Vergegnung*) — between Buber and Levinas, a dialogue that fell prey to mutual misunderstanding on more than one occasion.[1] I propose instead to occupy the "narrow ridge" — to borrow a favorite expression of Buber's[2] — *between* Levinas and Buber by reassessing Levinas's criticism of Buber's alleged formalism as it relates to the question of the other animal.[3] I shall argue that Levinas's criticism seriously underestimates a major strength of Buber's philosophy, which is precisely to have included the possibility of extending ethical consideration to other animals in their own right. This is not to privilege Buber's philosophy over Levinas's. Although I do not argue the point here, I continue to regard Levinas's dialogical philosophy as the stronger and more sophisticated of the two, one that is ultimately better equipped to move beyond the ontotheological tradition. My aim on this occasion is simply to call into question Levinas's treatment of animals by juxtaposing it with Buber's. Is Levinas right to reject the Buberian possibility of an I-Thou — or face-to-face — with the animal? I shall claim that he is not, and that as a result his objection to Buber's philosophy is specious — and *speciesist.*

"AND YOU, POOR FLOWERS, ARE NOT EVEN THERE" — PAUL CELAN

Critics, such as Levinas, who reject the possibility of addressing "Thou" to anything other than human beings are likely to regard the relation to the nonhuman realm as an I-It relation or some other type of relation irreducible to the twofold ontology of *I and Thou*. Certainly, Buber himself was aware of the difficulty of including the nonhuman in a relation whose paradigm is the interhuman relationship characterized by mutuality (*Mutualität*) and reciprocity (*Gegenseitigheit*). Indeed, in the 1957 Postscript to *I and Thou*, he sought to distinguish the relation to nature from the relation that exists between persons through the introduction of the term threshold (*Schwelle*). The plant and mineral world ("from the stones to the stars" [*IT*, 173]) were said to be at the "pre-threshold" (*Vorschwelle*) of mutuality; the animal at the threshold; and the human at "over-threshold" (*Überschwelle*). The fact that human beings alone are capable of *complete* mutuality, and thus are said to participate in the life of what Buber calls "spirit," explains why the I-Thou relationship with the human other enjoys a certain privilege in Buber's descriptions: "When I face a human being . . . everything else lives in *his* light" (*IT*, 59). But it is clear that the regions of nature — from rocks to plants to animals — are still defined in terms of their capacity for mutuality, and that is presumably the reason why Buber felt he could simply revise the twofold ontology of *I and Thou* rather than abandon it altogether.

Why, then, did Levinas feel it necessary to exclude the relation to nature from the I-Thou? A short essay by Levinas appearing in 1972 under the title "Paul Celan: From Being to the Other" not only makes clear Levinas's uncompromising refusal to include nature within the relationship of dialogue, it also provides a striking example of his tendency to confine Buber's dialogue within the very anthropological limits that Buber himself attempted to go beyond.

The essay opens with Levinas citing approvingly an observation made by Celan in a letter written to Hans Bender: "I cannot see any basic difference between a handshake and a poem" (*PN*, 40).[4] Levinas is struck by the remark because for him the poem described in this way has all the hallmarks of ethical speech. In contrast to the famous Heideggerian "language that speaks"[5] — the *logos* of Being in general (ontology) that speaks to no one in particular — the poem is speech in the first person, "a saying without a said" (*PN*, 40) that goes toward the Other. It is "a moment of pure touching, pure contact, grasping, squeezing — which is, perhaps, a way of giving" (*PN*, 41). The reading is corroborated by Celan's famous apologia for his muse, *The Meridian*, written in response to his winning the Büchner Prize in 1960. There Celan describes the poem as "dialogue, often impassioned dialogue . . . meetings, paths of a voice toward a vigilant Thou" (*PN*, 42).[6] Levinas seizes upon these "vibrant formulas" (*PN*, 41) in order to introduce Buber into the discussion. He immediately brands them "Buber's categories!" (*PN*, 42) — adding an exclamation point lest his readers should forget that Buber was the first to make the point about meeting a Thou through dialogue.

A few sentences later, Levinas invokes Buber again — this time to denounce what he calls the "poetics of the avant-garde, in which the poet has no personal destiny" (*PN*, 42). "To them," writes Levinas, "Buber is preferred without doubt" (*PN*, 42). Levinas appears unperturbed by the fact that many elements in Buber's philosophy would also make Buber a target of criticism as much as an ally in criticism. Buber's Thou-saying in reference to a tree (*IT*, 57 passim), for example, is simply left out of consideration in the essay under discussion. As is the fact that it would be easy to cite numerous places in Celan's poetry and prose where the human and nature are conflated. ("Tall poplars — human beings of this earth!";[7] "Bury the flower and put a man on its grave."[8]) What Levinas finds in both authors' work is attestation of the "essentially Jewish" (*PN*, 45) movement where one human being goes toward another human being to the exclusion of everything else — namely, nature.

To illustrate this poetic movement of Hebraic "depaganization" (*PN*, 45) in contrast to the "poetic dwelling" (Hölderlin) of the early Greeks, attuned to the "self-blossoming emergence"[9] (Heidegger) of nature as *physis*, Levinas turns to Celan's prose piece "Conversation in the Mountains." Two Jews are having a face-to-face while walking through the mountains. They are so engrossed in conversation that they are oblivious to the resplendent nature that surrounds them. I quote the passage that is quoted piecemeal by Levinas (*PN*, 41, 45):

> So it was quiet, quiet up there in the mountains. But it was not quiet for long, because when a Jew comes along and meets another, silence cannot last, even in the mountains. Because the Jew and nature are two, have always been and still are, even today, even here. [*Denn der Jud und die Natur, das ist zweierlei, immer noch, auch heute, auch hier.*]
>
> So there they are, the cousins. On the left, the turk's-cap lily blooms, blooms wild, blooms like nowhere else. And on the right, corn-salad, and *dianthus superbus*, the maiden-pink, not far off. But they, those cousins, have no eyes, alas. Or, more exactly: they have, even they have eyes, but with a veil hanging from them, no, not in front, behind them, a moveable veil. . . .

> They are tongue and mouth as before, these two, and in their eyes
> there hangs a veil, and you, poor flowers, are not even there, are not
> blooming, you do not exist, and July is not July.[10]

Leaving aside the problematic gesture of using a particular culture to speak of that which allegedly transcends cultural differences, which is repeated by Levinas elsewhere when he elevates Judaism to the status of an existentiale,[11] we are obliged to ask the following question: Would Buber, a Jewish thinker, informed by Hasidism and the mystical ideal of *Hislahavus* ("bursting into flame" or "fervor"), accept the claim that "the Jew and the nature are two, have always been two?" To be sure, Buber never ceased from *I and Thou* onward to claim that the terms of the I-Thou relation maintain their independence, and even renounced his early writings, e.g., *Daniel* (1913), for presenting the relation as one of unity.[12] To speak of the meeting as "within one," according to the later Buber, is to relegate it to an I-It relation. If, however, the claim "*Denn der Jud und die Natur, das ist zweierlei*" is meant to set up an opposition between the I and the Thou in the sense that would rule out the possibility of the "inclusion" (*Umfassung*) of nature within Thou-saying, then Buber would be the first to reject it.

The tendency to invoke Buber against Heidegger and "the philosophy of the Neuter" (*TI*, 298) also emerges in "Martin Buber and the Theory of Knowledge." This was Levinas's earliest and most sustained critique of Buber, drawing on *I and Thou* (1923), "Education" (1926), "Dialogue" (1929), "The Question of the Single One" (1936), "What is Man?" (1938) and "Man and His Image Work" (1957). Perhaps because of the philosophical anthropology that grounds these Buberian texts, Levinas sides with Buber everywhere against previous philosophizing and the tendency to treat the relationship with the Thou as a relationship with an It. He writes:

> The fact that the relation with the being that underlies objective knowledge leads not to the inhuman and neuter entity, Heidegger's *Sein des Seienden*, but rather to a *Seiendes* that is the other person, and therefore to society, seems to me to be of great spiritual importance. (*PN*, 23)

Buber's "fundamental contribution" to contemporary philosophy, according to Levinas, resides in his distinguishing the meeting with a

Thou from the experience of an object, as well as in the richness of the analyses underlying the distinction, and in the desire to ground experience in the meeting itself (*PN*, 23).

This approval notwithstanding, "Martin Buber and the Theory of Knowledge" ends with "a few objections." The "main criticism" is directed at the reciprocity of the I-Thou relation:

> How can we maintain the specificity of the interhuman *I-Thou* without bringing out [*faire valoir*] the strictly ethical meaning of responsibility, and how can we bring out the strictly ethical meaning without questioning the reciprocity on which Buber always insists? Doesn't the ethical begin when the *I* perceives the *Thou* as higher than itself? (*PN*, 32)

If the specificity of interhuman relation I-Thou (S) implies that responsibility has an ethical meaning (E), and if ethical responsibility is nonreciprocal (~R), then it follows that the specificity of interhuman relation can be maintained only if the I-Thou is nonreciprocal. Formally put: $S \supset E / E \supset \sim R // S \supset \sim R$. It should be noted that nonreciprocity is only a *necessary* and not sufficient condition for "bringing out" the ethical meaning of responsibility. If it were indeed a sufficient condition, then the relationship with the nonhuman would have an ethical meaning, something Levinas objected to earlier in the essay when he attributed the indeterminateness of what he called the "ethical elements" in Buber's work to the fact that "the I-Thou is possible in relation to things" (*PN*, 29). Buber denied that rocks, plants and animals — "things" in Levinas's vernacular — are capable of complete reciprocity, which he restricted to the interhuman I-Thou. Not that Buber thereby excluded the possibility of ethical asymmetry in Levinas's sense. Indeed, at times he even embraced it: "Now one can act, help, heal, educate, raise, redeem. Love is responsibility [*Verantwortung*] of an I for a Thou" (*IT*, 66). But even if we accept, as I do, that Levinas is substantially correct when he criticizes Buber for under-estimating "the strictly ethical meaning of responsibility" by presenting the I-Thou as a relation of "totally spiritual friendship" and "angelic spiritualism" (*PN*, 33),[13] is Levinas right to insist on what he calls "the specificity of the interhuman *I-Thou*" in the first place?

Not that Levinas completely excluded the nonhuman from the I-Thou — or what he prefers to call the face-to-face. Nor is he wholly disdainful of spirituality. In *Totality and Infinity*, he writes: "The dimension of the divine opens forth from the human face"; "Ethics is spiritual optics"; "The Other is not the incarnation of God, but precisely by his face, in which he is *disincarnate*, is the manifestation of the height in which God is revealed" (*TI*, 78, 79); "In this welcoming of the face (which is already my responsibility in his regard, and where accordingly he approaches me from a dimension of height and dominates me), equality is founded"; "The Other, in his signification prior to my initiative, resembles God" (*TI*, 78, 79, 214, 293). How is it possible to make these types of metaphysical statements and *not* draw a cardinal and hierarchical distinction between the human and the so-called lower animals? As soon as we say that the human Other is "spiritual" and "resembles God," do we not thereby imply that every other creature on earth is radically dissimilar to human/God, unequal and humble ("low to the earth" in the etymological sense)? Have we not immediately provided a justification for their domination, exploitation and use? In the Book of Genesis, following the creation of human beings in His own image, God immediately proceeds to give humans dominion (*râdâh*, literally "to tread down") over the fish and the fowl and all other creatures (Gen. 1:26). One wonders how much Levinas was influenced by this passage when he stated in "Is Ontology Fundamental?" (1951) that it is possible to murder the Other when one does not look the Other in the face: "I can in killing attain a goal; I can kill as I hunt or slaughter animals, or as I fell trees."[14] Or when he wrote in *Otherwise Than Being*: "The infinite cannot then be followed in the way of the trace like game by a hunter" (*OB*, 12; modified translation).

Levinas acknowledges that there are times when the shoe is on the other foot — or hoof — and human beings find themselves exposed to animal nature. Hunger, sickness and fear prey on human beings: "There is no question of doubting this human misery, this dominion [*empire*] the things and the wicked [*les méchants*] exercise over man, this *animality*" (*TI*, 35; emphasis added). Elsewhere Levinas speaks of "the hostile impulses of animal particularities [that] oppose one another" (*TI*, 253). It would appear, then, that when I do not look the Other in the face, when I no longer treat him or her as *homo spiritualis*, but merely as *homo animalis*, then in my wickedness I become *homo animalis*. Levinas here is quite close to Kant, who similarly made a distinction between human beings in animal nature and humans as moral beings, while attributing human wickedness to animality — naturally. But Levinas is no Kantian regarding the animal question, as we shall see in the next section.

THE FACE OF THE OTHER ANIMAL

Everything would seem to depend on whether an animal has a face. For if an animal has a face, then presumably it is owed obligations in the same way that the bearer of the human face — the Other — is owed obligations.[15] To understand what Levinas means by the fundamental concept of "face," we must glance briefly at *Totality and Infinity*. The face expresses itself "*kath auto*" (*TI*, 67 passim). Levinas almost certainly uses this term in the sense that Aristotle uses it in Book Δ of the *Metaphysics*, where it is defined as "whatever factor of a thing's being cannot be a factor of some other being. So, a man can be explained as an animal, a biped, but 'by himself' ['*kath auto*'] a man is a man."[16] The face signifies the "living presence" (*TI*, 66) of the Other "by himself," i.e., without reference to anything else. This is why Levinas calls the face-to-face an "immediate relation" (*TI*, 52) and a "relation without relation" (*TI*, 80). The face is characterized by a directness and ineffability that dispenses with — or is capable of dispensing with — the intermediary of concepts or symbolic communication (words, signs, ritual, music, and art). The directness of the face, however, is not entirely immediate for it cannot forgo the mediation of the senses. Hence, "the whole body — a hand or a curve of the shoulder — can express as the face" (*TI*, 262). Indeed, it is the eyes in their absolute frankness that best captures the *kath auto* of expression that is without words as such: "The eyes break through the mask — the language of the eyes, impossible to dissemble. The eye does not shine; it speaks" (*TI*, 66).

Prima facie, Levinas's description of the face as it is presented in *Totality and Infinity* would seem to augur well for the animal that is traditionally *zōon alogon*. For although the animal lacks speech, it could still be said to have a face insofar as it has the power of expression at its disposal — the very power of expression that Buber was able to find in the eyes of a cat, for example. In the third part of *I and Thou*, he wrote:

> The eyes of the animal have the capacity of a great language. *Independent, without any need of the assistance of sounds and gestures*, most eloquent when they rest entirely in their glance, they express the mystery in its natural captivity. . . . I sometimes look into the eyes of a house cat. . . . Undeniably, this cat began its glance by asking me with a glance that was ignited by the breath of my glance: Can it be that you mean me? Do you want that I should not merely do tricks for you? Do I concern you? Am I there for you? Am I there? What is that coming from you? What is that around me? What is it about me? What is that?! (*IT*, 144–45)

It is easy to dismiss this famous passage as an anthropomorphism. But even if Buber can be criticized here for attributing distinctively human characteristics to a cat, the question still remains whether Levinas has the critical resources at his disposal to rule out in principle the animal's having the kind of face from which something like an ethical address might proceed.

In the decade prior to *Totality and Infinity*, there is little doubt that Levinas did not consider this to be a possibility. The animal simply lacked a face able to address us. In "The Ego and the Totality" (1954), he spoke of "an animal freedom, wild, faceless" (*CPP*, 19), and in "Philosophy and the Idea of Infinity" (1957) he stated that "a face . . . differs from an animal's head in which a being, in its brutish dumbness, is not yet in touch with itself" (*CPP*, 55). However, in an important interview that took place in 1986, Levinas appeared to have changed his mind somewhat: "One cannot entirely refuse the face of an animal. It is via the face that one understands, for example, a dog. Yet the priority here is not found in the animal, but in the human face. . . . The phenomenon of the face is not in its purest form in the dog. . . . But it also has a face" (*PM*, 169). We might have expected

Levinas to go on to say that the dog is able to appeal to our goodness in roughly the same way as humans. Unfortunately for the dog, things are not that straightforward for Levinas. When his interviewers wanted to know whether the commandment "Thou shall not kill" is not also expressed in the face of an animal, Levinas equivocated: "I cannot say at what moment you have the right to be called 'face.' The human face is completely different [from the animal's] and only afterwards do we discover the face of an animal. I don't know if a snake has a face. I can't answer that question. A more specific analysis is needed" (*PM*, 172).

One cannot help but feel that Levinas is being less than ingenuous here. He does not know at what moment "the right to be called 'face'" occurs, but he knows that the human possesses the right first ("only afterwards do we discover the face of an animal"). He claims not to know whether a snake has a face *in the ethical sense*, though his failure to undertake the "specific analysis" required to answer the question during the 40 years or so he spent talking about the ethical significance of the human face naturally makes one doubt whether he was really as agnostic as all that. It also leaves one perplexed as to what such an analysis might have looked like had he seen fit to undertake it. As Matthew Calarco writes, "one perhaps wonders what kind of 'analysis' would help one to 'know' whether or not a given singular being has a face — as if the face were not precisely that which is irreducible to analysis and knowledge."[17]

Might we still not have obligations to animals even if analysis were to show conclusively that animals lacked a face in the ethical sense? In the interview under discussion, Levinas conceded that, "It is clear that, without considering animals as human beings, the ethical extends to all living beings. We do not want to make an animal suffer needlessly and so on. But the prototype of this is human ethics. Vegetarianism, for example, arises from the transference to animals of the idea of suffering. The animal suffers. It is because we, as human, know what suffering is that we can have this obligation" (*PM*, 172).

I assume by "all living beings" that Levinas does not mean the entire biosphere — though he may.[18] What seems more likely is that

Levinas is saying that we have obligations to all *sentient* beings — animals as well as humans. Our obligations to animals, however, are merely secondary and derivative inasmuch as they presuppose the "prototype" of human ethics. Not that Levinas here is simply following Kant, who argues in his *Lectures on Ethics* that so-called duties to animals are really "indirect duties toward humanity."[19] Kant argued that kindness bestowed on animals helps us cultivate and strengthen our good will, thus making us more likely to do our duty to each other. Levinas appears to be arguing, by contrast, that we have an obligation to animals simply because "the animal suffers." In doing so, he seems quite close to Bentham and Singer, who both argue that the fact that an animal can suffer is evidence that it has interests (in *not* suffering) that we are obliged to take into account when deciding how to act.[20] However, whereas the principle of equal consideration of interest underlying Jeremy Bentham's and Peter Singer's position generates positive obligations to animals, Levinas suggests that our obligations to animals are purely negative duties of omission. He says "we do not want to make an animal suffer *needlessly*." This, of course, begs the question of whether we are justified in making animals suffer when we eat them, farm them, wear them, hunt them, race them, ride them, stick picas in them, sacrifice them, encage them, or use them for scientific and medical purposes. I shall come back to this question later. First, I wish to return to the interview, if only because it is Levinas's most indepth response to the animal question, and shows the extent to which Levinas, despite his self-professed departure from the philosophical tradition (*TI*, 269), retains the great twin leitmotifs of the tradition — anthropocentrism and humanism.

Levinas does not deny that we have obligations to members of other species. What he denies is that those obligations are primary in the sense that we can have them independently of our ethical relations with each other. Recall, "the prototype of this is human ethics. Vegetarianism, for example, arises from the transference to animals of the idea of suffering. The animal suffers. It is because we, as human, know what suffering is that we can have this obligation." The implication is that our relations with each other require no such vicarious identification. The reader familiar with Levinas's *Otherwise Than Being* will know that when confronted with human suffering, according to Levinas, I am immediately affected by the affection of the Other. I do not project onto the Other my own suffering through "analogical appresentation" (Husserl) and "empathy" (Stein),[21] but am exposed to the Other's suffering directly though "contact," "the caress" and "maternity" (see *OB*, chap. 3). By contrast, my relation with the other animal is never immediate or direct. The animal affects me only through the face of the Other, who teaches me the evil nature of suffering. Unable to express itself *kath auto*, and without the support of the Other, the face of an animal is no more than a pelt. "In stroking an animal," writes Levinas, "already the hide hardens in the skin" (*CPP*, 119).

For Buber, by contrast, the experience of stroking an animal, e.g., a horse, puts one in contact with it in a manner that is no less direct and immediate than the I-Thou with a person. In the essay "Dialogue" (1929), Buber wrote:

> What I experienced in touch with the animal was the Other, the immense otherness of the Other, which, however, did not remain strange like the otherness of the ox and the ram, but rather let me draw near and touch it. When I stroked the mighty mane. . . it was as though . . . something that was not, was certainly not akin to me, palpably the other, not just another, really the Other itself: and yet it let me approach, confided itself to me, placed itself elementally in the relation of *Thou* and *Thou* with me. . . . I considered myself judged.[22]

It is not clear what criterion is available that would recommend Levinas's phenomenological description of the face-to-face with the other human over Buber's description of the I-Thou with the other than human. The fact that the overwhelming majority of Westerners eat meat, apparently in good conscience, is not decisive here. For while it is difficult to explain how animals are treated so cruelly when their "eyes have the capacity of a great language" (*IT*, 145), it is also not easy to provide a convincing account of how humans in history have been victims of such appalling violence (war, genocide, racism, etc.) when the face would appear expressly to forbid such an "inversion." ("Whatever the motivation which explains this inversion, the analysis of the face as I have just made, with the mastery of the Other and his poverty, with my submission and my wealth, is primary.")[23] In short, the evidence of animal cruelty does not show that animals are any less capable of prohibiting mistreatment than are humans, and perhaps attests to the very repugnance of alterity that Levinas attributes to *all* violence, as when he claims in *Totality and Infinity* that "violence can only aim at a face" (*TI*, 225)? A non-Levinasian, of course, would find this last point unconvincing. It is not the alterity of animals that makes them victims of violence — quite the opposite. From a psychoanalytic point of view, animal cruelty is a defense mechanism used to cope with the fact that we are more closely related to them than we would like — a kinship that Nietzsche dubbed a "painful embarrassment," and Freud called a "biological blow to human narcissism."[24]

Levinas fiercely denies this biological kinship. Not even as staunch a humanist as Kant appears to have been as hostile to animality as Levinas is.[25] Whereas Kant at least saw fit to speak of man's duties toward himself in his "animal nature,"[26] Levinas in the interview under discussion repudiates the idea of the animal in the human:

> The widespread thesis that the ethical is biological amounts to saying that, ultimately, the human is only the last stage of the evolution of the animal. I would say, on the contrary, that in relation to the animal, the human is a new phenomenon. And that leads me to your question. You ask at what moment one becomes a face. I do not know at what moment the human appears, but what I want to emphasize is that the human breaks with pure being, which is always a persistence in being. This is my principal thesis. A being is something that is attached to being, to its own being. That is Darwin's idea. The being of animals is a struggle for life. A struggle of life without ethics. . . . However, with the appearance of the human — and this is my entire philosophy — there is something more important than my life, and that is the life of the other. That is unreasonable. Man is an unreasonable animal. (*PM*, 172)

The story is both traditional and untraditional. Human beings are different from animals because they have the ability to rise above their instincts. This ability, however, does not come from reason — a trait both Darwin and Freud considered naturally selected for survival —

but from their ability to *ignore* reason by putting the needs of "the other" (human) first and transcending their "animal perseverance in being."[27]

It might be asked whether such unreasonableness might not also be attested by extending ethical consideration to other animals. ("It is man's sympathy with all creatures that first makes him truly a man" — Albert Schweitzer.) For what could be more unnatural (and hence more ethical?) than caring for a dumb animal (*zōon alogon*)? As Michael Ruse says, "one would certainly expect the emotions to grow more faint as the blood ties loosen. The obligations would loosen."[28] Nothing in Levinas's work appears to thwart this expectation. Indeed, deconstruction might show that in his repudiation of the idea that we have immediate obligations to members of other species, Levinas resorts to the very naturalism and biology that his ethics is intended to go beyond.

Ethical Cynicism[29]

Despite his rejection of the Greek conception of human being as *zōon logon echon*, there seems little doubt that Levinas is still a humanist in his valorization of the human above the animal. There is, however, one important exception — a short essay entitled "The Name of a Dog, Or Natural Rights" (1975). The essay first appeared in a collection published in honor of the Dutch expressionist painter Bram Van Velde (1895–1981), entitled *Celui qui ne peut pas se servir des mots* (*The One Who/Which Is Not Able To Use Words*). As John Llewelyn[30] and David Clark[31] have already written on the essay, I will here confine myself to the story of Bobby, the stray dog that befriended Levinas and his companions for a few short weeks during their internment in a camp for Jewish prisoners of war in Nazi Germany in 1943.

Bobby appeared

> at morning assembly and was waiting for us as we returned, jumping up and down and barking in delight. For him — it was incontestable — we were men.
>
> Perhaps the dog that recognized Ulysses beneath his disguise on his return from the Odyssey was a forebear of our own. But no, no! There,

they were in Ithaca and the Fatherland. Here, we were nowhere. This
dog was the last Kantian in Nazi Germany, without the brain needed to
universalize maxims and drives. (*DF*, 153)

It is difficult to know what to make of this story, whether Levinas
meant it to be taken literally or whether he was anthropomorphizing
Bobby and using him as a foil to show how it is possible for the human
to fall well beneath the status of humanity. The story is further
complicated when Levinas writes, "The other men, called free, who
had dealings with us or gave us work or orders or even a smile — and
the children and women who passed by and sometimes raised their
eyes — stripped us of our human skin. We were merely a quasi-humanity
[*une quasi-humanité*], a gang of apes" (*DF*, 153; modified translation).

Notice that implicit in his account is the claim that to be like animals
("apes") is not to have the Kantian dignity and autonomy of the human;
it is "a quasi-humanity." It seems fairly clear that Levinas wishes to
imply that humanity stands above animality, even though it would
appear that some humans (Nazis) "called free" are altogether incapable
of recognizing the humanity of Levinas and his fellow prisoners.
Thus — and here Levinas comes closest to elevating the animal — the
Nazis failed to attain the humanity of Bobby, who is an animal. But
notice too that, according to Levinas, they fail to measure up to the
human (and Bobby) only because they falsely attempt reduce the
human to the status of an animal (and Bobby), thus implying once
again that the human is morally superior.

But why is it assumed that the human has greater moral worth and
value than the animal? To be sure, Bobby is *zōon alogon*; Levinas makes
a point of telling us that he is altogether incapable of universalizing his
maxims. But, pace Kant, what does that really matter *ethically*? Many
human beings are in the same boat as Bobby. Human infants have
little or no capacity to act as moral agents; many schizophrenics find
themselves compelled to act in certain ways. Yet they are not thereby
precluded from having certain "natural rights" and obligations owed
to them as moral patients. Buber speaks of "anxiety — the stirring of
the creature between the realms of plantlike security and spiritual risk"
(*IT*, 144). Do not animals feel anxiety, too? Is the suffering and distress

of animals — from the rainforests to the slaughterhouse — any less painful than the anxiety felt by infants and adults who are mentally deficient, and thus incapable of having a face-to-face in the manner that Levinas describes so well? We know that Levinas says that the "prototype" of ethics is the interhuman relation, but we have yet to show the extent to which his philosophy is capable of countenancing a less anthropocentric response — and one that is more in line with Buber's philosophy.

ANIMALS, INFANTS AND THE "PSYCHICALLY DEPRIVED, BACKWARD, HANDICAPPED" — LEVINAS

Clearly it is not simply the possession of reason that makes the human beings the center of Levinas's moral universe — though it is equally clear that he is reluctant to give equal consideration to beings in possession of anything less. Only human beings are capable of being morally obligated because only they are capable of transcending instinctual needs, of being "unreasonable" as well as reasonable. But why are human beings the primary beings *to whom* moral obligations are owed? Why am I more obligated to the neighbor than to the animal next door? Is it because my neighbor, like me, has the capacity to be reasonable/unreasonable whereas the dog or the horse stands outside the orbit of reason altogether?[32] Levinas never says that I am obligated to the Other because we have the same mental capacities. On the contrary, "The Other as Other is not only an alter ego: the Other is what I myself am not." This is not to define the Other in terms of me, of course, using the familiar logic of negation. That the Other is what I am not means that I will never be able to reduce him or her to one of *my* ideas. As Sartre puts it, the Other is "a little particular crack in my universe"[33] through which he or she seeps away from me; he or she is no longer fully "present" (to consciousness) in that I am no longer able fully to comprehend him or her. But does not the animal also constitute a similar hemorrhage of intelligibility and meaning? Indeed, are not animals — from ants to antelopes — more other than the Other? In *The Gift of Death*, Derrida makes the following throw away remark: "without speaking of animals that are still more other than my fellows."[34] If animals are more other than the Other, then why are my fellows more dear than fallow deer — currently farmed in New Zealand, the United States, and South Africa for breeding and hunting purposes, slaughter stock, antler velvet, as well as livestock, skin, leather, and oddities such as "pizzles" (whips made from penises), testicles and tendons?

To be sure, fallow deer are inarticulate. They cannot entreat the gamekeeper to let them alone or beseech someone to help them. They are as dumb as wood. But then so are infants. Deer cannot reason; again, neither can the severely mentally impaired. In one of his most beautiful and touching essays, "Useless Suffering" (1982), Levinas spoke of the malignancy of pain where "the integration of other psychological states does not bring any relief."

> But one can go further — and doubtless arrive at the essential facts of pure pain — by evoking the "pain-illnesses" of beings who are psychically deprived, backward, handicapped, in their relational life and in their relationships to the Other, relationships where suffering, without losing anything of its savage malignancy, no longer covers up the totality of the mental and comes across novel lights within new horizons. These horizons nonetheless remain closed to the mentally deficient, except that in their "pure pain" they are projected into them to expose them *to me*, raising the fundamental ethical problem which pain poses "for nothing": the inevitable and preemptory ethical problem of the medication which is my duty. (*US*, 158)

It matters little that the persons who are "psychically deprived, backward, handicapped, in their relational life and in their relationships to the Other" are incapable of making an appeal for friendship and medication through speech. The suffering of the Other, despite the Other's inability to express it in words, finds a way of getting to me, getting under my skin (*OB*, 84–85, 109) and causing me to suffer. "In this perspective a radical difference develops between *suffering in the Other*, which for *me* is unpardonable and solicits me and calls me, and suffering *in me*, my own adventure of suffering, whose constitutional or congenital uselessness can take on a meaning" (*US*, 159).

Levinas goes on to call suffering for the unjustified suffering of the Other the "supreme ethical principle — the only one which it is not possible to contest" (*US*, 159). But can we not question its exclusive application to the "inter-human" (*US*, 159)? Is the pain an animal feels any less useless than the pain felt by a human being? Levinas's statement that "we do not want to make an animal suffer needlessly" implies that "we" *would* be prepared to make an animal suffer on the condition that it served a purpose. Not all animal suffering is therefore unjustified — unlike the suffering of the neighbor, which is never justified. Levinas couldn't make the point any stronger: "the justification of the neighbor's pain is certainly the source of all immorality" (*US*, 163). When is the suffering of animals justified? The typical response from individuals who care enough to treat it as a serious question in the first place, is that it is justified when it is necessary to stop the suffering of human beings. Even individuals who refuse to eat or wear animals often feel that using animals in biomedical research is morally acceptable, as long as there are some tangible medical benefits for human beings somewhere down the road, no matter how restricted. They argue in non-Benthamite fashion that those benefits outweigh the suffering undergone by the animal as long as the animal doesn't suffer beyond what was required to produce those benefits.

Is the "malignancy" of pain any less malignant when the pain pertains to an animal? Is pain somehow worse when human beings are feeling it — whether or not they can speak? One thinks of Nietzsche, who, upon seeing a horse being beaten mercilessly by a coachman on the morning of January 3, 1889, at the Piazza Carlo Alberto, in Turin, threw his arms around the horse's neck and collapsed, irrevocably insane. His final breakdown — and break with the world of humans — was brought on by the sight of a horse being tormented. He suffered for the unjustifiable suffering of a horse.[35]

FINAL REMARKS

We have seen that there is an anthropocentric strain in Levinas's ethics that might have been eliminated had he considered, as Buber did, the potentiality of the animal — or some animals — to address us independently of our relation to one another. Buber's philosophy of

the I-Thou, while certainly making the interhuman relation primary
among all the relations to the Thou, did not reduce the relationship
with nature to an I-It, the relation with things. To Buber, "our
relationship to domestic animals with whom we live, and even to the
plants in our garden, is properly included as the lowest floor in the
ethical building."[36] To be sure, Buber's descriptions are shrouded in
metaphor and obscurity, the I-Thou presented in a language heavily
imbued with mysticism and religious inspiration without providing a
more robust account of what "ethics" might mean. If there is an irony
here, it is that Levinas was better equipped to interpret and represent
the relationship with the nonhuman other than was Buber. He had at
his disposal a more serviceable and sophisticated philosophical
vocabulary, a better understanding of the history of philosophy, and
deeper appreciation of the challenge posed by Heidegger's thinking
than did Buber, despite his kind words about Buber's "epistemology."
But, like so many philosophers before him — and unlike Buber —
Levinas did not make much of an attempt to extend ethical
consideration to animals. Very much to his credit, Buber did in a way
that merits serious attention from a Levinasian point of view if only
because the very questions he (Levinas) poses concerning otherness
invite meditation on the suffering of victims of hatred everywhere,
not just of anti-Semitism, but also of imperialism, oppression and
racism. If I add "speciesism" to the list — to choose Richard Ryder's
term[37] — it is because I see no reason to discount the suffering of
animals merely because, like Bobby, they cannot universalize their
maxims.

In the same year Buber published *I and Thou*, Rilke published his
Duino Elegies, a work in which he caught sight of the face of the animal
as an openness to the outside, calling for a response that is nothing
less than ethical — and perhaps nothing less than *human*.

> *Mit allen Augen sieht die Kreatur*
> *das Offene. Nur unsere Augen sind*
> *wie umgekehrt und ganz um sie gestellt*
> *als Fallen, rings um ihren freien Ausgang.*
> *Was draußen ist, wir wissens aus des Tiers*

Antlitz allein; denn schon das frühe Kind
wenden wir um und zwingens, daß es rückwärts
Gestaltung sehe, nicht das Offene, das
im Tiergesicht so tief ist.
[With all its eyes the animal world
beholds the Open. Only our eyes
are as if inverted and set all around it
like traps at its portals to freedom.
What's outside we only know from the animal's
countenance; for almost from the first we take a child
and twist him round and force him to gaze
backwards and take in structure, not the Open
that lies so deep in an animal's face.]

       — Rainer Maria Rilke, "The Eighth Elegy"[38]

NOTES

Notes to Introduction

1. Maurice Friedman, *The Confirmation of Otherness: In Family, Community, and Society* (New York: Pilgrim Press, 1983), Chap. 2.

2. For this reason James Walters calls Buber a "transcendental empiricist." For an excellent, balanced discussion of Buber and Kant, see James W. Walters, *Martin Buber and Feminine Ethics: The Priority of the Personal* (Syracuse, NY: Syracuse University Press, 2003), 1–7.

3. As Maurice Friedman has shown at length in *Martin Buber's Life and Work: The Early Years — 1878–1923* (New York: E. P. Dutton, 1983).

4. This point is demonstrated at length in Maurice Friedman's *The Worlds of Existentialism: A Critical Reader* (Atlantic Highlands, N.J.: Humanities Press International, 1991).

5. Jacques Derrida, *Of Grammatology*, trans. Gayatri Chakravorty Spivak (Baltimore: The John Hopkins University Press, 1976), 70.

6. Martin Buber, *Two Types of Faith*, trans. Norman P. Goldhawk (New York: Collier, 1951), 40.

7. Jerry Lawritson, "Martin Buber and the Shoah," in *Martin Buber and the Human Sciences*, eds., Maurice Friedman and Pat Boni (Albany: SUNY, 1996).

8. *Modern Judaism* 23, 2 (2003): 156–79.

9. Tamra Wright points out in chapter 11 of this volume that Buber's approach to both Judaism and the Holocaust is consistently biblical in that it remains centered on the theme of the encounter with God, although, we might add, the meeting with God is central to Buber's philosophy of dialogue, as it is expounded in *I and Thou* and *Between Man and Man*, and not just to his interpretation of the Hebrew Bible.

10. For a thorough discussion of Buber's response to the Shoah and his concept of "the eclipse of God," see Maurice Friedman, *Martin Buber's Life and Work: The Middle Years — 1923–1945* and *The Later Years — 1945–1963* (New York: E. P. Dutton, 1983 and 1984).

11. Levinas described his life in his brief autobiography "Signature" (1961) as "dominated by the presentiment and memory of the Nazi horror." *DF*, 291.

Notes to Chapter 2/Levinas

1. I have here adopted the dominant practice of translating "*autrui*" as "Other" and "*autre*" as "other." — Trans.

282

2. The ellipsis dots are used to mark Levinas's references to comments made earlier in the interview. — Trans.

3. See Fyodor Dostoyesky, *The Brothers Karamazov*, trans. David Magarshack (London: Penguin, 1982): "every one of us is responsible for everyone else in every way, and I most of all" (338). — Trans.

4. Deuteronomy 25:19 in the King James Version of the Bible. — Trans.

Notes to Chapter 3/Strasser

1. See in this connection Grete Schaeder, *Martin Buber: Hebrew Humanism* (Detroit: Wayne State University Press, 1968).

2. Hans Kohn, *Martin Buber: Sein Werk und seine Zeit* (Köln: Joseph Melzer Verlag, 1961), 14.

3. Immanuel Kant, *The Critique of Judgement*, trans. James Creed Meredith (Oxford: Clarendon Press, 1952), 38.

4. Immanuel Kant, *The Critique of Pure Reason*, trans. Norman Kemp Smith (London: Macmillan, 1992), B1.

5. The question as to whether Buber has correctly represented Hasidic theology is irrelevant for our purposes.

6. Martin Buber, *For the Sake of Heaven*, trans. Ludwig Lewisohn (Philadelphia: The Jewish Publication Society, 1945), 117.

7. In this connection, see Edith Wyschogrod, *Emmanuel Levinas: The Problem of Ethical Metaphysics* (New York: Fordham University Press, 2002), Chap. 7, "Philosophy and the Covenant," 176–221.

8. Theo de Boer, *Tussen filosofie en Profetie. De wijbegeerte van Emmanuel Levinas* (Baarn, 1976).

Notes to Chapter 4/Tallon

1. Besides the work of Emmanuel Levinas, I will mention only the following sampling. Michael Theunissen's book, *Der Andere. Studien zur Sozialontologie der Gegenwart* (Berlin: de Gruyter, 1965) is an example of a generally positive appreciation of Buber, though it faults Buber for not following through his project. In Hans Duesberg's *Person und Gemeinschaft: Philosophisch-systematische Unter-suchungen des Sinnzusammenhangs von personaler Selbständigkeit und interperso-naler Beziehung an Texten von J. G. Fichte und M. Buber* (Bonn: Bouvier, 1970), the confrontation staged between Fichte's transcendental interpersonalism and Buber is interesting to compare with Simons's (see below) use of Fichte for dia-logical theology (contra Rahner), and with Heinrichs's (see below) attempt at a transcendental dialogic. See also, Bernhard Waldenfels, *Das Zwischenreich des Dia-logs: Sozialphilosophische Untersuchungen in Anschluss an Edmund Husserl* (Den Haag: Nijhoff, 1971). See also Klaus Held, "Das Problem des Intersubjektivität und die Idee einer phänomenologischen Transzendentalphilosophie," in Ulrich

Claeges and Klaus Held, eds., *Perspektiven transzendentalphänomenologischer Forschung: Für Ludwig Landgrebe zum 70. Geburtstag von seinen Kölner Schulern* (Den Haag: Nijhoff, 1972), 3–60.

2. On the failure of Husserl's attempt to substantiate his phenomenology in the only way he said he could, that is, by intersubjectivity, see Levinas's *The Theory of Intuition in Husserl's Phenomenology*, trans. A. Orianne (Evanston, IL.: Northwestern University Press, 1973). See also: Alfred Schutz, "The Problem of Transcendental Intersubjectivity in Husserl," in *Collected Works: Studies in Phenomenological Philosophy*, ed. I. Schutz (The Hague: Nijhoff, 1966), 3: 51–91; Schutz's very relevant essays on Scheler (on intersubjectivity and the alter ego) and on Sartre (on the alter ego) in *Collected Works I, vol. 1*. Hans Wagner, "Critical Observations Concerning Husserl's Posthumous Writings," Ludwig Landgrebe, "Husserl's Departure from Cartesianism," both in *The Phenomenology of Husserl: Selected Critical Readings*, ed. and trans. R. O. Elveton (Chicago: Quadrangle Books, 1970); Paul Ricoeur, *Husserl: An Analysis of His Phenomenology*, trans. Edward G. Ballard and Lester E. Embree (Evanston, IL.: Northwestern University Press, 1967), 84–85, 105–06, 115–42; and Stephan Strasser, *The Idea of Dialogal Phenomenology*, trans. Henry J. Koren (Pittsburgh: Duquesne University Press, 1969), xi–xii.

Strasser mentions that Max Scheler, Adolph Reinach, Wilhelm Schapp, Martin Heidegger, Karl Löwith, Jean-Paul Sartre and Maurice Merleau-Ponty are all witness to "the inability of Husserl's transcendental phenomenology to solve the problem of intersubjectivity" (xi). This problem was "Husserl's major difficulty" (xi), as he himself recognized. Strasser also points out, "Husserl declared that his transcendental idealism stands or falls with the possibility of solving the problem of intersubjectivity by means of the method of intentional analysis" (xii). It is by recourse to Buber that Strasser (like Theunissen) tries to make a contribution to phenomenology through the dialogical principle.

3. The much abused concept of space, the very mention of which triggers a knee-jerk criticism from some who accuse its users with "spatializing," a disdainful and offhand dismissal of all further discussion, is nonetheless almost inexhaustibly rich, as will be shown later, especially with reference to the human (that is, social) sciences.

4. "The Between actualized in relation is the central notion of Buber's thought." See Robert E. Wood, *Martin Buber's Ontology: An Analysis of I and Thou* (Evanston: Northwestern University Press, 1969), 41. On the between, see also my "Person and Community. Buber's Category of the Between," *Philosophy Today* 17 (1973): 62–83.

5. Hence, the point of contact of existential phenomenology with Buber and the evolution of a transcendental dialogic.

6. See Richard M. Zaner, *The Problem of Embodiment: Some Contributions to a Phenomenology of the Body* (The Hague: Martinus Nijhoff, 1964), on Marcel, Sartre, and Merleau-Ponty.

7. See Erazim Kohák, "Phenomenology as Rigorous Humanism: Edmund Husserl in Context of History," mimeograph, 1973 (adapted from his *Pheno-*

menology as Tool and Perspective). Kohák points out that in Husserl's Czechoslovakia *Sinngebung* would not suggest a dispensing (or bestowal) of meaning; "*Sinngeben* in ordinary usage means in the first place 'to make sense'" (8).

8. For the sake of clarity, I reserve until later mention of the social sciences. Within philosophy, between the classic Greek preference for vision and the Sartrean "look," there is the hardly noticed history of this visual dominance in thought. See Don Ihde, *Sense and Significance* (Pittsburgh: Duquesne University Pres, 1973), especially 23–68.

9. See Hans Jonas, "Sight and Thought: A Review of *Visual Thought*," in *Philosophical Essays: From Ancient Creed to Technological Man* (Englewood Cliffs: Prentice Hall, 1974), 224–236. See also Jonas's sixth and seventh essays in his *The Phenomenon of Life: Towards a Philosophical Biology* (New York: Harper & Row, 1966), 135–82.

10. Following Theunissen, Waldenfels calls this Husserlian limitation of intentionality, a *Horizontintentionalität* (*Das Zwischenreich des Dialog*, 51).

11. Kohák, "Phenomenology as Rigorous Humanism," 14 (emphasis in original).

12. See *TI*, esp. John Wild's introduction to this work (11–21). Levinas's "infinite," like Buber's "between," maintains the *otherness* of the other.

13. Robert Perkins's paper on Kierkegaard and Buber, presented at the Buber centenary in Israel in January, 1978, pointed out Buber's misinterpretation of Kierkegaard in important places. Perkins also refers to the parallel work of Rabbi Halevi, which confirmed this flaw.

14. Strasser, *Dialogal Phenomenology*, 117.

15. On the idea of uniting transcendental philosophy and dialogical thought into a transcendental dialogic, see Johannes Heinrichs, "Sinn und Intersubjektivität. Zur Vermittlung von transzendentalphilosophischem und dialogischem Denken in einer transzendentalen Dialogik," in *Theologie und Philosophie* 45 (1970): 161–91. Also relevant is Hans Duesberg's treatment of Fichte's transcendental philosophy alongside Buber's in his *Person und Gemeinschaft* (see n. 1). Theunissen's study mentioned above is, of course, basic. Note that once the strong Kantian, Fichtean and Hegelian influence on transcendental theology is also recognized, then an extremely rich trend in ecumenical theology is identified. The same transcendental interpersonalism that, for example, Eberhard Simons in *Philosophie der Offenbarung: In Auseinandersetzung mit Hörer des Wortes von Karl Rahner* (Stuttgart: W. Kohlhammer Verlag, 1966) brings from Fichte into critical dialogue with Karl Rahner (not Fichtean enough for Simons), becomes the inspiration for Alexander Gerkin in *Offenbarung und transzendenzerfahrung: Kritische Thesen zu einer künftigen Thesen zu einer künftigen Dialogischen Theologie* (Düsseldorf: Patmos Verlag, 1969). This is not the place to pursue this best of theological trends, but for further discussion the interested reader can refer to Peter Eicher, "Immanenz oder Transzendenz? Gespräch mit Karl Rahner," in *Freiburger Zeitschrift für Philosophie und Theologie* 15 (1968): 29–62 (on Simons 42–52), and *Die anthropologische Wende: Karl Rahners philosophischer Weg vom Wesen des Menschen zur personalen Existenz* (Freiburg [Switzerland]: Universitätsverlag,

1970). See also Klaus P. Fischer, *Der Mensch als Geheimnis. Die Anthropologie Karl Rahners* (Freiburg: Herder, 1974), esp. 193–205.

16. Strasser, *Dialogal Phenomenology*, 53.

17. A recent essay by Strasser on Levinas says some of this again. See "Antiphénoménologie et phénoménologie dans la philosophie d'Emmanuel Levinas," in *Revue philosophique de Louvain*, 75 (1977): 101–25.

18. See *Imagination: A Psychological Critique*, trans. Forrest Williams (Ann Arbor: University of Michigan Press, 1962), esp. 134–45; 146. Also *The Psychology of Imagination* (Secaucus, NJ: Citadel Press, 1948), 7–8; 134.

19. Sartre, *The Psychology of Imagination*, 96–104, 98 (emphasis in original); *The Emotions: Outline of a Theory*, trans. Bernard Frechtman (New York: Philosophical Library, 1948); *Being and Nothingness*, trans. Hazel E. Barnes (New York: Washington Square Press, 1953), 7, 9, 11, 15.

20. Dietrich von Hildebrand, *Metaphysik der Gemeinschaft* (Regensburg: Verlag Josef Habbel, 1955), and *Ethics* (Chicago: Franciscan Herald Press, 1953). A helpful presentation of von Hildebrand's rich thought on intersubjectivity is Thomas J. Owens, *Phenomenology and Intersubjectivity: Contemporary Interpretations of the Interpersonal Situation* (The Hague: Martinus Nijhoff, 1970), 111–49.

21. Maurice Merleau-Ponty, *The Structure of Behavior*, trans. Alden L. Fisher (Duquesne University Press, 1983), 171; *Phenomenology of Perception*, trans. Colin Smith (London: Routledge and Kegan Paul, 1962), ix, xv, 24, 242, 326, 404, 121, 316.

22. For a sample of anthropology and sociology on the languages of space and time, see the trilogy of Edward T. Hall, *The Silent Language* (Garden City, NJ: Doubleday Anchor, 1959), *The Hidden Dimension* (Garden City, NJ: Doubleday Anchor, 1966), and *Beyond Culture* (Garden City, NJ: Doubleday Anchor, 1976). See also Albert E. Scheflen, *How Behavior Means* (Garden City, NJ: Doubleday Anchor, 1974) and Scheflen and Norman Ashcraft, *People Space* (Garden City, NJ: Doubleday Anchor, 1976). The terms "kinesics" (Ray Birdwhistell), "proxemics" (Hall), "metacommunication" (Scheflen), and so forth suggest their analyses. Interesting too, on "ethical" and "philosophical" space, is Roger Poole, *Toward Deep Subjectivity* (New York: Harper Torchbook, 1972).

23. Tony Schwartz's provocative media analyses in *The Responsive Chord* (Garden City NJ: Doubleday Anchor, 1973) directly tie in with Hall's concept of "extension transference" (*Beyond Culture*, 28).

24. Heinrichs, "Sinn und Intersubjektivität," 166.

25. Karl Rahner, *Theological Investigations III*, trans. Karl H. and Boniface Krüger (London: Darton, Longman and Todd, 1967), 332, 335; see also 325, 327, 331–37. See also Robert E. Wood's "Introduction" to Strasser's *Phenomenology of Feeling* (3–22). This "old news" about affective intentionality — the heart — offers us a concept around which we can organize the manifold of work being done on human relations.

26. See the sections on Marcel on feeling and embodiment in Zaner's *Problem of Embodiment* (see 33–56). Marcel's *Urgefühl*, in my interpretation, is intentional

because, consonant with the ambiguity of being and having in relation to my embodiment, that embodiment is first otherness. That is to say, it is the first emanation or exteriorization of my finite spirituality becoming itself through otherness, the otherness of embodiment and sensibility, so that I am given to myself in affectivity. On the notions of first and secondary otherness, see my *Personal Becoming: Karl Rahner's Metaphysical Anthropology* (Milwaukee: Marquette University Press, 1982).

27. Blondel's *L'Action* is the *point de repère* for this idea, of course, as developed in contemporary thought and seminal for the thought of Maréchal, Rousselot, Rahner, et al. A neglected study that explicitly works out the implications of the restless heart philosophically is Hunter Guthrie's *Introduction au problème de l'histoire de la philosophie: La métaphysique de l'individualité a priori de la pensée* (Paris: Librairie Félix Alcan, 1973). Guthrie, inspired by Kierkegaard and Heidegger, and trying to identify an experience of existence most apt for a hermeneutic of human being, chose the feeling of disquiet (*sentiment de l'inquiétude*). Although it is highly problematic, Michel Henry has written an entire philosophy based on subjectivity as affectivity. See Georges Van Riet, "Une nouvelle ontologie phénoménologique. La philosophie de Michel Henry," in *Philosophie et religion* (Louvain: Publications universitaires de Louvain, 1970), 251–72. Van Riet is quite critical of Henry's *L'essence de la manifestation* and *La philosophie et phénoménologie du corps* (published in 1963 and 1965 respectively).

28. Strasser, *Phenomenology of Feeling*, especially 81–82, 150, 155, 157. *Das Gemüt* seems an important influence on Levinas and Ricoeur.

29. Joseph Maréchal, *Studies in the Psychology of the Mystics*, trans. Algar Thorold (Albany: Magi, 1927), 55–145. Auguste Poulain, *The Graces of Interior Prayer*, trans. Leonora L. Yorke Smith (St. Louis: B. Herder Book Co., 1910), 64–87.

30. See Carlos Cirne-Lima, *Personal Belief: A Metaphysical Inquiry*, trans. G. Richard Dimler (New York: Herder and Herder, 1965).

31. See Jacques Maritain, "On Knowledge through Connaturality," in *The Range of Reason* (New York: Charles Scribner's, 1942), 22–29. Specifically named instances of such experience, which Maritain traces back to Aquinas while admitting that it certainly goes back much further, are mystical experience (24–25), poetic knowledge (25–26), and moral experience (76–79).

32. See Ceslaus Spicq, *Agape in the New Testament*, trans. Marie Aquinas McNamara and Mary Honoria Richter (St. Louis: Herder: 1966).

Notes to Chapter 5/Bernasconi

1. The fullest study of Levinas's relation to Buber is "Buber und Levinas: Philosophische Besinnung auf einen Gegensatz" by Stephan Strasser (chapter 3 of this volume). It appeared alongside Levinas's *BP* in the same issue of *Revue Internationale de Philosophie* 32 (1978): 512–25, and so was unable to take account of it. Strikingly, Levinas in *APB* refers the reader to "Martin Buber and the Theory of Knowledge" in *NP*, and to "the fine study" by Strasser, but not to *BP* itself

(*APB*, 133). Philip N. Lawton's "Levinas's Reading of Buber," *Philosophy Today* 20, no. 1 (1976): 77–83, is hampered by the fact that he was apparently unaware of "Martin Buber and the Theory of Knowledge" and the discussion in *PI* which were the major sources then available. His account of Levinas closely follows Derrida's footnote on Buber in "Violence and Metaphysics" which I discuss in the third section of this study. Most of the interest in Andrew Tallon's, "Intentionality, Intersubjectivity, and the Between: Buber and Levinas on Affectivity and the Dialogical Principle," *Thought* 53, no. 210 (1978): 292–309 (see chapter 4 of this volume) resides in the fact that he makes no reference to any of Levinas's discussions of Buber — not even those in *TI* — and so exhibits in absolute purity the proximity (Tallon calls it "complimentarity" [309]) of Buber and Levinas as it appears to the external observer, independent of the observations of the participants themselves.

2. Martin Heidegger, *Unterwegs zur Sprache* (Pfullingen: Neske, 1959), 188; *On the Way to Language*, trans. P. D. Hertz (New York: Harper & Row, 1971), 83.

3. In most cases I follow Kaufmann's translation with minor revisions, but I have not kept with his decision to translate *Du* as "you." While granting that this translation has clear advantages for the reading of Buber, the contrast with Levinas makes it essential to maintain the difference between the second person singular and the second person plural, and so I have returned to the "Thou" which is still more familiar to readers of Buber.

4. See note 14.

5. Levinas would not have known this letter of Rosenzweig, which was not published until 1973. Six years later the letter was republished in a critical edition, F. Rosenzweig, *Der Mensch und sein Werk. Gesammelte Schriften. Briefe und Tagebücher* (The Hague: Martinus Nijhoff, 1979), 824–27, and made the subject of an essay by Bernhard Casper, "Franz Rosenzweigs Kritik an Bubers 'Ich und Du,' " *Philosophisches Jahrbuch* 86 (1979): 225–38. Levinas praised Casper's article and discussed the letter briefly in "Façon de Parler" in *OGM*, 179–80/*DVI*, 268–69. For an English translation of the letter, see Rivka Horwitz, *Buber's Way to "I and Thou"* (Heidelberg: Lambert Schneider, 1978), 253–56. See also M. Friedman, "Martin Buber and Franz Rosenzweig: the Road to I and Thou," *Philosophy Today* (1981): 210–20.

6. It is significant in this regard that in "Martin Buber and the Theory of Knowledge" Levinas suggested that spiritual friendship was the apogee of the I-Thou relation for Buber (*PMB*, 148/*NP*, 47), and referred to the latter's essay "Education," where, as the third of three forms of the dialogical relation, Buber wrote of friendship "based on a concrete and mutual experience of inclusion" (*DL*, 285/*W*, 806/*BMM*, 128). Buber in reply wrote that he regarded this relationship as winning its true greatness "precisely there where two men without a strong spiritual ground in common even of very different kinds of spirit, yes of opposite directions, still stand over against each other so that each of the two knows and means, recognizes and acknowledges, accepts and confirms the other, even in the severest conflict, as this particular person. In the common situation,

even in the common situation of fighting with each other, he holds present to himself the experience-side of the other, his living through this situation. This is no friendship, this is only the comradeship of the human creature, a comradeship that has reached fulfillment. No 'ether,' as Levinas thinks, but the hard human earth, the common in the uncommon" (*PMB*, 725/*MB*, 619–20). Presumably the comradeship of philosophical debate is included.

7. Buber's postscript, dated October 1957, first appeared in the special edition of *Ich und Du* prepared in connection with Buber's eightieth birthday on 8 February 1958. Levinas, who wrote "Martin Buber and the Theory of Knowledge" in the same year, cites there the collection of Buber's writings called *Dialogisches Leben*, which was compiled in 1947.

8. Written in 1958, it was published in German in 1963 (*MB*, 119–34), in English in 1967 (*PMB*, 133–50), but the French original first appeared in 1976 (*NP*, 29–50). However sympathetic one might be to translators of Levinas, it has to be said that neither of these translations does justice to the original. In their defense it could be said that the translators, working without a knowledge of *Totality and Infinity* where the importance of many of the concepts Levinas uses in the essay is established, were not well placed to know what needed to be preserved and what could be sacrificed in the process of translation. Of course, it would be possible to argue in the same way that Buber's failure to recognize all that lay behind Levinas's "objections" this too was a consequence of his not being aware of the way Levinas developed the notions of asymmetry and separation in *Totality and Infinity*. But even though Buber's comments would no doubt have been different had he had the opportunity to study the thinking from which Levinas's objections arose, we should beware of assuming that it would have brought the thinkers into closer proximity or — and it is not the same thing — would have improved the possibility of dialogue between them. Failure of communication is an essential character of the dialogue between thinkers — as well as lovers — although Buber might well have been among those who would not have understood such an observation.

9. The evidence that half of Buber's reply never reached its destination may be found in the fact that Levinas referred to only one of the two comments — both in a letter he wrote to Buber at the time and in comments that he attached to the letter on the occasion of its publication 13 years later in 1976 (*NP*, 51, 53). See also note 13 below.

10. "Dialogue avec Martin Buber," *Les Nouveaux Cahiers* 1 (1965): 1–3; reprinted with the omission of the first two paragraphs in *NP*, 51–55. The article consisted of an introduction, a further short paragraph introducing a brief extract from his essay "Martin Buber and the Theory of Knowledge" in which he opposed the notion of solicitude to Buber's model of spiritual friendship (*PMB*, 148/*NP*, 47–48), and Buber's reply — an extract from his "Reply to my Critics" also quoted in note 6 above — which began, "Levinas errs in a strange way when he supposes that I see in the *amitié toute spirituelle* the peak of the I-Thou relation" (*PMB*, 723). Alongside these documents Levinas published a respectful letter he had written to Buber in 1963 trying again to explain to Buber his differences together

with Buber's reply, a letter which seems to have been addressed to all the contributors to the "Library of Living Philosophers" volume. This letter contained some Heideggerian reflections on the relation between "thinking" and "thanking" and a postscript acknowledging receipt of Levinas's letter. In a short introduction, Levinas noted with an exclamation mark the irony in the fact that the "Library of Living Philosophers" volume on Buber was to appear after his death. But there was no hint of irony or mockery in the way Levinas put together these documents under the title "Dialogue avec Martin Buber." One is reminded of Levinas's own words in *Totality and Infinity*: "The claim to know and to reach the other is realized in the relationship with the Other that is cast in the relation of language, where the essential is the interpellation, the vocative. The other is maintained as confirmed in his heterogeneity as soon as one calls upon him, be it only to say to him that one cannot speak to him" (*TI*, 69/*TeI*, 41). Levinas's only complaint was that following "la Discourtesie par excellence" — Buber's death — "the interruption of the dialogue but lately begun was clothed with a profound silence" (*NP*, 51). Again, Levinas does not seem to have regarded failure of communication as a deficiency.

11. Levinas here rejoins a theme of his thinking which was already pronounced in *De l'existence à l'existant* in 1947 — the tendency of modern philosophy "to sacrifice for the sake of the spirituality of the subject its very subjectivity, that is its substantiality" (*EE*, 97/*DEE*, 168).

12. See also the essay "Transcendance et Hauteur," *Bulletin de la Société française de Philosophie* 54 (1962): "Our effort does not consist so much in bringing out the originality of the I-Thou relation as in showing the ethical structures of this relation" (99).

13. The only indication that Levinas was aware of Buber's reply to this specific passage (see also note 9 above) is to be found in the fact that there is nothing in the French text corresponding to the English phrase "as Buber asserts" (or the German *wie es Buber will*). Did Levinas, when publishing the French original in 1976, drop the phrase in deference to Buber's denial? A rough examination of the English and German translations does not suggest that Levinas revised the text before publishing the French version, but the translations are so free that it is not always easy to be sure.

14. "La pensée de Martin Buber et le judaïsme contemporain," in *Martin Buber, l'homme et le philosophe* (Bruxelles: Editions de l'Institut de Sociologie de l'Université Libre de Bruxelles, 1968), 56–57. Levinas here defends Heidegger, as he had already done in "Martin Buber and the Theory of Knowledge" (*PMB*, 148/*NP*, 47–48), against Buber's charge that *Fürsorge* does not offer access to the Other of itself, but only where that access is already secure (*DL*, 401–02/*W*, 367–68/*BMM*, 296–97/*MB*, 620/*PMB*, 723). It is striking to see how quickly Levinas, who wastes no opportunity of his own to attack Heidegger, nevertheless rushes to his defense when he is attacked by someone else or from another perspective.

15. In questioning Buber's use of the word "relation," Levinas found himself on common ground with Rosenzweig, who had already put the point to Buber

when reading *I and Thou* prior to its publication. See R. Horwitz, *Buber's Way to 'I and Thou'* (256). Marcel in his contribution to the volume of the "Library of Living Philosophers" dedicated to Buber made a similar observation (*PMB*, 44). For Buber's own defense of his use of the word, see *PMB*, 705/*MB*, 603.

16. The lectures are published in Horwitz's *Buber's Way to 'I and Thou'* (41–152).

17. Levinas, *OT*, 46, EDE 202. See B. Casper, "Illéité," *Philosophisches Jahrbuch* 91 (1984): 273–88.

18. Levinas's sensitivity to the ontological character of experience (insofar as it is inscribed with the value of presence) seems to be a consequence of Derrida's remarks in "Violence and Metaphysics." For example, he asks, "Has not the concept of experience always been determined by the metaphysics of experience?" (*WD*, 152/*ED*, 225). Before that Levinas himself used the word, albeit with a recognition of certain difficulties. For example, he wrote in the preface to *Totality and Infinity*, "The relation with infinity cannot be stated in terms of experience, for infinity overflows the thought that thinks it. . . . But if experience precisely means a relation with the absolutely other, that is, with what overflows thought, the relation with infinity accomplishes experience in the fullest sense of the word" (*TI*, 25/*TeI*, xiii).

19. Buber in his "Reply to my Critics" dismissed the conclusions Marcel drew from this section of *I and Thou* (*PMB*, 705–06/*MB*, 604), but he did not address the question of how this section should be understood. It is not simply another statement of the "progressive increase of the It-world," which I discussed briefly in the second section above, because it joins that theme with the question of the status of dialogue in Buber. This silence of the "unformed (*ungeformten*), undifferentiated pre-linguistic word" (*IT*, 89/*DP*, 42) — which comes second to the longing for relation — would appear to be the same as the "wordless anticipation (*Vorgestalt*) of saying Thou" (*IT*, 78/*DP*, 31). But this would serve to show the fragility not just of the I-Thou itself; but also of Buber's distinctions. Buber was denying that one must choose *either* the silent anticipation of the I-Thou *or* the response which already subverts the I-Thou. When he dismissed Marcel's discussion, but such statements of intent are no final court of appeal.

20. The essay first appeared as "Le Dialogue: Conscience de soi et proximité du prochain" in *Archivio di filosofia* 48 (1980): 345–57. The following year it was published in German as "Dialog" in *Christlicher Glaube in moderner Gesellschaft* (Freiburg: Herder, 1981), 61–85. The French version was republished in *DVI*. In this essay Levinas does not attempt to divorce himself from so-called "dialogical thinking," and this raises the question of its relation to his subordination of dialogue to the "responsibility of being-in-question" elsewhere. When Levinas in *AE* posited the latter as "prior to dialogue, to the exchange of questions and answers," dialogue was conceived as "the thematization of the said" (*OB*, 111/*AQE*, 142). In other words, Levinas in this place upheld the priority of saying over the said, just as in "Dialogue" it is the *saying* of dialogue which is the original mode of transcendence (*OGM*, 147/*DVI*, 225). See also Emmanuel Levinas, "Le mot je, le mot tu, le mot Dieu," *Le Monde* 19–20 (mars 1978): 2. However, note Levinas's rather

292 Notes to Pages 87–96

different comment earlier in *AQE*. There he contrasted, on the one hand, "the presence of interlocutors to one another in a dialogue in which they are at peace and in agreement with one another" with, on the other hand, subjectivity as "the restlessness of the same disturbed by the other" (*OB*, 25/*AQE*, 32). The first phrase describes the conception of "dialogue" which emerges from the "philosophy of dialogue." Levinas's relation to Buber, however, is more readily assimilated to the second of these descriptions.

21. So, for example, instead of voicing his suspicions concerning the appropriateness of situating the divine person in the Thou of dialogue (*APB*, 132/*TO*, 46/*EDE*, 202), he might have observed that in so far as all Thou-saying addresses the eternal Thou ("in every Thou we address the eternal Thou" [*IT*, 57/*DP*, 10]), the relation is asymmetrical. Perhaps it was the way the single Thou provided a glimpse of the eternal Thou (*IT*, 123/*DP*, 10) which led Levinas in *Philosophical Interrogations* to characterize the original relation in Buber as a relation where one of the terms remains absolute. Levinas's reference on that occasion is insufficiently specific to allow for a clear identification.

22. "I agree with him not in his criticism, to be sure, but in the general tendency of his interpretation of Buber. Even Levinas tries to see Buber in the context of the philosophical endeavors of the twentieth century. However, he brings the dialogic back too closely to fundamental ontology and does not distinguish sharply enough between Buber's attempt at an overcoming and Heidegger's attempt at a grounding of intentionality" (*O*, 405 n. 27/*A*, 260 n. 27). Again, "That the interpretation of the 'sphere of subjectivity' with the help of Husserlian terminology is not arbitrary and irrelevant is confirmed by Levinas, who insists that it is 'characterized in Buber by the same expressions that Husserl utilizes for the designation of the intentional object'" (*A*, 405 n. 28/*O*, 260 n. 28).

23. Derrida attempted to impose this "transcendental symmetry" on Levinas in "Violence and Metaphysics" (*WD*, 126/*ED*, 185).

24. The language of conditions is one that Levinas himself frequently employed in the course of explicating his own thinking, but there are indications that even in *Totality and Infinity* he was not only aware of its problems — preeminently within that context that it is an ontological language — but engaged in an effort to counteract or "unsay" it by employing it only in ways whereby it destroys itself.

25. This relates back to the second of the objections in "Martin Buber and the Theory of Knowledge" where Levinas noted the way that, according to Buber (*IT*, 84/*DP*, 37), the I-It relation corrodes the I-Thou (*PMB*, 149/*NP*, 48). The saying and the said address this question by not being introduced as in opposition to each other.

26. This is a question that of course addresses not only to my efforts here, but more importantly Levinas's *account* of the "distinction," an account which can only present the saying and the said as a distinction. Levinas already addressed the problem of giving such a thematic account in *Totality and Infinity*: "The very utterance by which I state it and whose claim to truth, postulating a total reflection, refutes the unsurpassable character of the face to face relation, nonetheless confirms

it by the very fact of stating this truth of telling it to the Other" (*TI*, 221/*TeI*, 196). See also *OB*, 143/*AQE*, 182 for Levinas's own discussion of "saying saying the saying itself" (*Dire disant le dire même*).

Notes to Chapter 6/Gordon

1. See Levinas's essays on Buber in *PI, PMB* and *OS. Philosophical Interrogations* consists of a series of questions posed to famous philosophers. Levinas is among the questioners in the section dedicated to Buber. The chapters in *The Philosophy of Martin Buber* are followed by a 55-page section called "Replies to My Critics" in which Buber dedicates two short answers to Levinas. Note that Levinas's questions in *PI* were written after his essay in *PMB*.

2. The only study that I am aware of that discusses all of Levinas's essays that deal with Buber's philosophy is Robert Bernasconi, "'Failure of Communication' as a Surplus: Dialogue and Lack of Dialogue between Buber and Levinas" (chapter 5 of this volume). Earlier studies like Philip Lawton, "Love and Justice: Levinas's Reading of Buber," *Philosophy Today* 20, no. 1 (1976): 77–83; Andrew Tallon, "Intentionality, Intersubjectivity, and the Between: Buber and Levinas on Affectivity and the Dialogical Principle," (reproduced as "Affection and the Transcendental Dialogical Personalism of Buber and Levinas" in chapter 4 of this volume); and Jacques Derrida, "Violence and Metaphysics: An Essay on the Thought of Emmanuel Levinas," in *Writing and Difference*, trans. Alan Bass (Chicago: University of Chicago Press, 1978), 314–15 n. 37, were originally published before three of Levinas's five essays on Buber were written.

3. In "'Failure of Communication' as a Surplus," Bernasconi reveals several inconsistencies in Levinas's assessment of Buber's thought. Nonetheless, he argues that these inconsistencies are not due to a "refusal to listen to what is said, much as when one poses objections against a text from a totally different standpoint or when one assimilates a text to one's own standpoint," but rather that Levinas attempted to awaken "the 'saying' of Buber from the said" (124). He portrays Levinas's treatment of Buber as a Levinasian ethical relation, where Levinas awakens the saying of Buber through a cyclical process commencing with a separation from Buber, and leading "to exercis[ing] an orientation in favor of Buber." To re-read Buber in order to confirm or deny the correctness of Levinas's reading, Bernasconi asserts, "would be to pose the question at a level of simplicity that remains divorced from the 'dialogue between thinkers'" (124). By contrast, Bernasconi suggests that one should examine whether Buber reads differently after one has carefully thought through the so-called dialogue between the two thinkers. Despite Bernasconi's suggestion, I believe that it is more becoming to begin by reading Buber without assimilating him to Levinas. Only after one wrestles with Buber's ideas, after one understands his insights, does it become appropriate, I think, to criticize, expand on and develop his idea — or in Bernasconi's words, to awaken the saying from the said. This is, of course, a hermeneutical position, which I will adopt throughout this paper.

4. This is an echo of Levinas's understanding of the Cartesian cogito as receiving its certitude from the idea of God (infinity). See Descartes' "Third Meditation" and Levinas's discussion of it in *TI*, 212. Levinas's return to the Cartesian cogito and his appropriation of the notion of the idea of infinity as founding the certitude of the ego is problematic, particularly if one acknowledges the seriousness of Heidegger's criticism of the cogito. Already, in *Being and Time*, Heidegger claimed that the body of the Cartesian cogito is disengaged from the world, and attempted to move from the rationalist approach of disengagement. The body is not merely an object for intelligibility, he asserted, but a condition of intelligibility. Human beings are embodied and not disengaged. In this manner, Heidegger opposed the *res cogitans* and the *res extensa* dualism. By adopting Descartes' analysis in order to demonstrate the importance of infinity, Levinas resumes the mind-body dualism.

5. See note 1.

6. In *Philosophical Interrogations* (*PI*, 27), Buber refers Levinas to this essay which was originally published in 1951. See "Distance and Relation" (*KM*, 59–71).

7. As Robert Bernasconi pointed out, perhaps Levinas's major criticism in "Martin Buber and the Theory of Knowledge" was his claim that Buber's account of "the Other fulfilled the ambitions of the theory of knowledge in its ancient classical form. For Buber, only in the I-Thou relation did one succeed in grasping the independent other; only there did one enter into community with the totality of being" ("'Failure of Communication' as a Surplus," 113). Bernasconi implicitly agrees with Levinas, since he does not indicate that Levinas's conclusion is based on the latter's misunderstanding of Buber's notion of primal distance. But if it is following the first movement and not in the I-Thou relation that one sets things apart and grasps them as separate, it is not the case that only in the I-Thou relation one succeeds in grasping the independent other. On the contrary, the sphere of the first movement where the independent other is grasped is merely the presupposition of the second movement in which the I-Thou can occur; within the first movement one relates to the other as an It.

8. Bernasconi, "'Failure of Communication' as a Surplus," 111.

9. Following Bernasconi, I will use Walter Kaufman's translation of *I and Thou*, changing Kaufman's You to a Thou.

10. Buber, while characterizing the I-Thou relation as reciprocal, claims that the "'asymmetrical' is only one of the possibilities of the I-Thou relation, not its rule, just as mutuality in all gradations cannot be regarded as the rule" (*PI*, 28).

11. Bernasconi begins the discussion of Levinas's later writings on Buber claiming that Levinas "came finally to a recognition of the importance of the eternal Thou and of dialogue in Buber" ("'Failure of Communication' as a Surplus," 115). This is a dubious statement, particularly when one considers its author, and the argument that preceded it. It is not my intention to question Bernasconi's assertion that Levinas did not recognize the importance of dialogue in Buber when he was writing, for instance, his contribution for the Martin Buber edition

of the *Library of Living Philosophers*. I do, however, wish to emphasize that Bernasconi's claim undermines his insistence that one should not reread Buber in order to deny or confirm the correctness of Levinas's reading, since, as he states, such a reading poses the question at "a level of simplicity that remains divorced from the 'dialogue between thinkers'" ("'Failure of Communication' as a Surplus," 124). In my view, if Levinas indeed did not recognize the importance of the eternal Thou and of dialogue in Buber, then it would be hard to claim that the two thinkers had a dialogue. I believe that it is important to understand the other before objecting to what he or she is saying. In particular, we should understand the other before we assume the task of awakening the saying from the said. I believe that such an approach is not only in the spirit of Buber's thought, but also very close to Levinas's perspective.

12. See, for example, *IT*, 83–85.

13. Buber also mentions the technique of the tool and the weapon.

14. This part of Bernasconi's chapter ("'Failure of Communication' as a Surplus," 113–19) does not limit itself to the question of the I-Thou relation, but rather deals with many of the themes in Levinas's article. Most important is the question regarding the possibility of thinking beyond being. Thus, when Bernasconi claims that the failed dialogue was made good, he is referring to a variety of themes, of which I discuss only one.

15. Ibid., 115.

16. Levinas qualifies his use of the word "status," which, strictly speaking, is appropriate to a subject-object relation.

17. Levinas's concessions about responsibility and "meeting" in Buber both clearly support Bernasconi's argument that Levinas retracts his argument and enters into dialogue with Buber.

18. We are reminded of Heidegger's "letting beings be," which also captures the passive/active duality needed for an ethical relationship. See Martin Heidegger, "Letter on Humanism," in *Basic Writings*, ed. David Farrell Krell (San Francisco: Harper Collins, 1993).

Notes to Chapter 7/Friedman

1. Robert Bernasconi, "'Failure of Communication' as a Surplus: Dialogue and Lack of Dialogue between Buber and Levinas," in Robert Bernasconi and David Wood, eds., *The Provocation of Levinas: Rethinking the Other* (London and New York: Routledge, 1988), 124 (republished as chapter 5 of this volume).

2. Neve Gordon, "Ethics as Reciprocity: An Analysis of Levinas's Reading of Buber," *International Studies in Philosophy* 31, no. 2 (1999): 106 n. 4.

3. Buber is talking here about the "normative limitation of mutuality" which he posits when he says that although the teacher, the therapist and the pastor must practice "inclusion" — i.e., "imagine the real" in their relations to those they help — the pupil, the patient and the parishioner cannot do the same without changing the structure of the relationship and turning it into friendship.

4. I stress this point in response to a May 16, 2000 letter to me from the

Levinas scholar Jeffrey Murray who wrote: "For Buber, the problem seems to be an inability to draw meaningful boundaries. Since ethics arises out of the situation, I seem to have a moral obligation to each thing that comprises the situation — i.e., each thing with which I find my self in relationship. How then do I prioritize those obligations? (Note: if it is the situation itself that 'tells' me, then Buber has the same problem as Levinas.) For Levinas, the problem also seems to be an inability to draw meaningful boundaries. Since Ethics comes from the Other, I am not only obligated to things that can speak/call. How can be I sure that there are not calls that I do not, but should, hear? To be blunt, Buber seems to include too much in the moral area and Levinas too little."

5. See in particular "Society and the State" and in general the whole last section on "Politics, Community, and Peace" in *Pointing the Way*, ed. and trans. Maurice Friedman (New York: Harper, 1963); *Paths and Utopia*, trans. R. F. C. Hull (New York: Macmillan, 1988); the chapter on "Social Philosophy," in Maurice Friedman, *Martin Buber: The Life of Dialogue*, 3d ed. (Chicago: University of Chicago Press, 1976); the relevant chapters in the three volumes of Maurice Friedman, *Martin Buber's Life and Work* (New York: E. P. Dutton, 1982–84), and numerous other works (Bernard Susser and Lawrence Silberstein among others) on Buber's political and social philosophy. See also Maurice Friedman and Pat Boni, eds., *Martin Buber and the Human Sciences* (Albany: SUNY Press, 1996), Part IV — "Economics, Politics, and History."

6. See Buber, "With a Monist," in *Pointing the Way*.

7. See Buber, *Tales of the Hasidim: The Later Masters*, trans. Olga Marx (New York: Schocken Books, 1991).

8. François Poirié, *Emmanuel Levinas, qui êtes-vous?* (Lyon: La Manufacture, 1987), 125 (see chapter 2 of this volume).

Notes to Chapter 8/Meir

1. I would like to thank Prof. Rivka Horwitz for having read an earlier draft of this article that was enriched by some of her constructive remarks.

2. I agree with Pamela Vermes who states in *Buber on God and the Perfect Man* (London: Littman, 1994) that the correct translation of *Ich und Du* has to be *I and You*, and not Walter Kaufmann's *I and Thou*, which risks reducing relation to the relation with God (xviii).

3. In *Daniel*, the I-It as the world of ir-relation structured by time and space is pictured by the concept "orientation," the I-You as the world of relation by the concept "realization." Buber here distinguishes between "orientation," an attitude that situates everything in a context, and "realization," a "sign of the eternal" (*Signum des Ewigen*) through which one relates to everything according to its own content. Later, in *I and You*, he dropped the term "realization" because of its overly mystical tone. See Martin Buber, *Daniel: Dialogues on Realization*, trans. Maurice Friedman (New York: Holt, Rinehart, & Winston, 1964).

4. The presence of the teacher is most important for Buber, not as a content, but as a speaking voice. "Relationship educates" (*Beziehung erzieht*) (*BH*, 98, 101).

5. David Banon, "Une herméneutique de la sollicitation: Levinas lecteur du Talmud," in *Les Cahiers de La nuit surveillée, no. 3: Emmanuel Levinas,* ed. J. Rolland (Lagrasse: Verdier, 1984), 100–01.

6. Emmanuel Levinas, "'A l'image de Dieu' d'après Rabbi Haim Voloziner," in *L'au-delà du verset: Lectures et discours talmudiques* (Paris: Minuit, 1982), 187–88.

7. For Levinas's attitude toward Judaism, see Catherine Chalier, "Singularité juive et philosophie," *Les Cahiers,* ed. J. Rolland, 78–98. Chalier writes that Levinas wants to give to Judaism its philosophy, and to awaken philosophy to its "other"— the otherwise than being. See also Richard A. Cohen, *Elevations: The Height of the Good in Rosenzweig and Levinas* (Chicago: University of Chicago Press, 1994), 126–32. For his thinking on Jewish education, see Annette Aronowicz, "L'éducation juive dans la pensée d'Emmanuel Levinas," in *Emmanuel Lévinas: Philosophie et judaïsme, Pardès* 26 (1999): 195–210, and Shmuel Wygoda, "Freedom as Responsibility: On the Educational Thought of Emmanuel Levinas" (Hebrew), in *'Al dèrèkh ha-'avot: Articles On the Subject of Torah and Education* (Alon Shvut: Tevunot, 2001), 75–162. For Levinas's relation to other Jewish thinkers, see Edith Wyschogrod, *Emmanuel Levinas: The Problem of Ethical Metaphysics* (The Hague: Martinus Nijhoff, 1974), and "The Moral Self: Emmanuel Levinas and Hermann Cohen", *Da'at* 4 (1980): 35–58; J.-L. Schlegel, "Levinas et Rosenz-weig,", in *Les Cahiers,* ed. J. Rolland, 50–70; Robert Bernasconi, "'Failure of Communication' as a Surplus: Dialogue and Lack of Dialogue between Buber and Levinas" (see chapter 5 of this volume); Susan Handelman, *Fragments of Redemption: Jewish Thought and Literary Theory in Benjamin, Scholem and Levinas* (Bloomington: Indiana University Press, 1991); Robert Gibbs, *Correlations in Rosenzweig and Levinas* (Princeton: Princeton University Press, 1992); Richard Cohen, *Elevations.*

8. Vermes, *Buber on God and The Perfect Man,* 29.

9. On Levinas as post-Holocaust philosopher in comparison with Emil Fackenheim, see Tamra Wright, *The Twilight of Jewish Philosophy: Emmanuel Levinas's Ethical Hermeneutics* (Amsterdam: Harwood, 1999), 97–109.

10. I follow here the argument of Rivka Horwitz, "Gnosticism and The Theory of Creation In The Thinking of Martin Buber" (Hebrew), in *Da'at* (1979): 229–40.

11. Rivka Horwitz, *Buber's Way to "I and Thou": The Development of Martin Buber's Thought and his "Religion as Presence" Lectures* (Philadelphia: Jewish Publication Society, 1988). This remarkable study investigates Ebner's influence on Buber's *I and You.*

12. See Rivka Horwitz, "Revelation and the Bible According to Twentieth-Century Jewish Philosophy," in *Jewish Spirituality: From the Sixteenth-Century Revival to the Present,* ed. A. Green, (New York: Crossroad, 1987), 348–51.

13. For Buber on revelation, see "Fragments on Revelation," in *BH,* 113–16.

14. Friedrich Nietzsche, *Ecce Homo,* in *Sämtliche Werke, Kritische Studienausgabe,* Band 6 (Berlin: de Gruyter, 1980), 339: "Man nimmt, man fragt nicht, wer da gibt."

15. Martin Buber, "The Man of Today and the Jewish Bible," in *WMB*, 247.

16. Herberg writes that Buber genuinely combines repentance (*teshuva*) and grace (*WMB*, 28–29). Yet, there is no doubt that in Buber's discourse on the relation the accent is on the gratuitous character of the encounter, which crowns the multitude of our meetings.

17. Martin Buber, "The Faith of Judaism," in Herberg, *WMB*, 254–56.

18. This vision also implies a political dimension, the realization of the lofty prophetic idea of justice. I maintain this against Haim Gordon, who thinks that Buber did not do justice to the realization of justice. See Haim Gordon, *The Heidegger-Buber Controversy: The Status of the I-Thou* (Connecticut: Westport, 2001), 144–46, 160–62. Gordon disregards Buber's writing on spiritual Zionism and on Israel's role among the nations.

19. This enigmatic person, apparently a Lithuanian Jew, was Levinas's teacher from 1947 until 1951. Levinas revered Chouchani, a brilliant, itinerant sage who appeared in France, but also in Israel (between others in Kibbutz Sde Eliyahu) and in South America. He was also Elie Wiesel's teacher. On Chouchani, see Salomon Malka, *Monsieur Chouchani: l'énigme d'un maître du XXᵉ siècle* (Paris: J. C. Lattes, 1994).

20. *Du sacré au saint: Cinq nouvelles lectures talmudiques* (Paris: Minuit, 1977), 18.

21. See Amos 3:2 to which Levinas refers.

22. Vermes, *Buber on God and The Perfect Man*, 157.

23. Paul Mendes-Flohr, *From Mysticism to Dialogue* (Detroit: Wayne State University Press, 1989), 78.

24. Ibid., 79. Mendes-Flohr remarks that Simmel did not consider religion to be a debasement of religiosity. Buber tended to characterize religion as perverted. See *BH*, 109–10.

25. The Buberian dichotomy between *emunah*, faith or confidence (*fides qua creditur*), and *pistis*, dogmatic institutionalized sayings (*fides quae creditur*), was criticized by Tsvi Werblovsky in "'Ways of Faith and Ways of Wisdom" (Hebrew), in *To The Memory of Martin Buber, Twenty Years After his Death* (Jerusalem: Israeli National Academy of Sciences, 1987), 28–33.

26. Martin Buber, *Der heilige Weg: Ein Antwort an die Juden und die Völker* (Frankfurt: Literarische Anstalt Rütten und Loening, 1920), 53.

27. Vittorio Hösle, *Praktisch Philosophie in der modernen Welt* (München: Beck, 1992), 59–86.

28. See Martin Buber, *Paths and Utopia*, trans. R. F. C. Hull (New York: Macmillan, 1988).

29. See Herberg's introduction to *WMB*, 35.

30. For a detailed account of Levinas's attitude toward the land and the State of Israel, see my article "The Place of the Land of Israel and the State of Israel in the Work of Emmanuel Levinas" (Hebrew), in *Metaphora* 4 (1993): 41–61.

31. Concerning the parallels and differences between Levinas's and Rosenzweig's view on Christianity, see J.-L. Schlegel, "Levinas and Rosenzweig," in *Les Cahiers*, ed. J. Rolland, 54–59.

32. Aronowicz reminds us of Levinas's Mendelssohnian understanding of Jewish singularity: Jews through their praxis of laws preserve and support this truth to which everybody has access through reason (*NTR*, 203–04). See also *DF*, 274. For Levinas's positive evaluation of Mendelssohn, see my "Moses Mendelssohn's *Jerusalem* from Levinas's Perspective," in *In Proximity: Emmanuel Levinas and the Eighteenth Century* eds., Melvyn New, Robert Bernasconi and Richard A. Cohen, (Lubbock: Texas Tech University Press, 2001), 243–59.

33. Buber, *Two Types of Faith*, 12–13.

34. Bernard Dupuy, "Le christianisme dans l'oeuvre de Martin Buber," in *Martin Buber: Dialogue et voix prophétique* (Strasbourg: Université des Sciences Humaines de Strasbourg, 1980), 148–60.

35. See *Die chassidischen Bücher* (Berlin: Schocken Verlag, 1927), where Buber writes that Jewish Messianism is not limited to the faith in a one time eschatological event (xxvi–ii). There are in each generation the humble and despised "servants of God" (*Gottesknechte*) who bear the filth of the world and purify it.

36. Banon, "Une hermeneutique de la sollicitation," 106.

37. Ephraim Meir, "The Idea of Revelation in Levinas's Thought," (Hebrew), in *Da'at* 30 (1993): 41–52.

38. Levinas was critical of the exclusiveness of the historical viewpoint. He saw the historico-philological approach and the science of Judaism as too preoccupied with their own methods, and thus unable to revive texts. He was impressed by the miracle of the confluence of the different biblical texts, which receive their unity through the traditional ethical way of life and point of view of the Jews. See *LR* 197–98.

39. See Vermes, *Buber on God and the Perfect Man*, 73.

40. Buber writes: "*Das Wesen liebt der Chassid, liebend hält / Er's fest in Gott, im Menschen, in der Welt* [The Hasid loves the Creature, lovingly he holds it / Fast in God, in Man, in the World]" (*BH*, 124–25).

Notes to Chapter 9/Fagenblat & Wolski

1. Following Robert Alter, Harold Bloom and others, the term Hebrew Bible will be used to refer to what Christians call the Old Testament, and what Jews regard as the entirety of the scriptural canon. Buber and Levinas employ a Judeo-centered approach to the Bible, though Levinas, when he is addressing a Christian audience, occasionally includes illustrations from the New Testament.

2. This aspect of Rosenzweig's thinking is especially well brought out by Leora Blatnitzki, *Idolatry and Representation: The Philosophy of Franz Rosenzweig Reconsidered* (Princeton: Princeton University Press, 2000). See also Stéphane Mosès, *System and Revelation: The Philosophy of Franz Rosenzweig*, trans. C. Tihanyi (Detroit: Wayne State University Press, 1992), which explores Rosenzweig's understanding of revelation, time, history and liturgy, discussed below.

3. Hans-Georg Gadamer, *Truth and Method*, ed. J. Weinsheimer and D. G. Marshall (New York: Continuum, 1994), 70.

4. A particularly apposite example of this line of thinking is developed by

Michael Walzer, *Thick and Thin: Moral Argument at Home and Abroad* (Indiana: University of Notre Dame Press, 1994), and *Interpretation and Social Criticism* (Cambridge, MA: Harvard University Press 1993), who draws on the biblical prophets to illustrate the idea of the engaged critic.

5. On "holy history," see *DF*, 226–27; *ITN*, 1, 3 ff., 20, 29, 88, 117 f., 121; *BV*, 6 ff., 21, 63, 112, 129 ff., 187, 192. When the argument for a moral temporal order beyond the ordinary historical plane is first made, its valence is decidedly ethical and nonliturgical; see *TI*, 52.

6. This is Levinas's claim (*OS*, 128). We are not convinced that a clear distinction between liturgical life and mythic life can be sustained, though we agree that life practices are the key to avoiding the reduction of positivist historicism and the abstraction of allegory. Interestingly, it was Buber who made the explicit argument that Jewish myth is precisely realized in liturgical practices ("Myth in Judaism," *OJ*, 95–107). Here too, however, as we shall see below, Buber's acclamation of myth goes hand in hand with his denunciation of "rabbinism, which has emasculated the Jewish ideal" (*OJ*, 100), and a counter affirmation of Lurianic and Hasidic mytho-theurgical ritual life (*OJ*, 103–07). It is not a coincidence, then, that Buber's other great Jewish love beside the Bible is the world of Hasidism, for according to Buber only pre-rabbinic biblical existence and "post-rabbinic" Hasidic existence realizes the ideal of life lived in the presence of divine reality, whereas the rabbis of the Talmud "so cruelly rationalized" "Jewish monotheism" (*OJ*, 105). Levinas, of course, prizes this rational monotheism, and equally rejects an unmediated approach to the Bible and to Hasidic "spirituality." In fact, no clear distinction exists between liturgical and mythic life, at least insofar as these terms are applicable to Jewish practices, because the very rabbis whom both Levinas and Buber wish to characterize as antimythic (while ascribing opposite values to this characterization) in fact develop a rich mythic consciousness that supplements and occasionally subverts "rational monotheism." See Yehuda Liebes, *Studies in Jewish Myth and Jewish Messianism*, trans. B. Stein (Albany: SUNY Press, 1993), 1–64; and Daniel Boyarin, *Intertextuality and the Reading of Midrash* (Bloomington, Ind.: Indiana University Press, 1990), chapter 6.

7. *CPP*, 92. This theme determines the temporal structure of Levinas's major early works (*Existence and Existents* [1947], *Time and the Other* [1947], and *Totality and Infinity* [1961]), all of which strive to articulate a desire that distinguishes itself from need by relating to a *future* that belongs to the other rather than oneself.

8. See especially "Revelation in the Jewish Tradition," *BV*, 146–48, and "The Temptation of Temptation," in *NTR*, 42–50. For a helpful discussion, see Tamra Wright. *The Twilight of Jewish Philosophy: Emmanuel Levinas's Ethical Hermeneutics* (Amsterdam: Harwood Academic Publishers, 1999), 109–18.

9. Robert Alter, *The Art of Biblical Narrative* (Basic Books: USA, 1981), 70.

10. The boldest argument beyond a theology of presence is undoubtedly Jean-Luc Marion, *God Without Being*, trans. T. A. Carlson (Chicago: University of Chicago Press, 1991), whose project is essentially indebted to Levinas. On the

problematic correlation between God and presence, see Kevin Hart, *The Trespass of the Sign: Deconstruction, Theology and Philosophy* (Cambridge: Cambridge University Press, 1989).

11. Levinas even rejects the term theology to describe what he is doing (*OGM*, ix, xi; *OB*, 196 n. 19). We use the term theology only to indicate Levinas's discourse on God without determining whether it is a positive or negative theology. On this, see Wright, *The Twilight of Jewish Philosophy*, and Jeffrey L. Kosky, *Levinas and the Philosophy of Religion* (Bloomington: Indiana University Press, 2001), and Michael Fagenblat, "Lacking All Interest: Levinas, Leibowitz, and the Pure Practice of Religion" (forthcoming).

12. Stephen Kepnes, *The Text as Thou: Martin Buber's Dialogical Hermeneutics and Narrative Theology* (Bloomington: Indiana University Press, 1993).

13. See, for example, Levinas's essay "On the Jewish Reading of the Scripture," *BV*, 101–05.

14. The tradition of *pshat* is, of course, both rich and well respected within the Jewish tradition, especially among the medieval commentators. However, for the main modes of Jewish biblical exegesis — Talmudic, Midrashic, Kabbalistic and Hasidic — literalness is not of primary exegetical interest. See Moshe Greenberg, *Studies in the Bible and Jewish Thought* (New York: Jewish Publications Society, 1995), xiiv–xv; David Weiss Halivni, *Peshat and Derash: Plain and Applied Meaning in Rabinic Exegesis* (Oxford: Oxford University Press, 1991); Uriel Simon, "The Religious Significance of the *peshat*," *Tradition* 23 (1988): 145–55.

15. Indeed, Levinas would have agreed with David Hartman's depiction of a development leading from biblical to rabbinic to modern Jewish theology as a process of increasing human responsibility that corresponds to a decrease in divine control. See David Hartman, *A Living Covenant: The Innovative Spirit in Traditional Judaism* (Woodstock, Vt.: Jewish Lights, 1997), and Jonathan Cohen, "Educating for Spiritual Maturity: Hartman's Interpretation of Judaism as a 'Religion for Adults,' in *Judaism and Modernity: The Religious Philosophy of David Hartman*, ed. Jonathan W. Malino, (Shalom Hartman Institute: Jerusalem, 2001).

16. For a characterization of the agonistic and dialogical character of the Talmud see Daniel Boyarin, *Carnal Israel: Reading Sex in Talmudic Culture* (Berkeley: University of California Press, 1995), 25–30.

17. There is some rabbinic, homiletic precedent that reduces the entire Bible to one or several principles, in the Babylonian Talmud, Tractate Makot, 24a or as in Rabbi Akiva's famous remark (in *Sifra* 2:4) that "You shall love your neighbor as yourself" (Lev. 19:18) is a principle standing for the whole Torah.

18. Simon, "The Religious Significance of the *Peshat*," 154.

19. Wright, *The Twilight of Jewish Philosophy*, 118–23.

20. Ibid., 111.

21. Yeshayahu Leibowitz has taken this fact as foundational for his neo-Orthodox theology. See his classic essay, "Religious Praxis: The Meaning of Halakhah," in *Judaism, Human Values, and the Jewish State*, ed. Eliezer Goldman (Cambridge: Harvard University Press, 1992), 3–29.

22. Levinas attempts to get out of this impasse by insisting on the ambivalence

of the term "Israel," which for him means not only Jews, but all moral people (e.g., *NTR*, 98). This apologetic gesture simply confirms the problem, for Levinas just as surely wants to preserve a sense of Jewish particularism.

23. Gershom Scholem, "Martin Buber's Conception of Judaism," in his *On Jews and Judaism in Crisis* (New York: Schocken Books, 1976), 165.

24. Martin Buber, *Moses: The Revelation and the Covenant* (Atlantic Highlands, N.J.: Humanities Press, 1988), 15–16.

25. Ibid., 18; emphasis added.

26. Buber, *Moses*, 74.

27. James Kugel, "Two Introductions to Midrash," in *Midrash and Literature* eds. Geoffrey Hartman and Sanford Budick, (New Haven: Yale University Press, 1986) 77–99.

28. Levinas adds: "The Bible — a volume inhabited by a people. But also a volume that has nourished that people, almost in the literal sense of the term, like 1. the prophet who, in Ezekiel 3, swallows a scroll. A singular digestion of celestial food! In the Jewish reading, episodes, figures, teachings, words, letters, receive — through the immediate meaning, as if it were transparent — other innumerable meanings. Parable and homily (genres known by philologists but which appear minor to them) have stored the treasures of Jewish thought and spirituality. Their diversity, their very contradictions, far from compromising the truths commented upon, are felt to be faithful to the Real, refractory to the System" (*OS*, 129–30).

29. Franz Rosenzweig, *On Jewish Learning*, ed. N. Glatzer (New York: Schocken Books, 1965), 103.

30. Levinas makes the same point in "The Strings and the Wood": "It may even be that a less naïve conception of the inspired Word than the one expiring beneath critical pens allows the true message to come through widely scattered human witnesses, but all miraculously confluent in the one Book" (*OS*, 126).

31. For an elaboration of this task and some modern responses to it, see *The Return to Scripture in Judaism and Christianity*, ed. Peter Ochs (New York: Paulist Press, 1993). For a wider range of Jewish responses, see also Nathan Wolski, "Keeping the Torah in Heaven" (forthcoming).

32. Peter Ochs, "An Introduction to Post-Critical Scriptural Integration," in *The Return to Scripture in Judaism and Christianity*, 3. Among Jewish exegetes, the task is best expressed and epitomized by Moshe Greenberg, e.g., "Can Modern Critical Bible Scholarship Have a Jewish Character?" and "To Whom and For What Should a Bible Commentator Be Responsible?" in his *Studies in the Bible and Jewish Thought*, 3–8 and 235–44, respectively.

33. We are indebted to Jonathan Cohen for pointing out to us this phrase of Fackenheim's — and for a seminar on this problematic in general.

Notes to Chapter 10/Gibbs

1. See Robert Bernasconi, "'Failure of Communication' as a Surplus: Dialogue and Lack of Dialogue between Buber and Levinas" (chapter 5 of this volume.) For a discussion of the polemic concerning biblical reading, see Eleanor Pontoreiro,

"On 'Loving the Neighbour': The Implications of Emmanuel Levinas' Intensification of Ethics after the Shoah" (Ph.D. diss., University of Toronto, 2002).

2. Dan Avnon, *Martin Buber: The Hidden Dialogue* (London: Rowan and Littlefield, 1998); Steven Kepnes, *The Text as Thou* (Bloomington: Indiana University Press, 1992); Jill Robbins, *Altered Reading: Levinas and Literature* (Chicago: University of Chicago Press, 1999); Richard A. Cohen, *Ethics, Exegesis and Philosophy* (Cambridge: Cambridge University Press, 2001); and Robert Gibbs, *Why Ethics? Signs of Responsibilities* (Princeton: Princeton University Press, 2000).

3. The texts are numbered consecutively and are broken into shorter pieces (lettered 1.a, 1.b, 1.c, etc.). The texts are all retranslated by me, although I cite both the original language publication and the available English translations.

4. Indeed, the greatest dialogue of twentieth century thought is the one that occurred between Rosenzweig and Buber during the translation. Each maintained his own distinctive personality, philosophy of language and hermeneutics, and theological vision of the Bible, but they met over the Bible and produced a translation together. There is both generosity and responsibility in Buber's invitation to the mortally ill Rosenzweig; Buber wants to offer Rosenzweig a task worthy of his last months, and to plumb Rosenzweig's mind in order to learn from him.

5. Martin Buber, *Werke*, (Munich: Kosel-Verlag und Verlag Lambert Schneider, 1962), trans. Lawrence Rosenwald with Everett Fox (Bloomington, Ind.: Indiana University Press, 1994), 2:73.

6. Of course, other languages are capable of being reconcretized in just this way, and such thinking is characteristic in some ways of Heidegger's poetics — but just how Hebraic that turn in Heidegger is is a topic for a different paper.

7. Martin Buber, *Buber Werke*, 2:869. *Scripture and Translation*, 21.

8. Emmanuel Levinas, *L'Au-delà du verset* (Paris: Editions de Minuit, 1982), 94–95. *BV*, 75.

9. Jean Halperin, ed., *La Conscience Juive: Données et débats* (Paris: Presses Universitaires de France, 1963), 53.

10. Emmanuel Levinas, *Hors Sujet* (Paris: Fata Morgana, 1987), 26–7. *Outside the Subject*, trans. Michael Smith (Stanford: Stanford University Press, 1993), 13.

11. For the moment I skip over the issue of contradictions and note simply preserving the letter requires facing that the text does not have a literal unity — that it includes diversity and, indeed, contradiction.

12. Halperin, *La Conscience Juive*, 149.

13. See the interview with François Poirié in *Emmanuel Levinas: Qui êtes-vous?* (Lyon: La Manufacture), 1987, 124–25 (chapter 2 of this volume).

14. Martin Buber, *Werke*, 2:241; *PF*, 6.

15. Martin Buber, *Werke*, 2:910. *On the Bible*, ed. Nachum N. Glatzer (New York: Schocken, 1982), 144.

16. Hermann Levin Goldschmidt, *Weil Wir Brüder Sind* (Stuttgart: Verlag Katholisches Bibelwerk, 1975) and *Die Botschaft des Judentums, Werke 3* (Wien: Passagen Verlag), 1994.

Notes to Chapter 11/Wright

1. Steven Katz, for example, in his article "Jewish Faith After the Holocaust: Four Approaches," discusses only Fackenheim, Rubenstein, Berkovits and Maybaum, all writers who were addressing the issues of post-Holocaust theology in the 1960s and 1970s. See Steven Katz, *Post-Holocaust Dialogues* (London: New York University Press, 1983), 141–73.

2. Richard Rubenstein, *After Auschwitz: Radical Theology and Contemporary Judaism*, (Indianapolis: Bobbs Merrill, 1966).

3. Emil Fackenheim, *To Mend the World: Foundations of Post-Holocaust Jewish Thought* (Bloomington: Indiana University Press, 1994), 260 and passim.

4. Emil Fackenheim, *The Jewish Bible after the Holocaust: A Re-reading*. (Manchester: Manchester University Press, 1990), 1–26. See also *To Mend the World*, 16–18.

5. Emil Fackenheim, *God's Presence in History* (New York: Harper & Row, 1970), 10.

6. Martin Buber, *On the Bible*, ed. Nachum N. Glatzer (New York: Schocken, 1982), 1.

7. Fackenheim, *God's Presence in History*, 61.

8. *OJ*, 224. Buber is quoting a verse from Psalms that is one of the refrains of Hallel, a liturgical expression of praise of God the Redeemer, which forms part of the service of Passover night.

9. Fackenheim, *To Mend the World*, 196.

10. *OJ*, 225; italics added.

11. The story, along with articles on its textual history, a translation of "Loving the Torah More than God" and other commentaries on the monologue, can be found in Zvi Kolitz, *Yossel Rakover Speaks to God: Holocaust Challenges to Religious Faith* (Hoboken, NJ: Ktav, 1995).

12. The translation in *Difficult Freedom* mistakenly has Yossel "echoing the whole of the Torah" rather than the Talmud. In addition, the same translation presents Yossel's exclamation as the "monologue's closing remark" rather than "the high point" (*"le point culminant"*) (*DF*, 144).

13. From a literary point of view, it is interesting to note that the Yossel Rakover story inverts the talmudic tale in interesting ways. In the Talmud, it is the people of Israel who have forsaken God, whereas Yossel Rakover refers to a situation in which the human being is disappointed by God.

14. Hilary Putnam, "Levinas and Judaism," in *The Cambridge Companion to Levinas*, eds. Simon Critchley and Robert Bernasconi (Cambridge: Cambridge University Press, 2002), 46; 60–61.

15. *OS*, 13; emphasis added.

16. *Kiddushin* 39b.

17. Richard J. Bernstein discusses these three quotations and argues that the concern with finding an ethical response to evil is the key to understanding the major thrust of Levinas's philosophical work. ("Evil and the temptation of theodicy," in *The Cambridge Companion to Levinas*.) I took a similar approach in

my *The Twilight of Jewish Philosophy: Emmanuel Levinas's Ethical Hermeneutics* (London: Routledge, 1999), chap. 1.

18. According to Jewish tradition, there are 613 divine commandments in the Torah. Fackenheim's trope suggests that a new obligation was revealed at Auschwitz. See Fackenheim, *God's Presence in History*.

Notes to Chapter 12/Kelley

1. Levinas explicitly mentions Buber in these books and articles: *Time and the Other*, trans. Richard Cohen (Pittsburgh: Duquesne University Press, 1985); "Martin Buber and the Theory of Knowledge," in *PMB*; *TI/TeI*; "Apropos of Buber: Some Notes," in *Outside the Subject*, trans. Michael Smith (Stanford: Stanford University Press, 1993); "Dialogue with Martin Buber," in *Proper Names*, trans. Michael B. Smith (Stanford: Stanford University Press, 1996); "Martin Buber, Gabriel Marcel and Philosophy," in *Outside the Subject*; Martin Buber's Thought and Contemporary Philosophy," in *Outside the Subject*, "Dialogue," in *Of God Who Comes to Mind*, trans. Bettina Bergo (Stanford: Stanford University Press, 1998); "Ethics of the Infinite," interview by Richard Kearney, *Dialogues with Contemporary Continental Thinkers* (Manchester: Manchester University Press, 1987).

2. Martin Buber, *Ten Rungs: Hasidic Sayings*, trans. Olga Marx (New York: Schocken Books, 1947), 82.

Notes to Chapter 13/Cohen

1. This chapter presents part of a larger monograph on Levinas and Buber by Richard Cohen. It has been edited by the editors of this volume.

2. Martin Heidegger, *Being and Time*, trans. John Macquarrie and Edward Robinson (San Francisco: Harper and Row, 1962), 435; 436; see paragraph 74 in general.

3. Martin Buber, *Paths and Utopia*, trans. R. F. C. Hull (New York: Macmillan, 1988), 134.

4. Ibid., 145.

5. Ibid., 134.

6. Arno Munster, "De la pensée Buberienne du je-tu vers la pensée de l'autre dans la philosophie d'Emmanuel Levinas," *Le principe dialogique: de la refiexion monologique vers la pro-fiexion intersubjective* (Paris: Editions Kime, 1997), 61–79.

7. See Paul Mendes-Flohr's *From Mysticism to Dialogue* (Detroit: Wayne State University Press, 1989), 147–48 n. 2. Levinas, in contrast to Mendes-Flohr, believes that "the adjective Hasidic seems inaccurate" to characterize Buber's actual insight. He writes: "Are not the instants transfigured by fervor, according to Buber (and all instants open themselves, according to him, to that natural magic to the point where one is no more privileged than another), the continually renewed springtimes of Bergson's duration?" (*OS*, 10). Levinas continues, "Meetings are, for Buber,

306 Notes to Pages 248-52

dazzling instants without continuity or content" (17). Mendes-Flohr, intent on showing the influence of Nietzsche and (above all) Gustav Landauer, only considers the influence of Bergson via the analyses of Hans Kohn in *Martin Buber: Sein Werke und seine Zeit* (Koln: Jacob Meltzner, 1961); see Mendes-Flohr, *From Mysticism to Dialogue*, 161–62 n. 234.

8. Buber clearly is greatly influenced by the popular sociological work by Ferdinand Tonnies (1887), *Community and Society*, trans. Charles P. Loomis (New York: Harper and Row, 1963). For Buber, however, genuine sociology is reduced to the intersubjective encounter of the "I-Thou." Paul Mendes-Flohr, referring to "Buber's tendency to emasculate sociological concepts" (78), writes: "Buber frequently employs sociological concepts. However, he introduces these concepts, essentially, only as rhetorical props . . . deprived of their sociological content. . . . External regulation, that is, a regime of instrumental aims, is antithetic to authentic human *Gemeinschaft*, which can only define itself in the immediacy of each moment" (*From Mysticism to Dialogue*, 76–77). For Buber's pre- and post-*I and Thou* relation to Tonnies, see *From Mysticism to Dialogue*, 76–78, 112–13.

9. Emmanuel Levinas, *Entre Nous: On Thinking of the Other*, trans. Michael B. Smith and Barbara Harshav (Columbia: Columbia University Press, 1998), 230.

Notes to Chapter 14/Calarco

1. See Friedrich Nietzsche, *The Will to Power*, trans. Walter Kaufmann (New York: Vintage, 1967): "We are in the phase of the modesty of consciousness" (357); and *On the Genealogy of Morality*, trans. Maudemarie Clark and Alan J. Swensen (Indianapolis: Hackett, 1998): "The sight of man now makes us tired — what is nihilism today if it is not *that*? . . . We are tired of man" (24).

2. I am here referring to contemporary neohumanists such as Luc Ferry. For Ferry's efforts at a recovery of humanism, see his coauthored work with Alain Renault, *French Philosophy of the Sixties: An Essay on Antihumanism*, trans. Mary H. S. Cattani (Amherst: University of Massachusetts Press, 1990).

3. For an excellent, albeit contentious, reading of Heidegger as an antihumanist, see Reiner Schürmann, *Heidegger on Being and Acting: From Principles to Anarchy* (Bloomington: Indiana University Press, 1987).

4. Martin Heidegger, "Letter on 'Humanism,'" in *Pathmarks*, ed. William McNeill (Cambridge: Cambridge University Press, 1998), 263.

5. See Heidegger, "Letter on 'Humanism'": "To think against 'values' is not to maintain that everything interpreted as 'a value' — 'culture,' 'art,' 'science,' 'human dignity,' 'world,' and 'God' — is valueless . . . [nor is it] to beat the drum for the valuelessness and nullity of beings. It means rather to bring the clearing of the truth of being before thinking, as against subjectivizing beings into mere objects" (265).

6. Anticipating Jean Beaufret's response to the paradoxical disavowal *and* employment of "the human" in his work, Heidegger writes:

But — as you no doubt have been wanting to rejoin for quite a while now — does not such thinking think precisely the *humanitas* of *homo humanus?* Does it not think *humanitas* in a decisive sense, as no metaphysics has thought it or can think it? Is this not a "humanism" in the extreme sense? Certainly. It is a humanism that thinks the humanity of the human being from nearness to being. But at the same time it is a humanism in which not the human being but the human being's historical essence is at stake in its provenance from the truth of being. But then does not the existence of the human being also stand or fall in this game of stakes? Indeed it does. (Heidegger, "Letter on 'Humanism,'" 261)

7. Aulus Gellius, *Noctes Atticae*, trans. J. C. Rolfe (Cambridge, Mass: Loeb Classical Library, 1967), 457–58. Cited in Tony Davies, *Humanism* (London: Routledge, 1997), 126.

8. In Buber's case, of course, this philanthropy is extended beyond the human to a bio- and theophilia.

9. One might argue, against Buber, that the dominant thrust of Heidegger's attempt to rethink the human must also be understood in terms of the relation between the human and other beings. For an indepth discussion of this theme, see Jean-Luc Nancy's *Being Singular Plural*, trans. Robert D. Richardson and Anne E. O'Byrne (Stanford: Stanford University Press, 2000).

10. In commenting on the themes of relation and meeting in Buber, Levinas helps to draw out their noncognitive aspect: "Buber's Meeting has suggested a relation that cannot be cast in the molds of consciousness. . . . If these molds, these forms of consciousness, determined all presence, nothing else would be able to enter our world" (*OS*, 19).

11. To cite Levinas again: "[Buber's] religiosity . . . stands opposed to religion, and leads him, in reacting against the fixed, rigid forms of a spiritual dogmatism, to place contact above its content, and the pure, unqualifiable presence of God above all dogma and rule" (*PN*, 29).

12. See Martin Heidegger, "The Question Concerning Technology," trans. William Lovitt and David Farrell Krell, in *Martin Heidegger: Basic Writings*, ed. David Farrell Krell (San Francisco: Harper, 1993), 332–33.

13. See Peter Atterton, "Levinas's Skeptical Critique of Metaphysics and *Anti-Humanism*," *Philosophy Today* 41, no. 4 (1997): 491–506.

14. *OB*, 127.

15. Albeit an abuse that leaves a "trace" of the saying in the said.

16. See chapter 15 of this volume.

Notes to Chapter 15/Atterton

1. See Robert Bernasconi's authoritative discussion of the *ethical* significance of this misunderstanding in "'Failure of Communication' as a Surplus: Dialogue and Lack of Dialogue between Buber and Levinas" (Chapter 5 of this volume).

2. Martin Buber, *The Legend of the Baal-Shem*, trans. Maurice Friedman (New York: Schocken Books, 1969). Cited by Maurice Friedman in *Encounter on the Narrow Ridge: A Life of Martin Buber* (New York: Paragon House, 1991), 43.

3. I use the expression "other animal" here and in my title, though I shall occasionally refer to nonhuman animals simply as "animals." I realize that in so doing, I risk giving the erroneous impression that humans are not animals. My reason for entertaining such a risk is merely to facilitate exposition and avoid too much repetition.

4. Paul Celan, *Collected Prose*, trans. Rosemarie Waldthrop (New York: Sheep Meadow, 1986), 25.

5. Martin Heidegger, *Poetry, Language, Thought*, trans. Albert Hofstadter (New Haven: Harper & Row, 1971), 210; cited by Levinas in German, *PN*, 40.

6. Celan, *Collected Prose*, 53.

7. Paul Celan, "Landscape," in *Paul Celan: Poems*, trans. Michael Hamburger (New York: Persea Books, 1980), 75.

8. Celan, *Collected Prose*, 12.

9. Martin Heidegger, *An Introduction to Metaphysics*, trans. Ralph Manheim (New Haven: Yale University Press, 1959), 4.

10. Celan, *Collected Prose*, 17–22 (18–19); modified translation.

11. "In Celan's writings," writes Levinas, "Judaism is not a picturesque particularism or a family folklore. Clearly, in the eyes of this poet, Israel's passion under Hitler . . . has the significance of humanity *tout court*, of which Judaism is the extreme possibility — or impossibility" (*PN*, 45). See also Levinas's assertion in *Difficult Freedom*: "[Israel] is a particularism that conditions universality, a moral category rather than a historical fact" (*DF*, 22). For a thought-provoking discussion of the problems surrounding this type of gesture in Levinas, see Robert Bernasconi, "Who is my neighbor? Who is the Other? Questioning 'the Generosity of Western Thought' " in *Ethics and Responsibility in the Phenomenological Tradition*. The Ninth Annual Symposium of the Duquesne University Simon Silverman Phenomenology Center, Pittsburgh, 1992, 1–31. See also Levinas's remark in *Difficult Freedom*: "Jewish existence itself is an essential event of being; Jewish existence is a category of being" (*DF*, 183).

12. For a discussion of Buber's repudiation of mysticism, see Maurice Friedman, *Encounter on the Narrow Ridge* (71–72, 81–83). Buber, however, never ceased to include nature within the I-Thou meeting, which Friedman says is "perhaps the most consistent thread in his entire philosophy" (67).

13. See the discussion of spirit at the beginning of the second part of *I and Thou*, where we read statements such as "Spirit in its human manifestation is man's response to his Thou" (*"Geist in seiner menschlichen Kundgebung ist Anwort des menschen an sein Du"*) and "Spirit is not in the I but between I and Thou" (*IT*, 89). It is surely these remarks and those like them that make Levinas's criticism of Buber not as easy to dismiss as many Buberians — including Buber himself (*PM*, 697) — have sometimes tried to do.

14. Emmanuel Levinas, "Is Ontology Fundamental?" trans. Peter Atterton, in *Basic Philosophical Writings* eds. Adriaan T. Peperzak, Simon Critchley and Robert Bernasconi (Bloomington, Ind.: Indiana University Press, 1996), 9.

15. This is not meant to imply that the animal and the human should both be treated the same way. As Peter Singer points out, giving ethical consideration

to animals as well as humans "does not require equal or identical *treatment*; it requires equal consideration" (*Animal Liberation* [New York: Ecco, 2002], 2).

16. Aristotle, *Metaphysics*, trans. Richard Hope (Michigan: The University of Michigan Press, 1952), 113.

17. See "Deconstruction is not Vegetarianism: Humanism, Subjectivity, and Animal Ethics," in *Continental Philosophy Review*, forthcoming. In this excellent essay, Calarco does a fine job of pointing out the shortcomings of both Levinas's and Derrida's work concerning the animal question, while finding in them the resources required "to thoroughly question discourses on animal ethics and vegetarianism concerning the consequences of the manner in which they regulate and determine the proper modes of ingestion and introjection, understood literally, symbolically and metonymically. In brief, the most pressing task is not to demonstrate that 'deconstruction is vegetarianism,' but to think through the *disjunction* of deconstruction and vegetarianism in order to bring deconstructive thinking to bear on the undisclosed anthropocentric and carnophallogocentric limits of the dominant discourses in animal ethics and vegetarianism."

18. For various discussions seeking to push Levinas's ethics in the direction of "deep ecology," see John Llewelyn, *The Middle Voice of Ecological Conscience: A Chiasmic Reading of Responsibility in the Neighborhood of Levinas, Heidegger and Others* (New York: St. Martin's Press, 1991); Roger Gottlieb, "Levinas, Feminism, Holocaust, Ecocide," in *Artifacts, Representations and Social Practices*, ed. Carol C. Gould (Dordrecht: Kluwer Academic Publishers, 1994); and Danne Polke, "Good Infinity/Bad Infinity: *Il y a, Apeiron*, and Environmental Ethics in the Philosophy of Levinas," *Philosophy and the Contemporary World* 7 (Spring 2000): 35–40.

19. Immanuel Kant, "Duties to Animals and Spirits," in *Lectures on Ethics*, trans. Louis Infield (New York: Harper and Row, 1963), 239–41.

20. See Singer, *Animal Liberation*; also Jeremy Bentham, *Introduction to the Principles of Morals and Legislation*, chapter 17 (quoted Singer, *Animal Liberation*, 7).

21. Edmund Husserl, *Cartesian Meditations*, translated by D. Cairns (Dordrecht: Kluwer Academic Publishers, 1988). Edith Stein, *On the Problem of Empathy*, trans. Waltraut Stein (Dordrecht: Kluwer, 1989). See also *TI*, 67.

22. *BMM*, 23.

23. Emmanuel Levinas, *Ethics and Infinity*, trans. Richard A. Cohen (Pittsburgh: Duquesne University Press, 1985), 89.

24. Friedrich Nietzsche, *Thus Spoke Zarathustra*, in *The Portable Nietzsche*, trans. Walter Kaufmann, (London: Penguin Books, 1982), sec. 3. Sigmund Freud, "A Difficulty in the Path of Psycho-Analysis," in *The Standard Edition of the Complete Psychological Works of Sigmund Freud*, trans. and ed. James Strachey (London: Hogarth Press, 1955), 17: 141.

25. It would be difficult to rebut the charge that Levinas is firmly entrenched in the tradition of what Nietzsche called "anti-natural morality" (*Twilight of the Idols*, trans. R. J. Hollingdale [London: Penguin, 1968], 45). See Levinas's repeated claim that ethics is "against-nature, against the naturality of nature" (*Of God Who*

Comes to Mind, trans. Bettina Bergo [Stanford: Stanford University Press, 1998], 171). See also *OB*, 197 n. 27.

26. In *The Metaphysics of Morals*, Kant writes that "there are impulses of nature having to do with man's **animality**. Through them nature aims at a) his self-preservation, b) the preservation of his species, and c) the preservation of his capacity to enjoy life, though still on the animal level." (*The Metaphysics of Morals*, trans. Mary Gregor [Cambridge: Cambridge University Press, 1993], 216.)

These natural impulses entail three perfect *ethical* duties of omission. Thus, 1) man is strictly forbidden to commit suicide, 2) to use sex for anything other than procreative purposes, and 3) to overindulge in sensuous pleasure, which would be to preclude him from enjoying similar pleasure in the future. To my knowledge, Levinas never speaks of an ethical obligation to follow such animal instincts in one's own person. On the contrary, Levinas mostly argues that ethics is the only thing that is capable of interrupting their triumviral governance. If there is one exception here, it is Eros, which is perhaps the sole example we find in Levinas's writing where ethics is interrupted by "animality" (qua the Feminine [*TI*, 263]) — and even that is not entirely certain. In the "Phenomenology of Eros" section of *Totality and Infinity*, amid a chaste description of voluptuousness, Levinas writes, "The beloved is opposed to me not as a will struggling with my own or subject to my own, but on the contrary as an irresponsible animality that does not speak true words. The beloved, returned to the stage of infancy — this coquettish head, this youth, this pure life, 'a bit silly' [*'un peu bête'*] has quit her status as a person. The face fades, and in its impersonal and inexpressive neutrality is prolonged, in ambiguity, into animality. The relations with the Other are enacted in play; one plays with the Other as with a young animal" (*TI*, 263). Since the relationship with the Feminine lacks the seriousness of ethics, it amounts to a reciprocal relationship of love and friendship. This arguably explains why Levinas likens it to Buber's I-Thou relationship: "The I-Thou in which Buber sees the category of the interhuman relationship is the relation not with the interlocutor but with feminine alterity" (*TI*, 155).

27. *OGM*, 152.

28. Michael Ruse, "Evolution and Ethics: The Sociobiological Approach," in *Ethical Theory: Classic and Contemporary Readings*, ed. Louis P. Pojman (Belmont, Cal.: Wadsworth, 2002), 657.

29. An extended discussion of this topic is due to appear in an essay entitled "Ethical Cynicism," in *Animal Philosophy: Essential Readings in Continental Thought*, eds. Matthew Calarco and Peter Atterton (New York: Continuum, 2004). I also address Levinas's 1986 interview at greater length.

30. John Llewelyn, "Am I Obsessed by Bobby (Humanism of the Other Animal?)," in *Re-Reading Levinas*, eds. Robert Bernasconi and Simon Critchley (Bloomington: Indiana University Press, 1991), 234–45. An expanded version appears in John Llewelyn, *The Middle Voice of Ecological Conscience*, 49–67.

31. David Clark, "On Being 'The Last Kantian in Nazi Germany': Dwelling with Animals after Levinas," in *Animal Acts: Configuring the Human In Western History*, eds. Jennifer Ham and Matthew Senior (New York: Routledge, 1997).

32. See Heidegger's remark in his 1942–1943 Parmenides lecture course: "For oppositions, even the most extreme, still require one same domain in which to be opposed to each other." He immediately goes on to say in reference to the segregation between the animal and the human, "Precisely that is missing here." (Martin Heidegger, *Parmenides*, trans. André Schuwer and Richard Rojcewicz [Bloomington: Indiana University Press, 1998], 152).

33. Jean-Paul Sartre, *Being and Nothingness*, trans. Hazel E. Barnes (London: Methuen, 1957), 256.

34. Jacques Derrida, *The Gift of Death*, trans. David Wills (Chicago: University of Chicago Press, 1995), 69; modified translation.

35. For a touching literary account of this episode, see Milan Kundera, *The Unbearable Lightness of Being* (New York: Harper and Row, 1983), 290. The whole of part 7, chapter 2 (from which it is taken) reads as a powerful defense of animal liberation.

36. *PI*, 28.

37. Richard Ryder, *Victims of Science* (London: Davis-Poynter, 1975).

38. Rainer Maria Rilke, *Duino Elegies*, trans. Edward Snow (New York: North Point Press, 2000), 46–47.

PETER ATTERTON teaches philosophy at the University of California, San Diego. He has translated several essays by Levinas and publishes in the field of Continental philosophy. With Matthew Calarco, he is author of *On Levinas* (2004), and editor of *The Continental Ethics Reader* (2003). He is currently writing a book on Levinas entitled *Ethics Beyond the Limits of Reason Alone.*

ROBERT BERNASCONI is the Lillian and Morrie Moss Professor of Philosophy at the University of Memphis. He is author of *The Question of Language in Heidegger's History of Being* (1985) and *Heidegger in Question* (1993). He recently edited *The Idea of Race* (2001), *Race* (2001), and *The Cambridge Companion to Levinas* (2002) and is the author of numerous essays on Levinas and Derrida.

MATTHEW CALARCO is assistant professor of philosophy at Sweet Briar College. He has published extensively on leading figures in contemporary Continental thought, including Agamben, Derrida, Levinas and Nancy. With Peter Atterton, he is author of *On Levinas* (2004), and editor of *The Continental Ethics Reader* (2003). He is currently completing a book entitled *The Animal After Derrida.*

RICHARD A. COHEN is the Isaac Swift Distinguished Professor of Judaic Studies at the University of North Carolina at Charlotte. He is author of *Ethics, Exegesis and Philosophy: Interpretation After Levinas* (2001) and *Elevations: The Height of the Good in Rosenzweig and Levinas* (1994). He has translated several books by Emmanuel Levinas, including *Time and the Other* (1987) and *Ethics and Infinity* (1985), and edited *Face to Face with Levinas* (1986). He is director of the Levinas Center at the University of North Carolina at Charlotte.

MICHAEL FAGENBLAT is lecturer at the Australian Centre for the Study of Jewish Civilization, Monash University. Previously he was a Jerusalem

Fellow at the Mandel School for Social and Educational Leadership. His doctoral thesis *How is Ethics Possible? Levinas, Heidegger and the Responsibilities of Transcendence*, was written at Monash University, after which he was a Golda Meir Postdoctoral Fellow at the Hebrew University, Jerusalem. He has published in philosophy and social criticism.

MAURICE FRIEDMAN is professor emeritus of religious studies, philosophy and comparative literature at San Diego State University. He is translator of several works by Martin Buber, and is author of innumerable books and articles on Martin Buber, existentialism and philosophy. His *Martin Buber's Life and Work* won the National Jewish Book Award. Among Friedman's other works are *Worlds of Existentialism: A Critical Reader* (1991) and *Religion and Psychology: A Dialogical Approach* (1992). He is codirector of the Institute of Dialogical Psychotherapy in San Diego.

ROBERT GIBBS is professor of philosophy at the University of Toronto where he teaches Continental philosophy and Jewish thought. His writings include *Correlations in Rosenzweig and Levinas* (1992) and *Why Ethics? Signs of Responsibilities* (2000). His most recent book is *Suffering Religion*, coedited with Elliot R. Wolfson (2002). His current research includes a larger project on law and ethics, and a book entitled *Messianic Epistemology*.

NEVE GORDON teaches in the department of politics and government at Ben-Gurion University in Israel. He specializes in the field of political theory and human rights, and is a contributor to *The Other Israel: Voices of Refusal of Dissent* (2002). His research includes a theoretical analysis of social control, with particular emphasis on the writings of Antonio Gramsci, Hannah Arendt and Michel Foucault. He also teaches and writes about feminism and human rights, emphasizing both the theoretical underpinnings of these topics and how they manifest themselves in the international sphere.

ANDREW KELLEY is assistant professor in the Department of Philosophy and Religious Studies at Bradley University. He has published articles on Kant, Maimon, Levinas, and the philosophy of peace and war. In 1995, his translation of Josef Popper-Lynkeus's *The Individual and the Value of Human Life* was published. He is currently translating Vladimir Jankélévitch's *Le Pardon*, and coediting a book on the philosophy of peace.

EPHRAIM MEIR is professor of modern and contemporary Jewish philosophy at Bar-Ilan University. He has translated Levinas's *Ethics and Infinity* into Hebrew and has written numerous essays and lectured throughout the world on contemporary Jewish thought. He is also the author of *Star from Jacob: The Life and Work of Franz Rosenzweig* (in Hebrew, 1994) and *Modernes jüdisches Denken* (1996).

STEPHAN STRASSER was Chair of Pedagogy at the University of Nijmegen until his retirement in 1975. Among several volumes, he published *Phenomenology and the Human Sciences* (1963), *The Idea of Dialogical Phenomenology* (1969) and *Understanding and Explanation* (1985).

ANDREW TALLON is professor of philosophy at Marquette University. He is the author of *Personal Becoming: Karl Rahner's Metaphysical Anthropology* and *Head and Heart: Affection, Cognition, Volition as Triune Consciousness* (1982), and the translator of Pierre Rousselot's *Intelligence: Sense of Being, Faculty of God.*

NATHAN WOLSKI is currently associate director of education at Harvard Hillel. He received his doctorate in aboriginal archaeology from the University of Melbourne, Australia. The recipient of a Jerusalem Fellowship with the Mandel School in Jerusalem, Israel, he focused there on Jewish education. He has lectured in contemporary Jewish thought at Monash University, Australia with the Australian Centre for Jewish Civilization.

TAMRA WRIGHT is Bradfield Lecturer in Jewish Studies at the London School of Jewish Studies, and a London School of Jewish Studies Fellow in the Department for the Study of Religions, School of Oriental and African Studies, University of London. She is the author of *The Twilight of Jewish Philosophy: Emmanuel Levinas' Ethical Hermeneutics* (1999).

INDEX

237–45; and collectivity of side by
side, 126; critique of humanism,
251–53; on fallenness, 86; on
intentionality, 55, 64; and
Jemeinigkeit, 59, 243; Levinas's
criticism of, 266; on metaphysics,
251–53, 256; Nazi affiliation of,
239; and question of being, 237–
38; on relation of things, 66; and
solicitude, 105; against transcendental idealism, 54
height: Buber's criticism of, 110; of
God, 226; morality and dimension
of, 12, 99; neediness of other and,
120; relation to other and, 227,
230
Heinrichs, Johannes, 57
Herder, Johann Gottfried von, 191
hermeneutics. *See* interpretation
Heschel, Abraham Joshua, 15, 129,
203–4
history: Buber versus Levinas on,
160–61, 170–77; Heidegger and,
239–40; interpretive tradition and,
190; of religion, 197–200
Hölderlin, Friedrich, 239
Holocaust, 203–25; Buber and, 19–20,
34, 128, 138, 203–12; delay in
discussion of, 203–5; Levinas and,
20–21, 138, 212–24
Horwitz, Rivka, 138
Hösle, Vittorio, 147
human condition: animal nature and,
274; ethics and, 274–75; finitude
of, 54, 58; as relational, 254–55
humanism, 250–61; animal inferiority
and, 272, 275–76; Buber's
"believing humanism," 253–57;
Buber versus Levinas on, 142;
decline of, 250, 258; Heidegger's
critique of, 251–53; Levinas and,
258–60
"Humanism and Anarchy" (Levinas),
258
Humanisme de l'autre homee
(Levinas), 258
Husserl, Edmund, 50, 52, 53–54, 56,

64, 85–86, 94–95, 273

I and Thou (Buber), 17, 77, 235–36
Ichud, 148
idealism, 38
I-It relationship: I-Thou versus, 66–
67, 74, 94–95, 134, 209, 228–29;
Levinas on insufficiency of
Buber's, 71; positive aspects of,
228; primal distance and, 102
illeity, 68–69, 90, 126, 137
infinite, 232
institutions: ethics and, 147–48; evil
countered by, 147; religious, 144–
46
intellectualism, 52
intentionality, 50, 52–56
interpretation: Buber's practice of
biblical, 171–72, 180–87, 190, 197–
200, 205–6, 216; community of,
169–70, 192–97; familiarity as
problem in, 183–84; Jewish
hermeneutics, 153; Levinas's
practice of biblical, 164, 173–76,
180, 187–97, 213, 215–16; reading
and textuality in Buber and
Levinas, 180–81; revelation and,
161–63, 164, 168, 189
introspection, 50
Irigaray, Luce, 10
Israel, 148–49, 166, 207–8
I-Thou relationship, 2–3; animals
and, 270, 273, 279–80; asymmetry
of, 33, 81–82, 103–4, 110, 119–21,
267; Buber's biblical interpretation
and, 205–6; comradeship versus
friendship in, 120, 229; ethical
action in, 113–14, 121; formalism
of, 41–43, 70–71, 76, 102–6, 119,
262–63; "I" in, 92–93; I-It versus,
66–67, 74, 94–95, 134, 209, 228–
29; and I-We relationship, 246–49;
justice in, 112; language and, 83–
84, 184; Levinas on, 6–8, 33, 41–
45, 68–80, 100–106, 126; nature in,
262–64, 267; reciprocity of, 7, 33,
44–45, 68–72, 76–79, 81–82, 90,